Economics Directorate
Information Directorate
(eds.)

 NATO (North Atlantic Treaty Organization)

CMEA: Energy, 1980-1990

Colloquium
8-10 April 1981
Brussels

 OTAN

CAEM: Energie, 1980-1990

Colloque
8-10 Avril 1980
Bruxelles

Oriental Research Partners
Newtonville, Mass. 02160
USA

Library of Congress Card No. 81-86626
ISBN # 0-89250-341-6

For Further Information
Write: Dr. P. Clendenning, Editor
Oriental Research Partners
Box 158, Newtonville, Mass. 02160 USA

Typesetting and Layout by:
INDEPENDENT TYPESETTING, INC.
2204 Government Street
Mobile, Alabama 36606

10027450 66

Preface
CMEA:
Energy, 1980-1990

James Ellis
NATO Economics Directorate

The annual Colloquium, held on 8-10 April 1981 at NATO Headquarters, sponsored by the Economics and Information Directorates, benefited from the participation of noted academics, businessmen and government officials; they presented authoritative papers on a topic which has been foremost in the minds of many economic analysts, namely that of the development of energy in CMEA.[1]

The Colloquium in session: From left to right, Dr. Theodore Shabad, Editor, Soviet Geography; Professor Leslie Dienes, University of California; Mr. Michael Roeskau, International Energy Agency, OECD; Mr. Jean-Noel Gibault, Director, NATO Economics Directorate; Mr. Glenn R. Cella, Director and Deputy to ASG for Political Affairs, NATO; Mr. Philip Joseph, Deputy Director, NATO Economics Directorate.

Foremost among world producers of energy, thanks to the USSR's leading position, the CMEA area nonetheless in the 1980s faces the prospect of growing energy constraints. Energy-poor Eastern Europe will have to continue relying on Soviet supplies of oil and natural gas in particular, whose vast reserves are becoming increasingly more expensive to develop. For these supplies, the Eastern European nations will have to give up more of their exportable goods to the USSR, at a time when their economies are already burdened by adverse foreign trade balances. In addition, they will be called on to contribute heavily to CMEA's ambitious programme of nuclear energy development, which will produce significant returns only over a long term. Even the energy-rich Soviet Union will be forced to find means to curtail its often wasteful use of oil, as its existing sources of supply become depleted. In short, the CMEA area, like the rest of the world, will have to contend with growing problems of energy availability.

With respect to the rest of the world, CMEA should be able to maintain its present relatively advantageous energy position[2]. Throughout the 1980s the OECD nations will most likely have to continue importing approximately half of their huge energy needs, principally from the OPEC; the CMEA area, however, should remain energy self-sufficient, with possible imports of small amounts of oil being balanced, in caloric terms, by exports of natural gas[3].

Within CMEA, however, Eastern Europe's energy position is not so sanguine, since it may be forced to import more oil from world markets at high prices. Consequently, growth in Eastern Europe's economic output may further slacken, and might give rise to additional consumer discontent. In addition, Eastern Europe will increasingly be tied to Soviet supplies of natural gas and eventually, of nuclear electricity, leaving it little room to develop alternative energy suppliers.

For the West, the implications of the CMEA energy situation in the 1980s are far-reaching. While Eastern Europe could become a more frequent competitor on world oil markets, the USSR may become an important supplier of natural gas to Western Europe. Both of these potential developments raise anew the question of the security of Western energy supplies.

To gain an idea of the magnitude and impact of the projected energy situation on the CMEA economies and with respect to the rest of the world, one has to investigate CMEA energy production and use in considerable detail, as was done at the NATO 1980 Colloquium. The papers assembled here, which were presented at the Colloquium, provide revealing insights, not only as to probable trends in CMEA energy developments, but also as to the potential for interaction between the East and the West in the field of energy.

Notes

[1]The Council for Mutual Economic Assistance, comprising Bulgaria, Cuba, Czechoslovakia, the German Democratic Republic, Hungary, Poland, Romania, the USSR and Vietnam.
[2]See adjoining graphs of world energy production and consumption in 1979.
[3]See adjoining graphs of plausible world energy production and consumption in 1990.

Contents

Synopses of Papers

Exxon Energy Outlook for USSR and Eastern Europe

Clara S. Szathmary

Each year Exxon Corporation prepares a new world energy outlook. In 1980, for the first time, energy supply and demand projections for the centrally planned economies were published in the outlook.

Energy growth in the USSR is slowing down from about 5% between 1965 and 1980 to slightly over 2% yearly in the 1980-2000 period. Coal and oil are losing their share of total output; nuclear power is gaining, but from a low base; gas is expected to be a major source of energy growing at better than 4% yearly, based primarily on large Siberian gas reserves. Coal growth will continue to be moderate, possibly accelerating to 2% in the 1990-2000 period. Oil production is expected to be relatively stable in the 11-12 mbd range through 2000. The USSR's unexploited energy is in Siberia. The Soviet ability to develop and transport oil, coal and gas to the Western section and for exports will be a primary determinant of production levels.

In the USSR, utilization of energy is very different from other industrial nations. A much larger share of energy is used by industry and electric power generation. Switching from oil to gas and coal in these sectors is implied in order to accommodate no growth in oil.

Net energy exports will continue. Oil exports are likely to remain about the same to Eastern Europe, but decline to the West. Gas exports are likely to increase to both areas; to the West they will make up for hard currency losses due to lower oil exports.

Energy use in Eastern Europe is expected to grow at a modest 2% rate through 2000. Coal is likely to remain the major contributor; nuclear power, with Soviet help, shows the fastest growth potential. Eastern Europe is supplementing decreasing oil production by OPEC and USSR imports.

Total net energy exports to the West will decline. Oil exports will about balance imports from 1985 on, with East European imports at about USSR export levels. Gas exports, all from the USSR, are expected to increase. Overall, the USSR remains an energy exporter but Eastern Europe will be a net importer.

*   *   *   *   *   *

1

Forms and Dimensions of Soviet and East European Trade and
Cooperation in Energy with Third World Economies

John B. Hannigan and Carl H. McMillan

Following a trend initiated in the 1960s, the USSR and the East European
CMEA countries intensified their energy relations with Third World
countries through most of the endowments and import requirements, both
followed separate paths in the development of these relations. Diversifying
its petroleum exports, the USSR emerged as a major supplier to some
developing economies. At the same time, it concluded large-scale, long-
term agreements for the import of natural gas from Iran and Afghanistan.
Its East European allies, for their part, entered into a variety of
arrangements with the Arab OPEC countries and Iran aimed at diversifying
their imports of petroleum and reducing their dependence on Soviet oil.
Both the USSR and Eastern Europe were active in developing the energy
sectors of certain Third World economies.

In the late 1970s, CMEA energy relations with the Third World began to
undergo significant changes. A tightening Soviet oil supply situation raised
the prospect of an upper limit on oil exports to Third World countries. The
revolutionary government in Iran unilaterally abrogated the agreements for
export of natural gas to the USSR, causing supply problems which could
not be fully offset despite Soviet control of Afghanistan's gas industry.
Events in the Middle East caused serious problems for Eastern Europe,
disrupting oil supply arrangements and raising the price of oil. The USSR
and Eastern Europe continued to participate in the development of Third
World energy sectors, both to fulfill commitments to the development of
these countries and to secure compensatory fuel deliveries.

The prospects are not bright for increased Soviet and East European fuels
imports from Third World suppliers, at least in the medium term (through
1985), unless a pro-Soviet government should come to power in Iran.
Eastern Europe will find it increasingly difficult to finance even present
import levels of Third World oil. The unreliability of Middle Eastern supply,
and the rapidly rising price of OPEC oil, make sourcing from the Soviet
Union a more attractive alternative to Third World countries. The levelling
off of Soviet oil production will, however, limit Soviet ability to take
economic or political advantage of the opportunities thus afforded. In these
circumstances the USSR is likely at least to exact special economic terms
for its oil deliveries (oil-for-grain barter agreements, for example). Increases
in Soviet natural gas exports to Eastern and Western Europe could, to the
extent that they can substitute for oil exports, free some additional Soviet
oil for the Third World.

*   *   *   *   *   *

Oil: Demand in the CMEA Economies in the 1980s

Tony Scanlan

The market economists claim that demand for oil is a function of the demand for goods and services using petroleum, but it is availability of supply that determines future growth in demand for oil at the primary energy level. The dynamics of oil demand growth are a combination of consumption and supply, but the outcome may have as much to do with national objectives for trade or infrastructure as with market preference and this is especially the case in centrally planned economies.

The paper reviews the oil scene inside CMEA in the 1970s which commenced with the expectations of major developments in supplies from Western Siberia. The decade also began with forecasts that the combined growth in the three major areas of demand, USSR indigenous, Eastern European and CMEA export markets would, by 1980, begin to outstrip this supply potential and require a choice to be made between them. These predictions have been borne out by events.

Looking ahead into the 1980s the outlook for annual increases in economic growth is only half that of ten years ago, but oil supply prospects have also diminished — a similar position to the rest of the world. Success in Western Siberia has made the USSR the leading oil producer at 12 million barrels per day. This requires a new "Samotlor equivalent" every three years to sustain even zero growth but unlike 1970 there is little sign of this level of discovery occurring. It is not surprising therefore that ways of conserving oil through greater efficiency and by using alternate fuel sources now feature in many Soviet articles. The paper will try to examine how this might be achieved and a major distinction is perceived between the position of the USSR and that of Eastern Europe.

*   *   *   *   *   *

Electrical Energy: Supply and Demand in the CMEA Economies in the 1980s, including Nuclear Energy Prospects

Theodore Shabad

Pending the realization of Soviet proposals for inter-connection with West European electricity systems, the CMEA remains essentially a closed electric-power economy, facing a number of specific problems in the 1980s. On a geographical level, the concentration of demand in the Western region of the CMEA system and the availability of supplies in the eastern regions will give rise to a growing flow of electrical energy both from Siberia to the European USSR and from the European USSR to Eastern Europe. The East-West transmission within the Soviet Union will be dependent on completion of the long delayed extra-high voltage lines from lignite-fired power stations situated next to eastern strip mines; the transmission from the European USSR to Eastern Europe will require an expanding network of 750 KV lines feeding nuclear power from Soviet stations near the western border into the East European grid.

Because of growing constraints not only on the use of oil and gas for power generation, but also on the use of the limited solid fuel supplies in the western region of CMEA, increasing stress will be placed on development of nuclear generating capacity both in the European USSR and in Eastern Europe. The need for rapid nuclear capacity growth will mean a shift in reactor size from standarized 440 MW units to 1,000 MW or even 1,500 MW units. This shift is already underway in the Soviet Union, and is to be extended in the 1980s to Eastern Europe on the basis of growing cooperation in the manufacture of nuclear equipment. Nuclear power is to be used not only for electricity generation, but also for the production of steam heat in combined heat and power plants and in nuclear boiler plants. The increasing stress on nuclear power raises problems with respect to the transportation of nuclear fuel from the Soviet Union to Eastern Europe, the disposal of spent fuel, and the choice of suitable nuclear power station sites.

*   *   *   *   *   *

Oil: Resources, Exploration and Projected Production through 1990.

Jochen Bethkenhagen

It is improbable that the Soviet oil production will decline in the early 1980s. On the contrary, a production growth of 1% per year is expected until 1990 (1985: 633 million tons, 1990: 665 million tons).

A prerequisite for this development is the accelerated procurement of new equipment for the oil industry. The efforts towards modernization could be facilitated by additional imports. A restrictive export policy of the West on the other hand can render the Plan fulfillment more difficult. This would have negative repercussions on East-West trade.

Reliable information on the reserve situation is not available. Both the pessimistic estimates of the CIA (4,500 million tons) and the optimistic estimates of Petro Studies (16,000 million tons) contradict Soviet sources. In view of the uncertain data, no well founded information can be given on the range of Soviet reserves. Estimates could easily lead to incorrect economic and political conclusions.

The Soviet oil industry can look back on a successful decade. Since 1974 the USSR has been the largest oil producer in the world. In 1980 it accounted for 20% of the world oil production (1970: 15%). However, production growth has slowed down. This was not caused by a shortage of capital but by a faulty production policy. For example, well density was increased albeit too strongly. Owing to this the yields per well and the recovery rates sank. As a result, the Five-Year Plan could not be fulfilled (Plan 1980: 640 million tons, fulfilled: 603 million tons). The USSR will further improve its monopoly position—it produces 98% of the oil—within the CMEA. A further fall in production can be expected for Romania; it may be partially offset by additional production in Poland.

*   *   *   *   *   *

Solid Fuels: Resources, Production and Demand in the 1980s

Theodore Shabad

The solid fuels are being looked to in the CMEA countries as an increasingly important fuel for power generation in the 1980s as the use of fuel oil is to be cut back, especially in the Soviet Union, in light of the growing tightness of oil supply. However, while the production of coal appears to be holding its own in East Europe it has been declining in the Soviet Union at the very time when planners are looking to solid fuels as a more significant factor in thermal power generation. After having reached a peak in gross mine output of 723.6 million metric tons in 1978, coal production in the Soviet Union slipped to 716 million in 1980. The new five-year plan 1981-85 projects not only stabilization of this coal mining decline, but renewed increase to 775 million by 1985. However, coal production goals since the mid-1970s appear to have been unusually optimistic and performance has fallen far short.

The basic problem in the Soviet union is that the most easily accessible coal beds in some of the older coal basins in the European part of the country, notably the Donets Basin, are being depleted requiring the construction of increasingly deeper mines, which has been both costly and time-consuming. In the meantime, the largely untapped eastern basins have been unable to compensate for the western capacity depletions. Future expansion will be concentrated in the Kuznetsk Basin, the main main source of high-grade coking and steam coals after the Donets Basin, and in the huge strip-mine operations of the Ekibastuz Basin of northeast Kazakhstan and ultimately in the Kansk-Achinsk Basin of southern Siberia.

In Eastern Europe, the need for high-grade coal has to be met almost entirely by Poland's Upper Silesian basin while the other countries produce mainly the inferior brown coal or lignite, suitable only for use in mineside power stations. However, Eastern Europe's reserves are limited and few significant increases in production can be projected.

*   *   *   *   *   *

CMEA Energy Production and World Energy Balance in the 1980s

Michael Roeskau

As a result of soaring prices and of policy efforts, the industrialized countries of the West may be able to curb the secular trend of growing energy consumption effectively and reduce it to a minimum. The objective, which they are committed to for 1990, i.e., to use only 0.6% more energy for any additional percentage point of economic growth, is quite likely to be achieved. It would mean that total primary energy requirements would increase at a pace of less than 2% p.a. At the same time, the structure of energy supply and demand should change significantly. If the production and the use of coal, gas and nuclear can be increased, the share of oil should be further reduced from a current 50% to 40% by 1990 and perhaps 29% by 2000. In absolute terms, primary oil consumption would not only stagnate, but actually decrease and the oil imports of these countries might fall by as much as 250 million tons in 1990 as compared with 1979 imports.

By contrast, the Third World will need more and more energy to fuel its development process. A steep increase in energy requirements is to be expected and annual energy growth rates may be in the order of 5-6% for non-OPEC developing countries as a whole. OPEC's own energy consumption will rise even faster and annual increases between 8.9% and 7.6% appear warranted. But while there are basically good prospects for greatly expanded indigenous energy production in non-OPEC developing countries, OPEC energy production is likely to show a more stable profile. In particular, there is not much hope that OPEC's annual oil production will exceed the 30 mbd mark ever again.

Thus, with OPEC oil exports decreasing at a rate close to the reduction of oil demand in industrialized consumer countries, present tight market conditions are likely to continue to prevail as a long term trend and there will be continued interest for additional supplies.

While the future role of the USSR in world energy markets has been subject to controversial discussions, the difference of opinions seems to be narrowing now. There is not much doubt that, due mainly to Soviet production of natural gas, the European CMEA as a whole has a potential for remaining a net energy exporter. But this would involve a basic shift in the structure of energy exports and natural gas would have to replace oil in its role as the predominant export item. In fact, even official Soviet figures suggest by now that oil production in the USSR is about to level off. With domestic oil demand continuing to grow in spite of conservation efforts, availability of Soviet oil for exports to the West and the Third World will decline. Whether natural gas exports can make up for these losses depends on both accelerated Soviet production and the attitude of Western customers. While the former is likely, additional gas imports from diversified sources would fit in with Western industrialized countries' energy strategy away from oil. The overall volume of East-West energy trade would presumably not be affected by this and would remain stable rather than increase significantly over present levels. In fact, other energy exports by the East, such as coal and electricity generated from both coal and nuclear, will only play a marginal role in the decade ahead.

At the same time, while maintaining a net energy export position, the CMEA's role in world oil markets might become that of a more important buyer. The energy-poor European CMEA countries may be forced to cover their growing oil requirements by direct purchases from surplus oil producers. But there would also be an option for the USSR to act as an intermediate, i.e., to buy oil against hard currency, which it can more easily earn than the other CMEA countries, and resell it at softer conditions to its East European allies. The Soviets might thus be in a position both to establish closer commercial ties with Middle East producers and to maintain control over vital supplies to the East European economies.

* * * * * *

Natural Gas Resources, Production Possibilities and Demand in the CMEA in the 1980s

Jonathan P. Stern

Natural gas is a relative newcomer in the energy balances of CMEA countries, but in the 1980s it is likely that this source of energy will substantially increase its share of primary energy consumption throughout the region. This is almost entirely due to the USSR which possesses around one-third of world proven reserves, mainly concentrated in a number of extremely large fields in Western Siberia. The inaccessible location of these reserves means that the biggest problem for the industry lies in the development of the production and transportation infrastructure required to bring the gas many thousands of kilometres to markets. The industry performed this task remarkably well in the 1976-80 period, but the targets for 1981-85 are extremely ambitious in terms of pipelines and compressor stations which will be required to fulfill them.

The recent stagnation or slowdown of production of other Soviet fuels has brought the role of gas to the fore as the major incremental contributor to the Soviet and overall CMEA energy balance in the 1980s. Not only will Soviet gas need to compensate for other fuels in the CMEA energy balance, it will also be exported for hard currency in order to compensate for a possible decline in Soviet oil exports to the West. Nevertheless, while its contribution will be extremely substantial in the 1980s, natural gas cannot be expected to fill the gap completely if other energy forms fall dramatically short of production targets. While Soviet gas production and exports will increase rapidly, particularly in the latter part of the decade, the fuel is far from a complete answer to CMEA energy problems in the 1980s.

* * * * * *

The Cost of Soviet Oil

Peter Wiles

Costs are far too often neglected in talking about oil, but not in actually extracting it (except perhaps in USSR). The aleatory element in oil costs is of course unusually high. But without a vast excess over Saudi costs in, say, Northern Western Siberia or the North Sea there would be no oil crisis at all. Nevertheless we can speak guardedly of the long-run marginal cost of Soviet oil. It is rising very rapidly indeed but still seems to be some way below "world" price. Soviet accountancy obscures this fact, but possibly not at Gosplan level.

*   *   *   *   *   *

East-West Energy Trade and Technology Transfer: A Security Perspective

Tyrus W. Cobb

This paper examines the volume and nature of energy trade between the developed countries of the West and the Soviet bloc, with particular attention to the ramifications of this trade on the foreign policies of the individual nations and implications for respective alliance cohesion. The study focuses on the energy trade between the United States and the Soviet Union, then proceeds to address the larger question of East-West energy trade patterns. Policy issues relating to technology transfer, use of economic "leverage" as an instrument of national strategy, and economic dependency as a security concern are analysed.

The evolution of American policy on trade with the Soviet Union has undergone several significant changes in the last 15 years, ranging from a "Cold War" denial policy across-the-board to a detente-inspired encouragement of trade between former adversaries in order to promote a politico-economic interdependence. More recently, the American energy trade to the Soviet Union, which consists almost entirely of US exports of technology and products to the USSR, has been viewed as a potential lever in the arsenal of foreign policy instruments by which the Soviet Union might be persuaded to alter its domestic and international political behavior. From the perspective of Moscow the view of this trade has been more unilinear—it is vitally necessary to obtain Western credits, investment, and technology in order to solve pressing structural problems in the economy, especially in the energy sector.

A closer examination of this trade demonstrates the low volume of the Soviet-American energy trade and the comparatively minor role of these sales compared to overall East-West trade. The study finds a potential for leverage enjoyed by the Western "camp" given the extent of Soviet bloc vulnerability and possession of advanced technology and financing in the developed countries. However, the paper also discusses the numerous areas of disagreement between Alliance members that serve to place real limitations on the ability of the West or any individual nation to exercise influence over Soviet behavior. This problem is likely to be exacerbated in this decade as Western dependence on the USSR for energy supplies grows and the Kremlin begins to integrate its own energy "lever" into the Soviet national security arsenal.

In the 1980s the Soviet Union will be a major actor in international energy flows. Despite a continuing requirement for advance technology and extensive financing, the Soviet Union will significantly expand the output of energy resources. Petroleum sales will gradually diminish, but exports of natural gas will rise rapidly. The Kremlin will seek to translate this export of natural potential into a viable security instrument by intertwining its raw material base with military power. Brezhnev's recent proposals relating to Persian Gulf security and frequent calls for a "High-Level" Energy Conference are indicative of this resource diplomacy in which the USSR will engage.

It is incumbent upon the West to develop a broad-based policy that recognizes common interests, both political and economic, of the industrialized countries in addressing Soviet initiatives. Neither a "denial" policy nor a "laissez-faire" approach will suffice to adequately treat the complex security issues that will surround energy and technology transfers in this decade. Rather, the West must engage in regular discussions designed to formulate longer term cooperation in integrating economic and security policy toward the Soviet bloc.

*   *   *   *   *   *

Implications of CMEA Energy Prospects for Soviet Economic Growth

Joseph Licari

Growth in Soviet energy supplies is expected to slow considerably during the 1980s. Western interest in the emerging Soviet energy plight stems from the impact it will have on both Soviet economic growth and Moscow's ability to remain a major exporter of energy. These linkages between Soviet energy and growth prospects for the 1980s can be examined through a simulation model of the Soviet economy. The model generates a set of internally consistent energy demand, economic growth and foreign trade projections for any given assumptions regarding domestic energy production.

The outlook for Soviet energy is very uneven. While gas and electric power output are likely to increase by about 50% by 1990, the rise in coal production may not exceed 15%. Oil production is actually expected to decline from its present level of 12 million barrels per day (mbd) to around 10.5 mbd in 1985 and 8 mbd in 1990. Given this outlook for energy supplies, Soviet growth during the '80s will be energy-constrained. This situation in oil would be particularly accute, as oil imbalances developed by the mid-'80s from an inability to adjust the energy-consuming capital stock fast enough to a changing energy supply mix. Under these conditions, GNP growth would trend around 2.5% a year for the first half of the decade and somewhat less than 2% for the second half. By mid-decade, the Soviets could shift to a net import position on oil with the West to try to relieve some of the pressure on domestic oil use, but these oil imports would force imports of Western machinery, steel and other industrial goods down to little more than half their recent levels.

Guidelines for energy production in the 11th Five-Year Plan imply much more optimistic prospects for economic growth and energy trade. With gas, coal and especially oil production higher than our basic supply assumptions, annual GNP growth could average almost a percentage point more through 1985 and there would be no constraint imposed by energy. Hard currency oil exports still could be as high as a half million BPD in 1985. Growth rates above 3% a year would mean that the USSR would be roughly on a balanced growth plateau during the 11th Five-Year Plan—the shares of GNP devoted to consumption, defense and investment would change little over the five years.

While the Politburo may view this condition longingly, it is not likely to occur. If problems in energy supplies develop as we now foresee, there is little short of slashing energy exports to Eastern Europe that Soviet policymakers could do to contain the ensuing negative effects on economic growth and trade with the West.

*　*　*　*　*　*

Les Transports d'Energie dans le CAEM: Problèmes et Perspectives

Hervé Gicquiau

Les stratégies soviétique et est-europeenes de l'énergie vont être confrontées dans la décennie 1980-1990, peut-être plus qu'auparavant, aux problemes jamais résolus des transports.

Un volume accru de combustibles solides et un tonnage elevé—quoique stabilisé—d'hydrocarbures non expédiés par conduites, seront transportés essentiellement par les chemins de fer, la voie d'eau accusant un retard de développement qui sauf exception, ne pourra lui permettre d'absorber une part substantielle du trafic.

Les réseaux ferroviaires vont longtemps connaître une situation critique, au moins égale à cette observée ces dernieres annèes, les transporteurs pouvant cependant dans certains cas tabler sur des accroissements de production locale ou nationale moins importants que prévu. Néanmoins les difficultés matérielles de la voie ferrée persisteront malgré la possibilité d'appliquer divers remèdes complémentaires les uns des autres, remèdes qui ne font pas systématiquement appel ou alors modérément à l'investissment — dont on sait qu'il se fait toujours plus rare dans le secteur des transports traditionnellement défavorisé — mais plus à une rationalisation de l'organisation.

Les perturbations dans la fourniture de courant électrique dans tous les pays du CAEM font accueillir favorablement les réalisations en cours (interconnexion des réseaux) pour le transport d'électricité. La création de ligner nouvelles de grande puissance ameliorera les conditions et les coûts d'exploitation, mais des limites techniques et économiques pourraient remettre en cause certains projets sovietiques de long terme. Les systèmes de transport d'électricieté semblent etre cependant en mesure de réduire les contraintes d'emploi de cette energie.

Alors que le transport du pétrole brut par oléo-ducs apparaît désormais, de même que les flux, stabilisé, et que l'ère d'établissement de grandes conduites est, sauf découverte majeure, achevée, plus d'attention pourrait être accordée a là distribution des produits de raffineries pour libérer quelque peu les chemins de fer.

Il est vrai que l'attention va se porter au cours de la décennie essentiellement sur le transport à grande distance du gaz sibérien. Mais les problèmes techniques et sourtout financiers que la poursuite de cet objectif va poser à l'URSS sont généralement considérés comme impossibles à surmonter. Construire quelques 33,000 km des seuls gazoducs de grand diamètre dans les pires conditions signifie certes que l'exploitation des grands gisements siberiens devra tout à la fois permettre a l'URSS de compenser le fléchissement des ressources pétrolières du bloc socialiste et rapidement être en mesure par des livraisons accrues à l'Ouest de peser sur la situation enérgétique de l'Europe. Malgré ces bonnes raisons susceptibles de rendre prioritaire aux yeus des Soviétiques la création des nouveaux gazoducs, on peut s'enterroger sur les possibilites réelles de fourniture en 10 ans à l'industrie du gaz de plus de 33 milliards de roubles et des tubes, matériaux et équipements nécessaires à la réalisation de ces projets.

*   *   *   *   *   *

Energy and Economic Growth in Eastern Europe in the 1980s

Robin A. Watson

Sluggish productivity growth and declining increments to the labor force are constricting East European growth prospects for the 1980s. The transition to slower growth and the search for improved efficiency is seriously complicated by the rising cost and uncertain availability of energy. We have attempted to trace the connections between energy and growth with the help of a set of small macroeconomic models. It appears that likely energy supplies will degrade significantly the already unfavorable prospects for GNP growth and living standards over the next five years.

East European energy demand is likely to increase at somewhat less than 3% per year, much more slowly than in the 1970's. Increased demand would have to be met by either more Soviet oil (currently three-fourths of the region's oil imports) or more oilpurchased for hard currency. Unless the Soviet Union increases annual allocations, Eastern Europe will need over one million barrels per day of non-Communist oil to satisfy energy requirements by 1985 as its production cannot meet demand.

Hard currency oil purchases of this magnitude could cost about $US15 billion at current prices—nearly half the region's 1979 hard currency earnings. Yet Eastern Europe's limited ability to expand exports, continuing requirements for grain, technology and spare parts from the West, already burdensome debt-service obligations, and rising oil prices will probably limit imports of non-Communist oil during the next five years to somewhat less than the current level of around a half million barrels per day.

Thus constrained by energy shortages, economic growth might average less than 2% per year through 1985, about one percentage point below potential growth with energy requirements fully met and much less than half the growth rate of the 1970s. Of course, the impact of the regional energy problem varies a good deal from country to country. Czechoslovakia and Hungary, in particular, appear to face almost stagnant living standards for the first half of the decade. Moreover, cutbacks of Soviet oil deliveries at concessionary prices could cause per capita GNP to actually decline in Hungary, Czechoslovakia, and Poland.

Eastern European leaders seem painfully aware of their poor economic prospects, yet the options which they have available to lessen the problem—expanded hard currency exports, constricted imports, larger credits, improved energy efficiency, more conservation, and accelerated productivity growth—hardly seem promising especially in light of Polish domestic problems. Their realistic alternatives are unlikely to prevent near stagnation in living standards over the next five years.

*   *   *   *   *   *

Planning and Management of Energy R and D in CMEA

Robert Campbell

All the alternatives for solving energy problems in the CMEA countries in the nineties involve substantial technological progress. To assess the degree of success to be expected, the best evidence available is their track record on innovation in the energy sector to date. Most new technology in the energy sector in CMEA has originated in the USSR, and this is likely to continue to be the case. An extensive study of this record over a wide range of energy technologies suggests several generalizations.

Development histories for pipeline compressor equipment, excavating and haulage equipment for surface coal mining, and many others show that that programs characteristically fall many years behind schedule and often never meet the design criteria planned for equipment. There is a great inertia in Soviet development programs that inhibits changes in direction as the technological problems change. The coal processing program is a case in point. The system does support bold work at the speculative end of the R and D spectrum, but smooth movement through successive stages of the cycle is not often achieved. Work in any given area often continues with little direction or progression until top level decisions are made to move ahead with a crash program for commercialization, at which time development stages get telescoped, and expensive investments are made on the basis of too little work at intermediate R and D stages. R and D work is often concentrated on one element of a system, ignoring associated equipment which is developed only later. Often it is never developed and existing production equipment is substituted even though it is poorly integrated with the new elements. There are many examples in the energy R and D experience of a poor match-up between the choices the developers of new technology make, and the priorities and needs of those who must employ it in the energy producing and transforming sectors.

Specific conclusions from this record regarding future energy policy include the following. Most of the R and D tasks posed by energy policy will be performed behind schedule, and will meet the needs that inspired them only partially. These efforts are not likely to alter the relative advantage of alternative options in a way that will move the main features of CMEA policy much away from that elsewhere in the world. In the past the Russians have bypassed these domestic R and D failures by technology transfer and it is likely they will continue to do so.

*   *   *   *   *   *

Implications for the West, Including Defense, of CMEA Energy Prospects

Freidemann Müller

Soviet energy-production in the 1980's will likely have lower though still positive growth rates. To maintain even the reduced growth rates the Soviet Union will have to shift from oil to gas, which in turn will drastically affect the structure of exports to the West and increase the Soviets' need for closer cooperation with the West in developing the infrastructure required for the production and transportation of gas. Increasing investment costs within the Soviet Union will make Mid-East oil seem that much more attractive; to protect that option, the USSR will likely stimulate rather than help subdue crises in the region. Western willingness to cooperate with the Soviet Union in developing her energy resources (which generally would help to alleviate a world-wide decline in energy output) should, therefore, be linked with Soviet restraint in a region of critical importance for Western energy supplies.

*   *   *   *   *   *

CMEA Energy Demand in the 1980s: A Sectoral Analysis

Leslie Dienes
Nikos Economou

Energy consumption in the COMECON states is more closely tied to the production of goods, to the sinews of the economy, than in the West. It reflects the goals and priorities of central planners rather than the consumer, though in the rising and now generous deliveries to agriculture through most of the Bloc planners and most of the populace may not be far apart. Clearly, the COMECON countries must look, above all else, to industry for reduction in waste and attempts at energy savings, particularly since private motoring in recent years has been restricted even further. At the same time, the backward state of energy supply to households outside large cities and the necessity of modernizing that neglected sector should result in a rising claim on centrally furnished resources.

Energy consumption in the Soviet Bloc, also reflects structural peculiarities in resource use and transformation characteristics of given countries. The very high share of lignite and/or coal in aggregate energy demand through East Germany, Poland and Czechoslovakia reflects both resource endowment and government policy. In the GDR, the intensity of electrification, expressed both in the end use pattern and the very high share (53% in 1978) of the aggregate fuel demand supplied to power plants, is the structural consequence of such dependence in a modern economy on very poor lignites. So are the roughly 50% processing and conversion losses plus internal consumption by the energy industries, the unavoidable price paid for turning this wretched fuel into usable forms of energy. The rapid growth of nuclear power will lead to still higher levels of electrification throughout COMECON, but especially in the smaller states of Eastern Europe.

The impressive development of energy efficient cogeneration and district heating in the USSR and its rapid growth in some of the smaller countries of the Bloc is another structural peculiarity, reinforced by living patterns and government policy. If the intensive research underway on atomic heat and power plants and pure heating stations bears fruit, the already significant role of power plants in furnishing energy at both high and low temperatures (via electricity and steam respectively) should increase much further. Higher levels of electrification are also envisaged and are clearly necessary through mechanising auxiliary work, in view of the great deal of hand labor in lifting, loading etc. operation and internal transport still common throughout the COMECON. At least in the USSR, however, the current huge efforts at resource developments in remote Siberia, are also raising the share, not to mention the quantity, of high quality fuels (nearly all hydrocarbons) used for mechanical energy in the thermodynamically inefficient IC engines and gas turbines. The sectoral and structural consumption patterns and trends will continue to have a very significant influence on attempts at energy savings and the feasibility of substitution for increasingly scarce petroleum.

Biographies of Authors

Name: Dr. Theodore SHABAD

Current position: Editor
                       Soviet Geography Journal
                       145 East 84th Street
                       New York, NY 10028
                       USA

Main field of work: Publication of *Soviet Geography* journal. Research and writing on natural resource and energy policy of the USSR.

Publications during last two years: (with Leslie Dienes) *The Soviet Energy System,* London, John Wiley & Sons, 1979 "Soviet Regional Policy and CMEA Integration" in Paul Marer and John Michael Montias (eds.) *East European Integration and East-West Trade,* Bloomington, Ind., Indiana University Press, 1980, pp. 223-244.
"Some Aspects of Central Asian Manpower and Urbanization", *Soviet Geography*, February 1979.
"Preliminary Results of 1979 Soviet Census (urban-rural and interregional migration by republics; male-female ratios)", *Soviet Geography*, September 1979.
"Magaden and the Upper Kolyma Country", *Soviet Geography*, February, 1980.
"Ethnic Results of the 1979 Census of the USSR", *Soviet Geography,* September 1980.

Name: Professor Robert W. CAMPBELL

Current position: Chairman and Professor of Economics
Indiana University
Ballantine Hall
Bloomington, Indiana 47405
USA

Main field of work: Teaching and Research on Soviet and East European
Economic Affairs

Publications during   *Soviet Energy R & D: Goals, Planning and*
last two years: *Organizations*, Rand Corporation, R-2253-DOE, May
1978, 98 pp.
Soviet Energy Balances, Rand Corporation,
R-2257-DOE, December 1978.
Soviet Energy Technologies: Planning, Policy,
Research and Development, Indiana University
Press, 1980.
"Energy in the USSR to the Year 2000", a paper to
be included in a conference volume, edited by Abram
Bergson and Herbert Levine.

Name: Mr. Jeremy L. RUSSELL

Address: Shell International Petroleum Co. Ltd.
Shell Centre
London
SE1 7 NA
England

Main field of work: The Comecon energy situation and geopolitics

Publications during
last two years: (all internal)

Name: Dr. Friedemann MÜLLER
Current position: Senior Researcher
Stiftung Wissenschaft und Politik
8026 Ebenhausen
Germany
Ford Foundation Fellow (1980-81) at
The Rand Corporation

1700 Main Street
Santa Monica, Ca. 90406
USA

Main field of work:

Energy Situation in Soviet Bloc.
Economic Aspects of Military Expenditure
Politics of East-West Trade.

Publications during last two years:

"Die Situation des Energiesektors in der Sowjetunion mit Blick auf die 80er Jahre", *Osteuropa Wirtschaft,* Vol. 24, no. 1, 1979, p. 24-34; English translation in *Soviet and Eastern European Foreign Trade,* Vol. XVI, No. 1, Spring 1980.
"Gesamteuropäische Zusammenarbeit im Energiebereich. Ein neuer Ansatzpunkt für die Ost-West-Kooperation", *Europa Archive,* Vol. 34, no. 11, 1979. p. 171-181; English in English edition.
"Abhangigkeit und Vertrauen als sicherheitspolitische Komponente der Ost-West-Wirtschaftsbeziehungen", in: Bruno Simma, Edda Blenk-Knocke, (eds.), *Zwischen Intervention und Zusammenarbeit,* (Berlin 1979), p. 319-336.
"The Interests of the Federal Republic of Germany in East-West Cooperation in Energy", in *Christopher T. Saunders (ed.), "East and West in the Energy Squeeze",* The Macmillan Press Ltd., London 1980.
"Das Energieproblem der Sowjetunion." Ansatzpunkt für eine starke Verflechtung zwischen Ost und West? *Europa Archiv, Vol. 36, No. 3, 1981.*

Name: Professor Carl H. McMILLAN

Current position:

Director and Professor of Economics
Institute of Soviet and East European Studies
Paterson Hall
Carleton University
Ottawa K1S 5B6
Canada

Main field of work: Comparative economics

Publications during last two years: *Partners in East-West Economic Relations — The Determinants of Choice,* New York, Pergamon Press, 1980, 476 (co-editor with Z.M. Fallenbuchl) "Growth of External Investments by the Comecon Countries", *The World Economy,* Vol. 2, no. 3 (Sept. 1979), pp. 363-386. "Soviet Investment in the Industrialized Western Economies and in the Developing Economies of the Third World", in Joint Economic Committee, US Congress, *Soviet Economy in a Time of Change,* Washington, DC, Government Printing Office, 1979, pp. 625-647. "Joint Investment in Resource Development: Sectoral Approaches to Socialist Integration" in Joint Economic Committee, US Congress, (ed.), *East European Economic Assessment,* Washington, DC, 1980 (co-author with J. B. Hannigan).

Name: Mr. John B. HANNIGAN

Current position: Research Associate
Institute of Soviet and East European Studies
Paterson Hall
Carleton University
Ottawa K1S 5B6
Canada

Main field of work: Current problems and issues in Soviet and East European economies, and East-West economic relations

Publications during last two years: "The Participation of Canadian Firms in East-West Trade: A Statistical Profile", *East-West Commercial Relations Series,* Ottawa, Carleton University, June 1979 (co-author).
"The Orenburg Natural Gas Project and Fuels-Energy Balances in Eastern Europe", *East-West Commercial Relations Series,* Ottawa, Carleton University, July 1980.
"Joint Investment in Resource Development: Sectoral Approaches to Socialist Integration", in *Joint Economic Committee,* US Congress, (ed.), *East European Economic Assessment,* Washington DC, 1980 (co-author with C.H. McMillan).

Name: A. F. G. SCANLAN

Current position: Economic Adviser
                        Public Affairs and Information Department
                        The British Petroleum Company Limited

Main field of work: Graduate in economics from London University and
                        Fellow of the U.K. Institute of Petroleum. After flying
                        training in Canada, he spent 25 years with BP in
                        many aspects of international oil trading and
                        strategic planning including 6 years in charge of
                        energy supply forecasting. A strong believer in a
                        "total world" approach to energy economics, he has
                        been producing specialist analyses of Comecon
                        energy since 1967.

Name: Dr. Jochen BETHKENHAGEN

Current position: Senior Researcher
                        Deutsches Institut fur Wirtschaftsforschung
                        Königin-Luise-Strasse 5
                        1000 Berlin 33
                        Germany

Main field of work: CMEA: Energy Policy and Integration; East-Trade of
                        West Germany.

Publications during   "Stagnation des Exports in die RGW-Lander halt an.
last two years: Zum Osthandel der Bundesrepublik Deutschland im
                        Jahr 1978." In: *Wochenbericht des DIW,* Nr.
                        13/1979.
                        "Zunehmende Wachstumsschwierigkeiten im RGW
                        (mit M. Lodahl, H. Machowski und M. E. Ruban)."
                        In: *Wochenbericht des DIW,* Nr. 20/1979.
                        "Ausbau der Kernenergie soll Autarkie der
                        Energieversorgung des RGW sichern." In:
                        Wochenbericht des DIW, Nr. 35/1979.
                        "Handel DDR-UdSSR im Zeichen verminderten
                        Wachstums (mit H. Lambrecht)." In: *Wochenbericht
                        des DIW,* Nr. 7/1980.
                        "Preissteigerungen begunstigen Bemuhungen der

RGW-Lander um Verminderung ihres Defizits. Zum Osthandel der Bundesrepublik Deutschland 1979." In: *Wochenbericht des DIW*, Nr. 15/1980.

"Zur Wirtschaftslage im RGW: Erneute Wachstumsabschwachung engt Spielraum für Lebensstandardsverbesserungen ein (mit M. Lodahl, H. Machowski und M. E. Ruban)." In: *Wochenbericht des DIW*, Nr. 20/1980.

"Wachstumsfordernde und wachstumshemmende Effekte der Integration der DDR in den RGW (mit H. Lambrecht)." In: *Vierteljahrshefte zur Wirtschaftsforchung des DIW*, Nr. 3/1979, S. 261-273.

"Die Entwicklung der Wirtschaftsbeziehungen zur Sowjetunion." In: Hans-Adolf Jacobsen, Gert Leptin, Ulrich Scheuner, Eberhard Schulz (Hrsg.): *Drei Jahrzehnte Aussenpolitik der DDR.* (Munchen-Wien 1979), S. 381-402.

"Die Aussenwirtschaftsbeziehungen der DDR vor dem Hintergrund von Produktion und Verbrauch" (mit H. Lambrecht). *Berichte des Bundesinstituts für Ostwissenschaftliche und Internationale Studien.* Nr. 19/1979, 56 S.

"Ausbauplane der Kernenergiegewinnung im Rahmen der allgemeinen Energiepolitik der Lander des RGW." In: Arnold Buchholz (Hrsg.): *Kernenergiepolitik der Lander des RGW. Konferenzbericht. Sonderveroffentlichungen des Bundesinstituts für ostwissenschaftliche und internationale Studien,* Oktober 1979, S. 3-10.

"Uber den Zusammenhand von aussenwirtschaftlichen Interessen und Entspannung (mit S. Kupper und H. Lambrecht)." In *Die DDR im Entspannungsprozess/Lebensweise im realen Sozialismus. 13. Tagung zum stand der DDR-Forschung in der Bundesrepublik,* 27-30 Mai 1980. Köln 1980.

"Die Energiepolitik der UdSSR im Rahmen der weltwirtschaftlichen Entwicklung. Die Rolle der Kernenergie." Paper given at the Zweiter Weltkongress für Sowjet- und Osteuropastudien. Garmisch 30.9 bis 4.10.1980.

Name:	Professor Leslie DIENES
Current position:	Department of Geography University of Kansas Lawrence, Kansas 66044 USA
Main field of work:	Geography of the USSR and Eastern Europe. Specialization: Energy, industry, regional development.
Publications during last two years:	With Theodore Shabad, *The Soviet Energy System: Resource Use and Policies* (Winston and John Wiley), 1979, 298 pp. "The Soviet Energy Policy" in US Congress, Joint Economic Committee, *Soviet Economy in a Time of Change* (Washington, DC: US Government Printing Office), 1979, pp. 197-230. "Soviet Energy Policy and the Hydrocarbons: Comments and Rejoinder", in Association of American Geographers, Discussion Paper no. 7. Project on *Soviet Natural Resources in the World Economy* (Syracuse University) 1979, Rejoinder by Leslie Dienes, pp. 66-94. The Regional Dimensions of Soviet Energy Policy (With Emphasis on Consumption and Transport)'' in Association of American Geographers, Discussion Paper no. 13. Project on *Soviet Natural Resources in the World Economy* (Syracuse University), 1979, 65 pp. "Energy and Modernization in the USSR", *Soviet Geography,* March 1980, pp. 121-158. "Energy Conservation in the USSR" in John P. Hardt, (ed.), *Energy in Soviet Policy* (Congressional Research Service). Prepared for the Subcommittee on International Economics, US Congress, Joint Economic Committee. In press.
Name:	Mr. G. Michael ROESKAU
Current position:	Principal Administrator International Energy Agency IEA/OECD 2 rue Andre-Pascal

75775 Paris
France
(on secondment from the Federal Government, Bonn)

Main field of work: Analysis of energy prospects and policies of non-IEA/OECD countries.

Publications during last two years: "Pespektiven der Energieproduktion Osteuropas," in *Zeitschrift für Energiewirtschaft,* January 1980 (Köln, FRG)

Name: Mr. Jonathan P. STERN

Current position: Consultant and Analyst
Conant and Associates Ltd.
Flat 1
157 Stapleton Hall Road
London
N4 4QS
England

Main field of work: Soviet and East European Energy.
World Natural Gas Trade.

Publications during last two years: *Soviet Natural Gas Development to 1990: The Implications for the CMEA and the West* (Lexington, Mass., Lexington Books/D.C. Heath & Co., 1980).

Name: Professor Peter WILES

Current position: Professor of Russian Social and Economic Studies
London School of Economics and Political Science
Houghton Street
London
WC2A 2AE
England

Main field of work: Communist Economies

Name: LTC Tyrus W. COBB

Current position: Associate Professor
                           Department of Social Sciences
                           US Military Academy
                           West Point, NY 10996
                           USA

Main field of work: Energy and National Security.
                           Soviet National Security Policy.
                           Comparative Defense Strategies.

Publications during   "The Soviet Energy Dilemma: Extent of the
last two years: Crisis and Implications for US National Security
                           Policy", *ORBIS,* (Vol. 23, no. 2, Summer, 1979).
                           "Power and Policy in the Soviet Union", chapter to
                           appear in Jordan and Taylor, editors, *US National
                           Security: Policy and Process.*
                           "Tactical Air Defense: A US—Soviet Net Assess-
                           ment", *Air University Review,* March-April, 1979.
                           "Perspectives on the Soviet Energy Situation",
                           Keynote Address to the *Energy and National Securi-
                           ty Seminar,* co-sponsored by the Ohio State Univer-
                           sity and the US Department of Energy, Washington,
                           DC, May, 1980.
                           "Military Power and Soviet Foreign Policy: The View
                           from the Kremlin", address to the Boston World
                           Affairs Council, Boston, MA, May, 1980.
                           "The Soviet Union and the Middle East: Some
                           Security Considerations", paper presented to the
                           New York State *Air Force Association* annual
                           meeting held at West Point, NY, March 1980.
                           "The Political Economy of Contemporary Soviet
                           Security Policy", presented to a panel on *Issues in
                           Soviet-American Security* at the national convention
                           of the International Studies Association (ISA), Los
                           Angeles, Calif., 18-22 March 1980.

Name: Monsieur Hervé GICQUIAU

Current position: Chargé d'Etudes au Centre d'Etudes et de Documen-
                           tation sur l'URSS, la Chine et l'Europe de l'Est.
                           Documentation Francaise

29 quai Voltaire
75340 Paris
France

Main field of work: Industrie de l'URSS (Organisation - Branches -Produits - Entreprises)

Publications during last two years: "Fondements et pratique de la réorganisation de l'industrie soviétique," *(Courrier des Pays de l'Est, no. 215),*
"Panorama de l'URSS" (en collaboration), *(Courrier des Pays de l'Est,* fevrier-mars, 1979).
"Sidérurgie soviétique: Nouvelles stratégies du métal et de l'investissement," *(Courrier des Pays de l'Est,* mai 1980).
"La direction de la qualité dans l'industrie soviétique: cadre d'organisation et formes d'incitation," *(Economie et société,* série G, 1980).

Name: Dr. Robin WATSON

Current position: CIA, Washington, D.C. 20505

Main field of work: Robin Watson's research has been focused on the use of quantitative methods to simulate economic phenomena. He has constructed regional macroeconometric and mathematical programming models of the United States, particularly concentration on energy issues. He is currently interested in the macroeconomic adjustments being made in planned economics to compounding economic constraints — especially energy supplies.

Name: Joseph LICARI

Current position: CIA, Washington, D.C. 20505

Main field of work: Dr. Joseph Licari has spent more than ten years in quantitative economic research. Much of this work has involved applications of computer modelling and statistical analysis to the study of centrally planned economies. Prior to his present position with the Central Intelligence Agency, Dr. Licari held positions in private industry and academia.

CMEA Energy Production and World Energy Balance in the 1980s

Michael Roeskau

There are numerous aspects in the energy situation of the CMEA countries which warrant attention. Political and geopolitical questions are linked to it. This paper, however, is more limited in scope. Its purpose is to put forward some background against which the CMEA's energy performance may be estimated. What matters with respect to the world energy balance is not only to what extent Eastern countries will or will not produce more than their aggregate energy requirements, but also whether prospective energy demand and supply policies in other parts of the world will create supply deficits or surpluses. It is on the latter question that the paper concentrates. The analysis suggests some weakening of demand in future energy markets which, in turn, may ease the need for oil but not necessarily for other energy imports from Eastern countries.

Trends in World Energy Demand (Table 1)

Between 1975 and 1981, the energy outlook for the world changed dramatically. The oil crises of 1973-74 and 1979-80 had two immediate consequences. First, the sudden reductions of OPEC oil production and exports triggered erratic price increases: the average OPEC government sales price rose form around $2.30/barrel in summer 1973 to $35/barrel in the 1st Quarter 1981; in the period after 1978 alone, the nominal oil price grew by 170 per cent. Secondly, these experiences woke industrialized consumer countries to the awareness of the growing equilibrium in energy supply and demand trends which would expose the world economy to continued upward pressures on oil prices unless major efforts were made to improve energy efficiency in all sectors and to encourage rapid fuel switching.

These enormous price rises dampened oil and energy demand. A few numerical examples, taken from industrialized countries, may illustrate this. An analysis of energy demand between 1960 and 1973 showed that, if past trends had continued, primary energy demand in OECD countries would have reached more than 5000 mtoe (million tons oil equivalent) in 1980. Yet, our latest estimates indicate that OECD primary energy demand, in 1980, was 3830 mtoe, i.e. 3.2 per cent below the level of 1979. On average, this amounts to an annual growth rate of total energy requirements of 1.2 per cent for the period since 1973 which compares to the average of 5.2 per cent a year up to 1973. Oil demand was more directly hit, and hence, reacted faster: after 1973, oil consumption in industrialized countries grew only by an average 0.6 per cent a year as compared to almost 8 per cent annually in the period before. Oil demand growth was negative in 1974 and 1975 and again in 1979. In 1980, a dramatic reduction of 8 percent was recorded and it is expected that, in 1981, oil consumption will be about 2 per cent below the 1980 level.

TABLE 1
IEA Secretariat Scenario for Total Primary Energy Requirements
(including bunkers; in mtoe)

	1979	1985	1990
IEA	3725	3920	4300
Other OECD	230	230	250
TOTAL OECD	3955	4150	4550
OPEC	190	320	460
Non-OPEC LDCs	560	780	1040
Total	4705	5250	6050

Memorandum Items (in per cent p.a.):

Economic Growth	1979-1985	1985-1990
OECD/IEA	2.75	3.2
OPEC	6.8	6.0
Non-OPEC LDCs	4.5	4.4
Energy Demand Growth		
OECD/IEA	0.8	1.9
OPEC	8.9	7.6
Non-OPEC LDCs	5.8	5.5

It is true that an important part of the energy savings achieved have occurred because of low economic growth. In fact, the contractive effects of soaring oil prices constrained overall demand which, in turn, led to stagnation, and even to temporary reductions, in economic output. After the first oil crisis, the average rate of economic growth in OECD countries fell to 0.5 per cent in 1974 and to −0.4 per cent in 1975. Between 1976 and 1979, a recovery period followed but economic growth was again as low as

1.1 per cent in 1980. Yet, this still amounts to positive economic growth and it was achieved with decreasing energy input. In fact, during the period from 1973-1979, the overall efficiency of energy use (as measured by energy requirements per unit of GNP) had already improved by 7 percent. Moreover, while between 1960 and 1973 for each 1 per cent growth in GDP, OECD economies experienced an average 1 per cent increase in energy use, this coefficient decreased to about 0.4 in the period from 1973-1979. This is evidence that the oil shocks have not only triggered temporary, cyclical reductions, but have set in motion structural changes which will have a continuing effect on energy demand. Thus, it is expected that the overall energy efficiency will improve by a further 14 per cent over the next decade and that the energy coefficient for the entire period should remain low, in a range of 0.4 to a maximum average of 0.6.

Against this background, the IEA Secretariat has developed "plausible scenarios" for 1985 and 1990. These scenarios are not projections, but are designed to illustrate the possible results which may be obtained if determined efforts are made and strengthened policies are adopted. They are based on an analysis, and eventually a revision, of estimates submitted by IEA member countries. Allowance has been made for remaining OECD countries so as to present these scenarios in a comprehensive picture for the industrialized world. For the period to 1985, economic growth in industrialized countries is likely to be considerably lower than previously expected, and an average real economic growth of 2.75 per cent p.a. is assumed. Taking into account growth rates of about 1 per cent in each of 1980 and 1981, this would require annual growth of about 3.6 per cent over the period 1982-85 which would be similar to the average economic growth experienced during the last recovery between 1977 and 1979. As a result of limited economic growth and a high degree of price elasticity in energy consumption, growth in overall energy demand should not exceed an average of about 0.8 per cent a year. This would lead to total primary energy requirements of roughly 4150 mtoe for the IEA/OECD area. Over the second half of the decade, the OECD countries are assumed to achieve average annual economic growth rates of 3.2 per cent. At the same time the potential for relatively simple and less expensive energy conservation measures will progressively be reduced and it will become more difficult to maintain the high rate of energy improvements expected to take place in the early 1980's on the basis of the 1979/80 oil price increases. Therefore, a higher energy demand growth rate of about 1.9 per cent a year is possible. Total primary energy requirements might thus be in the vicinity of 4550 mtoe at the end of the decade. This would represent an annual growth in energy demand of 1.2 per cent for the entire period. If this trend could be maintained, total primary energy requirements should not exceed an order of magnitude of 5400 mtoe by the year 2000.

CMEA

Energy demand trends in industrialized countries are not necessarily indicative of what will happen in other parts of the world. One example is the centrally planned economies of the CMEA where no sufficient incentives for energy conservation are set by the price mechanism, but must be translated into the economic fabric of these countries by means of shifts in planning decisions which, in turn, may create problems of priorities and sectoral distortions. The continuing high growth of energy and oil demand, which prevailed in the USSR even after the first oil shock at average annual rates of 4.2 and 4.6 per cent respectively, are evidence of a lower degree of flexibility and a slower working of the adjustment process than in market economies. Even if future growth rates should be lower than those of the 1970s, official observers agree that total energy requirements in the CMEA countries are bound to rise significantly faster than in the industrialized countries of the West.

OPEC

OPEC energy consumption will grow at a faster rate than in industrialized countries. While OECD countries may be heading for a prolonged period of limited economic growth, OPEC economies can be expected to sustain much higher economic growth rates. This expected favorable economic performance will be due to the availability of both energy at comparatively low cost and capital derived from oil exports. By the same token, energy consumption will increase considerably in OPEC countries. However, even for OPEC one should not assume that the relationship between economic growth and growth in energy consumption will remain stable. Industrial development in these countries, while concentrating on energy intensive industries, is based on technology from industrialized countries where energy is scarce, resulting in increased energy efficiency of all capital equipment. At the same time, OPEC countries are becoming increasingly aware of the need for energy conservation in their own economies. Internal oil prices, which so far have attained world market levels only in Algeria and Nigeria may be allowed to increase in the future. A declining coefficient between economic and energy demand growth is therefore probable. It is assumed that it will be 1.32 in 1985 and decline thereafter to 1.27 in 1990, showing a gradual move of OPEC economies to more mature industrial economies. As a result, total energy consumption growth rates in OPEC countries may average 8.9 per cent per annum between 1979 and 1985 and fall to an average 7.6 per cent per annum in the second half of the decade. Thus, OPEC commercial energy demand which was estimated roughly at 190 mtoe in 1979, may more than double over the coming decade and rise to 320 mtoe in 1985 and 460 mtoe in 1990. By the end of the century it might almost double again and reach more than 800 mtoe.

Non-OPEC Developing Countries

The problem of economic and, in particular, industrial development is common to OPEC countries and other developing countries. For that reason, underlying trends of economic growth and energy demand are comparable. The early stage of development of non-OPEC developing countries and the enormous unfilled material requirements of their populations leave scope for economic growth. Starting from a low base, these countries may in fact have to maintain higher economic growth rates than industrialized countries. But the process of gradual industrialization and mechanization will be accompanied by even faster growing energy requirements. At the same time, the absolute potential for energy savings is low and will largely be overtaken by the needs of further development. For the "have-nots" among these countries, growth in energy requirements will therefore represent a serious constraint on development and demand estimates are based on the assumption that, on average, it will in fact be possible to considerably increase energy availability from indigenous sources of hydrocarbons and coal as well as from new and renewable sources of energy. In that case, total primary energy requirements of non-OPEC developing countries could grow from an estimated 560 mtoe in 1979 to about 780 mtoe in 1985 and to approximately 1000 mtoe by the end of the decade. For the year 2000, the underlying trend would suggest a range of 1700 to 1800 mtoe.

Changes in the Supply Pattern (Table 2)

Satisfying the amount of overall energy demand will only be possible if significant changes in the supply pattern and, conversely, in the structure of energy use occur. This is where demand and supply scenarios imply joint actions by governments, companies and private users to bring about structural changes in the energy economy. In fact, it is recognized among industrialized countries that oil supplies from Third World producer countries will at best stabilize, but are more likely to fall over time. All of these countries have therefore pledged to reduce the share of oil in their energy supply from the present 50 percent to 40 percent by 1990. Once this goal is achieved, it may be possible to push the trend further towards an oil share of less than 30 percent by the end of the century.

IEA SUPPLY STRATEGIES

Such a scenario, however, would require conservation efforts to reduce oil use in electricity generation, industry and the residential sector (so that oil use in these sectors would be 811 mtoe rather than the 922 mtoe which may otherwise be expected for IEA countries by 1985). It would also necessitate the following supply strategies for IEA countries:

— Coal would have to play a major role, providing about 27 per cent of TPE in 1990 and 35 per cent in 2000, compared with about 20 per cent today. This would require an increase of 60 percent in coal use by 1990 and of more than 240 per cent (over 1978 level) by the end of the century.

— Nuclear would be a second major building block — accounting for 8 per cent of TPE in 1990 and 12 per cent in 2000, compared with less than 4 per cent today. This would require about 250 GW of installed capacity in 1990 and 485 GW in 2000 — a two-and-a-half-fold increase over the next decade and almost a fivefold increase by the end of the century.

— Domestic oil production is expected to be maintained approximately at current levels through the end of the century.

— A large increase in natural gas use is expected, primarily through increased imports equivalent to about 205 mtoe by the year 2000.

— Hydro and geothermal energy would have to increase by almost 50 per cent over the next 20 years. Other energy sources (mainly solar) would make an increasing contribution by the end of the century.

Only if all these policies succeed and assuming that overall OECD energy demand will not grow more than about 1.2 per cent p.a., will it be possible to limit dependence on imported oil and to reduce oil imports to less than 1100 mtoe (i.e. less than 22 mbd for OECD or 19.5 mbd for IEA) by 1990.

TABLE 2
Plausible OECD Energy Outlook
(including bunkers; mtoe)

	1979	1985	1990
OECD Primary Energy Demand	3955	4150	4550
OECD Indigenous Supply			
Coal	730	865	1110
Oil	720	700	680
Gas	695	685	710
Nuclear	130	275	400
Hydro/Geo/Others	250	285	330
Total	2530	2810	3230
OECD Net Imports			
Coal	30	45	80
Oil	1350	1200	1090
Gas	45	95	160
Total	1425	1340	1330

Whether the corresponding oil exports will be available on the world market depends mainly on production policies in OPEC countries. In 1980, OPEC oil production (including NGL) fell from 1575 mtoe (= 31.5 mbd) to approximately 1378 mtoe (= 27.6 mbd). As this was mainly due to slackening demand and disruptions related to the war between Iran and Iraq, underlying productive capacity may still be in place or could be repaired if hostilities stopped. This, in turn, leaves theoretical scope for annual production levels up to 1500 mtoe (= 30 mbd) in both 1985 and 1990 provided adequate demand and moderate production policies. At the same time, OPEC's commercial production of natural gas is likely to increase rapidly over the next decade. As OPEC countries are more and more concerned about the wastefulness of present flaring practices, efforts are underway in most OPEC countries towards gathering and marketing natural gas. From current levels of roughly 90 mtoe, gas production could grow two-fold by 1985 (175 mtoe) and three-fold by 1990 (268 mtoe). Other energy sources, while increasing in absolute figures, will continue to be confined to a marginal role in OPEC energy production and consumption.

But while OPEC energy production as a whole may not increase significantly, OPEC domestic demand is likely to grow two-and-a-half fold over the next decade. Less would then be available for exports. And, even in the case of continuing high production levels, oil exports by OPEC would fall to 1250 mtoe in 1985 and to 1170 mtoe in 1990. While natural gas exports starting from a low basis may more than treble over the next decade this would not suffice to maintain the overall energy exports at 1979 levels and a diminishing, contribution of OPEC to world energy supplies is predictable (see Table 3).

Unlike OPEC countries, the non-OPEC developing countries use and produce a variety of energy sources. While oil and gas are very important, coal, hydropower and renewable energy sources are of similar importance. In some countries, particularly in Africa, unrecorded renewable energy is responsible for a much larger proportion of energy production and consumption than are oil and gas. Therefore, the attempt to strike an overall balance is not designed to reflect the complexities of developing countries' energy problems, but merely to assess possible strains on world energy markets. The main feature arising from tentative IEA estimates (Table 4) is that there is a potential for LDC oil production to grow at roughly the same pace as soaring oil consumption. While oil production will probably be concentrated in a relatively small number of countries such as Mexico, Brazil, Argentina, Egypt, Angola, Cameroon, Malaysia, Brunei, the aggregate LDC supply deficit would not grow further and possibly diminish slightly due to a gradual move to other commercial energy sources. In fact, the oil component in the LDC energy mix is expected to fall from over 60 per cent to about 50 per cent on the demand side by the end of the century. In parallel to growing oil production, natural gas will increasingly be gathered and marketed. At the same time, prospects for higher coal production exist in countries such as India, Pakistan, Vietnam, Korea, Taiwan, Brazil, Chile and Colombia. By 1990, Bangaladesh, Malaysia, Thailand, Angola, Zimbabwe, Botswana, Swaziland and Argentina could also become coal producers. With their coal production growing at estimated rates of 7-8 per cent annually, coal exports from these countries could play a more important role and an aggregate surplus may arise for LDCs as a whole.

TABLE 3
Projected OPEC Energy Supply-Demand Balances [a]
(mtoe)

	1979	1985	1990
Energy Consumption			
Oil and NGL	115	190	270
Natural Gas	68	120	175
Solid Fuels	2	6	8
Others [b]	3	4	4
Total	188	320	457
Energy Production			
Oil and NGL	1575	1475	1480
Natural Gas	90	175	268
Solid Fuels	2	6	8
Others [b]	3	4	4
Total	1670	1660	1760
Energy Imports (-)/Exports (+)			
Oil and NGL	+ 1435	+ 1250	+ 1170
(includes bunkers	-25	-35	-40)
Natural Gas	+ 22	+ 55	+ 93
Solid Fuel	—	—	—
Others [b]	—	—	—
Total	+ 1457	+ 1305	+ 1263

(a) Assumptons (in % p.a.)

	1978-85	1985-90
Economic Growth Rate	6.80	6.00
TPER/GDP Growth Rate Ratio	1.32	1.27
Energy Demand Growth Rate	8.90	7.62

(b) "*Others*" include hydroelectric, nuclear, geothermal and solar power.

TABLE 4
Projected Non-OPEC LDC Energy Supply-Demand Balances [a]
(mtoe)

	1979	1985	1990
Energy Consumption			
Oil and NGL	347.5	470.0	575
Natural Gas	42.5	60.0	100
Solid Fuels	102.5	145.0	200
Others [b]	67.0	110.0	150
Total	559.5	785.0	1025

	1979	1985	1990
Energy Production			
Oil and NGL	253.5	435.0	525
Natural Gas	53.5	77.5	110
Solid Fuels	102.5	157.5	230
Others[b]	67.0	110.0	150
Total	476.5	780.0	1015
Energy Imports (-)/Exports (+)			
Oil and NGL	-119.1	-60.0	-80
(includes bunkers	-25.0	-25.0	-30)
Natural Gas	+ 11.5	+ 17.5	+ 10
Solid Fuel	—	+ 12.5	+ 30
Total	-107.5	-30.0	-40

(a) Assumptions (in % p.a.)	1978-85	1980-90
Economic Growth Rate	4.50	4.40
TPER/GDP Growth Rate Ratio	1.29	1.25
Energy Demand Growth Rate	5.81	5.48

(b) "Others" include nuclear, geothermal and hydropower but not solar or biomass.

Towards more equilibrium in world energy markets?

It is worthwhile to try to juxtapose the different trends described above. Of course, the figures in Table 5 represent only very rough estimates and their absolute values hardly exceed a reasonable margin of error. Yet, their aggregate result may serve as one indication in which direction world energy markets could be expected to move. In fact, they confirm the outlook for some easing of the oil supply situation accompanied by increasingly scarce supplies of natural gas:

TABLE 5
Estimate Import/Export Balances by Fuel Source
(excluding Centrally Planned Economies; in mtoe)

		1979	1985	1990
Oil	OECD	-1350	-1200	-1090
	OPEC[1]	+ 1410	+ 1215	+ 1130
	LDCS	-120	-60	-80
	Total	-60	-45	-40
	[1]excluding bunkers			
Gas	OECD	-45	-100	-160
	OPEC	+ 22	+ 55	+ 93
	LDCs	+ 11	+ 17	+ 10
	Total	-12	-28	-57
Coal	OECD	-30	-45	-60
	LDCs	—	+ 15	+ 30
	Total	-30	-30	-30

— The deficit shown for oil supply in 1979 coincides with the tight market situation in that year and the price rises which actually occurred. Not surprisingly, the deficit is in the same order as OECD net imports of crude and products from European CMEA countries (see Table 6). However, this picture might improve slightly over the decade. If slackening demand in industrialized consumer countries is superseded by structural change in their energy economy, oil import requirements might actually fall to about 1100 mtoe. In that case, the supply deficit would narrow even in the face of growing domestic demand in OPEC countries.

— The gas situation, at present, seems less tense. A certain deficit is visible, but it is easily covered by gas imports from Eastern countries. With growing gas requirements in industrialized countries, the supply deficit may widen gradually, even if sizable increases in the gas exports from OPEC and other developing countries are assumed. If OECD countries do not step up their domestic gas production, this deficit would have to be filled by increased contributions from outside.

— Coal plays a minor role in an analysis of aggregate area requirements because the main expansion in supply streams has to take place among OECD/IEA countries themselves. Yet, the slight deficit left over after consideration of a certain coal surplus in Third World countries indicates a scope for coal deliveries from other parts of the world.

TABLE 6

OECD Net Imports of Crude and Petroleum Products by Origin
(million metric tons)

		1978	1979	1979	1980
		year		1st three quarters	
USSR					
	Crude	36.3	36.9	27.4	24.4
	Products	23.9	21.8	15.8	15.7
		60.2	58.7	43.2	40.1
Eastern Europe					
	Crude	0.6	1.4	0.9	1.7
	Products	7.5	9.9	6.7	10.3
		8.1	11.3	7.6	12.0
Total		68.3	70.0	50.8	52.1

However, one should not be misled by smallness of these deficits. Rather they should be interpreted in the light of the optimistic policy assumptions made. In fact, numerous risks are involved and deviations from this scenario are quite likely. In particular, uncertainties exist with respect to changes in the structure of energy use and supply and, without exception, they point to the downward side, i.e. to widening deficits. While demand behavior and related price elasticities are fairly well known and, hence, allow reasonable forecasting of overall requirements, implementation of policies to restructure the energy economy may more easily escape economic projections.

In this respect, major uncertainties lie with strategies in consumer countries themselves. For it is by no means certain that the present level of domestic oil production will actually be maintained, that coal production and use can be expanded, that nuclear energy will come onstream at desirable levels and that oil use can be reduced in all sectors. Failure by industrialized countries to make determined and ultimately successful efforts in these directions would inevitably build up higher oil demand and there are indications that oil imports might be more than 1200 mtoe by 1990 in such a case. At the same time, OPEC countries bear a great part of responsibility. These countries are in a position to make any supply surplus disappear from world oil markets, but they may also reduce oil production further and create deficits if this should meet their purpose. If, for reasons such as depletion concern, OPEC governments decided to produce less than the assumed quantities by 1990, substantial strains would appear. Also, much depends on whether energy exploration and production will advance rapidly in developing countries.

Finally, the CMEA energy situation may well represent an additional risk: the extent to which CMEA countries appear as additional buyers in world oil markets would add to already existing market tensions and would not necessarily be compensated by possible deliveries of other fuel sources. Whether CMEA countries will contribute to narrowing or widening deficits in the world energy balance, depends on their domestic energy production. With overall energy demand likely to continue to grow at a relatively rapid pace, exports can only be maintained or expanded if production increases accordingly or even faster. Yet, the USSR as the main producer country of the CMEA presents favorable production prospects for the 1980's mainly with respect to natural gas. In the case of other energy sources, official estimates submitted by the USSR in the framework of the UN Economic Commission for Europe (Senior Advisers to ECE Governments on Energy) contrast with decreasing increments or reductions in actual output (Table 7).

TABLE 7
Soviet Energy Production

	1978	1979	1980	1981	1985	1990
	(Preliminary Actuals)			(Planned)	(5-Year-Plan)	(Official Estimates)
Oil (mtoe)	572	586	603	610	620-645	620-700
Gas (bcm)	372	407	435	458	600-640	705-820
Coal (mt)	724	719	716	738	770-800	1000-1250
Electricity (TWh)	1202	1239	1290	1335	1550-1600	1900-2050

— The fact that gas production has always achieved or even over-achieved planned targets over recent years is evidence for the technical and managerial capabilities of the Soviet gas industry. Further increases over the 435 bcm (362.5 mtoe) produced in 1980 are therefore likely. Official estimates for 1990 range from 710-820 bcm (590-685 mtoe) and are consistent with new Five-Year-Plan target of 600-640 bcm for 1985 (500-530 mtoe). At least the lower ends of these ranges should not be out of reach.

— By contrast, oil production has been continuously below target and official figures seem to acknowledge the likelihood of a flat production profile. In fact, estimates range from 620-700 mtoe for 1990 and from 613-722 mtoe for 2000. The lower ends of these ranges practically include the present production level which was 603 mtoe in 1980 and is planned to be 610 mtoe this year. The new Five-Year-Plan target of 620-645 mtoe is also in line with this cautious approach.

— Official estimates for Soviet coal production are more optimistic. According to them, production would raise from 487 mtoe in 1978 to 675-845 mtoe (475-595 mtoe) by 1990. This would imply average growth rates of 2.8-4.7% p.a. which have never been realized in the past. By contrast, the Five-Year-Plan target of 770-800 tons or 518-538 mtoe (365-379 mtoe) is more prudent and suggests a growth rate of only 0.9 per cent p.a. in the lower case. Yet, the reductions in coal output recorded over the last two years make it doubtful whether even this modest goal can be achieved.

— Electricity production is officially estimated to grow by roughly 4 per cent p.a. to some 1900-2050 TWh by 1990. This would be a slightly faster pace than has been achieved over the last two years. Moreover, it would imply a greatly-increased share of nuclear-generated electricity. In fact, the nuclear goal for 1985 is 220-225 TWh as compared to the 71-72 TWh expected for 1981. Yet, there are serious doubts about the ability of the Soviet nuclear industry to provide the necessary 25000 MW of new nuclear generating capacity which will have to be commissioned before end-1985.

Despite the positive outlook for increased gas production, the Soviet authorities have omitted to define the amount set aside for exports. Neither consumption nor exports have been broken down by oil and gas, but are presented for aggregate hydrocarbons. Thus, hydrocarbon exports are officially estimated to range from 165-259 mtoe by 1990. While the ceiling would allow for a considerable increase, the lower case is slightly below present Soviet exports of oil and gas. In addition, if one accepted the ECE Secretariat's approach of attributing 50 per cent of exports in the lower case to oil and gas respectively, future Soviet oil exports would almost entirely be absorbed by other CMEA countries, but gas exports might double over the decade. What lies ahead then seems to be a switch in, rather than an expansion of, Soviet energy exports and much will depend on Western countries attitude towards such a change in energy trade patterns.

CMEA Energy Demand in the 1980s: A Sectoral Analysis

Leslie Dienes
Nikos Economou

The process of economic development is associated with complex changes in energy consumption through every stage. Not only does per capita usage increase, but the demand pattern undergoes significant shifts both among economic sectors and among end uses distinguished by different thermodynamic characteristics. The evolution of energy demand patterns, however, is greatly affected by variations in resource endowment among the different countries and by government policies, direct and indirect. Since the mobilization of energy resources provides a crucial underpinning to the economic and military strength of a modern state, government goals and priorities in the Soviet Bloc had an especially far-reaching impact on energy consumption.

In analyzing the sectoral pattern of energy demand it is important to separate aggregate consumption from that of delivered energy, i.e. energy available to other sectors of the economy. Because of decreasing quality and/or accessibility, non-renewable primary energy sources are subject to diminishing returns, which technological progress and scale economies may only partially counteract within a given time span. Growing production losses and self use by the energy producing branches are, as a rule, an expression of such a trend. The efficiency and applicability of the many sources of primary energy also vary greatly in the diverse technological processes and end uses demanded by an economy. To increase economic utility, convenience and utilization efficiency at the consumer end, the bulk of primary energy products are refined and converted today, but at the cost of significant energy waste. Electrification via conventional power plants fired by fossil fuels, in particular, is payed for by large thermodynamic losses.

The Sectoral Pattern

The industrialization drive followed by the leadership of the USSR and the European COMECON countries shifted the main locus of energy demand from the household-municipal to the industrial sector. A similar sectoral change took place in the US between 1880 and 1920, though manufacturing and mining here never achieved the degree of preponderance in energy use as they have in the USSR and East Europe. Moreover, the dominance of US industry decreased dramatically since 1920 and today this sector consumes roughly similar quantities of energy as transportation or the household-municipal (including commercial) sector.[1] In Western Europe considered as a unit, industry does represent the highest claimant, but only in about half of these states does this sector receive more than two-fifths of distributed energy and in none more than one half.[2] In the COMECON, on the other hand, the relative share of industry is not only much higher, but has continued to grow right up to the present, albeit at a slowing rate. With construction, it receives over three fifths of all delivered energy in the USSR and over one-half even in Eastern Europe as a whole (Tables 1 and 2).[3]

Such hypertrophy of industry clearly owes much to the Stalinist model of economic development, which stresses the rapid growth of basic manufacturing and the huge expansion of its capital stock. Czechoslovakia assumed the role of the chief metal and heavy equipment and the GDR the main machinery and heavy chemical supplier of the region. Poland and Romania, while far less developed but with comparatively rich resources have, similarly sought to industrialize in a like manner. It is in fact the excessive share and energy intensity of industry, together with very great conversion losses and/or self use (see below), which are responsible for the deceptively high per capita level of energy demand in the COMECON. They also help to explain the high energy intensity of these countries' GNP,[4] about which so much concern has been expressed recently in their literature. The issue is not an idle one. It may be assumed that energy consumption in mining and manufacturing is more technology-specific than in other sectors and has close interdependence with the existing capital stock. Thus apart from the elimination of some obvious wastes by better housekeeping rules industry may be quite resistant to conservation measures, at least in the short and medium term.

Data about energy demand in agriculture are much more limited. In developed countries, the latter invariably is but a very minor direct consumer, though when indirect uses, i.e. energy incorporated in fertilizers and agricultural equipment, are added the role of this sector increases greatly. In most of the COMECON states agriculture has now become a high priority claimant on the respective nations' resources and, with the probable exception of Romania and Poland[5], is no longer slighted in the allocation of energy either. In 1975, Soviet agriculture, not counting domestic use by the farm population, directly accounted for slightly over 5

Table 1

LOSSES AND SECTORAL DISTRIBUTION OF ENERGY CONSUMPTION

	Area	1970 Million tons of SF	%	1978 Million tons of SF	%
Gross	USSR	1029	100.0	1630	100.0
Domestic	US	2243	100.0	2653	100.0
Availability	WE	1474	100.0	1753	100.0
Losses and Internal	USSR	128	10.6	194	11.9
Consumption by Fuel	US	122	5.4	198	7.5
Producing Industries	WE	116	7.9	134	7.6
Conversion and Line	USSR	186	15.4	273	16.7
Losses Plus Station	US	350	15.6	448	16.9
Consumption by the					
Electric Power Industry	WE	229	15.5	228	13.0
Non	USSR	47	3.9	68	4.2
Energy	US	91	4.1	74*	2.8*
Uses	WE	89	6.0	41*	2.3*

DELIVERED ENERGY

	Area	1970 Million tons of SF	%	%	1978 Million tons of SF	%	%
All	USSR	848	70.1	100.0	1095	67.2	100.0
Demand	US	1656	73.8	100.0	1860	70.1	100.0
Sectors	WE	1009	68.5	100.0	1264	72.1	100.0
Industry	USSR	495	40.9	58.4	685	42.0	62.6
and	US	573	25.5	34.6	548	20.7	29.5
Construction	WE	433	29.4	42.9	498	28.4	45.5
Transport	USSR	98	8.1	11.6	120	7.4	11.0
	US	498	22.2	30.1	666	25.1	35.8
	WE	199	13.5	19.7	275	15.7	21.8
Agriculture	USSR	72	6.0	8.4	86	5.3	7.9
	US	40**	1.8	2.4	53**	2.0	2.8
	WE	15***	1.0	1.4	25	1.4	2.0
Household and	USSR	183	15.1	21.5	204	12.5	18.6
Municipal	US	545**	24.3	32.9	593	22.4	31.9
Economy (includ-							
ing commercial)	WE	362***	24.6	35.9	466	26.6	36.9
Unaccounted	US	24	1.1	1.4	73	2.6	3.9
Discrepancy	WE	31	2.1	3.1	86	4.9	6.8

* These declines are due to the exclusion of naptha from the non-energy category at the later date.

** Agricultural consumption estimated from 1974 share of agriculture in energy demand by ''other'' sector. USDA, Economic Research Service, *Energy and US Agriculture 1974 Data Base.* FEA/D-761459. (Washington, Sept. 1976) , p. 2.

*** Total of ''others'' category that comprises the two sectors distributed according to relative rations of 1974 from OECD Energy Balances.

Sources: Data for USSR in 1970 from R. Campbell, *Soviet Energy Balance,* p. 7; for 1978 estimated from 1975 and 1980 consumption figures and forecast on *Ibid.,* and Campbell, ''Energy in the USSR to the year 2000''. Paper prepared for the conference on the Soviet Economy, October 23-25, 1980. Airlie House, Virginia. Campbell's figures for household consumption were modified by incorporating appreciably larger quantities of self-produced fuel as given by Ryps, *Ekonomicheskie problemy,* p. 20. Data for the USSR and West Europe, defined as OECD Europe, from OECD, *Energy Balances of OECD Countries.* 1960/74 and 1974/1978 (Paris 1976 and 1978).

percent of all internal demand (6.3 percent of all fuels, 5.3 percent of electricity, plus some hot water and steam, amounting to about 76 million tons of standard fuel) and 7 percent of delivered energy.[6] In the three northern states of East Europe and Romania agriculture used 3-4 percent of the total, but in Hungary this sector claimed over 7 percent of gross consumption and almost 9 percent of all energy delivered.[7] The greatest demand is for oil products, which comprised over 70 percent of total energy furnished to agriculture in the Soviet Union and more than 86 percent in Hungary.[8] Both Soviet and Hungarian specialists expect consumption by this sector to grow at an annual rate well exceeding that for the economy as a whole, leading to still greater portions of energy flowing into agriculture during the 1980's.[9]

These are extremely high shares, surpassing those claimed by farming in the US and Western Europe several times. However, only when coupled with the value of GNP so produced can their magnitudes be appraised. Per $1 of national income produced, agriculture in the East European states still uses only a fraction of the energy as this sector in the United States (only in Hungary does the energy intensity exceed a quarter of the American level).[10] By contrast, the energy intensiveness of Soviet agriculture surpasses that of its US counterpart, the most mechanized one in the world, by a very significant margin. Indirect demand, i.e. energy embodied in machinery and fertilizers, inflates direct use appreciably in every country. In the USSR the two combined again seem to be larger than in the US and, therefore, must be very much larger per $1 of GNP produced.[11]

In sharp contrast to the high shares of industry and agriculture stands the transport sector with its modest claim on both total and delivered energy in every COMECON country. On a per capita basis, transport uses but a fraction of the energy consumed by this sector in West Europe, let alone the United States, and less even than in Spain, Greece and Portugal.[12] Small size does not in itself explain the discrepancy in the case of East Europe and the undeveloped state of private motoring and trucking must be the chief cause. In the vast USSR, the claim of the transport sector in 1960 was only one half of the corresponding American share, dropping to below one third by the end of the 1970's (Table 1). The sharp relative decline is largely explained by the shift in railroad haulage from steam to diesel and electric traction, which are far more efficient in energy use. Since 1960, the rapid spread of car ownership and trucking almost doubled the quantity of energy delivered to the transport sector in non-communist Europe. In the USSR and East Europe it remained virtually constant.[13] The absolute decline in Czechoslovakia in the 1970's resulted from the belated near elimination of some steam hauls using brown coal. The relatively heavy use of coal even in the past decade explains the higher transport shares in Poland and, to a lesser extent, in the GDR.[14]

At first blush, the position of household-municipal consumers in the COMECON appears favorable. Their shares in total demand and delivered energy approximate these in the United States and West Europe. Such a position, however, is clearly illusiory, and especially so in the USSR. This sector has modernized its energy use to a much smaller degree than manufacturing, and outside large cities it remains woefully backward. According to Soviet specialists, in 1975 solid fuels burned in individual stoves or under miniboilers of apartment blocks still comprised a full half of all energy used by household-municipal consumers in the USSR. Steam from cogenerating plants, pipeline gas plus small quantities of refinery liquids and LPG made up the other half.[15] Though their share declined somewhat since the mid-1960's, the quantity of solid fuels so burned actually increased. In Hungary, coal and wood used on the premises also furnished half of all energy to the domestic sector during 1975;[16] in Czechoslovakia at least as much.[17] And in Poland, over 20 million tons of coal and coke are utilized by the population directly (one third as much as is burned in power stations, which run overwhelmingly on coal), an amount that comprises roughly three-quarters of the total energy consumed by Polish household.[18]

In the current era of labor shortages, ranging form serious to severe among the various COMECON states, the further modernization of the still backward household energy sector is considered essential. Both the USSR and East Europe are planning to expand cogeneration and district heating, with the most ambitious program underway in the GDR.[19] Yet in recent years the increase of cogenerated power and heat has slowed dramatically in both the USSR and Hungary, though in the latter less than one tenth of all electricity and low temperature heat are produced by dual purpose turbines.[20] In these two states, but probably also in Romania and Bulgaria, the majority of heat and power plants are fired by hydrocarbons (their most important fuel source), which are experiencing mounting costs and pressure from other sectors of the economy.[21] The three northern countries of East Europe fuel nearly all such plants by coal, but the share of heat and power stations in total installed capacity is still much lower than in the USSR.[22]

The rapid expansion of coal-fired cogeneration for urban heating is and will be hampered by costly, complicated equipment, storage difficulties and the increasing length of heating pipes made necessary by the size of coal-fired stations.[23] In the southern states of East Europe, but also in Czechoslovakia and the whole European USSR, it will also be hampered by the shortage of coal whose production now encounters great difficulties. Both the USSR and Czechoslovakia regard nuclear heat-and-power stations and district heating plants as the only solution. With vigorous research underway, each has already announced construction start on pilot projects to utilize nuclear heat.[24] However, it will be at least a decade before such plants can make a significant immpact even in the small countries of East Europe and certainly longer in the vast USSR.

None of this, however, will help the neglected household sector in the countryside where, outside the GDR and Czechoslovakia, a large part of the

TABLE 2

Losses and Sectoral Distribution of Energy Consumption, Selected East European Countries

		Gross Domestic Output	Net Trade	Gross Domestic Industries	Losses and Internal Consumption by Fuel Producing Consumption	Conversion and Line Losses + Station Uses	Non Energy Sectors	Energy Delivery to All Demand	Construction	Industry and Transport	Other Uses	Household and Communal Economy *
		Million Tons of Standard Fuel										
Poland	1970	134.3	-16.5	117.8	10.8	18.9	1.6	86.5		43.9	11.9	30.7
	1978	213.7	-12.8	200.9	16.6	49.6	2.0	132.7		71.0	12.9	48.8
Czechoslovakia	1970	64.2	14.2	78.4	4.2	15.1	0.4	58.7		37.1	4.1	17.5
	1978	68.7	33.7	102.4	9.8	19.8	1.6	71.2		44.1	2.6	9.6
GDR	1972	88.8	26.7	107.5	6.2	49.8	1.8	49.7	22.7	7.7	19.8	27.3
	1978	83.3	43.8	127.1	13.9	51.6	1.6	60.0		24.5	8.2	
Hungary	1970	20.4	9.7	30.1	2.4	5.9	0.7	21.1	8.9	2.6	9.6	16.3
	1978	22.2	19.7	41.9	1.4	5.3	1.3	33.9		14.9	2.7	
		Percentages of Gross domestic Availability							Percentages of Delivered Energy			
Poland	1970	114.0	-14.0	100.0	9.2	16.0	1.4	73.4		50.8	13.7	35.5
	1978	106.4	-6.4	100.0	8.3	24.6	1.0	66.1		53.5	9.7	36.8
Czechoslovakia	1970	81.9	18.1	100.0	5.3	19.3	0.5	74.9	(100.0)	63.2	7.0	29.8
	1978	67.1	32.9	100.0	9.6	19.3	1.6	69.5	(100.0)	61.9	3.7	34.4
GDR	1972	75.2	24.8	100.0	5.8	46.3	1.7	46.2	(100.0)	44.7	15.5	39.8
	1978	65.5	34.5	100.0	10.9	40.6	1.3	47.2	(100.0)	40.8	13.7	45.5
Hungary	1970	67.8	32.2	100.0	8.0	19.6	2.3	70.1	(100.0)	42.2	12.3	45.5
	1978	53.0	47.0	100.0	3.3	12.6	3.2	80.9	(100.0)	42.2	12.3	45.5

For notes and the primary source, see Appendix. List of supplementary sources and assumptions can be furnished by the authors on request.

COMECON population still reside (Even today, over two-fifths of the Soviet population and 45 percent of the Polish population for example, live in settlements under 5000 persons, with the majority of these in villages under 1000).[25] It is admitted that the bulk of rural residents, who rely today almost exclusively on decentralized heat supply, must continue to do so in the future. Even in principle, settlements under 1000 inhabitants cannot be economically provided with heat and hot water from boilers. According to Soviet specialists, for all these settlements economic comparisons of fuel use favor refinery products (in case of proximity to pipelines also gas) over coal.[26] In time of great concern with agricultural performance and food supplies, the modernization of energy use by the rural population is becoming an urgent task and is claimed to be the subject of intensive research.

Self Use, Production and Conversion Losses

The production and distribution of energy, its processing and conversion into more flexible and valuable forms are placing increasing demand today not only on the capital and scientific resources of these nations but on their energy resource base itself. The production of primary fuels with worsening quality, accessibility and size distribution requires growing energy inputs. In addition, the substitution of hydrocarbons for solid fuels having come to an end, more of the increment in COMECON fuel supplies will have to come from coal and lignite than was the case in the past two decades. Wastage of heat form the burning of coal and lignite is much greater than from the combustion of oil products and gas and the former are still less efficient as chemical feedstocks.

In spite of the common problems confronting the smaller countries of the Eastern bloc and, to a degree, the USSR, the response of the former to the challenge of the seventies has been diverse. The differences in the energy strategies pursued by individual countries express themselves on the levels of efficiency of the energy system and the type and share of losses incurred. Energy wasted in fuel production and processing and in conversion to electricity is shown in Tables 1 and 2.

Loss in mining and fuel processing is inevitable in every relatively developed economy. However, the size of this loss can be minimized if the country opts for relying on foreign trade as a source of its fuels. This option is particularly attractive for smaller countries, but it requires a break with the tradition of autarkic development. Circumventing energy waste in this manner has been characteristic of Hungary, the only nation among those appearing in Table 2 to reduce both the quantity and share of energy losses. In Hungary, lignite and hard coal mining operations have been reduced. Oil output has increased insignificantly, but natural gas production registered a sustained growth. The associated loss in gas production is lower than in the extraction of other fuels, and this has helped to reduce waste in the energy economy.

Conversion and line losses and station consumption are the necessary price for the upgrading of primary sources to more versatile electricity. This loss has also been reduced in Hungary to the level lowest among the countries in question, except for Bulgaria. Once again, the more than doubling of oil and gas imports (in calorific content) made it possible to boost the share of hydrocarbons in the input to electric power generation from 37.5 percent in 1970 to 57.4 percent in 1978.

The synthetic measure of Hungary's success in increasing the overall efficiency of energy use is a spectacular 10 percent jump in the energy actually delivered to all sectors of demand. From the point of view of energy efficiency, the success is tremendous. It should be borne in mind, however, that imports of hydrocarbons and the resulting strain on the balance of payments put a limit to that energy efficient import strategy. This indicates a problem that is not confined to Hungary alone: some energy efficient changes, feasible and technologically attainable as they are, cannot be implemented because of sheer financial constraints.

The GDR represents the opposite strategy of energy development. The country is clinging to whatever self-sufficiency it can provide at a heavy cost to the economy in terms of processing and conversion losses. Lignite being its only abundant source of primary energy, the GDR has become a unique case on a world scale. No other country at a similar level of development meets 60 percent of its energy needs with that low-grade fuel or, for that matter, derives from it 80 percent of its electricity supply.[27] With the deterioration of mining conditions, keeping up the attained lignite output has only been possible with increased resource allocation into mining.[28]

At the same time, the very low quality of this fuel necessitates its extensive upgrading (e.g. briquetting, carbonization, production of semi-coke), some of which involves two-step processes with cumulative losses. For example, the process used at the major lignite-producing combine Schwarze Pumpe (briquetting and subsequent gasification of the briquette) results in a mere 45 percent thermal efficiency.[29] Although the energy efficiency of two other treatments, applied to lignite elsewhere (low-temperature carbonization and high-temperature coking) is appreciably higher — approximately 75 percent,[30] these also contribute to overall losses. A still larger portion of aggregate energy is lost in converting the very poor lignite to electricity. While the exact portion cannot be calculated, due to the closely intertwined stages of fuel processing and power generation within the same production unit, power production seems to be responsible for the lion's share of the losses.[31]

Yet, as long as lignite remains the "single crop" of East German energy economy, putting up with the abnormally high conversion loss may be regarded as a rational economic choice.[32] The energy locked in this fuel can hardly be harnessed in any other way in modern plants with stringent technological requirements. Lignites must be processed and/or turned into electricity[33], briquettes or liquids. In the GDR, the ratio of fuel input into power generation to the domestic availability of aggregate energy was 52.6 percent in 1978. By comparison, the ratio was only 31.2 percent in Hungary, 28.7 percent in Czechoslovakia and 33.1 percent in Poland in the same year. Similarly, the contribution of electricity to end-uses is unparalleled anywhere, except in some overwhelmingly hydro countries, such as Norway. The "single crop" energy economy also explains the high priority given to co-generation in the GDR: recapturing waste heat in a heavily electrified economy appears to be the most immediate source of energy savings. As Table 2 testifies, some success has been achieved along that line.

The other two countries in the northern tier, Czechoslovakia and Poland, overall show greater efficiency (i.e. a higher share of aggregate energy delivered to consuming sectors). This efficiency, however, declined between 1970 and 1978. The policies of the two countries represent certain combinations of the "Hungarian" and "East German" approaches, with Czechoslovakia rapidly becoming more energy deficient and Poland loosing its former status as a country with an energy surplus[34]. Loss in fuel processing in Czechoslovakia increased for essentially the same reasons as in the GDR[35]. In Poland, processing and mining loss (8.3 percent in 1978, down from 9.2 percent in 1970) appears doubtful in light of the tremendous growth of coal production during that period. Apart from the common statistical problems, an explanation for the decline may lie in the crash mining methods employed in the country (concentrating on the best seams, wide use of the roof-collapse method etc.) leading to the abandonment of up to 2/3 of minable coal reserves and, incidentally, some equipment in the ground[36].

Of special interest is the sharp growth of conversion losses in Poland. This country in fact was the only one among the East European members of the COMECON to experience such a trend in electric power generation despite a sizable relative shift form lignite to coal in firing power plants. Through miscalculation, the demand of electricity was allowed to outrun supply. The continuous operation of all available capacities, regardless of age and condition, adversely affected conversion efficiency[37].

Conversion rates in the southern tier of COMECON have generally been more favorable than in the northern countries. In Romania, the conversion loss dropped from 15.7 percent in 1970 to 13.3 percent in 1977, aided by the practically unchanged share (around 66-67 percent) of electricity generated by oil and gas[38]. The Bulgarian case is more instructive, a small scale model of the impact of nuclear power generation on the energy economy. A nuclear power plant commissioned in 1974 brought about a dramatic decline in conversion losses from 14.6 percent in 1970 to 9.8 percent in 1977. An additional factor acting in the same direction has been the high share of hydroelectricity (11.0 and 14.2 percent respectively). Tempting as the prospect of going nuclear might be, it will be some time before new nuclear stations can bring about a comparable decrease in conversion losses in larger economies, such as the GDR or Poland.

Though different for particular countries, prospects for the future are generally bleak. In Czechoslovakia, new allocations of oil to stationary devices are going to be denied and the increment is planned to be used for chemical processing. The relative share of conversion losses here is expected to remain constant, though an absolute increase of 2-3 million tons SF (Standard Fuel) is anticipated by 1985. In Hungary, the wisdom of heavily leaning on imported fuels is being questioned. A common consensus seems to exist in that lignites (if and when Hungary reverts to using them) can only make some difference in the five-year plan for 1986-1990, but hardly before[39]. If this resource is opted for, Hungary could go the "East German" way later on. East Germany has secured increasing supplies of Soviet natural gas, but no incremental oil. Conversion of some energy equipment from oil to gas is already underway[40]. Increased infusion of Soviet gas to East Germany and Czechoslovakia might contribute somewhat towards higher overall efficiency, but hardly to spectacular improvement. In Poland, a significant rollback of coal production to 162 million tons in 1981[41] is reckoned with, so mining loss may stablize as far as its relative share is concerned. Shortfalls in electric power generation and delay in putting new power generating facilities on line jeopardize the Polish program of retiring obsolete plants[42]. This, together with the policy of switching to more brown coal and not constructing electric stations fired by hard coal after 1985 will still augment conversion losses. Nuclear power generation holds no promise of quick solution.

Energy Consumption by Temperature and End-use Categories

An equally useful way of looking at the structure of consumption is by the thermodynamic character of the tasks energy performs and the form in which the latter is applied. Improvements in the technological efficiency and speed of modern operations have often been purchased at the price of rising energy inputs and increased enthropy. The Second Law effcieny of low temperature processes, such as space heating, is inherently higher than that of high temperature processes, while the transformation of heat to mechanical energy (whether for its own sake in mobile and stationary engines or for the generation of electricity) inevitably entails very large thermodynamic losses. High inherent efficiency, as in space heating, does not, however, rule out great wastage where energy is used in a dispersed fashion, particularly from solid fuels, since the capture and control of heat form these solids in such a case is very ineffective. Because data availability for these technological categories in East Europe is very poor, the bulk of this section deals with the Soviet Union, with only a brief look at the smaller states in the Bloc.

The organization of their economy and a high degree of centralized control over personal consumption and the household-municipal economy have given COMECON planners certain advantages in the furnishing of

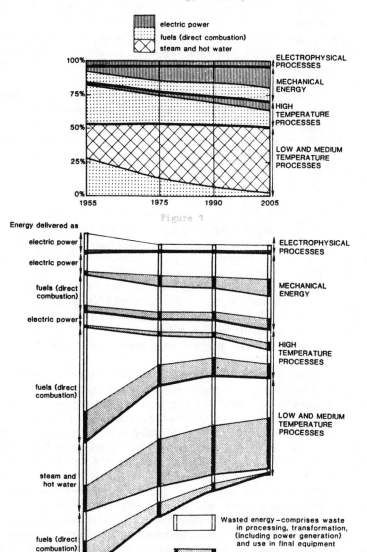

Soviet Union: Energy Consumption

Figure 1

Energy delivered as

Figure 2

Source: After A.A. Makarov and A.G. Vigdorchik, *Toplivnoenergeticheskii komplekns.* (Moscow: "Nauka," 1979), p. 128 and A.A. Makarov and L.A., Melent've, "Issledovaniia perspektivnoi struktury toplivnoenergeticheskogo balansa SSSR v osnovnykh zon strany," unpublished paper submitted to joint US-Soviet seminar under energy agreement, mimeo, 1979.

energy. Particularly in the supply of low and medium temperature heat to urban consumers and certain types of mechanical energy, they were able to make thermodynamically efficient choices. In the USSR, for example, nearly all increase in the provision of low and medium temperature heat since 1950 has been satisfied by steam and hot water, with an efficiency of energy transfer of almost 90 percent[43]. A growing share of that steam and water (today exceeding three-quarters) was furnished by cogenerating and district heating plants.[44] Through the last three decades, the quantity of solid fuels burned directly in small inefficient installation and at huge expense of labor time remained virtually constant, dropping sharply in areas, and their relative contribution declined drastically.[45] Soviet specialists expect this trend to continue and plan to expand the share of central heat supply via steam in low and medium temperature processes, reducing the need for stoves and furnaces fired on the premises to a small fraction of total consumption (Figures 1 and 2).

Heat much above 250°C cannot be conveyed via steam because vapor pressure soon becomes unacceptibly high. It must be applied via hot gases, air or directly to the materials being processed from fuels under combustion, or supplied in the form of electricity. Not only do these processes require specialized, often complex equipment, but when direct heat is involved, they are accompanied by significant energy waste. Electricity, once delivered can be applied with near 100 percent efficiency, but to generate it from fossil fuels very large thermodynamic losses must be incurred. The use of electric power for heat, even at high temperatures, is still very costly and is justifiable only in special smelting and electrolytic operations.

The heavy industrialization drive of the Stalin era greatly increased the share of high temperature processes in Soviet aggregate energy use. The consequent growth of thermodynamic losses thus largely counteracted other efficiency improvements in the energy system. Since the early 1950's, however, the proportion of high temperature uses stabilized, with some reduction expected in the future (Figure 1). Because even in 1975 only 6.5 percent of demand in this temperature category was satisfied by electric power[46] (and probably no more than 4 percent by electricity from thermal plants) this stabilization has helped to reduce the portion of energy wasted, improving the thermodynamic efficiency of the Soviet energy economy. While in the future the reduction in the share of high temperature processes will be accompanied by the increasing application of electric smelting and electrochemical technology, most of the incremental electricity so applied will come from nuclear and Siberian hydropower plants and will not enhance thermodynamic losses.

Economic modernization involves the whole-scale replacement of muscle-power by machines. It is, therefore, not surprising that the provision of mechanical energy (for stationary power tools and mobile machines) has been the most rapidly growing portion of the Soviet energy economy. It should remain so till the end of the century. By Soviet account,

42 percent of the industrial labor force in 1975 (and nearly all in auxiliary operations) worked by hand without machines and power tools.[47] The portion of unmechanized manpower in agriculture (actually mostly womanpower) must surely be larger. The worsening labor shortage throughout the Slavic Republics of the USSR makes the further application of mechanical energy in the economy essential and it is called for in Soviet plans.

Government policy and the structure of the economy have greatly influenced choices in the types of mechanical energy supplied. Because of the high priority and symbolic significance attached to electrification in the USSR, a higher share of total energy is delivered to the economy in the form of electric power than is the case either in the US or in Western Europe.[48]. And unlike in the US, where only two-fifths of that power is for mechanical drive, over 60 percent is so used in the USSR.[49] Not only are stationary operations in industry mostly electrified, but the dominance and high density of railway freight has led to electrification of half of all rail haulage as measured by ton-kilometers.[50] The relative contribution of electric traction can be expected to increase somewhat in the future. Soviet planners are anxious to substitute coal and nuclear generated power for diesel fuel,[51] in addition, electric locomotives have proven more reliable than diesels.

By contrast, the low priority assigned to private motoring and trucking means that the internal combustion (IC) engine, whose work efficiency is very low, makes comparatively small demands on energy resources. In 1975 it was responsible for only 16-17 percent of gross energy use versus some 23 percent in the United States. And over a third of the fuel burned by IC engines in the USSR is consumed not in transport but in agriculture and construction, which are very small consumers in the West.[52] Counteracting somewhat this parsimony in the supply of motor fuels (with very high scarcity value) through the thermodynamically inefficient IC engine is the unfavorable resource geography of the country. The latter results in unusually high direct fuel expenditures for mechanical power in construction, drilling and pipeline operations.[53]

Data by such thermodynamic categories in the East European COMECON states are very scanty. It seems that in the highly industrialized countries of the GDR and Czechoslovakia an ever greater share of energy is used at higher temperature ranges where steam can no longer be applied. Twenty-eight percent of all energy in the GDR is used in stationary processes over 400 °C and another 17 percent in the 100 °C-400 °C range. In the USSR, high temperature processes accounted for 26 percent of energy consumption in the mid 1970's.[54] In Czechoslovakia, despite the importance of heat intensive smelting, glass, ceramic, etc. industries, high temperature heat accounts for a much smaller share of useful energy (i.e. energy captured and incorporated in the products) than low temperature heat for space heating and hot water.[55] This suggests great losses and low efficiency in high temperature processes.

Countries with already developed basic industries, especially iron and steel, can be expected to stabilize their respective shares of high temperature processes, barring any large scale switches to electric smelting. A likely candidate to increase the share of these processes is Romania with its ambitious heavy industrial program, unless the leadership alters its current energy policy.[56]

Prospects of Substitution and Savings in Petroleum Demand in East Europe

In theory, savings of oil in the national economies of the smaller COMECON members might further economic stability. However, it does not seem that those countries have any significant reserves of oil savings. Due to the belated advent of the oil era in East Europe (with the notable exception of Romania) the oil crunch came at the time when boiler use of refinery products had not yet developed to the level found in the Soviet Union (where in 1976 over 180 million tons of oil or one third of all apparent consumption, including field and refinery losses, was burned under boilers. Without such losses, boiler use of oil amounted to some 37 percent of the total.[57]

Fuel oil is burned in some cogenerating plants for environmental and social reasons (especially within larger agglomerations). Its substitution with lower grade fuels may be unacceptable. Nor is it technologically possible to replace existing equipment throughout these countries. It is in this use that increased deliveries of Soviet natural gas can make a difference. Although only the less valuable heavy fractions can be released in this manner,[58] such replacement still appears rational.

One of the ways to assess the oil intensiveness of the COMECON economies is to compare their petroleum requirements per unit value of national income. Bulgaria in 1977 consumed 860 grams of oil per 1 rouble of national income—next only to the Soviet Union with 1060 grams. The other countries ranged from 326 grams in Poland to 716 grams in Romania.[59] At the same time, Bulgarian specialists estimate that 35 percent of refinery products was in uses where no replacement whatsoever is possible.[60] (This does not imply any judgement as to the feasibility of substitution for the remaining 65 percent). It may be conjectured that in less oil intensive economies the share of unsubstitutable liquid fuels is much higher than in Bulgaria.[61]

Conclusion

Energy consumption in the COMECON states is more closely tied to the production of goods, to the sinews of the economy, than in the West. It reflects the goals and priorities of central planners rather than consumer, though in the rising and now generous deliveries to agriculture through most of the Bloc planners and most of the populace may not be far apart.

Clearly, the COMECON countries must look, above all else to industry for reduction in waste and attempts at energy savings, particularly since private motoring in recent years has been restricted even further.[62] At the same time, the backward state of energy supply to households outside large cities and the necessity of modernizing that neglected sector should result in a rising claim on centrally furnished resources.

Energy consumption in the Soviet Bloc also reflects structural peculiarities in resource use and transformation characteristic of given countries. The very high share of lignite and/or coal in aggregate energy demand through East Germany, Poland and Czechoslovakia reflects both resource endowment and government policy. In the GDR, the intensity of electrification, expressed both in the end use pattern and the very high share (53 percent in 1978) of aggregate fuel demand supplied to power plants, is the structural consequence of such dependence in a modern economy on very poor lignites. So are the roughly 50 percent processing and conversion losses plus internal consumption by the energy industries, the unavoidable price paid for turning this wretched fuel into usable forms of energy. The rapid growth of nuclear power will lead to still higher levels of electrification throughout COMECON, but especially in the smaller states of East Europe.

The inpressive development of energy efficient cogeneration and district heating in the USSR and its rapid growth in some of the smaller countries of the Bloc is another structural peculiarity, reinforced by living patterns and government policy. If the intensive research underway on atomic heat and power plants and pure heating stations bears fruit, the already significant role of power plants in furnishing energy at both high and low temperatures (via electricity and steam respectively) should increase much further. Higher levels of electrification are also envisaged and are clearly necessary through mechanizing auxiliary work, in view of the great deal of hand labor in lifting, loading, etc. operation and internal, in-plant transport still common throughout the COMECON. At least in the USSR, however, the current huge efforts at resource developments in remote Siberia, are also raising the share, not to mention the quantity, of high quality fuels (nearly all hydrocarbons) used for mechanical energy in thermodynamically inefficient IC engines and gas turbines. The sectoral and structural consumption patterns and trends will continue to have a very significant influence on attempts at energy savings and the feasibility of substitution for increasingly scarce petroleum.

Sources for Table 2

1. UN, *Annual Bulletin of General Energy Statistics for Europe* (1970, 1972, 1978).
2. UN, *Annual Bulletin of Electric Energy Statistics for Europe* (Same years).
3. *Statisticheskii ezhegodnik stran-chlenov SEV*. Moscow. (various years).
4. Various sources (mainly technical literature of East European countries).

(1) can only be used with extreme care, but many hours of laborious calculations convinced the authors that the figures were not deliberately distorted. However, several unusual entries and inconsistencies in the tables could be traced, by and large pointing to major areas of inefficiency in the respective countries' energy systems. For example, in the column "steam and hot water", the GDR enters all steam flowing through the turbines of thermal plants of every variety, thus doublecounting cogenerated heat and the energy attributable to the electricity produced. In the same column, Hungary includes the output of pure heating plants for which the fuels have already been counted. The Czech and Polish heat generation and distribution patterns had to be reconstructed from the date for earlier years.

The figures for oil in Czechoslovakia and Poland had to be obtained from other statistical publications and periodicals. Due to the impossibility to cover fully all the data gaps, some estimates and adjustments also had to be made.

Consequently, Table 2 cannot be regarded as 100 percent reliable. However, the authors feel that, if judiciously interpreted, the Table gives as clear a picture of the energy balance of East Europe as we can hope to get with the data base available today.

NOTE: Due to the imperfect separation of pure heating plants from cogenerating plants in the GDR, the share of "Household plus other uses" in the energy delivered may be slightly inflated relative to the "Industry" column.

Footnotes

1. Sidney Sonenblum, *The Energy Connection: Between Energy and the Economy* (Cambridge, Mass.: Ballinger Co., 1978), pp. 82-83 and 234-235.
2. United Nations, Economic Commission for Europe (henceforth UN ECE) *Increased Energy Economy and Efficiency in the ECE Region* (New York, 1976), pp. 42 and 46 and UN ECE, *Economic Survey of Europe, 1979* (New York, 1981), Table 3.10.
3. UN ECE, *Increased Energy Economy.*, p. 44. The diagram gives an energy flow chart for East Europe as a whole, excluding Bulgaria, but without separating losses in production and transport. The latter are shown for individual countries in Table 2 of text.
4. UN ECE, *Economic Survey of Europe, 1979.* Tables 3.9 and 3.10 and UN, World Energy Supplies. 1973-1978. New York, 1979. In 1978, average per capita consumption of aggregate energy in the CMEA was 13 percent higher than in Western Europe; the USSR and the East European averages were nearly identical. All countries, except Hungary and Romania, exceeded the West European mean and Romania's lag was negligible. The energy intensity of the GDP in all the CMEA states of Europe, save Hungary, surpassed the same in West Germany and the UK by a very substantial margin. Even Hungary required as much energy expenditure per comparable unit of national income as France. yet these countries were clearly less economically advanced than either West Germany or France.
5. During the 1970's, however, allocations to agriculture in Poland have increased rapidly. Expenses grew faster than in all other East European states except Hungary. Thad P. Alton et al., *Agricultural Output, Expenses and Depreciation, Gross Product and Net Product in Eastern Europe.* 1965-1979. (New York. L.W. International Finance Research Inc. 1980), pp. 30-62.
6. *Vestnik Statistiki* (Moscow), No. 1, 1978, p. 9 and Table 1 in text.
7. *Revista economică* (Bucharest), November 1979, No. 47, p. 12; *Gospodarka Paliwami i Energia* (Warsaw), No. 1, 1980, p. 8 and *Energia és atomtechnika* (Budapest), No. 4, 1980, p. 174.
8. Robert Campbell, *Soviet Energy Balances* (Santa Monica, Ca: Rand Corporation. Research Report R-2257 — DOE, December 1978), p. 8 and *Energiagazdalkodas* (Budapest), Nos. 1-2, 1980, p. 3. In the USSR agriculture consumes one-tenth of all liquid fuels, in Hungary one-eighth and in Bulgaria over a quarter. *Referativnyi zhurnal* (Moscow), No. 6, 1979, E 59; *Energiagazdálkodás*, Nos. 1-2, 1980, p. 3 and Boris Popov, *Bulgaria's Power Generation* (Sofia Press, Balkan State Printing House, 1978), p. 27.

9. L.A. Melent'ev et al., "The Relationship between Economic Growth and Energy Development", 11th World Energy Conference, 8-12 Sept. Munich, Division 4. Energy Society and the Environment, Preprint, Table 1 and Energiagazdálkodás, No. 4, 1978, p. 143. Melent'ev's data refers to final (net) and not gross consumption. However, it is highly unlikely that energy efficiency improvements in agriculture would much (if at all) exceed that in the economy as a whole.

10. GNP series at constant 1979 prices for East European states, sectoral 1968-69 weights plus growth rates till 1979 given in Thad Alton et. al., Economic Growth in Eastern Europe 1965-79 (New York. Economic Studies, L.W. International Financial Research Inc., 1980), pp. 8-15. Shares of total energy consumed by agriculture from sources in footnote 7. Apparent consumption of aggregate energy from US CIA, Energy Supplies in Eastern Europe. A Statistical Compliation. ER 79-10624, December 1979.

11. Folk Dovring, "Capital Intensity in Soviet Agriculture, "Paper given at the Fifth International Conference on Soviet and East European Agriculture. October 5-7, 1978, Lawrence, Kansas.

12. UN ECE, Economic Survey of Europe, 1979, Table 3.10.

13. Robert Campbell, Soviet Energy Balances, pp. 16 and 22.

14. UN ECE, Annual Bulletin of General Energy Statistics for Europe, 1978, pp. 36, 52 and 90 and earlier issues of same tables.

15. G.S. Ryps, Ekonomicheskie problemy raspredeleniia gaza (Leningrad, "Nedra", 1978), p. 20.

16. Energiagazdálkodás, No. 10, 1978, p. 435.

17. In 1970, solid fuels accounted for over 70 percent of all energy supply to households in Czechoslovakia. The 1975 share, therefore, must still have been over one half. Hospodárské noviny. No. 39 (September 1972), p. 1. In the entire "non-productive" sphere of the economy accounting for 29 percent of all energy demand, more than two-fifths of all energy needs were to be met by brown coal alone, amounting to a supply of 16 million physical tons to that sphere. Hospodárské noviny, No. 37, 1978, pp. 8-9 and Plánovane Hospodářstvi (Prague), No. 1, 1979, p. 21.

18. Zycie Gospodarcze (Warsaw, No. 34, August 1980, p. 5 for coal and coke consumption). Household consumption alone in Poland is unavailable, but the household-municipal-communal sector combined used 310.8 x 10^{12} kcal in 1977. Assuming that on a per capita basis Polish household demand is not much above the Hungarian level, 60-65 percent of the nearly 311 x 10^{12} kcal must have been consumed by the population in their homes. Gospodarka Paliwami i Energia, No. 1, 1980, p. 8 and Energiagazdálkodás, No. 10, 1978, p. 435.

19. From the late 1970's to 1985, the GDR plans to increase the number of flats heated by centrally supplied steam by six fold, from one million to 6 million. By 1990 close to half of all flats are to be so heated. Energietechnik, No. 9, 1979, pp. 337-38.
    A Hungarian report on centralized heat supply in the GDR, however, gives only 32 percent by that date. Energia és Atomtechnika, No. 5-6, 1978, p. 203.
    One third of all energy consumed by the household-municipal sector as a whole will come from cogenerating and district heating plants. Hydrocarbons for heating purposes reportedly are completely denied to this sector in the GDR. Energia és Atomtechnika, No. 7, 1977, p. 324.

20. Teploenergetika, No. 12, 1978, p. 3; Robert Campbell, Basic Data on Soviet Energy Balances (Santa Monica, CA: Rand Corporation. Research Note N - 1332 - DOE, December 1979), pp. 18-20 and Energia és Atomtechnika, Nos. 2-3, 1980, pp. 52, 55-57 and 72. The built-in rigidities of a dual regime at cogenerating plants and the mismatch for the respective load curves of heat and power are important limiting factors in the USSR. In search for greater flexibility, Soviet energy planners are actually trying to decouple some heat and power production at older existing cogenerating plants and construct new ones with lower heat loads. This, of course, will boost the need for auxiliary boilers which produce only steam but no electricity. Elektricheskie stantsii, No. 8, 1979, pp. 13-17 and Teploenergetika, No. 4, 1979, pp. 18-19.

21. A.A. Makarov and A.G. Vigdorchik, *Toplivnoenergeticheskii kompleks* (Moscow: "Nauka", 1979), p. 137 and *Energia és Atomtechnika*, Nos. 2-3, 1980, p. 53.

22. *Energia és Atomtechnika*, No. 7, 1977, pp. 324-325.

23. The proposed radii of heat delivery for new plants are amazingly long—up to 35 km in Hungary *(Energia és Atomtechnika*, No. 5, 1980, pp. 221-227), 35-40 km in Czechoslovakia (*Energetika*, No. 2, 1980, p. 52), 20 km in the GDR (*Energeitechnik*, 1979, No. 3, pp. 71-74).

24. See *Plánované Hospodářstvi,* 1980, No. 3, pp. 1-7, *Izvestiia*, March 2, 1980, p. 6; *Energia és Atomtechnika*, Nos. 2-3, 1980, p. 67 and T. Shabad, "News Notes", *Soviet Geography*, June 1980, p. 396. An unusual proposal, indicating the urgency of the problem of heat supply, concerns a nuclear plant for heat and power projected jointly by Czechoslovakia and Hungary. It would furnish power and steam for both Bratislava and Gyor (70 km apart) in the two states. *Energia és Atomtechnika*, Nos. 2-3, 1980, p. 67.

25. *Rocznik Statystyczny. 1979* (Warsaw: Glowny Urząd Statystyczny), p. 33.

26. Makarov and Vigdorchik, *op. cit.,* pp. 113-115.

27. See *Życie Gospodarcze*, 1979, No. 47, p. 13.

28. 3.2 cubic meters of overburden had to be removed for 1 ton of lignite in 1970. The figure for 1980 stands at 4.5 m³/ton, with further increase projected for 1990, 5.3 m³/ton. See *Koks, Smola, Gaz* (Poland), 1979, Nos. 2-3, p. 37. In addition, 6 m³ of water is pumped out of the pits for every tone of lignite mined. See *Die Wirtschaft* (GDR), 1979, No. 7, p. 24.

29. See *Koks, Smola, Gaz,* 1979, Nos. 2-3, p. 41. Had it not been for a decrease in briqueting form 57.1 million tons in 1970 to 48.7 million tons in 1977 the loss in fuel producing industries would have been still higher. See *Górnictwo odkrywkowe* (Poland), 1979, Nos. 5-6, p. 45-50.

30. See *Koks, Smola, Gaz,* 1979, No. 5, p. 117.

31. Apparently, East German statistics are able to claim very low heat rates for such plants (275-300 grams SF/Kwh) because the plants are fueled by lignite already converted to liquids and/or gases. The heat rates may look efficient, but the loss is simply shifted to the previous processing stage (Ibid., p. 114.)

32. An East German source puts conversion loss in *lignite-based* power generation at 35 percent of domestic availability, which seems to substantiate the rather high figures in Table 2. See *Die Wirtschaft,* 1979, No. 7, p. 24.

33. 60 percent of the calorific content of lignite is converted to electricity in the GDR. Only 3 percent of lignite is used in its raw state. See *Koks, Smola, Gaz,* 1979, No. 5, p. 114.

34. The traditional energy surplus was lost in 1980 due to the shortfall in coal production (193 million tons out of the 205 planned were mined). See *Życie Warszawy*, January 21, 1981, p. 3. Even some of the earlier surpluses might have been due to statistical inconsistencies and outright swindling. It was revealed recently that adding rock to railway cars loaded with coal in order to boost weight was a common practice. According to the calculations of Czeslaw Mejro, one of the leading Polish energy specialists, there were 17 millions tons less coal available than the official data would indicate (*Życie Gospodarcze*, 1980, No. 48, p. 8). The average heat content of coal is claimed to have gone down by 15 percent over the last several years (*Trybuna Ludu*, 1980, No. 229, p. 2). There is no evidence to suggest that practices of this kind are exclusively confined to Poland.

35. The loss could have been even greater had not the process of brown coal carbonization at Žaluzi been terminated. See *Plánované Hospodářstvi,* 1979, No. 1, p. 19.

36. See *Życie Gospodarcze*, 1980, No. 48, p. 8.

37. See *Życie Gospodarcze*, 1978, No. 41, p. 9. Power plants with a heat rate of up to 542 grams SF/Kwh had to be kept on line in 1978 when the average heat rate stood at 360 grams SF/Kwh.

38. See *Buletinul institutului de studii si proiectari energetice* (Romania), 1979, No. 1, p. 27.

39. Earlier plans to open up a record large lignite field south of Bukk Mt. have been

postponed because of difficulties with this fuel and uncertainties about terms of COMECON cooperation in the nuclear field (*Energia és Atomtechnika*, No. 7, 1979, pp. 309-321).

40. See *Novoye Russkoe Slovo*, (New York), 1980, January 26, p. 2.

41. See *Życie Warszawy*, , 1981, October 22, p. 1. The 188 million tons mark initially offered by the government was criticized as unrealistic and subsequently revised downward in March 1981. See *Trybuna Ludu*, 1981, March 21/22, p. 1.

42. 800 megawatts were planned to be retired in 1981-1985 (*Energietechnik*, 1979, No. 5, pp. 161-164). Because a deficit of up to 2000 MW installed capacity was expected (and indeed occurred) during the 1980/1981 winter season, such retirement is most unlikely. See *Polityka*, 1980, No. 45, p. 4 and *Życie Gospodarcze*, 1981, February 22, p. 12.

43. Computed from A.A. Beschinskii and Iu.M. Kogan, *Ekonomicheskii problemy elektrifikatsii* (Moscow: "Energiia", 1976), pp. 413-415 and Makarov and Vigdorchik, *op. cit.*, p. 109.

44. A.M. Nekrasov and M.G. Pervukhin, eds., *Energetika SSSR v 1976-1980 godakh* (Moscow: "Energiia," 1977), p. 65.

45. Computed from Makarov and Vigdorchik, *op. cit.*, p. 109. This does not apply to the household sector, where the amount of solid fuels used increased marginally even between 1965 and 1975, the drop in self-produced fuels being entirely compensated by coal. Households accounted for about half of all energy consumption in the low and medium temperature range in the 1965-1975 period. This shows the relatively low priority assigned to household consumption even in the Brezhnev era. Ryps, *Ekonomicheskie problemy*, p. 20.

46. Makarov and Vigdorchik, p. 109.

47. *Ekonomicheskaia gazeta*, No. 48, November 1978, p. 10.

48. Campbell, *Soviet Energy Balances*, p. 17.

49. Makarov and Vigdorchik, p. 118 and Stanford Research Institute, USGPO, Report to the Office of Science and Technology, *"Patterns of Energy Consumption in the United States,"* (Washington, DC, January 1972).

50. Ibid., p. 92 and *Narodnoe khoziaistvo SSSR v 1978 godu*, p. 108.

51. Beschinskii and Iu. Kogan, *Ekonomicheskie problemy*, pp. 297-99 and Makarov and Vigdorchik, pp. 95-96. The latter source claims that a twofold growth in the length of electrified railway lines is considered rational by specialists.

52. In 1975, 73.6 percent of all diesel fuel in the USSR was consumed in transport, agriculture and construction. Nearly all of this plus a small fraction of the 22.3 percent used by industry was assumed to be consumed in IC engines *(Vestnik statistiki)*, No. 1, 1978, p. 9. Almost all gasoline was also assigned to IC engines. Diesel and gasoline output from Campbell, *Soviet Energy Balances*, p. 98. Because of the low octane quality of Soviet gasoline, exports should not distort this distribution greatly. In the US, the private car and trucking along comprises about 18 percent of total energy demand.

53. Gas pipelines alone consume one tenth of all natural gas output in the USSR today. *Ekonomika gazovoi promyshlennosti*, No. 3, 1980, p. 16.

54. *Energietechnik*, July 1978, p. 254 and Makarov and Vigdorchik, *op. cit.*, p. 97.

55. See *Energetika* (Czechoslovakia), 1980, No. 2, p. 49. Efficiency of final end-use is generally far form the thermodynamic efficiency threshold. In Poland only 47 percent of the energy locked in solid fuel was captured as useful heat at the consumer end. The figure for liquid fuels was 72.2 percent (see *Koks, Smoła, Gaz*, 1979, No. 9, p. 241).

56. The share of iron and steel industry in the consumption of *primary energy* in that country is expected to reach 13.5 percent in 1985 (12 percent in 1975), that of the chemical industry 21 percent (15 percent in 1975). See Popescu I., Turcu E., *Energia, încotro* Craiova (Romania), 1978, p. 254.

57. For the problems and prospects of fuel substitution and energy conservation in the USSR see L. Dienes and T. Shabad, *The Soviet Energy System*, New York, John Wiley and Sons, 1979, chapter 8, and L. Dienes *"Energy conservation in the USSR"*, in John P. Hardt et al. *Energy in Soviet Policy*, Congressional Research Service, Washington, D.C., 1981.

58. Czechoslovakia, for example, has occasional *seasonal* excesses of heavy fuel oil even under the present tight supply situation. Allocation of fuel oil in Czechoslovakia for steam and power is planned to be 0.3 million tons less in 1985 than in 1980. The situation is going to be especially difficult in light fuel oil (a decrease of 19 percent). See *Hospodářské noviny*, 1980, No. 3, p. 9.

59. The ratios for other COMECON countries were as follows: Hungary - 690 grams, the GDR - 560 grams, Poland - 326 grams, Romania - 716 grams, Czechoslovakia -685 grams. See Vorob'ev E.A., Kheifets B.A., *Otraslevaia struktura khoziaistva stran SEV i nauchno-tekhnicheskii progress*. Moscow, 1979, p. 92.

60. See P. Tsvetanov. *State, Problems and Achievements of Energy Development in the People's Republic of Bulgaria*. Paper given at the XVI International Seminar "Problems of Energy Policy: East and West". Milan, Italy, September 25-27, 1980, p. 9.

61. For instance, it has been estimated in Poland (presumably on the basis of the pre-1977 trends) that by the year 2000 18 million tons of fuel oil would be needed for "the normal functioning of the economy", whereas the economically desirable quota would be 24 million tons. Taking the former as the minimal and the latter as the maximum requirement, one can arrive at the possible substitution of only 25 percent. See *Gospodarka paliwami i energią*, 1979, No. 5, p. 7-8.

62. In the last few years, the growth of gasoline consumption by the population has been greatly dampened both by administrative measures and the sharp rise in prices throughout COMECON. In Hungary, the most liberal and one of the most consumer oriented states of the Bloc, the average *annual* rate of increase dropped from 18.7 percent in the 1970-75 period to 9.3 percent in 1976-78 and 1.5 percent in 1979-80. *Közgazdasagi Szemle*, No. 109, 1980, pp. 1164-65.

Solid Fuels: Resources, Production and Demand in the 1980s

Theodore Shabad

(Soviet Geography, New York)

The solid fuels are being looked to in the CMEA countries as an increasingly important fossil fuel for power generation in the 1980's as the use of fuel oil, especially in the USSR, is to be cut back in view of the growing tightness of oil supply. However, while the production of coal appears to be holding its own in some of the East European countries, it is posing a problem in the Soviet Union at the very time when planners are envisaging solid fuels as a more significant factor in thermal power generation. After having reached a peak production in 1978, Soviet coal production has been declining. To counter this trend, the new 1981-85 five-year plan projects not only stabilization of output, but renewed increase. However, coal production goals since the mid-1970's have been unusually optimistic, and performance has fallen far short.

In discussing the solid fuels situation in the CMEA countries it is important to distinguish between two basic categories of coal: (1) high-grade hard coal, which includes anthracite and high-heating value steam coals as well as the special-purpose coking coal for the iron and steel industry; (2) low-grade brown coal or lignite, which cannot be economically transported over long distances, is suitable only for power generation, and is used most efficiently in electric stations situated directly in the mining area. The general tendency has been for an increasingly tight supply of hard coal, which for the most part is mined underground, and for slow, but steady expansion of the lower-grade brown coal reserves, which tend to be extracted in surface mines.

A comparative discussion of coal production in the CMEA countries is hampered to some extent by differences in statistical reporting. While the East European countries tend to report net production (marketed mine output after the mine's own needs and losses are discounted), the Soviet Union uses gross mine output data, especially in regional statistics. For international comparisons, Soviet national production has been converted to net figures (Table 1),[1] but regional or coal-basin data in the Soviet Union are expressed in gross output. The difference is negligible for brown coal or lignite, but in the case of hard coal, net production runs around 90% of gross mine output.

59

The CMEA countries are facing problems with their solid fuels supply even though they include some of the world's largest producers. The Soviet Union is among the top three producers of hard coal (with the United States and China) and Poland ranks fourth. In brown coal or lignite, East Germany is the No. 1 producer in the world, followed by the USSR (with West Germany third). The other East European countries have moderate to negligible hard-coal production and larger volumes of brown-coal output. Among the isolated members of CMEA, Mongolia and Vietnam are minor producers, and Cuba has a virtually coal-less economy, relying mainly on imported oil for its fossil fuel needs. The following discussion will be limited largely to the present situation and outlook in the Soviet Union and in the East European countries.

I. Soviet Union

In the USSR, the basic problem is that the most easily accessible coal beds in some of the older coal basins in the European part of the country, notably the Donets Basin, are being depleted requiring the construction of increasingly deeper mines. This has been both costly and time-consuming. In the meantime, the largely untapped eastern basins in the Asian part of the Soviet Union have not been developed rapidly enough to compensate for western capacity depletions. Furthermore growing Soviet reliance from coal in the remote eastern basins poses serious problems of transportation to the populated and industrial regions in the western Soviet Union. Nevertheless, future coal-capacity expansion will have to be concentrated in the Kuznetsk Basin of southern Siberia, the main source of high-grade steam coals and coking coal after the Donets Basin, and in huge strip-mine operations of the Ekibastuz of northeast Kazakhstan and ultimately in the Kansk-Achinsk Basin of southern Siberia.

After having reached a record gross mine output of 724 million metric tons in 1978 (664 million tons net), the Soviet Union experienced an unusual decline in production to 703 million tons in 1981. The decline was all the more striking in view of the optimistic five-year plan goals that had been set for the 1976-80 period. Under the initial projections, Soviet output had been scheduled to rise from 701 million tons in 1975 to 805 million in 1980. As performance lagged far behind goals, annual plans were scaled down, and the revised 1980 target was 745 million tons, but even this reduced goal was missed by a full 29 million tons. Unrealistic coal planning appears to persist in the new five-year plan 1981-85. After having been tentatively projected in the range of 770-800 million tons, the 1985 goal was fixed at 775 million, up from 716 million in 1980. In light of recent performance, the 1985 target appears overly ambitious and unrealistic. Some uncertainty surrounding

TABLE 1
Net Coal Production and Trade in the CMEA Countries
(millions of metric tons)

| | Production | | | 1979 Trade | | Indicated 1979 Demand |
	1970	1975	1979	Import	Export	
USSR						
Hard coal	433	485	497	(10)	(25)	(480)
Brown coal	145	160	161			
POLAND						
Hard coal	140	172	201	1	41	161
Brown coal	33	40	38			
EAST GERMANY						
Hard coal	1.1	0.5	– –	8.7	– –	9
Brown coal	262	247	256			
CZECHOSLOVAKIA						
Hard coal	28	28	28	5.5	4.0	30
Brown coal	81	86	96			
RUMANIA						
Hard coal	6.4	7.3	8.1			(9)
Brown coal	14	20	25			
BULGARIA						
Hard coal	0.4	0.3	0.3	6.4	– –	7
Brown coal	29	28	28			
HUNGARY						
Hard coal	4.2	3.0	3.0	1.9	– –	5
Brown coal	24	22	22			
VIETNAM						
Hard coal		5.2	5.5			
MONGOLIA						
Hard coal	0.1	0.2	0.4			
Brown coal	1.9	2.6	3.7			

the coal industry is also suggested by the fact that the reporting of coal production for the two principal producing republics — the Russian Republic and the Ukraine — ceased in 1981. Indirect indications are that RSFSR output is planned to grow from 391 million tons in 1980 to 430 million in 1985, and Ukrainian production from 197 million to 207 million.

The production delcine has been most serious in the Donets Basin, dropping from a high point of 224 million tons in 1976 to around 203 million tons in 1980. Since Donets coal represents 85% or more of Ukrainian coal production—some 30 million tons of Donets coal is mined in the Rostov Oblast section of the RSFSR—the downward trend has been reflected in Ukrainian coal production as a whole. Soviet planners evidently hope to stablize Ukrainian production, although no specific output goals have been announced. The problem is to complete new and deeper mines fast enough to compensate for capacity depletions. In the 1971-75 period, when Donets production was still rising, 29 million tons of new capacity was completed. In the 1976-80 period, completions of about 28 million tons were planned, but only 14 million tons was added. This was evidently not enough to compensate for depletions and accounts for the output decline through the second half of the 1970's. Capacity depletions in the Donets Basin now appear to be running at the rate of up to 5 million tons a year so that a major mine construction effort is required just to slow the decrease in mine output. It was reported in early 1981 that 37 out of the 93 mines in Voroshilovgrad Oblast were in an "extremely difficult situation," evidently referring to capacity depletions.[2] For the 1981-85 period, 24 million tons of additional capacity is planned in the Ukraine, barely enough to keep pace with depletions; moreover the commissioning of new mines has been falling consistently below plans.[3]

The decline of production has made it increasingly difficult for the Donets Basin to meet demand within its marketing area in the European USSR and export commitments. The Soviet Union exports around 25 million tons of hard coal a year (5% of net production), and much of it originates in the Donets Basin. More than half of the exports go to Eastern Europe, where the USSR has been supplying virtually all the coal imports of Bulgaria, 60% of the imports of East Germany, half of the imports of Czechoslovakia and one-fifth of those of Hungary. The decline of Donets coal production has had the effect of narrowing the market area of the basin and of requiring more long hauls of Kuznetsk Basin coal from southern Siberia to the European USSR. Because of the high quality of Kuznetsk coal, some of it is even exported, mainly to Western Europe, and Kuznetsk coal accounts for around 15% of Soviet coal exports, or close to 4 million tons.[4]

At the present time, the Donets Basin meets about 38% of the Soviet Union's demand for high-grade steam coals and around 45% of the coking coal for the iron and steel industry; the Kuznetsk Basin contributes 29% of the high-quality steam coals and 32% of the coking coal. The two other major basins that yield good hard coal are the Karaganda Basin in central Kazakhstan (16%) and the Pechora Basin in northern European Russia (9%).

The growing westward shipments of coal from the Kuznetsk Basin (as well as from the Ekibastuz Basin, see below) have become a burden on the railroad system. Because of the coal traffic, the Trans-Siberian railroad west of the Kuznetsk Basin as well as the Middle Siberian Railroad west of the Ekibastuz Basin are among the most heavily used freight lines in the Soviet Union. Coal represents about 20% of all Soviet rail loadings, and the increasing volumes of long-haul coal are reflected in the sharp growth of the average length of haul in recent years. There is a high degree of correlation between mining trends in the Donets Basin and trends in average length of haul. In the first half of the 1970's, as Donets output was still rising, the average length of coal hauls by rail remained virtually the same (692 km in 1970 and 695 km in 1975). In the second half of the 1970's, as Donets production began to decline, the average length of coal hauls grew by 123 km, to 818 km in 1980.

Despite the evident need for having Kuznetsk coal compensate for declines in Donets production, the development of the Kuznetsk Basin has not received high priority. Reserves are adequate for several centuries and mining costs, because of a relatively favorable geology, are much lower than in the Donets Basin, enabling Kuznetsk coals to absorb the high transport costs to the west. Moreover the Kuznetsk Basin is the only hard-coal basin in the Soviet Union with substantial strip-mining capacity; close to one-third of Kuznetsk coal, mainly steam coal, is strip-mined. However, the construction of new mines has been lagging, and gross mine output, which had been projected at 162 million tons in 1980, was only about 150 million tons. Soviet writers have said that the Kuznetsk Basin has enough reserves to support a production of 500 million tons a year.[5] But it was disclosed in 1979 that no deep-mine construction had started since 1960 and no strip-mine construction since 1968.[6] It is evident that a considerably greater development effort will be required if the potential of the Kuznetsk Basin is to be brought into play.

The only other major coal prospects for the 1980's are in the Ekibastuz Basin of northeast Kazakhstan and in the Kansk-Achinsk Basin of southern Siberia. Both are entirely surface-mined operations and will support large mineside electric power complexes. But the quality of coal at Ekibastuz is superior to that in the Kansk-Achinsk Basin, and the development of Ekibastuz is also much further advanced.

In the first stage of Ekibastuz development, from the early 1950's to 1980, the basin reached a gross output level of 67 million tons. Although Ekibastuz coal is not of high rank and has a high ash content—it is properly classified as subbituminous, but the Russians classify it has hard coal—it has been shipped to electric power stations as far away as the Urals (over a distance of 1,400 to 1,500 km).[7] However, coal traffic has reached a saturation point, with up to 3,000 rail cars being loaded daily, two every minute. Further expansion of mining at Ekibastuz to what is envisaged as an output level of 150 million tons sometime in the 1990's will require the construction of four giant mineside power generating stations of 4,000 MW each and the construction of extra high voltage transmission lines to carry the electricity to the west. The first of these mineside electric stations began producing power in 1980, and Ekibastuz mine expansion is projected to about 85 million tons by 1985[8]. As will be noted again in the discussion of electrical energy, much of the success of the Ekibastuz project will depend on close coordination of power-station construction, mine expansion and the completion of the extra high voltage transmission lines.

Over the longer term, a similar coal-by-wire project is planned for the Kansk-Achinsk Basin in southern Siberia. This basin has huge reserves, but its lignite is of such low rank that it cannot support hauls of more than a few hundred kilometers. At present technological levels, the only use for Kansk-Achinsk lignite is in mineside power stations, with electricity being used in local power-intensive industries or transmitted over extra high voltage lines.

An even more ambitious coal and electric power complex is envisaged here. Soviet writers have suggested an ultimate mining capacity of 350 million tons of lignite and an electrical generating capacity of 50,000 MW, to be attained sometime in the 21st century.[9] For the immediate future, the five-year plan 1981-85 sets a more modest beginning — the start of production in the first giant strip mine and in the first power station by 1985, with more intensive progress expected in the second half of the 1980's.

To sum up the Soviet coal situation, it would appear that the economy will be hard pressed, at least over the short term, to foster development of the nation's vast coal reserves to the point where coal will begin to play a more significant role in the fuel supply. During the period of upsurge of oil and natural gas, the share of coal in the Soviet fuels budget declined from 66% in 1950 to 25% in 1980. Although the proclaimed policy is to arrest this decline and to raise the coal share to perhaps 30%, the time lag required in expanding mining capacity and providing the necessary infrastructure appears to be slowing the renewed coal orientation of the Soviet economy.

Two other solid fuels need to be briefly mentioned in the Soviet Union, oil shale and peat. Oil shale, though potentially of greater significance over the long term, is so far of local importance in Estonia, where it is used to fuel two large thermal power stations and experimental work is under way to develop economical methods of extracting oil from shale. Peat has traditionally been used as a power station fuel in Central Russia, which is poor in fossil fuels, but reserves in the area are being depleted, and a policy change allocates a greater share of available peat to agricultural uses. Oil shale and peat each represent less than 1% of the Soviet fuels budget.

II. East Europe

Although coal reserves in Eastern Europe are only a small fraction of the vast resources of the Soviet Union, the East European countries continued to rely much more heavily on coal as an energy source even during the period of easy availability of oil from the Soviet Union. Compared with the abrupt decline of coal in the Soviet fuels budget, coal still represents nearly 60% of the fuels budget in Eastern Europe.[10] The percentage of coal consumption is highest in countries with the largest coal production, namely Poland, East Germany and Czechoslovakia. It declined most rapidly in countries with limited coal resources, such as Bulgaria and Hungary, and it has been consistently below hydrocarbons production in Rumania.

Poland

Poland, the fourth among the world's coal nations, is by far the most important producer in CMEA after the Soviet Union. Steadily increasing production of hard coal, concentrated almost entirely in the Upper Silesian basin, reached the 200 million ton level in 1979. But it declined in 1980 under the impact of labor unrest, to 193 million tons and early reports show that 1981 output will be 162 million. About one-fifth of the hard coal is of coking quality, and four-fifths is high-grade steam coal. Tentative projections to 1990 envisaged an increase to 260 million tons, but there may be a question whether the demands of the new independent labor movement, such as a reduction in working hours, will make it possible to maintain the earlier rate of growth. Because of the high value of Polish coal in foreign trade, one-fifth of production was exported in 1979 and represented a major source of foreign exchange. Exports in 1980 and 1981 were, however, considerably lower.

There has been a tendency to reduce domestic consumption in the power generation sector by developing the strip-minable brown coal resources. The trend began after World War II with the development of the Turoszow brown coal district, at the border of East Germany and Czechoslovakia, and continued with the Konin-Turek district in central Poland in the late 1950's. By the late 1970's, about 18% of Poland's thermal power generating capacity consisted of lignite-fired mineside stations, and the trend is expected to continue. A new strip-mined lignite and power complex is being developed at Belchatow near Łodz, and projections for the 1980's envisage an increase in brown-coal production from some 37 million tons in 1980 to 115 million in 1990.[11]

East Germany

East Germany has an unusual coal situation in being the world's largest producer of brown coal and having had a negligible output of hard coal (in the Zwickau-Elsnitz district), which finally ceased in 1979. The brown coal production, which has ranged around 250 million tons in the 1970's, is concentrated in two basins—the Leipzig-Halle region west of the Elbe and the Lower Lusatian region near Cottbus. The brown coal is either burned in mineside thermal stations or is briquetted. The East Germans have also developed a technique for coking brown coal, but most of the coking coal needs for the East German iron and steel industry are being met by imports from both the Soviet Union and Poland—a total of 8.7 million tons of coking coal, yielding 6.5 million tons of coke. An additional 3 million tons of coke was imported.

Czechoslovakia

In Czechoslovakia, both hard coal and brown coal are being produced, but hard coal mines, concentrated in the Ostrava-Karvina district (a southern extension of the Upper Silesian Basin), have operated at a peak level of 28 million tons a year, with no prospects for expansion. Although Czechoslovakia both exports and imports hard coal, it is a net importer, thus supplementing its domestic production. In keeping with the overall trend in CMEA, brown coal resources are being actively developed for use in mineside power stations, with the focus of expansion in the North Bohemian Basin (three-fourths of total brown coal output) around Most and Chomutov, and in the Sokolov district (one-fourth).

Hungary

Hungary has very limited prospects for coal production, both hard coal and brown coal. Its domestic output of hard coal, near Pecs, meets only 60% of demand, with the rest imported from Czechoslovakia and the Soviet Union. Brown coal production, scattered in several basins, has stabilized at around 23 million tons, half of which is burned in mineside power stations.

Rumania

In Rumania, alone among the East European countries, coal has traditionally played a secondary role in energy consumption because of significant domestic resources of natural gas and oil. However, since the middle 1960's, brown coal deposits have been developed in the Oltenian district of southwest Rumania for use in local power stations, and mine output rose steadily through the 1970's to 25 million tons. Rumania also has some hard-coal production, centered in the Petrosani district in the Transylvanian Alps (8 million tons a year), but four-fifths is suitable only for power generation, and Rumania must import both coking coal and coke for its iron and steel industry.

Bulgaria

Like East Germany, Bulgaria has virtually no hard-coal production and is entirely dependent on imports (6 million tons a year, from the Donets Basin) for both high-grade steam coal and coking coal. But, in keeping with the general pattern, Bulgaria has also developed its brown coal resources, including some very low-ranking lignite in the East Maritsa Basin, for use in mineside power stations. The higher-ranking brown coal, in the Pernik and Bobovdol basins, reached an output peak of 11 million tons around 1960, and now runs around 7 million tons a year. The lower-ranking lignite of the East Maritsa Basin has stabilized at around 21 million tons, for a total production of 28 million tons.[12]

Overall the coal situation in the CMEA countries will face problems in the 1980's. In the Soviet Union, where reserves are plentiful, but remote from centers of population and industry, the main issue is the development of the eastern basins to compensate for production declines in the west and the overcoming of the huge distances, for example by the coal-by-wire approach. In Eastern Europe, with few exceptions (Poland, in particular) there seems little room for expansion in view of limited reserves and the use of increasingly low-ranking brown coals and lignite. Both in the European USSR and in Eastern Europe, therefore, recourse is being sought in the accelerated development of nuclear power generation, as will be shown in greater detail in the discussion of electrical energy in this Colloquium volume.

References

1. *Statisticheskiy yezhegodnik stran-chlenov SEV 1980* (Statistical Yearbook of the CMEA Member Countries 1980). Moscow: Statistika, 1980, p. 83.
2. *Pravda Ukrainy,* Feb. 2, 1981.
3. *Soviet Geography*, April 1981.
4. *Vneshnyaya Torgovlya* (Foreign Trade), 1976, No. 1
5. *Pravda*, Aug. 25, 1978; Gudok, April 2, 1980; Dienes and Shabad, *The Soviet Energy System*. (New York: Halsted Press, 1979), pp. 112-114.
6. *Izvestiya*, Dec. 1, 1979.
7. Shabad, *Basic Industrial Resources of the USSR.* (New York: Columbia University Press, 1969), pp. 292-293.
8. *Soviet Geography*, April 1981.
9. *Sotsialisticheskaya Industriya*, April 30, 1976, and June 24, 1978; *Ugol'*, 1980, No. 3; Shabad and Mote, *Gateway to Siberian Resources (the BAM).* (New York: Halsted Press, 1977), pp. 45-51.
10. *Energy Supplies in Eastern Europe: A Statistical Compilation.* (Washington: Central Intelligence Agency, ER 79-10624, December 1979).
11. *Ekonomicheskoye sotrudnichestvo strans-chlenov SEV* (Economic Collaboration Among the CMEA Member Countries), 1980, No. 5, p. 38.
12. V. P. Maksakovskiy. *Toplivnaya promyshlennost' sotsialisticheskikh stran Yevropy* (The Fuel Industry in the Socialist Countries of Europe). (Moscow: Nedra, 1975), pp. 119-120.

Oil in COMECON: Development of Production and Reserves to 1990

Jochen Bethkenhagen

Soviet Oil: Lack of Information Causes Speculation

Hardly any Soviet energy raw material causes as much publicity and scientific interest as oil. Yet, it should be noted that the two other energy sources had more extreme production developments during the 10th five-year plan: *gas production* expanded in accordance with the plan with a very high rate of growth of almost 9% per year, while the *coal production* remained clearly 10% below plan (actual production 716 million tons). In comparison, the 5% below target figure for oil production was relatively modest and an annual average growth of 4% was still reached. However, since the beginning of the 1970s the question regarding the future development possibilities of Soviet oil production has repeatedly been asked. This is by no means solely a domestic Soviet problem. Because of the great importance of oil for the Soviet foreign exchange balance — exports to the OECD countries yield about 60% of all the earnings — this product is a stabilizing factor in the USSR's trade with the West. Also under foreign policy aspects, the future production capabilities of the Soviet oil industry are of great importance. In this connection the USSR has an interest in the Gulf region in order to be able to compensate for the forecast decline in the oil production. Even if these speculations are considered unjustified it should be borne in mind that the USSR contributes to the uncertainty by its restrictive information policy: insufficient information is often replaced by speculation.

The initial considerations are relatively trivial in this connection: oil is a non-renewable resource; production growth has to reach a limit one day and then to decline. The decisive question is only when this high-point will be reached. The answer depends on several factors, among them:

— Oil in place,
— Exploration and/or opening up of deposits, i.e. scope of the economically exploitable reserves,
— Investment ability,
— Production strategy (eg., conservation versus maximum gain of foreign exchange).

However, the economic and political repercussions of any declining Soviet oil production should not be considered in isolation. Such an approach could easily lead to wrong conclusions and it is therefore also politically dangerous. The time frame depends primarily on the existing alternatives. In the most favorable cause, negative consequences for the balance of payments and domestic supply could be excluded. A precondition for this is an above average production growth of other energy sources (such as gas and nuclear energy). The medium-term plans of the USSR do at least provide for such a development. Undesired repercussions on the balance of payments and the domestic supply can therefore only be the result of unplanned developments. It appears almost impossible to forecast them due to the inefficiency of the planning bureaucracy and the lack of information on the Soviet oil industry.

The Development of Soviet Oil Production from 1970 to 1980

The Soviet Union is the largest oil producer within COMECON. Output of 603 million tons (12.06 b/d[1]) in 1980 corresponded to 98% of the production in European part of COMECON.[2]

Regional Structure of the Oil Production in COMECON (European COMECON countries from 1970 to 1980: mmt.)

	COMECON (7) Production	Share in %	USSR Production	Share in %	Romania Production	Share in %	Hungary Production	Share in %	Bulgaria, GDR, CSSR, Poland Production	Share in %
1970	369.5	100	353.0	95.5	13.4	3.6	1.9	0.5	1.2	0.3
1971	393.9	100	377.1	95.7	13.8	3.5	2.0	0.5	1.0	0.3
1972	417.5	100	400.4	95.9	14.1	3.4	2.0	0.5	1.0	0.2
1973	446.3	100	429.0	96.1	14.3	3.2	2.0	0.4	0.9	0.2
1974	476.5	100	458.9	96.3	14.5	3.0	2.0	0.4	1.0	0.2
1975	508.4	100	490.8	96.5	14.6	2.9	2.0	0.4	1.0	0.2
1976	537.4	100	519.7	96.7	14.7	2.7	2.1	0.4	0.9	0.2
1977	563.5	100	545.8	96.9	14.7	2.6	2.2	0.4	0.8	0.1
1978	588.1	100	571.5	97.2	13.7	2.3	2.2	0.4	0.7	0.1
1979	600.6	100	585.6	97.5	12.3	2.0	2.0	0.3	0.7	0.1
1980	617.2	100	603	97.7	11.5	1.9	2.0	0.3	0.7	0.1
1985[1]	647	100	633	97.8	10	1.5	2.0	0.3	2.0	0.3
1990[1]	677	100	665	98.2	8	1.2	2.0	0.3	2.0	0.3

[1]Estimate
Sources: Statistical Year Books of the COMECON countries.

When the development in the USSR is compared with that of the world market, the Soviet oil industry can look back on a successful decade: Since 1974 the USSR has has been the leading oil producer in the world. It clearly increased its production share last year: while in 1970 it produced only 15% of world production this share climbed to 20% in 1980.

Measured by the USSR's own targets, however, the result has been unsatisfactory. Less serious is the fact that the annual plans have no longer been fulfilled since 1974, since the shortcomings amount to less than 1% of the production. More important seems to be the clear difference of almost 40 million tons between the five-year plan target for 1980 (640 million tons) and the realized result (603 million tons). This result cannot be regarded as the expression of a deliberate policy of conservation; rather, it indicates that there have been difficulties in the oil industry which have not been sufficiently recognized in advance. If one regards the Soviet oil production in terms of periodical achievements production increased by 250 million tons between 1970 and 1980, but its growth has clearly slowed down. In 1979 and 1980 the absolute growth of production was only half as high as in 1975 when it reached its maximum yearly increase (32 million tons).

Causes of the decline in Growth: Production Methods

It is worth noting that in West Siberia increase in the oil production has been achieved according to plan. More than 300 million tons, i.e. 50% of the Soviet or 10% of the world oil production, were produced there in 1980. In the traditional oilfields production possibilities were obviously overrated. Although the plans foresaw a small decline in production, this decline was, in fact, three times higher than originally planned; this affected in particular the Volga-Ural region:

Oil Production in Million Tons

Region	1975	1980	1980	1985	Differences		
	(1)	(2)	(3)	(4)	3./.1	2./.1	4./.2
		Actual		Plan	Plan	Actual	Plan
USSR	491	603	640	633	+ 149	+ 112	+ 30
of which							
West Siberia	148	315[1]	315	390	+ 167	+ 167	+ 75
other regions	343	288	325	243	./. 18	./. 55	./. 45

[1]Provisional data

Sources: Leslie Dienes, Theodore Shabad, *The Soviet Energy System* (Washington, D.C. 1979), p. 47; *Izvestiya*, 24.1.1981; *Pravda*, 13.2.1981.

There is little Soviet information on the reasons for these incorrect forecasts. Critical remarks were published, amongst others, by the Academy of Science[3]. The key criticism is the production method applied: while formerly the drilling productivity was substantially increased by reducing the number of drillings per oilfield, an opposite production policy has been observed recently. To obtain favorable results in as short a time as possible the well density has been extended too rapidly. This, however, reduced the scope of the exploitable reserves and the efficiency of the oil production declined as all the 'easy oil' was immediately exploited leaving behind vast quantities of oil that required more substantial drilling. If this policy of 'over drilling' is continued oil production will soon reach its maximum and will then decline. This development has probably been caused by the calculation system which makes the plan fulfilment dependent on the number of drilled meters. If difficulties arise when drilling a well, no efforts are often made to overcome them. Instead, it is easier to increase the production by drilling a new well. In addition, the projected recovery rates have often been assessed too high, because of insufficient information about the deposits. In order to come as near to these recovery rates as possible, the Soviets prefer a drilling method which obtains short-term success but in the long run, leads to reduced overall productivity.

A further problem — the quantitative importance of which is difficult to estimate — is caused by Soviets production techniques. In order to maintain a rapid flow of oil, the oilfields are water-flooded. Due to the dilution of the oil caused by this procedure, special pumps have to be used and the water has to be separated from the oil. In 1977 the average water in the oil production was more than 50%. This method makes it possible — according to Soviet information — to produce more than 40% of the oil in place.[5] Newer techniques such as gas lift procedure are being developed but they are not yet of any importance since only 2% of the oil are reportedly being produced by this method. Up to now the equipment used for this method had also to be imported from abroad. Other modern procedures such as steam injection or the use of chemical agents are still in the experimental stage.[6]

The decline in the oil production in the traditional oilfields, which was stronger than expected, was probably the result of a faulty production policy which is an offshoot of the inefficienet use of capital. this thesis is supported by the development of *investments* for the oil industry. In the 10th five-year plan, this sector received over 60% more funds than during the 1971-75 five-year plan period. The investments for the oil industry thus increased twice as rapidly as those for the entire industrial sector. Thus, 13% of all industrial investments were devoted to the oil industry alone in 1980; in 1970 the share was only just 9%. The Soviet Union has thus reacted to the growing importance of the oil industry in terms of foreign growing importance of the oil industry in terms of foreign trade and to the increasing cost of the oil production by allocating additional funds. However, these funds have not been used efficiently.

Investments of the Soviet Oil Industry from 1971 to 1980

	In million rubles	Change[1]	Share in industrial investments in %
1971 to 1975	15,981	144.4	9.5
1976 to 1980[2]	26,100	163.3	12
of which			
1976	4,066	6.9	10.0
1977	5,270	10.7	10.6
1978	5,270	17.0	11.6
1979	5,860	11.2	12.9
1980[2]	6,400	9.2	13

[1]Compared with the year before and/or the previous planning period
[2]1980 estimated
Source: *Narodnoe khoziaistvo SSSR.*

The investment volume in the oil industry of 20,000 million domestic rubles during the period 1976 to 1979 is contrasted with imports amounting to 700 million transfer rubles (including imports for the gas industry; the Soviet foreign trade statistics do not give any separate data for the oil industry). About one fourth of the imports came from Romania. Judged by their value, equipment imports for the oil industry did not play a major role. With regard to the technological standard, western supplies are probably of greater importance. A substantial dependence on western technology however, cannot be deduced from these scarce data.

It is worth noting, however, that the USSR has raised the value of its equipment imports for the oil and gas industry to a higher level since 1975. While the average value of the years 1970 to 1974 was still 33 million transfer rubles the figure for the period 1975 to 1979 was about 170 million transfer rubles. This gave these industrial branches the possibility to profit at least to a small extent from the heavily increasing export earnings. On the other hand, oil industry difficulties have not induced the Soviet Union to increase the import of drilling equipment; in 1979 imports were the same as in 1975.

Imports of Equipment for the Oil and Gas Industry of the USSR in Million Transfer Rubles

Supplying country	1970	1975	1976	1977	1978	1979
Total	21	133	199	126	251	136
of which:						
Romania	13	25	31	39	52	70
USA	–	36	30	21	38	22
Federal Republic of Germany	–	35	53	15	10	1
France	2	17	16	12	1	15
Great Britain	5	5	16	12	101	14

Source: Statistical Foreign Trade Yearbooks of the USSR

The volume of investments for the oil industry increased by 63% during the period 1976 to 1980 compared with the 9th five-year plan, while the volume of production increased by 31%. Thus, the capital co-efficient in the oil industry has further increased: in the 19th five-year plan 24% more capital had to be invested for the growth of production by 1 ton of oil than during the period 1971 to 1975. This is not much more than had been planned on average for the entire industry (15%)[7].

Soviet cost data have their own problems. They can, on principle, not be compared with western calculations. In addition, the enormous expenditures for infrastructure measures—especially in West Siberia —are external effects which helps the oil industry. If these expenditures were included at least partially in the oil industry calculation— which is unusual in general—the production costs would certainly have increased more rapidly during recent years. This applies also to the inclusion of the transport costs which have tripled since 1965 to about 0.7 rubles per ton per 1,000 km according to Soviet data.

The overall production costs per ton, on the other hand, rose by only 50%[8] during the same period. However, the export earnings for each produced ton of crude oil increased from 4 to 24 transfer rubles between 1965 and 1979. Even if the two values are not fully comparable because of their differing initial level, the following conclusion can nevertheless be drawn: The increase in the average costs of oil production has been relatively small[9]. It was more than compensated by the heavily increased export earnings.

The Reserve Situation

Since 1947 the scope of Soviet oil reserves has been treated as a state secret by the Soviet Union. Information is therefore always based on estimates and the methods of arriving at these estimates are frequently obscure. It is therefore hardly surprising that the estimated values of different institutions differ strongly. The CIA estimates proven oil reserves are very low: only 4,100 to 4,800 million tons[10]; these figures correspond to those of the USA. On the other hand, the estimate by the Swedish institute, Petro Studies[11], is very optimistic. This institute estimated Soviet proven oil reserves as of 1 January 1976 were 16,000 million tons. Although Petro Studies explained its estimating method very extensively and relied mainly on Soviet sources, there are doubts as to its consistency because it is by no means a fact—as stated in the study—that the estimated values are not in contradiction to the cited Soviet statements on the development—not on the level—of the explored oil deposits. Proof: From statement no. 5[12] it can be concluded that the oil reserves of the categories A + B + C may have increased by a maximum of 42% between 1966 and 1976. The estimated values of Petro Studies[13], however, show an increase of 85%. Therefore, an essential precondition for the estimating method—namely the lack of contradiction—is no longer fulfilled. It can therefore not be claimed that these estimated values show the actual reserve figures. The estimates of *World Oil* and the *Oil and Gas Journal* hold a "medium position". Their estimate of the Soviet reserves are 8,000 and 9,700 million tons (1.1.1979). This represents about 11% of world reserves and twice or 2.5 times respectively as much as shown for the USA.

These striking differences are also due to the differing evaluation of the Soviet reserve categories. These categories are not comparable with the classification scheme used in the West (proved, probable, possible). The CIA regards the group A and a portion of group B as corresponding categories to the proved reserves; Petro Studies is of the opinion, however, that A, B and a portion (70%) of C_1 belong to the proved reserves. The Institute bases its opinion on a Soviet source. According to this source the Academy of Science of the USSR considers that the categories A + B plus a portion of C_1 correspond to the western concept of "proved reserves"[14]. The estimates of the *Oil and Gas Journal* relate presumably to the categories A + B + C_1. The basis of comparison for the information of *World Oil* is not clear. In view of this total confusion it is not very useful to develop a new estimate of the Soviet oil reserves within the framework of this work.

The following facts seem to be of importance in estimating the future Soviet oil production with regard to the reserve situation:
— The USSR occupies about one third of the area of the world where one can hope to find oil and about 2½ times greater area than the USA.
— According to Soviet information the oil reserves should be sufficient to safeguard supply for more than 100 years[15].
— The steep price increase on the world market must also have led to an increase in the economically exploitable reserves in the Soviet Union — an effect which is hardly reflected in the current US estimates of Soviet reserves.
— Since the introduction of the new Soviet reserve classification of May 1970 the categories B and C_1 have gained economic importance. A-reserves need no longer be explored before the industrial opening of a new deposit. The share of the B-reserves is said to amount to a maximum of 30%; in the case of complicated deposits B-reserves can be abandoned completely.[16]
— The tempo of exploratory drilling has stagnated in recent years. On the other hand, the scope of production drilling has more than doubled between 1970 and 1979[17].

The following conclusions can be drawn from these developments:
— From the decreasing share of the A-reserves in overall "industrial reserves" (A + B + C_1) — indicated by Soviet sources — it cannot be concluded that there has been a decline in explored oil reserves. In order to save costs the new reserve classification especially calls for a limitation of the exploration effort. The CIA thus has under-estimated the reserve development alone for methodical reasons.

— The stagnation of exploratory drilling, however, is not only due to the new reserve classification. There are also substantial backlogs— for instance of 30% in West Siberia in 1979[18] in planned exploratory drillings.
— In view of the uncertain data it seems impossible at present to calculate the level in reserves production ratios—i.e. using the statistical range of the explored reserves. There is the great danger that this may lead to wrong economic and political conclusions.[19]
— This unsatisfactory situation which results solely from the Soviet policy of secrecy is reduced to a small extent by the fact that the USSR publishes data on its medium-term planning. However, these data is of limited use for any well-founded prognosis on long-term trends.

The Soviet Oil Production until 1990

According to the draft of the 11th five-year plan (1981-85), the oil production is to be increased to between 620 and 645 million tons by 1985. The Soviet leadership, including the former oil minister and present chairman of GOSPLAN, Baibakov, thus does not expect that the oil production will reach its zenith in the 11th five-year plan and then decrease. However, the increase in production will be clearly slow.

Soviet oil production: Average annual growth		
	in million tons	in %
1961-1965	19.0	10.4
1966-1970	22.0	7.8
1971-1975	27.4	6.8
1976-1980	22.6	4.2
1981-1985	3.4-8.4	0.5-1.4

In view of this trend two questions arise:
(1) will the Soviet Union be able to realize the planned increase until 1985?
(2) does the oil production in this decade show a definite trend towards stagnation?

In the 11th five-year plan West Siberia will again have to provide the increase in the oil production. Here, the planned production growth for the period (+ 75 million tons)[20] is 2.5 times higher than the average growth for the whole country (+ 30 million tons; average figures). In the other regions a smaller overall decline (minus 45 million tons) is planned than in the previous five-year plan (minus 55 million tons). Since the decline in production will presumably be more pronounced in the Volga-Ural region, the production in the north of European Russia and in Kazakhstan is to be further increased. A limited increase in new investment capital will be available to realize the production targets. In 1981-85, average annual increases in investments of only about 2% will be possible. In view of the high investment requirements in the agricultural and possibly also in the armaments sector it will probably no longer be possible to increase the funds for the oil industry above average as during the previous plan. In addition, the following developments will have an aggravating effect: the gas industry is to receive more investments than the oil industry in West Siberia;[21] the labor force will increase only to a very small extent. This applies primarily to West Siberia where the housing shortage alone impedes an intensified settlement policy. For the resettlement of one worker the state has to invest up to 20,000 rubles, equal to about four annual average wages. Thus, the need to increase labor productivity rather than simply augment the labor supply plays a central role in fulfilling the plan. In the drilling sector the quality of the drilling equipment has to be improved. Soviet geologists have complained that the present equipment is of inferior quality and often breaks in the drilling holes. In order again to increase the rate of exploitation—as required in the draft plan—new oil production methods have to be further developed and increasingly applied. One of them is the gas lift method. More capital is also required for the planned extended exploration and production of oil in the shelf regions. The targets here are the Caspian Sea, the shelf region off Sakhalin and along the coast of the Baltic Sea.

The oil industry thus requires an accelerated provision of new technical equipment. The desired modernization can be accelerated by the extension of imports from western countries. The extent to which this will be possible does not only depend on the Soviet import policy but also on the western willingness to supply the equipment. A restrictive export policy can thus lead, at least temporarily, to a slow-down of the Soviet oil production—a development which is certainly not in the western interest.

Against the background of these problems and in view of the only modestly expanding overall investments it appears realistic not to regard the maximum goal but at best the medium forecast for oil output—i.e. 633 million tons—as the probable production figure of 1985. Only if the planned increase in the gas supplies to West Europe of 40,00 million cu.m proves impossible, the USSR might try to compensate for the lost foreign exchange earnings by stepping up its oil exports. In that case investment funds would have to be transferred from the gas to the oil industry.

If oil production increases of 1% per year were to continue until 1990 a production of 665 million tons would result with production of 450 to 500 million tons in West Siberia in 1990[22]. The realization of this target (average value) would mean that the production in the other regions would fall by almost 50 million tons in the 12th five-year plan. Even if this target is feasible, there remain a number of uncertainties. Among them is the question of the development of production and consumption in the other energy sectors as well as the future export possibilities of these sectors. The sooner the USSR succeeds in replacing its foreign exchange earnings from oil exports by earnings from the gas sector, the sooner it can permit itself to attach greater importance to the conservation aspect in its oil production. This would be reflected in a smaller growth in production.

The Development in East Europe

In East Europe, only Romania and Hungary have oil deposits of meaningful size. In addition, Poland was recently able to essentially expand its reserve claim of 10 million tons[23] by a spectacular discovery of oil near Karlina by the Baltic coast. According to first reports this oilfield may lead to an annual output of 2 million tons (present oil output in Poland 0.3 to 0.4 million tons). Poland hopes to find more oil. Since 1980, test drillings have been carried out in the Baltic shelf off the Hela peninsula from a drilling platform built in the Netherlands. The operator of this drilling platform is "Petrobaltic". This international economic organization was set up by the USSR, the GDR and Poland in 1975 with the aim of carrying out oil and gas exploration in the Baltic Sea. However, one major problem is transportation. Due to the lack of rail connections, the oil cannot be taken to the refineries in Gdansk and Plock for processing; rather it has to be transported to four smaller and less efficient refineries in southern Poland.

For years, the output in Hungary has been 2 to 2.2 million tons per year. Approximately three quarters of the production come from the neighborhood of Szeged in southern Hungary. The exploitable reserves are said to be 43 million tons (1.1.1977)[24] which means that the present production can be maintained for about 20 years. According to Hungarian information the cost of production for the domestic oil (600 forint per ton) in 1978 amounted to only one sixth of the import costs[25].

Romania's oil industry is in a critical situation at present. Production reached its peak in 1976/77 with almost 15 million tons but has been steadily declining since then. In 1980 it reached with 11.5 million tons the lowest value since 1960. This decline in production had not been planned; on the contrary, a 25% higher target had been set. Gradual exhaustion of the old deposits and "unsatisfactory drilling and production activities" have made the problem more serious. Additional material incentives are to improve performance again: since 1981 special bonuses are being paid for overfulfilment of the plan — for oil they amount to 15% of the production value[26]. However, the plan already foresees an increase of 9% compared with the year before. The five-year plan 1981/85 has not yet (as of mid 1981) been published. However, it is obvious from official announcements, that one has to be prepared for a reduction in Romania's oil production over the long run[27].

In view of the reserve situation such a policy is urgently required. Romania's exploitable reserves are estimated at only 150 million tons[28]. One of the aims is an improvement of the recovery rate from the present 31.5% to 37% in 1986 and to 40% by the end of this century. For this purpose more steam and carbon dioxide injections are to be carried out.

Since onshore exploration has been disappointing in recent years it is hoped to improve the reserve situation by exploring in the Black Sea continental shelf. After a search of five years the first oil was found in the Black Sea in 1979. A second oil drilling platform started operation in 1980.

This platform is a domestic Romanian construction, with only the lifting facilities based on a US license. Indeed the main emphasis of the production of oil equipment is to shift gradually towards the off-shore. Nevertheless, Romania oil production will continue to lose importance as long as there is no major exploration success. The country will increasingly depend on imports in order to make full use of its refinery capacities.

Footnotes

1. 1 ton of oil corresponds to 0.02 b/d.
2. The study is limited to that part. Mongolia, Cuba and Vietnam are not included.
3. A.P. Krylov: "O tempakh razrabotki neftyanakh mestorozdeniy," In *Eno*. Nr. 1/1980, p. 66 et seq.
4. *Economist*, No. 3/1980 p. 76.
5. *Sotsialisticheskaya Industriya*, 31.1.1979.
6. See "Nachrichten für den Aussenhandel" (Reports on foreign trade), 19.3.1980.
7. See V.E. Orlov: "O nekotorykh voprosakh ekonomiki otrasley toplivno-syrevogo energeticheskogo kompleksa". *Finansy SSSR* No. 8/1979, p. 19.
8. *Ibid.*, p. 19.
9. In 1979 the average production costs for 1 ton of oil amounted probably to 4 rubles. See Jochen Bethkenhagen: "Importance and Possibilities of East-West Trade with Energy Raw Materials." Special publication 104 of the *DIW*, Berlin, 1975, p. 72.
10. Central Intelligence Agency, *Prospects for Soviet Oil Production. A Supplemental Analysis*. (Washington, D.C. 1977), p. 30.
11. See Petro Studies, *Soviet Proved Oil Reserves, 1946-1980*. Malmo 1980.
12. *Ibid.*, p. 158. Original source: *Planovoe khoziaistvo*, No. 5/1975, p. 87 et seq.
13. Petro Studies, *op. cit.*, p. 106.
14. See Academy of Science of the USSR: *Fuel and Energy Resources of the Capitalist and the Developing Countries* (Russ.) Moscow 1978, p. 87-90. For a contrary view, see John P. Hardt, Ronda A. Bresnick and David Leving, "Soviet Oil and Gas in the Global Perspective". In: *Project Independence: US and World Energy Outlook Through 1990*. (Washington 1977), p. 835.
15. See N.V. Melnikov: *Toplivno-energeticheskie resursy SSSR*, (Moskva 1971), p. 17.
16. See Bethkenhagen: "The Importance . . ." *op. cit.*, p. 30.
17. See *Neftnoye khoziaistvo*, No. 2/1977, No. 4/1978, No. 4/1979, No. 4/1980, No. 5/1980.
18. See V. Filanovski, "Zapadno-sibirskiy neftegasoviy kompleks: Rezultaty i perspectivy." In: *Planovoe khoziaistvo*, No. 3/1980, p. 21.
19. The evaluation of the Soviet complaints about the decrease of the R/P ratio depends certainly on its absolute volume. In view of the Soviet efforts towards autarky in the raw material sector it appears likely that a decline on a high level is already regarded as alarming by the Soviet leadership. Moreover, the large oil discoveries in West Siberia in 1966/70 seem to have led to non-realizable expectations. Since corresponding discoveries were not made in the 1970s the R/P ratio had to decrease. See also Robert W. Campbell: *Trends in Soviet Oil and Gas Industry*. (Baltimore and London 1976), p. 13.
20. *Pravda*, 13.2.1981.
21. "Osnovnye problemy kompleksnogo razvitiya zapadnoy Sibiri," In: *Voprosy ekonomiki*, No. 8/1978, p. 15 et seq.
22. *Pravda*, 13.2.1981.
23. See "Bundesanstalt für Geowissenschaften und Rohstoffe (Edit.) *Rohstoffwirt schaftliche Länderberichte* (Raw material economic reports) Vol. XXII: "COMECON. Rohstoffwirtschaftlicher Uberblick (Raw material survey)" Hannover 1979, p. 117.
24. *Ibid.*, p. 180.

25. See *Budapester Rundschau*, 16.4.1979.
26. See *Neuer Weg*, 2.11.1980.
27. See "Programmdirektive für Forschung und Entwicklung im Bereich der Energie für den Zeitabschnitt 1981 bis 1990 und die Hauptausrichtungen bis zum Jahr 2.000) (Programme Directives for Research and Development in the Energy Sector for the Period from 1981 to 1990 and the Main Prospects until the year 2000". In: *Neuer Weg*, 25.7.1979.
28. See "Bundesanstalt für Geowissenschaften und Rohstoffe," *op. cit.*, p. 135.

CMEA OIL DEMAND
BALANCE TO 1990
Tony Scanlan

Introduction

Any view of CMEA oil demand prospects over the next ten years is inevitably going to be determined to some extent by the expectation of supply. As this colloquium is entirely about CMEA energy I can leave to others the details of the overall energy balance except where other forms of energy are substitutable for oil. Furthermore, I shall mainly be concerned with the USSR itself, which accounts for over 80% of the oil consumption in the "contiguous CMEA" and for nearly all of the incremental supply potential in the next decade. By "contiguous CMEA" I mean USSR and the six full members in Eastern Europe referred to hereafter as CMEA. I should also like to make it clear that, while acknowledging the help of colleagues, the views here are purely a personal interpretation at a time of greater uncertainty than at any time in the past decade.

As usual, units are either natural units or are in oil equivalent and a short glossary of conversion factors is appended. Tons are metric tons and billion is one thousand million. Tons of standard fuel (7000 kilocalories) are converted to oil (10,000 kilocalories) using the abbreviation MMTSF for million metric tons of the former to m.t.p.a. for million metric tons per annum of the latter.

*   *   *   *   *

The 1980 Oil Balance in CMEA

The Soviet oil scene has, until recently, been one of the more predictable areas of the world. For example my paper here in 1974, looking at 1980, estimated the range of oil balances as follows:

TABLE 1
1980 (as seen in 1974)

TABLE 1
1980 (as seen in 1974)

	USSR	Eastern Europe	Million metric tons Total
Production	600-640	20-25	620-665
Domestic Demand	500-600	100-150	600-750
Export surplus	+140/Zero	-75/-130	+65/-130

In the event USSR demand fell away drastically in the 10th 5-Year Plan period, but a lower end of the range forecast for the other factors, including demand in Eastern Europe, has broadly been achieved:

TABLE 2
1980 (provisional end 1980)

	USSR	Eastern Europe	Million metric tons Total
Production	603	17	620
Domestic Demand	450	104	554
Export (gross)	153	-87	66

The Eastern Europe balance involves imports of about 97m tons of which 77m tons came from the USSR and about 20m tons from non-CMEA sources. However about 10m tons is estimated to have been re-exported as finished products. These figures are still provisional, because the extraordinary effect of world oil prices doubling in 1979/80 caused great uncertainty, both to the actual level of oil demand and through the effects upon demand of the economic recession, from which Eastern Europe has not been immune.

Seven years ago the forecast perceived the need for the USSR, by 1980, to choose between USSR internal demand, CMEA exports and hard-currency exports (essentially Eastern and Western Europe respectively). This has been partly resolved by the growth in gas deliveries to Eastern Europe which exceeded the absolute growth in oil deliveries from the USSR during the 10th Five Year Plan. USSR oil supplies to Eastern Europe are not expected by these countries to rise in future above the 1980 level, although total energy supplies (gas and electricity) are scheduled to go up by 20% between the 10th and 11th Plans.

Oil exports to non CMEA countries, which had doubled in the decade up to 1975, have tended to level off and in 1980 there were reports that some importers were having their supplies reduced. However, the disturbances in the world market, the Iranian revolution and the cessation of IGAT gas exports to the USSR and of oil exports to CMEA in 1979 from Iran, and later from Iraq, with the onset of the Iraq-Iran war of 1980, together with the fact that the USSR can now obtain its foreign currency needs for fewer barrels of oil, all combine to suggest it would be premature to declare on this evidence that there is, or will be, a long term decline in USSR oil production. The program to bring Samotlor to full production at 150 million t.p.a. was brought to a successful conclusion, despite unexpected difficulties, and this directly enabled the lower end of the All-Union production target range of 600-640 million tons (12 m.b.d.) to be achieved in 1980.

CMEA Oil Production Prospects to 1990

Any prospect of improving crude oil production depends totally upon the USSR. Romania is the only other producer of significance, at about 13 million t.p.a., but its production is publicly admitted to be in decline. Remaining reserves are equivalent to only ten more years output at the current level. None of the other East European states has any oil potential that can offset this decline with the exception of Hungary which may continue to find minor fields of the type found also across the border in Austria and Yugoslavia, and the new fields in Poland north of Warsaw. However the production prospects these new areas offer are about 10% of requirements and will inevitably leave Hungary and Poland heavily dependent on imported oil, while production in Bulgaria, Czechoslovakia and the DDR is less than 1m t.p.a. in total.

USSR production is basically comprised of two giant production regions, West Siberia and Volga-Urals, and a group of smaller areas, some of them new, others among the world's oldest producers. It is worth noting the trends in these areas that have occurred during the 10th 5-year Plan, using 1979 reports and Soviet comments on the more promising areas to assess 1980, and then to take a reasoned view of 1985 output by area in the light of the Plan targets.

TABLE 3
USSR Oil Production Forecast by Region
Million Metric Tons

	1980 (provisional)	1985 (forecast range)
West Siberia	312	350-390
Volga-Urals	190	140-160
Baku & Offshore Caspian	15	25-15
Kazakhstan East Caspian	25	35-25
North Caucasus	21	20-17
Georgia	3	4-3
Ukraine White Russia & Baltic Offshore	11	10-6
Komi	23	30-26
Far East	3	6-3
	603	620-645

West Siberia, according to a Soviet source at the end of 1979, would add 600,000 barrels per day in 1980: this is reflected above. After that, however, the rate of increase declines to the equivalent of one or two more increments of this size in the entire Plan period and not every year. By 1985 all the known producible giant fields will have peaked unless the eastern part of the West Siberian plain can provide a major discovery very soon.

The Volga-Urals decline of 500,000 b/d that has already taken place in three years, 1976-79 is expected to continue. The 1980 figure estimated here shows only half the rate of decline from the previous year as occurred between 1978 and 1979. If that rate were extrapolated it would result in only 125 million tons of Volga-Urals output in 1985 but since the area is likely to continue to add some minor new fields it is unlikely to be so low.

The minor areas take account of rising optimism in the offshore areas of Azerbaijan and Sakhalin, and the newer production areas of Komi and Georgia. For the older areas where no such news exists the recent trends in decline are either shown as arrested or continuing. If all areas except Western Siberia only achieve the lowered end of the forecast, the upper target in Western Siberia would just enable the lower All-Union Plan target to be met. There is also considerable potential to add to total liquid hydrocarbon production from natural gas liquids (NGL) associated with the Plan target to increase gas output by over 40%. Improved secondary oil recovery by additional "tertiary" or enhanced oil recovery (EOR) is not likely to have much effect up to 1985. This is a question of lead time rather than potential, especially as only 3 million tons or 0.5% of 1980 production was achieved in this way (according to Oil Minister Maltsev).

Some evidence that Western Siberia may indeed have to provide the increase in production and that additional assisted recovery in the Volga-Urals area is unlikely to intervene, came from an interview in *Soviet News* on 27 January 1981 with the Minister of Construction of Oil and Gas Enterprises in which he is reported as stating: "Another specific feature of the eleventh (planning) period is that all our efforts will be channelled into Western Siberia in general and the Tyumen Region in particular. These regions will account for all the increases in oil and gas production, including those which will make up for the reduction in oil production in other regions." Mention of the Plan details of a 390m tons target for oil and NGL's in Western Siberia by 1985 appears to be consistent with this trend, but it also implies a continuing decline in the Volga Urals even at the top of the All-Union target range. Soviet planners include higher recovery of oil among "conservation" or "oil saving".

Looking beyond 1985 it is worth recalling that the USSR is the world number one oil producer, or, to put it another way, draws down its oil reserves faster than any other nation. Output of oil during the 11th 5-Year Plan will amount to 24 billion barrels. For comparison the recoverable reserves of Samotlor have been reported at 15 million barrels which places it among the top five fields ever discovered in the world. If production continues at this rate until 1990, the depletion of oil in the USSR in this decade will be equivalent to three times Samotlor reserves or equal to the total remaining oil reserves in the USA (as published by the American Petroleum Institute).

Therefore, while the prospect of another supergiant field in the remaining, eastern, part of the West Siberian plain cannot be ruled out, time is running out for any such development if it is to make any contribution to production in this decade. It is already too late for any more remotely located Arctic or East Siberian major discovery of the future to have any impact until at least the early 1990's. In this connection note that Samotlor itself was discovered twenty years ago but only reached full production recently.

The dynamic interaction of supply and development lead times, the random—and rare—distribution of supergiant fields and the constant drawdown of 5 billion barrels each year at current levels of All-Union production presage that even if a multiplicity of fields of the average size already found in the Tyumen region are about to be discovered and developed in the eastern part of the West Siberian sedimentary basin, (which has over one million square kilometres of potential oil bearing area awaiting the drilling rigs)—these discoveries will be necessary to maintain All-Union production after 1985 at the current level. By that time normal oilfield profiles will see the production peak for Samotlor and other "first generation" West Siberian fields begin to decline. Without new fields by 1990 the area will resemble the current profile of the Volga-Urals. If that occurs, All-Union production will not be able to compensate for decline in its two major provinces: it too will decline.

Some indication of one high level Soviet attitude was given in a paper presented by Minister Neporozhnyi at the Moscow energy symposium in October 1979 (released with an English text). It deals with the whole spectrum of Soviet energy over the rest of the century, based upon total output in 1975, and projects two "scenarios" of national income at 3¾ % p.a.—and up to 5% p.a. These the paper foresees requiring energy consumption to rise at 2.8-3.3% p.a., or above 4% p.a. in the upper case, both clearly implying an improvement in the energy co-efficient below parity.

The 11th Plan, for comparison, appears to project both national income and energy production growth, at 3.7% p.a. —broadly in line with the lower scenario but without any noticeable improvement in the ratio. None of the projections of total energy production in the paper—given in precentages only but deducible from the 1975 base— appear to expect oil and NGL's production to exceed 700 million tons except at the very top of the high scenario. It is also noticeable that all three fossil fuels are projected at the end of the century to have similar shares of total USSR energy production, with non fossil fuels not exceeding one-sixth of the total. Natural gas increases its share very rapidly, reaching the same level as oil by 1990, but does little more than maintain its percentage after that, while after 1990 the proportion of coal and nuclear continue to rise, especially in the high growth case. This is an important pointer to Soviet attitudes to fuel substitution in the long term. I quote Minister Neporozhnyi: "We should adopt a very cautious attitude towards the use of gas and especially oil as fuels. Already it is necessary to curtail to a maximum the use of these fuels at large power production plants".

If we develop the "unique uses" concept and apply it to our rather limited perceptions of Soviet internal consumption, which we estimate last year was about 450 m. tons of oil, we can broadly group consumption into:
a) Heat and electricity
b) Industrial outlets including oil and chemical processing and
    building construction.
c) Transport and agriculture.

The categorization is quite different from any in non-CMEA areas and it happens to come out that broadly one-third of the total consumption lies in each group. The pattern of USSR internal oil consumption that follows owes acknowledgement to Leslie Dienes' October 1979 paper on Soviet energy policy and to papers given by Soviet energy officials and comments made at the Soviet Energy Symposium in that same month.

(a) Firstly, space heating and domestic needs for energy. Apart from any oil-fired power stations in the background, or oil fired boilers for district heating, there is very little evidence of oil in the energy mix. The typical new city apartment uses district heating for which nuclear power stations are beginning to be utilized as well as thermal stations. Use of very large diameter pipes enables "waste heat" to be transmitted up to 40 kilometers according to the observations of Symposium delegates in 1979. Regulations of the heat received is not so effective but the sight of windows open in Moscow in sub-zero temperatures in order to reduce room temperature, while offending the conservation-minded visitor, is not comparable to western practice because we fail to collect the heat at source. The actual electric power produced is used in the apartment for lighting and appliances only and cooking is done by gas, for which a purely "flat rate" nominal charge of a few kopecks a month is levied, with no variation for actual use. The cost of electricity is related to the amount used but I was told that a typical cost would be 8-9 roubles a month—as much as the rent; but with two or more wage earners per apartment all these sums are insignificant. Electricity costs are rising but any "market sensitivity" through price response appears to be non-existent.

A check on the extent to which the modern apartment is typical comes from figures issued by the Central Statistical Bureau in Moscow. Flats and apartments are being built at an annual rate of about 2.2 million but the increase in the number with gas facilities has been rising at nearly 4 million annually, so that whereas 10 million apartments had gas laid on in 1965, by 1978 the figure was over 50 million and by the end of this year could reach 60 million. The number of apartments built between 1950 and 1980, is also about 60 million. Records of the number of citizens who received new flats annually shows a consistent average of just below four people per apartment. In addition about 3 million people annually received fresh accommodation in renovated buildings. The "gross" list of 300 million people rehoused from 1950-1980 (and the figures on gas retrofitting and new apartments) is equivalent to nearly double the total urban population of 165 million, which is nearly two-thirds of the total USSR population. With life expectancy of 60 years, changes in marital status and so forth, the entire urban population will have gone through at least one turnover since 1950. Add to this the statement in a symposium paper by V.P. Korytnikov and V.E. Arakelov of the Ministry of Power and Electrification, that 170 million people use gas for domestic purposes and the comprehensiveness of the penetration of gas and the ubiquitous nature of the new apartment becomes clearer. Gas Minister Orudzhev (over Moscow home service on 28/2/81) estimated the number of people who used gas "in the household" at nearly 200 million.

Unfortunately no figure was given in either case for district heating, although it is clear from the same paper that nuclear power station use for this purpose is only just beginning, e.g. at Odessa. But it was made clear that gas penetration was intended to take over district heating from oil wherever a supply is available and that in both electricity generation and other thermal boiler outlets natural gas was about to surpass oil as the main primary source of supply. Applying this to Dienes (cit.) estimate for 1980 of 420 MMTSF of combined oil and gas use in power stations and large boilers, if half of this is oil it implies the use of about 150-160m tons of oil. Another 40m tons of oil are required for smaller boilers (110 out of the 420) in remoter areas. Thus a total "heat sector" oil requirement for 1980 emerges at 190-200 MMTSF. This at once accounts for electricity, and the entire area of domestic use (except transport).

(b) Secondly, industrial outlets. Again, the symposium paper cited of Korytnikov and Arakelov is enlightening. "More than 55% of all energy is consumed by industry. Approximately 52% of the total energy consumed in industry goes to three branches which are conspicuous by their high energy consumption — oil refining, chemicals and steel. Approximately 22% of energy consumption is in building materials,, non-ferrous metals, food, paper and pulp. The remaining 26% are the low-energy consuming branches of industry." Their paper goes on to claim a 15% energy saving in oil refining and chemical plants since 1970 by saving electricity through new processes and more efficient use of recycling process heat at intermediate stages. The high level of electricity used in steel does not give the authors any overall hope of economies although they are more hopeful about non-ferrous metals such as aluminum, (10-15%

target savings during the 10th Plan). New processes in cement manufacture, and in papermaking show only marginal savings in the targets for the same period.

Secondary energy use in industry generally is expected to show up to 20% more harnessing of available waste heat between 1975 and 1985. But in general one cannot expect much practical energy saving from this list. Steel industry good housekeeping practices tend to disappear when the monthly targets are becoming urgent. Recycling in a variety of processes to improve the use of waste heat in other industries is again largely a matter of skilled and consistent practice on the site. The technical improvements in oil refining will be offset, as they are in the OECD, by the need to upgrade heavy fuel oil to distillate products. As the USSR backs out the use of mazut from power stations and aims to lighten the barrel, so the more complex refining processes will require more fuel.

Again, it is substitution, by gas, that is significant. Quoting the paper of Korytnikov and Arakelov: "Today 80% of steel, 85% of cast iron, 40% of rolled steel, 20% of non-ferrous metal and 60% of cement is produced with natural gas." The authors expect a doubling of the use of gas in industry in the "current" (10th) Plan period and this trend is expected to continue. Even higher figures were given by Orudzhev on 28th February this year: 93% of all iron and steel, 60% of cement and 95% of mineral fertilizers (a major category in which the USSR is world leading producer and which is planned to increase by 50% by 1985.) Dienes (op. cit.) estimates 50 MMTSF use of oil in industry in 1976 and 55 MMTSF of gas, and gives an aggregate of 170 MMFSF for 1980. In addition he shows various figures for oil used for chemical manufacture, oil refining, pipeline losses and fuel, etc. which the Soviet classification I am using includes in industrial uses. These additions double the totals of both oil and gas required in 1976 and raise the combined oil/gas figure for 1980 to about 420 MMTSF. Now, the increase in the use of oil and gas in industry is expected to be 230 MMFSF between 1976 and 1980 so that doubling the use of gas, as Korytnikov and Arakelov expect, would result in an increased demand for oil of 80 MMTSF in the 10th Plan period, only half the rise shown in the use of gas. Oil use in industry in 1980 (including the oil industry itself) would on this progression have amounted to 200 MMTSF or 140 million tons of oil. In industry, as in space heating and electricity generation, oil is being phased out of the energy intensive sectors, not by price but by allocation.

(c) In Transport, including the agricultural sector, dependence on oil is more difficult to limit for obvious reasons. Current estimates are that about 150 MMTSF of oil is used in transport and a further 50 in agriculture, about 140m tons of oil in total. Railways, in terms of freight ton/miles, are over 50% electrified and the rest are all diesel including passenger trains. In terms of the direct use of oil railway diesel is only 2-3% of total oil use. Aircraft, vital in the largest country, are more significant as a growth factor and in the absence of any firm data may be expected to grow at least double the rate of growth of national income in terms of freight and passenger miles. Introduction of wide-bodies jets will help to economize on fuel, but in practice the older aircraft they displace will tend to swell the secondary routes. Road transport and tractors showed the following annual increase in numbers in 1977/78:

Lorries	800,000
Passenger Cars	1,300,000
(Trolleybuses	2,000,000)
Other buses	100,000
Tractors, etc	600,000

The extent to which these productions figures represent net increases is difficult to judge but in the case of passenger cars and tractors the production rate probably is an increase in the total vehicle population. At this level, the increase in gasoline and diesel demand could amount to one million tons p.a. for cars and 3-4m tons p.a. for commercial vehicles of all types. This would require another 20-25 million tons of road fuels by 1985. Air, marine, river and rail increases might add another 15-20 million tons. This would raise total transport demand from 140m tons in 1980 to 175-185 million tons in 1985, after which the net increase in cars might flatten out. Electrified city increase in cars might flatten out. Electrified city transport by tramcar and trolleybus dominate urban commuting as the scale of trolleybus construction implies. Increasing urbanization will also see more cities passing the one million citizen level at which point they can, apparently, press for a Metro to be built — a further depressant to increased petrol or diesel use on the roads.

Summary of USSR Internal Oil Demand

(a) 1980

The foregoing results in an estimate of total USSR oil demand in 1980 of:

Oil	MMTSF	Million Tons OIL
Heating and electricity	200	140
Industry	200	140
Transport & agriculture	200	140
Non-energy uses,		
(bitumen, lubricants, etc)	30	20
	630	440

To this must be added a factor for losses and the first stockfilling of new pipelines and storage tanks of 2% of the total. This gives an adjusted total of nearly 450 million tons of oil as the level of USSR domestic consumption in 1980. The figures of course are not that precise; (a major uncertainty is military use) but there is a large degree of confluence about the various assessments from different Soviet statements.

(b) 1985

The minimum estimate would be to take the 1980 estimate of 450 million tons, add on the whole increment in section 4 for transport (35 to 40 million tons) plus chemicals and the increase in other non-energy uses (fertilizers, lubricants) as the sector that is largely unsubstitutable at 10 million tons. Secondly, to assume that conservation and substitution take care of potential oil growth in all other sectors. That puts a minimum value on 1985 demand of 495 million tons of oil. The maximum value is that in which oil demand across the economy advances at the same rate as national income. If this occurs 1985 oil demand could be 540m tons.

The higher projection is unlikely. The continuing phasing-out of oil in power stations and in energy-intensive industries, mainly by gas, is going to continue, and there may be curbs on the use of passenger cars and increased efficiencies in transport and industry. Equally unlikely however is that the USSR will be able to reduce demand for oil below the bottom of the range, 495-540 m.t.p.a. That is an average annual increase of 9-18 million tons, (190-280,000 b/d) throughout the 11th Plan, compared with an increase of between 3 and 8 million tons, (60-160,000 b/d) in annual production. Taking the mean of both sets of figures, oil demand will tend to grow at about twice the annual growth in oil supply if the economy meets its plan targets.

In the event, there is one other factor which may alleviate the pressure on oil, and that is the prospect of a slower economic advance. But the short-term economic results (3.8% national income advance in 1980 compared with 4.0% planned) do not in themselves presage dramatic slowdown beyond that which has already occurred.

Eastern Europe "The Six" Oil Demand 1980-1985

In the 1980 Colloquium, I commented upon the abnormally low use of oil in the energy balance. The three northern countries, Poland, Czechoslovakia and the DDR, averaged a mere 20% of oil in their energy mix while the three more southerly countries, Hungary, Romania and Bulgaria averaged between one-third and forty per cent—similar to the USSR. The OECD average is 50% of oil in the total energy mix. The decline in oil production expected in Romania has resulted in plans for all six nations to increase the use of Soviet gas imports, to raise the production of solid fuels and to embark on ambitious nuclear programs. The combined production of solid fuels in 1980 was in excess of 700 million tons (in natural units) compared with oil production of 20 million tons. For comparison the USSR, with 2½ times the population produced the same quantity of coal but thirty times the quantity of oil. This is a key difference between "the Six" and the USSR. While the USSR has sufficient flexibility in its primary energy mix to substitute for oil, Eastern Europe (except Romania) has little flexibility. For example the ability to reduce oil in electricity generation is almost non-existent: solid fuels alone provide 80% of total generating capacity in Bulgaria and the DDR and 90% or more in Czechoslovakia and Poland.

The second point emerging from the paper last year was the high use of energy per capita, especially in the DDR, Czechoslovakia and Poland on an absolute basis. On an adjusted standard of living basis (using the DDR at datum) Poland emerged as the highest user per capital with Romania second—the two nations with, up to now, significant energy export potential. Now, a year later, and with a further interruption of supplies as a by-product of the Iraq-Iran war, there is little relief for oil supply position of "The Six". figures are still provisional, but the level of consumption, expected a year ago to be 105-110 million tons in 1980 was probably only 103 m. tons. The Adria line appears hardly to have been used by the full CMEA members and supplies from the USSR have now reached a plateau. Prices of both sources of supply have doubled. However growth in the national income, although lower than planned everywhere except Bulgaria, was reasonably close to planned targets. I am endebted to the National Westminster Bank for the comparative table:

TABLE 4
USSR and Eastern Europe National Income Target (% p.a.)

	Annual Plan 1980 Target	Annual Plan 1980 Result	Annual Plan 1981 Target	Five-Year Plan 1981-85 Target
USSR	4.0	3.8	3.4	3.4-3.7
Poland	1.4-1.8	-3.0	Not yet published	— —
GDR	4.8	4.2	5.0	N/A
Czechoslovakia	3.7	3.0	3.0	3.0-3.1
Romania	8.8	6.0*	7.0	6.7-7.4
Hungary	3.0-3.5	1.0	2.0-2.5	3.0
Bulgaria	5.7	5.7	5.1	5.0 (1982 only)

*Estimate

This suggests that modified 1981 targets are being projected into the five year plans i.e. no further slowdown is predicted.

The Hungarian (6th) 5 year plan is an example: national income is to rise by between 14 and 17 percent and industrial output by between 19 and 22 percent, but energy is only due to grow at a maximum of 10-11 percent with a 4-8% percentage fall in hydrocarbons. The production of crude oil is to be "maintained" and oil imports, it is clear, are not expected to increase.

Acknowledgements that the USSR has placed a limit on oil exports have also been made by the DDR, Czechoslovakia and Poland. How absolute the 1980 level of supply will be remains to be seen, but extra quantities will apparently be priced at full world level.

The apparent improvement in the energy coefficient (0.7 units of energy growth for each unit increase in the economy) is a realistic target, given the high degree of energy use in Eastern Europe. Hungary emerged from last years analysis as the most efficient per capita energy user of "The Six" so that short-term energy coefficients as large as perhaps 0.5 to 1.0 could be achieved in the Romanian, Polish or East German economy who have a higher use of energy per capita.

There are also some spectacular, once-for-all, energy saving adjustments possible in the scope of total CMEA trade. One example is the potential for the DDR to switch from bauxite to alumina imports from the USSR, thus removing at a stroke the entire energy intensive process from Germany. Of course, the USSR will incure the burden, but perhaps—and this is significant—it can take on the process with hydro-power, avoiding the use of fossil fuels. If the accounting procedures for energy saving in the DDR also credit nuclear power stations with "saving" fossil fuels and if the import of electricity "saves" indigenous consumption of primary energy we could be about to experience a series of dramatic claims that economic advance is being achieved with negligible increases in the use of energy. But there are two problems with this type of accounting (a) it cannot last into the long term once the main list of "once-for-all" measures have been effected and (b) due to the structure of oil use which is limited to unique purposes, substitution is ruled out. Romania is the exception, with plans to virtually eliminate oil burning in power stations (oil and gas, now 30% of the total, to reduce to 4% combined by 1990).

The oil position in this regard is different to that in energy. Hungarian ability to limit use, when over one-third of national energy is oil-based, is going to be considerably easier than the position in the DDR, Czechoslovakia or Poland whose oil base is only 25% of total energy. If the five year plans are fulfilled, and assuming a target of about 3% p.a. for Poland and 4% p.a. for the DDR, the following oil pattern is projected.

TABLE 5
Potential Energy and Oil Growth Rates 1981-85

	Plan Target National % p.a. increase	1981-85 Oil Coefficient Potential	1981-85 Oil Increment
Bulgaria	5	0.7	19%
Romania	7	0.5	19%
Hungary	3	0.7	10%
DDR	4	1.0	22%
Czechoslovakia	3	1.0	16%
Poland	3	1.0	16%

In the composition of total 1980 oil demand in "The Six", Bulgaria and Hungary each represent about 10% of total demand with the other countries each about 20%. Thus a weighted average increase in oil use on this basis between 1980 (103 million tons) and 1985 would be 18% (19 million tons) i.e. a 1985 demand of 122 million tons. Last year my paper here estimated between 125 and 140 million tons — little change at the lower end. Energy demand however could reduce further the energy coefficient, partly due to "special effects" already mentioned but mainly because of the high intensity of use, could be drastically improved to as much as 0.5 to 1.0, reducing 1985 demand to little more than 500 million tons, compared with the previous estimate of 520-535 million tons oil equivalent.

These are not forecasts, as I said last year, but perspectives. The achievement of such sustained improvement in energy efficiency is a formidable task but practical. The problem with the oil targets however is that the end uses for all the new growth are technically inflexible — another aircraft, another road vehicle, another chemical feedstock plant. While space heating or the recycling of industrial process heat can adapt in a few months, new types of transport have to evolve by turnover. There can be little doubt that the upper end of the range forecast last year, 140m tons, would emerge if oil supplies were easier.

Summary of CMEA Oil Balance 1985

The result of sections 5 and 6 would be as follows:

TABLE 6
1985 Potential Oil Demand and Supply in CMEA
Millions of metric tons

	USSR	Eastern Europe	Total
Production	620-645	17-20	635-665
Domestic demand	495-540	122-140	617-680
Export surplus (net?	+ 150/ + 80	− 102/ − 123	+ 48/ − 43

The export surplus is expected to decline. Eastern European demand will have to allow for gross imports sufficient to provide re-export products to non-CMEA markets at about 10 m.t.p.a., mainly Romanian trade. If the USSR continues to limit exports to Eastern Europe to 80 million tons (approximately the 1980 level), some 35 m.t.p.a. of non-CMEA crude would have to be imported by Eastern Europe even at the lower level of 1985 demand. If demand within the USSR is also held at the lower level and 80 million tons of oil continues to be exported to Eastern Europe, only 50 million tons of oil would be left for export both to non-Communist and Communist areas (other than Eastern Europe). Since deliveries to Vietnam, North Korea, etc. cannot easily be reduced (as yet, none of these countries is a producer) the ultimate quantity available to sell for hard currency may be only half the 1980 level — despite the "freeze" on Eastern Europe. This loss of volume would be compensated by higher dollar prices and by gas exports. The key, of course, is higher production success in Western Siberia to alleviate the total oil balance.

Prospects for 1986-1990

a) Supply 1986-1990

The pattern after 1985 will put tremendous reliance on increasing production in Western Siberia. For example a senior economist with the Soviet Academy of Sciences, Abel Aganbegyan was quoted by Reuter as having said in Moscow as recently as 21st March that a 50% increase from 1980 to 1990 is anticipated. However he is also reported to expect this regional target to be 70% of All-Union production, i.e. 475m. tons out of 670m. tons. This would mean all other areas combined would produce less than 200 million tons. Allowing for some continuing successes in minor producing areas, the implication for the Volga-Urals could be that production is only expected to be half the level of recent years. If the forecast of Academician Aganbegyan is realized, West Siberia will be producing more crude oil than the entire USA does today, and by 1990 the comparison could be even more noteworthy. It would also mean that for twenty years, 1970-1990, the world's number one oil producer would have depended on this one region for its production growth.

Is this feasible? The potential resources of this vast sedimentary basin could have this sort of potential but unless some really giant oilfields emerge that are easy to develop, the time scale is barely adequate. Of the known giant fields, there are technical extraction problems at Salim. The USSR does not expect to be producing from Salim until 1986 when this highly viscous field is expected to yield 5 m.t.p.a. As Meyerhoff has noted, the Bazhenov shale formation underlies Salim at a depth of 3,000 meters, which is perhaps sufficient comment in the prospects for this location. The essential perspective on West Siberia at this point in time is that without substantial new developments or new discoveries USSR production could decline by 2 m.b.d. in 1990 due to decreases in other regions, and because Samotlor, currently 25% of USSR production, will be past its peak.

Enhanced recovery techniques and deep drilling may not be as important as the intention to treble the amount of exploration and development drilling in West Siberia and elsewhere. Of course, accelerated effort and higher quality equipment are always useful and better drilling techniques may save as much as a year in drilling below 15,000 feet. Soviet technicians claim to have achieved this depth off Baku, and most of the oil in the Volga-Urals and West Siberia is at half this depth. Enhanced oil recovery (EOR) is simply another set of methods to stimulate the "energizing" of the flow of crude oil from a reservoir either by increasing pressure or improving viscosity. Essentially EOR is used at a mature stage to maintain production profiles and arrest decline and may not increase production flow rates above the level of the "mature" profile. The significance of the limits to the effectiveness of EOR in daily production (as opposed to preventing its decline and increasing total recoverable reserves over time) is slowly being realized all over the world. It is not a panacea outside CMEA and it will not overturn the oil outlook within CMEA although its long term effects could be significant. This increase in drilling is partly a response to the public complaints of the oil producers that too little exploration drilling took place in the past few years. Exploration was sacrificed to development priorities at Samotlor etc. and the gap is now being felt.

b) Demand 1986-1990

After 1985 options to substitute oil by gas will be becoming very much more limited. The major energy consuming industries such as steel and cement, electricity generation and CHP for the main urban centers will already have been converted. All that will be left will be smaller outlets in areas remote from the gas grid and where oil is more accessible.

The logistics also require the phasing out of older refineries. Data produced by the CDPD in Paris shows about 470 million tons of refinery capacity in units over 2m tons. There is a great preponderance of refining at the 2 m.t.p.a. size, and the average size of plant is less than 4 m.t.p.a. The plants are spread widely throughout the Union Republics and the yield of 50% of the average barrel refined has been left as residual fuel oil, mazut, no doubt for the local power stations, etc. Now that gas is taking over this role, the mazut is not required and its heavy molecules need to be "cracked" to produce more light products for transport and chemicals feedstock. To do this effectively larger refineries with wider distribution networks are essential. The CDPD figures show an impressive total of 200 million tons of much larger plant, averaging 8 m.p.t.a. under construction, mainly in European city areas, Centre and Ukraine, and also in Western Siberia where there are several urban centers of one million or more inhabitants. The Plan details are flimsy, apart from calling for a better refinery yield of higher quality products, but they do include a six-fold increase in product pipelines (12,000 kilometers).

A lot will depend on the logistics and timing of further penetration by other fuels. Long distance high voltage electricity from Ekibastuz to the cities of the Urals and Central Asia is due to be in commission before 1985, so that its effectiveness (and thereby a major key to the use of coal and lignite from Karaganda and Kansk-Achinsk) will have been tested before the 12th Plan commences. The use of nuclear power for district heating will also have been put to the test, and for European Russia this is a vital development for the 1990's. In the same way the pace of development in the nuclear industry in Eastern Europe will be of prime concern as the limits to lignite production in the DDR becomes a medium term concern. And in the Asiatic USSR, the degree of success in producing oil from Kansk Achinsk lignite at Krasnoyarks will be establishing its viability as a source of major long term oil supply. It would be fascinating to compare the future costs of this source of liquid fuel with future exploration and development costs offshore in the Arctic basins. Both are likely to be extraordinarily high. But as liquid fuels are unlikely to be the mainstay of the 21st century economy, and can therefore be awarded a premium strategic value, these options will be taken up if technically feasible one way or another as we have seen before in other parts of the world. Neither can have any impact before 1990, but they do serve as a reminder of the potential long term Soviet energy resources. From 1985 to 1990, therefore, it appears that the USSR will be dependent upon the same areas of production as in the first part of the decade.

Economic growth is likely to be attempted at a similar level in 1981-85, about 3% p.a. National income, perhaps a little lower; but with many of the easier options for substituting other fuels for petroleum already exhausted, annual growth in oil demand is unlikely to be much below the 1981-85 rate of increase. Extensive road networks complementing the BAM and other TPK's are mentioned in the current plan and the rail network in other areas is likely to remain saturated, requiring more road (diesel) haulage. Air transport will continue to be an expanding sector. The situation in Eastern Europe is likely to be unchanged in all major respects except Romanian crude output will be lower. A possible 1990 oil balance would be:

TABLE 7
Projected CMEA Oil Balance
Million Metric tons

	USSR	Eastern Europe	Total
Production	600-675	10-15	610-690
Consumption	525-575	140-160	665-735
Export Surplus	+150/+25	-125/-150	+25/-125

Because of the potential supply constraints, and other depressants to general economic growth, the upper end of the demand range is unlikely to emerge. However, there are also doubts about the upper end of the supply range. Taking even the most comfortable combination, however, the trend towards the elimination of any export surplus (including the problem of non-European CMEA) is clearer implication of the basic balance. But unless, for example, Vietnam discovers oil, Eastern Europe is unlikely to take complete priority in CMEA and that implies that 1 million barrels per day of Eastern European demand will have to come from non-CMEA sources. The ability to pay for this size of acquisition is one of the major uncertainties in the entire CMEA energy balance.

However, if the costs of producing oil are rising steeply (some recent Soviet commentators have suggested a twenty-fold marginal cost increase) then the Eastern European nations may consider the real economic cost of acquiring crude from world markets is no worse than investing in or paying for marginal Soviet production. As if to ensure this comparison is made the Soviet Union is offering small incremental quantities of crude oil to the Six at world prices.

If the incentive exists, the trade necessary to achieve imports of crude from non-CMEA sources will almost inevitably develop under the aegis of existing trade deals. Once the Iran-Iraq conflict is over, the decline in oil demand in OECD will ease the problems of access. Last year I speculated on how the trade would evolve and suggested triangular East-West European deals with the developing world. Alternatively the USSR act for CMEA as a whole in external trade. We are no closer to the answer, and the price of oil in hard currency has risen still further. But the demand potential is there in Eastern Europe and although the USSR itself is unlikely to need oil imports, the prospects of easing the cost burden of incremental domestic production (if the opportunity to import arises in the course of opening trade doors for the rest of CMEA) must look very attractive. And if the prospects in the eastern part of the West Siberian plain are disappointing this attraction will grow.

Conclusion

A conclusion in such a speculative and vast subject can only be to try to give a final overall perspective on the trends in CMEA oil demand:
1. The high use of energy in CMEA and the absence of end-use prices which at least cover costs of supply are twin symptoms of a system without functional market feedback. Oil demand may be "contained" by allocation but the control of total energy demand is an equally great problem which allocation and substitution cannot deal with. The following comparison of CMEA (365 million people) and OECD (730 million people) incremental oil and energy use over the last 6 years illustrates the point:

TABLE 8
Comparative growth in oil and energy OECD and CMEA,
1973-1979
(Million metric tons of oil or oil equivalent)

	OIL			ENERGY		
	Total 1973	Total 1979	Increment 1973-79	Total 1973	Total 1979	Increment 1973-79
OECD	1950	1984	34	3722	3914	+ 194
CMEA	392	542	+ 150	1258	1590	+ 332

(Source: BP, *Statistical Review*)

Thus with only half the population the absolute increase in energy use in CMEA has been 50% higher and 450% higher in oil.

2. The USSR faces rising costs of oil production but it has considerable flexibility to substitute gas and an ambitious nuclear program which together will provide European Russia with most of the incremental energy required in the next ten years and eventually limit oil to unique uses only. A similar program based on gas and coal will be carried out in the Asiatic USSR. Soviet harnessing of energy produced e.g. combined heat and power, allocation of primary energy resources to sectors, replacement of oil by gas etc are part of the benefits of centralized planning. After 1985 the logistics of replacing oil by means of gas or electricity grids will become much more difficult, and by 1990 most of the current interfuel substitution flexibility will have been exhausted.

3. Whereas the Soviet Union does have the benefits of flexibility in primary fuel substitution and enjoys a natural advantage in the terms of trade for oil both inside and outside CMEA, "the Six" are in the opposite position. The economic burden on the Six, whether they obtain their oil from the USSR or non-CMEA sources, is increasing, despite the substantially lower economic growth rates projected for the whole of CMEA in the 11th (and no doubt 12th) Plan periods. More foreign trade to acquire minimum oil needs will be essential for economic development.

4. The oil potential of Western Siberia, if it continues to fulfill Soviet predictions, will constitute two-thirds of all-Union production by 1990 and equal current Saudi production. Higher priority for exploration drilling and field maintenance and restriction of oil use will help optimise oil resources; but by the middle of the decade it will become clear whether or not higher discovery/recovery rates can offset the decline in Samotlor and the Volga-Urals.

5. Unless there is further drastic reduction in economic growth even the best forecasts for oil and gas production—essentially West Siberia—will be insufficient to contain total CMEA oil demand. The USSR itself can remain self sufficient unless it chooses to engage in the energy trade needed by "the six". This also assumes that no undue impediment occurs to the nuclear/coal electricity program. West Siberian potential is often debated as though the outcome would make all the difference between a Soviet Bloc oil surplus or an import deficit. The perspective suggested here is that even if the best forecasts are fulfilled the Bloc will probably cease to be a net exporter; this will have inevitable repercussions throughout the oil world.

Natural Gas: Resources, Production Possibilities and Demand in the 1980s

Jonathan P. Stern

"Swift development of natural gas production has acquired special significance. Resources are immense, above all in Western Siberia. These resources will contribute to the solution of the fuels-energy problem and speed the development of the chemical and other industries. The expansion of gas deliveries can also contribute towards the needs of the countries of the socialist commonwealth."[1] Thus Leonid Brezhnev, describing the tasks of the 1981 plan, gave natural gas a special mention in the context of the Soviet and overall CMEA energy balances, but omitted to remark on the growing contribution of natural gas exports to Soviet hard currency earnings. In the West, natural gas has been called, ". . . the ace in Soviet energy plans and provides a critical cushion for the uncertainties faced by the planners with respect to other sources of (energy) supply."[2] Within a relatively short period, after having been neglected in both Soviet and western analyses of CMEA energy, natural gas has come to be seen as the critical fuel for balancing CMEA energy books in the 1980's.[3]

Resources.[4] Obtaining estimates of energy reserves for CMEA countries is no easy matter, although more information is available for gas than for oil reserves. Fortunately, the gas resource position of the CMEA is not a particularly controversial issue since, although actual numbers may be open to dispute, the situation is fairly clear cut in overall characteristics and orders of magnitude. As shown in Table 1, the vast majority of proven reserves are situated in the USSR. The two estimates show slight differences in the size of East European reserves, but these are quite small and unlikely to increase in any country, with the possible exception of Romania.

I. Soviet Gas Reserves

In 1980, proven Soviet gas reserves were variously estimated at 25-33 trillion cubic meters (TCM) or some 40% of world proven reserves.[5] In a submission to the United Nations Economic commission for Europe, the Soviets estimated proven reserves at 39.2 TCM and ultimated recoverable gas reserves at 228 TCM. This latter figure is interesting in that it represents considerable increase from a 1971 estimate of 150 TCM, comprising 124.7 TCM onshore and 25.5 TCM offshore (in the 1.9 million square miles of coastal shelf in waters no deeper than 200 meters).[6] Once again, while one may quarrel with the actual numbers, the orders of magnitude are generally accepted. Soviet natural gas resources are truly tremendous and have been identified in extremely large accumulations which can be exploited with technology available to the USSR at this time. It is these last two factors which distinguish the prospects for natural gas from those of other fuels and appears to make the 1980's a particularly promising decade for the gas industry.

Table I.
Proven Reserves of Natural Gas in CMEA
(billion cubic meters)

	USSR	Poland	Romania	Hungary	Czecho-slovakia	GDR	Bulgaria
CIA	28,600	135	243	100	15	100	25
Petroleum Economist	30,600	125	135	115	13	80	5

Sources: CIA figures for USSR, Poland and Romania are yearend 1979 from *Handbook of Economic Statistics 1980*, ER-10452, p. 121. Other countries from *Ibid*. 1976, p. 78.
Petroleum Economist figures are yearend 1979 from, Jeffrey Segal, "Natural Gas: Rapid Growth in Output Expected," *Petroleum Economist*, August 1980, pp. 336-337.

As with all Soviet energy deposits however, the bulk of the established natural gas reserve base, and by implication the bulk of probable future finds, is inconveniently located east of the Ural mountains.[7] Table 2 demonstrates this point by showing four fifths of the proven reserves located in the east of the country; more up to date figures would undoubtedly raise this figure even higher. Western Siberia holds about three quarters of total proven gas reserves in six giant fields: Urengoy (5 TCM), Yamburg (3 TCM), Zapolyarnyy (2 TCM), Medvezhe (1.5 TCM), Kharasevey (1 TCM) and Bovanenko (1 TCM); plus another ten fields where significant reserves have been located.[8] These figures represent the initial Soviet estimates of proven reserves at the deposits; an overall estimate by the Director of the Institute of Geology and Geophysics at Novosibirsk, suggests that in the West Siberian plain there is an ultimately recoverable total of 40 TCM of which 18 TCM are in North Tyumen.[9] According to the

Director of the Urengoy gas production association, the Urengoy field is reckoned to hold more than 10 TCM of ultimately recoverable reserves.[10] The 1976-80 plan target for discovering new reserves was completed a year and a half ahead of plan and it was reported that 10 TCM had been located in Tyumen during the plan period.[11]

TABLE 2

Soviet Natural Gas Reserves (A + B + C_1) Distribution

(billion cubic meters, beginning of year)

	1951	1960	1971	1974	1976
USSR[i]	173.0	2,202.4	15,750.1	22,413.6	25,800
European USSR and Urals:	167.5	1,554.4	3,026.2	4,221.4	4,200
Komi	20.8	18.1	405.6	367.1	
Bashkir	0	23.1	54.5	58.2	
Perm	0	0	40.8	61.5	
Kuibyshev	3.1	4.6	4.1	3.4	
Orenburg	4.3	16.9	1,124.9	2,108.0	
Saratov	21.3	66.9	59.4	62.2	
Volgograd	6.4	141.6	85.7	77.3	
Astrakhan'and Kalmyk	0	11.6	20.4	16.4	
Rostov	0	0	8.9	9.3	
Krasnodar	0	359.4	89.7	256.0	
Stavropol	26.8	249.6	198.6	171.3	
Dagestan	0.5	0.1	35.0	31.2	
Chechen-Ingush	4.9	2.0	8.3	8.2	
Ukraine	70.3	544.8	810.0	868.7	
Azerbaidzhan	9.1	115.7	80.3	122.6	
East of Urals:	5.5	627.2	12,506.9	18,026.1	21,600
Tyumen'*	0	50.2	9,252.3	13,749.5	
Tomsk and Novosibirsk*	0	0	231.2	256.3	
Krasnoyarsk	0	0	149.8	302.9	18,200
Irkutsk	0	0	12.9	12.9	
Yakutia	0	0	259.5	316.2	
Sakhalin	1.1	7.4	57.5	68.2	
Tadshikistan	0	3.4	31.7	29.0	
Kirghizia	0	7.7	15.6	15.3	
Kazakhstan	0	1.2	177.3	167.6	3,400
Uzbekistan	4.4	544.2	796.8	949.6	
Turkmenistan	0	13.1	1,522.3	2,158.6	

*Tyumen' plus Tomsk and Novosibirsk make up the energy-producing region of Western Siberia.

[i]totals do not necessarily add.

Sources: *USSR: Development of the Gas Industry*, Central Intelligence Agency ER 78-10393, July 1978, adapted from Table J-11, p. 68. 1976 figures from Dienes and Shàbad, *The Soviet Energy System,* (New York: Wiley, 1979), Table 17, p. 69.

Of the other regions east of the Urals, Central Asia will continue to be extremely important although finding rates have slowed considerably and it is unclear whether, there are sufficient reserves to compensate for depletion at the Gazli (Uzbekistan), Naip, Achak and Shatlyk (Turkmenistan) deposits. No other eastern regions have proven reserves of significant magnitide, although very considerable potential exists in Eastern Siberia and the continental shelf. The Yakutia deposits in Eastern Siberia, which have been considered primarily in connection with exports of liquefied natural gas to Japan and the United States, have been developed more slowly than planned. Soviet claims of 1 TCM proven have been disputed by a western authority on the subject, but if Trofimuk's assertion of 9 TCM of recoverable reserves in six gas and gas condensate deposits is correct, it may not be long before the required reserves are proven.[12]

West of the Urals, future developments will greatly depend on the Orenburg field which contains one half of all proven reserves in the west of the country. Interestingly, the five year plan spotlighted the development of the Astrakhan gas field (also known as the Shiryayev field) with apparently significant reserves of very high sulfur gas. The development of this field, where the sulphur content appears to be even higher than at Orenburg, will undoubtedly require imports of treatment plant from the West. In the rest of the country, the picture is one of poor finding rates and rapid decline in the resource base, with the exception of the Caspian Sea region, where offshore exploration and production equipment and technology is being purchased from the West in order to fully develop existing potential. Elsewhere on the continental shelf, the most promising areas appear to be in the north, particularly the Kara Sea. In addition, gas deposits have been identified in the joint Soviet-Japanese exploration offshore Sakhalin. However, the industry's onshore resource base is such that offshore development will not receive priority, particularly since much of the technology will need to be imported using scarce hard currency.

II. PRODUCTION TRENDS

As would be expected from the reserve position discussed above, the USSR produces the overwhelming majority of the gas within CMEA. As can be seen from Table 3, gas production in East European countries, with the exception of Romania, is small and in no country will totals do better than hold steady over the next decade. The best prospects for East European production are probably in the offshore joint venture in the Baltic between the USSR, Poland and the GDR. Likewise Romania's best prospects for future gas discoveries are in the Black Sea, but in the absence of new finds, production is likely to fall, slowly but steadily, throughout the 1980's. Thus the discussion of production possibilities centers almost exclusively on Soviet prospects.

TABLE 3.
CMEA Natural and Associated Gas Production 1960-79
billion cubic meters

	1960	1970	1975	1978	1979
Bulgaria	–	0.5	0.1	negl	negl
Czechoslovakia	1.4	1.2	0.9	1.2	0.7
Hungary	0.3	3.5	5.2	7.3	6.5
GDR	–	0.3	8.1	8.5	8.5
Poland	0.5	5.2	6.0	8.0	7.3
Romania	10.0	25.3	33.3	35.5	35.5*
USSR	45.3	197.9	289.3	372.2	407

*estimate
Sources: Individual country yearbooks and CMEA statistic yearbook.

TABLE 4
Soviet Gas Production 1960-1985
(billion cubic meters)

		Plan	Actual	Annual Percentage
	Orig*	Revised		Increase
1960	60	53	45.3	28.0	
1961		60.1	59.0	30.2	
1962		70.5	73.5	24.6	
1963		91.6	89.8	22.2	1961-65
1964			108.6	20.9	23.1%
1965	150	129.4	127.7	17.6	
1966	142	148	143.9	12.0	
1967	158.3	160	157.4	10.1	1966-70
1968	170.3	171.3	169.1	7.4	9.2%
1969	191.1	184.0	181.1	7.1	
1970	225-240	198	197.9	9.3	
1971	211	211	212.4	7.3	
1972	229		221.4	4.2	1971-75
1973	250	238	236.3	6.7	7.9%
1974	280	257	260.6	10.3	
1975	300-320	285.2	289.3	11.0	
1976	313		321.0	11.0	
1977	342		346.0	7.8	1976-80
1978	370		372.2	7.5	8.5%
1979	401	404	407	9.3	
1980	400-435	435	435	6.9	
1981	458			5.3	(plan)
1985	600-640	630			1981-85 (plan) 6.0-8.0%

Sources: J.L. Russell, *Energy as a Factor in Soviet Foreign Policy*, (Saxon House/Lexington Books, 1976), Tables 1.4 and 1.5 pp. 20-21. *Ekonomicheskaya Gazeta*, No. 6, 1977, p. 1. and No. 3. 1979, pp. 1-2. *Pravda*, October 23, 1980, p. 2. and December 2, 1980, p. 2.

*The ranges represent original five year plan targets. Intermediate figures are a mixture of annual targets set at the outset of the period (such as those for 1971-75 and 1977-80, set at year-end 1976) and annual targets set at the end of the year for the coming annual plan.

Table 4 is intended to make a number of points: firstly, that natural gas has little more than a twenty year history as a significant element in the Soviet energy balance. In 1950, natural gas accounted for only 2.3% of all energy produced in the USSR (less important than peat, hydroelectric power or firewood) and by 1960, the fuel still represented less than 8% of total energy supplies.[13] Secondly, the growth of production has been extremely rapid, whether measured by actual increments or in percentages, and within two decades gas production has expanded to provide one quarter of Soviet energy supplies.

Thirdly, up until 1975, the industry failed to fulfil a single production plan target, which led to the impression that natural gas had been a major disappointment overall, and minimized both the resource base and the very considerable production gains which had been achieved. In 1975, no doubt as a result of the industry's record of failure to meet targets, the tenth five year plan figures simply required the industry to replicate (in percentage terms) its performance in the previous quinquennium. At that time, few in the West disagreed with the U.S. view that, "The present plan appears as optimistic as those of the recent past, and production is unlikely to exceed 390 BCM."[14] In the event, the natural gas industry proved to be one of the major successes of the tenth plan period and delivered more than 20 BCM of gas over the planned volumes during the five years.

This does not mean that the industry solved all its problems in the late 1970's, but that it came some way towards solutions of a number of long standing obstacles which had held back production rates in the past. While many pages could be spent cataloguing the problems facing the industry, with limited space, it makes sense to single out those which seem to be of primary importance, both in explaining the past and predicting the future.[15] First must undoubtedly come the question of pipelines and compressor stations, the building of which has consistently lagged behind field development.

III. GAS PIPELINE NETWORK

The length of the Soviet gas pipeline network increased to about 132,000 kilometers by 1980, made up of a number of systems which bring gas from the major deposits in the Ukraine, Volga-Urals, Central Asia, Western Siberia and, most recently, from Orenburg.[16] Given the location of reserves and future production, great interest centers on the building of giant 56 inch trunk pipelines which will bring gas from Western Siberia to the west of the country. This is achieved by three routes: the "Northern Lights", which was originally built simply for the Vuktyl field in Komi ASSR, but subsequently linked with Urengoy and Medvezhe. The Urengoy-Centre and the Urengoy-Chelyabinsk systems which take gas through the Urals and European USSR, some of which is eventually channelled for export. The Orenburg pipeline, which was completed in late 1978, is exclusively for the export of gas to Eastern and Western Europe.[17]

While the average yearly length of pipe laid has increased continuously from 5100 km in the late 1960's, to 6300 km in the ninth five year plan and 6960 km during 1976-80, the important additional difficulties faced by the industry have been an increase in pipeline diameter and the harshness of the terrain through which the pipe must be laid.[18] A high percentage of the new pipelines to be laid are 48 and 56 inch diameter pipe, which the USSR does not produce in large quantities and therefore needs to import from Western Europe and Japan. In addition to pipe, there have been great problems with introducing sufficient compressor stations to move the gas through the lines at optimum speed and these units have also been imported from the west. As a result, Soviet pipeline capacity has been greatly underutilized, perhaps by as much as 25% of the entire system, and by much greater proportions in individual cases.[19a]

The Soviets are acutely aware of the need to improve the pipeline network and much discussion has taken place as to ways in which this might be achieved. Early suggestions of increased pipeline diameters have given way to the possibility of chilling the gas (with the effect of increasing its density, thus allowing more fuel to flow through the same diameter pipe), increasing the pressure from 75 to 100 atmospheres (and in some cases to 125 atm) and increasing the numbers of compressor stations to make this possible.[20] Experimental links of low temperature pipelines are in operation on the "Northern Lights" pipeline and at Urengoy, but these require increased strength from the pipe and the Soviets have experimented with the manufacture of multilayer pipe, especially to cope with gas at low temperatures.[21a]

Overall, one gets the impression that imported pipe and compressor stations will continue to be paramount importance because of a lack of Soviet capacity and technology to manufacture these items. In addition, rather than attempt to break new technological ground (important as this will eventually be), the industry must utilize current capacity to the full and pay greater attention to the needs of what is becoming a very much more complex gas distribution system. In the future, safety measures will need to be incorporated to take care of breakdowns in pipelines and gas surges, plus the problems that arise from mixing gases from different sources. This will be an essential adjunct to laying the mighty east-west trunk lines.

IV. LABOR AND INFRASTRUCTURE

Perhaps the other major area in which the gas industry has to succeed in the 1980's in order to increase output, is that of labor and infrastructure. This tends to be glossed over in western analyses, where the tendency is to concentrate on the physical shortage of labor. This will indeed be important for the gas industry which needs particularly pipelaying and welding personnel with the skill to handle large diameter pipe under Arctic conditions. (The experiment with the Orenburg pipeline, where the inexperience of East European labor in laying large diameter pipe on conditions which did not approach Siberian severity, greatly hampered the joint cooperation exercise and showed just how necessary it is that the Soviet labor force has the skills for the job.)

The more important task however, will be the provision of an adequate industrial, and especially social, infrastructure. The Soviet press is full of articles criticising delays in building permanent settlements for gas workers. Enormous cost overruns at deposits, on account of transportation of materials to sites and building of infrastructure for the deposit (specifically roads, rail access and provision of an electricity supply), has meant that funds have been insufficient and worker accommodation has lowest priority. A high official in the West Siberian oil and gas administration "Glavtyumenneftegaz" estimated that in 1979, of 90,000 workers in the region, only 27,000 lived in permanent accommodation.[22] The majority, and perhaps the overwhelming majority of gas workers (since the gas fields are even more remote), therefore live in temporary accommodation which usually consists of railway box cars or trailer caravans without permanent electricity, sanitation or amenities of any kind. Small wonder therefore, that labor turnover is high and that men seek this type of employment as a way of earning quick money and return to the west of the country with improved purchasing power. But this is no sort of labor force for the future in an industry which must be able to hold and improve the skills of its workers, as they move even further north to deposits such as Yamburg in the continuous permafrost zone. The 1981-85 plan calls for an increase in labor productivity of 30-35% fulfilment of which will obviously depend on the motivation of the labor force which will in turn reflect its conditions of work.[23]

There are signs that the industry is improving in this regard and the territorial-production complex at Nadym, the power station at Surgut and the Urengoy-Surgut railway will form the beginnings of the social and industrial infrastructure which may hold the key to the rate at which the big gas fields can be developed. However, the development of the region around Urengoy (particularly the town of Novyy Urengoy which will have a planned population of 70,000 in 1985 compared with 18,000 in 1980) is lagging badly behind schedule in both industrial and social infrastructure.[24]

V. PRODUCTION POSSIBILITIES

This infrastructural growth is extremely important since most recent data indicate a major acceleration of the West Siberian gas deposits, especially Urengoy, in order to obtain maximum possible gas production in 1985. Field development priorities in Western Siberia appear to have been changed as targets have become more ambitious. An article written at the beginning of 1979 illustrates the first stage in this process: "We reason thus. If on average up to 1990 we extract 300 BCM per year, then we can live on resources from Medvezhe, Urengoy and Zapolyarnyy. Add to these

Komsomolsk, Gubkin and Yubilyeynoy and in the twelfth five year plan (i.e. 1985-90) we will have to think about Yamburg."[25] The author criticizes the Ministry of the Gas Industry for neglecting smaller deposits which lie close to existing pipelines in order to hurry on to the bigger accumulations such as Yamburg, not recognizing how much more difficult these will be to exploit. But with the 1985 gas production plan for Western Siberia set at 330-370 BCM and Urengoy alone targeted at 250-270 BCM (compared with an original plan of around 185 BCM), one gains an idea of the extent to which gas is being accelerated as an option in the Soviet energy balance. Up to 1985, West Siberian gas is to come from just three fields: Medvezhe, Urengoy and Vengapur; in the latter part of the decade, Yamburg, Zapolyarnyy, Yubilyeynyy and Kharasevey are slated for production.[26] Thus practically all the investment for Western Siberia in the 11th Five Year Plan will be poured into the single field of Urengoy, a strategy which may yield the best results in terms of short run production gains (because of the savings in infrastructure which result form such a heavy concentration on one deposit), but which may not be optimal when considering overall field development for the province. One is reminded of the situation in the oil industry, where concentration on Samotlor has perhaps led to overly rapid development of the field (probably at the expense of ultimate recovery) and insufficient attention to alternative deposits. There is however, an important difference in that the gas industry has identified a number of extremely large fields to which it can turn after Urengoy.

On the other hand, the choice of field development also reflects the much more difficult conditions at Yamburg and particularly at fields such as Kharasevey in the north of the Yamal Peninsula.[27] In 1979, Altunin was already warning that the target of 35 BCM of gas from Kharasevey which had been provisionally set by the planners was unrealistic and that the industry was not yet ready to move into the Yamal Peninsula, where climatic and permafrost conditions are immeasurably harsher than at Urengoy and requires dramatically increased capital investments.[28] Even in early 1981 it is clear that the Yamburg pipeline project to carry gas to Western Europe cannot possibly bring gas from that field of the required quantity until the late 1980's and the gas will have to be found from Urengoy (or perhaps from Orenburg) if the project is to commence by the middle of the decade.

Table 5 illustrates the regional production of gas and the eastward shift of the past decade which will be greatly accentuated in the 1980's. As recently as 1976, the Ukraine was the most important gas producing region in the country with the Shebelinka field along with the deposits at Stavropol and Krasnodar in the North Caucasus region having dominated the production picture in the early years of the industry. By the mid-1970's, production in the west of the country had stabilized and the eastern regions had taken over thanks to the early development of the Central Asian gasfields (particularly Gazli in Uzbekistan) which predates the opening up of Siberia. From the regional targets for the 1981-85 period, it appears that the older

TABLE 5.
Soviet Gas Production by Region
(billion cubic meters)

	1960	1970	1979	1980	1981 plan	1985 plan
European USSR and Urals:	44.5	138.9	165	160*	158*	150*
Ukraine	14	61	60	51	47	
Azerbaidzhan	6	6	14	15	15	
North Caucasus	14	47	14	11		
Orenburg	1	1	48			
Komi	0	7	18	18		
East of Urals:	0.8	59.0	242	275*	300*	400-490*
Western Siberia	0	9	123	156	185	330-370
Kazakhstan	0	2	5	4.3	5	5.3
Uzbekistan	0	32	37	39	37	
Turkmenistan	0	13	70	70.5	69	81-83

*estimates

Sources: Jonathan P. Stern, *Soviet Natural Gas Development to 1990.* (Lexington Books: 1980) Table 2.5, p. 28. *Soviet Geography,* April 1981, Table 2, p. 276.

regions in the west of the country will be allowed to decline with all the investment being devoted to Siberia. This contrasts markedly with the situation in the oil industry where the older deposits are under secondary and tertiary recovery in order to maintain their production levels.

While regions such as the Ukraine and North Caucasus had reached their zenith in the early to mid-1970's however, two important discoveries were made which greatly bolstered production in European USSR. The first was the Vuktyl field in Komi ASSR and the second, and more important, was the discovery of nearly 2 TCM of gas at Orenburg. As the only new giant field to be discovered in a temperate region, it was developed relatively quickly and has played an important role in stabilizing production totals in the west of the country and compensating for the delays in bring Siberian deposits into full production. Production from Orenburg, about half of which is exported, will be supplemented by the new gasfield at Astrakhan.

From the above discussion, it should be clear that natural gas production is not constrained by the size of the resource base, but rather that the speed and quality of development of social, industrial and especially transportation infrastructure at, and between Siberian deposits and the energy consuming areas in the west of the country. Essentially, the 1981-85 plan hinges on the ability of the industry to construct six to seven strings of pipeline from Western Siberia to the Urals and beyond, plus all the infrastructure associated with delivering these massively increased volumes of gas to domestic and foreign customers. During the plan period the industry will have to lay 50,000 km of pipeline (of which at least 30,000 km will be 48 and 56 diameter trunk lines) and assemble 360 compressor stations.[29] This is an awesome task and there must be doubts about the ability of the industry to fulfill it.

Table 6 contrasts six western estimates of Soviet gas production possibilities with official Soviet projections. Given the high degree of uncertainty involved in this type of projections and the fact that all the western estimates were made prior to the publication of the five year plan targets, the degree of agreement between the authors is surprising. In general however, the western forecasts opt for the lower end of the planned range for 1985. The reason for this stems perhaps from a conviction that so much remains to be achieved in the Siberian north before all the various components of the exploration and production process become firmly and efficiently established, that delays will inevitably occur. One hesitates to predict, however, that the target of 640 BCM is impossible if only because critics, even the severest, of the Soviet energy system have been forced to admit that the progress of the gas industry has been remarkable. There is nothing to compare with the Soviet gas effort in Siberia anywhere in the world. The US and Canadian efforts in Alaska and the Arctic seem relatively puny by comparison. The fact that the Soviet gas effort has been acocmplished primarily with Soviet technology and equipment (large diameter pipeline and compressor stations being important exceptions), most of which does not measure up to western equivalents, makes the achievement even more impressive.

TABLE 6.
Soviet Natural Gas Production Estimates 1985-1990
billion cubic meters

	1985			1990		
	Production	Consumption	Net Exports	Production	Consumption	Net Exports
1.	605	550	55	750	670	80
2.	560-600		46.8	700-730		
3.	660	496-589	164.5			
4.	600		95	750		130
5.	598-647	456-481	141-166			
6.	600			765-785	635-640	130-145
7.	600-640			710-820		

Sources:
1. Leslie Dienes and Theodore Shabad, *The Soviet Energy System,* (Washington D.C.: V.H. Winston/John Wiley 1979,) Table 53. p. 252.
2. USSR: *Development of the Gas Industry*, CIA., ER 78-10393, July 1978.
3. Herbert L. Sawyer, "The Soviet Energy Sector: Problems and Prospects." Harvard University, January 1978, quoted in: George W. Hoffman, "Energy Projections — Oil, Natural Gas and Coal in the USSR and Eastern Europe," *Energy Policy*, pp. 232-241.
4. David Wilson, *Soviet Oil and Gas to 1990*, Economist Intelligence Unit Special Report No. 90. (Export figures are gross, the author expects small volumes of gas imports from Afghanistan throughout the 1980's.)
5. "Situation et Perspectives du Bilan Energétique des Pays de L'Est," *Le Courier des Pays de L'Est*. No. 216. March 1978. Median and low hypotheses only.
6. Jonathan P. Stern, *Soviet Natural Gas Development to 1990*, (Lexington: D.C. Heath/Lexington Books/Gower Publishing Co., 1980,) Table 15.1, p. 178.
7. Soviet projections submitted to the Secretariat of the U.N. Economic Commission for Europe.

To forecast production a decade hence, one needs a crystal ball and a good deal of luck, but it is interesting that western and Soviet forecasts coincide rather well. Once again, production will be dependent on pipeline capacities, but if successive strings of 56 inch diameter can be laid each year (plus some improvement in pressures and utilization of throughput capacity), there seems no doubt that 750 BCM could be achieved by the end of the decade. Much may depend on the progress of other fuels, particularly that of oil, where gas is a close substitute. If the planners sense that they will be short of oil in the late 1980's, extra resources may well be switched to the gas industry since, according to one well-placed Soviet expert, ". : . every ruble invested in the gas industry . . . assures a higher economic effect than if it were invested in the oil industry."[30] There is no reason why Soviet gas production totals should not continue to increase up to the end of the century; it is a truly remarkable resource.[31]

VI. GAS DEMAND IN CMEA

Forecasting gas demand in CMEA over the next decade is an extremely difficult task, not least because it is essentially an exercise in predicting how the Soviet planners will apportion total available energy resources between the Soviet domestic economy, Eastern Europe and the world market. The latter factor has become increasingly important over the past decade as the Kremlin has found it useful (some would maintain essential) to earn increasing volumes of hard currency by exporting fuels. By the end of the 1970's, exports of oil approached one half of total Soviet hard currency earnings; but with most observers expecting oil exports to diminish, if not to disappear entirely, during the 1980's, natural gas will assume an important role in this regard. When talking about CMEA gas demand it is therefore important to recognize that, ". . . exports play a major role in the planning balance, in financial rather than volume terms, and that any shortfall in production makes itself felt through a reduction in fuel available for domestic needs rather than a decline in exports."[32]

TABLE 7
Natural Gas as a Percentage of Primary Energy Consumption in CMEA

	1960	1970	1975	1980*
Romania	49.9	54.1	53.4	48.0
Poland	1.3	6.3	6.7	7.6
Hungary	3.3	13.8	19.0	27.1
GDR	negl	0.7	6.2	8.8
Czechoslovakia	3.8	3.4	5.8	10.0
Bulgaria	0	2.0	4.0	14.1
Total	6	11	14	16.6
Soviet Union	7.9	22.3	24.7	26.0

Sources: *Energy Supplies in Eastern Europe: A Statistical Compilation.* CIA., ER 79-10624 December 1979, Tables: 1, A-2, B-2, C-2, D-2, E-2, F-2. Soviet figures from *Handbook of Economics Statistics, 1980*, CIA, ER-80 10452, p. 118, *International Energy Statistics*, CIA IESR 80-016, December 30, 1980.
*East European figures are estimates.

As Table 7 shows, gas is of variable importance in the economies of the CMEA countries. In Romania, the share of gas in energy consumption is falling as domestic production declines and coal and nuclear power are brought into the energy balance to a greater extent. In Hungary, gas accounts for around one quarter of total consumption, while in other East European countries the proportion is 10% or less. In all six East European countries, the maintenance and expansion of the share of gas in the energy balance will be dependent on imports from the USSR. In addition, with the overall CMEA oil situation appearing extremely constrained in the 1980's, the USSR having pegged oil deliveries to CMEA at 1980 levels during the following five years (which does not rule out an actual decline in those deliveries in the latter part of the decade), it will be necessary to substitute natural gas for oil in the energy balances of all East European countries with the exception of Romania.[33]

Average annual increases in Soviet apparant gas consumption fell steadily from 9.2% per annum in the latter part of the 1960's, to 7.3% p.a. in the first half of the 1970's and further to 5.9% p.a. during the tenth five year plan. While it is clear that actual yearly increments available to the domestic economy rose during that period (from just over 14 BCM per annum in the late 1970's to 18.8 BCM p.a. during 1976-80), the expansion of gas utilization in the Soviet Union was not as great as production figures would lead us to expect, due to the dramatic expansion in Soviet gas trade.[34]

Part of the trade pattern, shown in Table 8, was expected in that exports to Eastern and Western Europe formed part of long term contracts, but the anticipated imports from Iran and Afghanistan were disrupted by political events in those countries. the most serious of these were in Iran where, after reduction of contracted volumes and much negotiation, deliveries to the USSR were halted entirely in March 1980 as a consequence of a pricing dispute between the two countries. More than a year later it is unclear whether these deliveries will ever resume, given the damage to oil and gas installations caused by the Iran/Iraq war. Unlike the proposed Trilateral exchange project (IGAT 2) between the USSR, Iran and three West European countries, the IGAT 1 contract has never finally been cancelled and resumption depends on readiness and repair of facilities, resumption of Iranian oil production (since the exported gas is associated with oil from the Ahwaz fields) and resolution of the price dispute.[35]

As far as deliveries to the West are concerned, negotiations are well advanced which would take an additional 40 BCM of gas from the Yamburg field in Western Siberia, to commence around 1985, to (as many as) seven West European countries. At the time of writing, commercial terms are still to be settled and political objections to West European dependence on Soviet gas have been raised.[36] If the deal were to be concluded, it would mean that in 1990, the USSR would be exporting around 70 BCM of gas to the West.

VII. GAS TRADE

TABLE 8
Soviet Trade in Natural Gas 1970-80
(billion cubic meters)

	1970	1974	1976	1980
Exports:				
Poland	1.0	2.1	2.5	5.3
Czechoslovakia	1.4	3.2	4.3	8.7
Bulgaria	—	0.3	2.2	4.6
GDR	—	2.9	3.4	6.5
Hungary	—	—	1.0	3.8
Romania	—	—	—	1.5
Yugoslavia	—	—	—	3.0
Austria	1.0	2.1	2.8	2.4
Federal Republic				
of Germany	—	2.2	4.0	10.7
Italy	—	0.8	3.7	7.0
France	—	0.4	1.0	4.0
Finland	—	0.4	0.8	0.9
Imports:				
Iran	1.0	9.1	9.3	1.0
Afghanistan	2.6	2.8	2.5	2.5
Net Trade*	-0.3	2.1	14.0	54.9

*totals may not add due to rounding

Sources: Figures through 1976 are from *Vneshnyaya Torgovlya SSSR*, for respective years. Others are estimates.

It is very difficult to predict Soviet gas exports to Eastern Europe, since this will depend on the quantity of Soviet (and non-Soviet) oil available for the socialist countries in the late 1980's. It may also depend on the movement of world natural gas prices, hitherto always well below those of crude oil, which may change the current motivation to maintain oil exports to the West and keep gas within the bloc. At the least, it appears that East European countries will be receiving an additional 15-20 BCM per year in the 1985-90 period bringing total yearly deliveries to the bloc to a minimum of 50 BCM by the end of the decade.

With exports of 120 BCM and production at around 750 BCM, this would suggest Soviet consumption of 630 BCM, which represents annual percentage increases of about 5.3% through the 1980's. This may not be sufficient to an economy where one of the most important issues in the next decade may be the extent to which gas can substitute for increasingly scarce oil in the structure of energy demand.[37] The most obvious area in which this can take place is in power stations, where natural gas can substitute for fuel oil which in the future must be further refined for essential transportation and petrochemical uses. Perhaps the biggest paradox of this situation, which has been the subject of some discussion within the industry, is that the least profitable use of gas is being burned under boilers or in power stations. It is argued that gas should be reserved for end uses where it can bring the greatest economic return, i.e. production of methanol, ammonia and glass.[38] Although this view is undoubtedly true in the narrow sense, it overlooks the overall energy situation in a country where an abundance of gas, compared with a scarcity of oil, and crucially coal, combine to indicate a greatly expanded utilization of gas, even in end uses which, in economic terms, are clearly suboptimal.

VIII. CONCLUSIONS

What has been attempted here is a sketch of the potential for natural gas in the CMEA energy balance, in the light of resource availability and the constraints on exploration, production and transportation. However, this paper tries to indicate that projections are somewhat artificial unless placed in the context of the likely options for, and constraints on, the CMEA energy situation as a whole.

In contrast to earlier writing on Soviet and CMEA energy matters, which tended to neglect the potential for natural gas, there is a growing temptation to focus on the resource base (which is admittedly massive) and assume that this will provide a solution to all CMEA energy problems. This view should be resisted. Natural gas will be of enormous importance in CMEA energy balances in the 1980's. According to Soviet plan targets, the fuel will provide nearly 75% of the increment in fuels production during 1981-85 (and probably more in reality, if oil and coal do not achieve their targets) and over 90% of the increase in Soviet fuel deliveries to other CMEA countries during the same period. Nevertheless, severe problems of equipment and infrastructure in exploration, production and, particularly transportation, will be limiting factors in the expansion of the industry in the 1980's. If Soviet energy (particularly oil) production should run into serious trouble in the 1980's in its threefold task of supplying the Soviet domestic economy, the East European countries, and hard currency earnings for the USSR (from exports to the West) there is simply no way that the natural gas industry, however impressive its performance, can fully bridge the gap.

SOURCES

1. *Izvestiia*, October 22, 1980, p. 2.
2. Leslie Dienes and Theodore Shabad, *The Soviet Energy System: Resource Use and Policies*, (Washington D.C.: V.H. Winston/John Wiley, 1979,) p. 287.
3. I have set out the reasons for this neglect in a larger work, Jonathan P. Stern, *Soviet Natural Gas Development to 1990: The Implications for the CMEA and the West*, (Lexington Books: D.C. Heath/Gower Publishing Co., 1980).

4. In this paper, "proven reserves" refer to the Soviet categories $A + B + C_1$, while "resources" or "ultimately recoverable reserves" refer to Soviet categories A through D_2.

5. The higher figure comes from, David Wilson, *Soviet Oil and Gas to 1990, Economist Intelligence Unit* (London) Special Report No. 90. 1980. Table 18, p. 44.

6. A.D. Brents, B.Y. Gandkin and G.C. Urinson, *Ekonomika gazodobivaiushchei promyshlennosti,* (Moscow 1975.) p. 24.

7. Elsewhere I have suggested that this spatial dimension is the single biggest problem in Soviet natural gas development and affects virtually every decision taken with respect to natural gas production and exports. Jonathan P. Stern, "Soviet Natural Gas in the World Economy," in Association of American Geographers Project on *Soviet Natural Resources in the World Economy,* (University of Chicago Press: forthcoming).

8. For full details of all the major gas fields in Tyumen see: *USSR: Development of the Gas Industry,* CIA ER-78 10393, July 1978, Table C3, p. 45.

9. A.A. Trofimuk, "Mineral'nye Resursy Sibiri— Na Sluzhbu Rodine." *Ekonomika i organizatsiia promyshlennogo proizvodstva* (henceforeth EKO), No. 6. 1980, pp. 6-34.

10. Interview in Tyumenskaya Pravda, *BBC Summary of World Broadcasts,* SWB/SU W1114/A/9 December 19, 1980.

11. *Ibid* and Wilson, *op. cit.* p. 48.

12. Trofimuk, *loc. cit.* The U.S. geologist Arthur Meyerhoff claims that only 0.57 TCM of reserves has been proven over a six year period.

13. I.F. Elliott, *The Soviet Energy Balance,* (New York: Praeger, 1974,) Table 1.2, p. 8.

14. Emily E. Jack, J. Richard Lee, Harold H. Lent, "Outlook for Soviet Energy," in *Soviet Economy in a New Perspective,* Joint Economic Committee, U.S. Congress, October 14, 1976, pp. 460-478.

15. Fuller accounts can be found in Stern, *op. cit.* Chapter 2.; Dienes and Shabad, *op. cit.* pp. 68-98. Also, Robert W. Campbell, *Trends in the Soviet Oil and Gas Industries,* (Baltimore: Johns Hopkins/Resources for the Future, 1976), especially Chapters 3 and 7.

16. *Ekonomicheskaya Gazeta,* No. 13, March 1981, p. 2. For full details of the pipeline systems, see: Stern, *op. cit.* pp. 40-41; CIA, ER-10393, *op. cit.* pp. 59-62.

17. A full account of the Orenburg pipeline project can be found in: J.B. Hannigan, *The Orenburg Natural Gas Pipeline Project and Fuels-Energy Balances in Eastern Europe.* (Research Report 13. East-West Commercial Relations Series, Institute of Soviet and East European Studies, Carleton University, July 1980.)

18. Figures are calculated from *Narodnoe Khoziaistvo SSSR,* for respective years.

19. For a full account of the deficiencies of the Soviet gas pipeline system see: Robert W. Campbell, *Soviet Technology Imports: The Gas Pipeline Case.* California Seminar on International Security and Foreign Policy, November 1980.

20. V.A. Smirnov, "Defining Progress in the Gas Industry,", and O.M. Ivantsov, "The Promise of Liquefied Natural Gas," *Current Digest of the Soviet Press,* Vol. XXVIII, No. 1. pp. 7-13.

21. For scenarios on the prospects of gas transmission using these new technologies, see the paper by Hervé Gicquiau in this volume.

22. F.G. Arzhanov, "Vokrug Burovoy," *EKO,* No. 2. (1979), pp. 23-31.

23. *Pravda,* December 2, 1980, p. 2.

24. L. Kostylev, "The Polar Region's Difficult Gas," and "Leadership Relay," in *Current Digest of the Soviet Press,* Volume XXXII, No. 8, pp. 13-14.

25. Ye. G. Altunin, "Strategiyu Vybirat' Segodnya," *EKO,* No. 2. (1979), pp. 12-22.

26. *Ekonomicheskaya Gazeta,* No. 13, March 1981, p. 2.

27. There is some confusion in western writings as to the location of the gas fields in north-western Siberia. The three major fields: Urengoy, Medvezhe and Yamburg are located on the Taz Peninsula (situated between the Gulf of the Ob' and the Gulf of the Taz), whereas another cluster of large fields including Kharasevey, Novyy Port, Arkticheskii, etc., are situated on the Yamal Peninsula (to the west of the Gulf of the Ob'). Due to similarity of names and inaccurate reporting, the *Yamburg* field has become confused

with the *Yamal* Peninsula. The distinction is not one of semantics but one of geography, particularly as the climate and terrain in the Yamal Peninsula are much harsher than those of Yamburg in the north of the Taz Peninsula which in turn is harsher than Urengoy, located further south.

28. Altunin, *loc. cit.*
29. *Ekonomicheskaya Gazeta*, No. 13, March 1981, p. 2.
30. Dimitry Wolfberg, "A Soviet View of Energy," *Wall Street Journal,* March 6, 1981, p. 18.
31. In a round table discussion on Siberian energy development, a senior Soviet commentator suggested that gas production might stabilize around the end of the century. *EKO*, No. 3. (1979), p. 12.
32. Wilson, *op. cit.* p. 130
33. The USSR has pledged 400 m. tons of oil to East European countries in the 1981-85 period, corresponding roughly to 80 m. tons of oil per year delivered in 1980.
34. Documentation of these figures can be found in, Stern, *op. cit.* Table 2.12, p. 5.
35. These agreements are discussed in much greater detail in, C.B. McMillan and J.B. Hannigan *The Soviet-Iranian Energy Relationship,* (Ottawa: Institute for Soviet and East European Studies, Carleton University, November 1979.)
36. Strategic implications of Soviet gas exports are discussed in, Stern, *op. cit.* pp. 125-6, 140-143.
37. Sectoral consumption and substitution possibilities for natural gas are discussed in, Dienes and Shabad, *op. cit.* Chapter 8.
38. V.A. Dinkov, "Povisit' effektivnost' ispolzovaniya gaza v narodnom khozyaistve." *Gazovaya Promyshlennost'* No. 6, 1978, pp. 2-4.

Electrical Energy: Supply and Demand in the CMEA Economies in the 1980s, Including Nuclear Energy Prospects

Theodore Shabad

(Soviet Geography, New York)

The electrical energy economy of the CMEA countries, an essentially self-sufficient system accounting for more than 20% of world electricity generation, faced increasing problems in the 1970s in meeting demand. In most of the countries, the production of electric power lagged behind overall industrial output.[1] In the 1980s, CMEA power generation faces further constraints related to changes in the fuel base, structural problems and the geographical gap between sources of energy supply and areas of demand.

The change in the fuel base, already discussed in this forum, derives from the need for arresting a relative decline in coal consumption that began in the 1960s, especially in the Soviet Union, and the associated increase in the use of oil under boilers. In the East European countries, there has been continuing heavy reliance on solid fuels, with low-calorific lignite becoming increasingly important. Even in Rumania, where hydrocarbons, especially natural gas, have been an important power station fuel, low-grade lignite has been increasingly used.[2] Growing constraints on oil production in the USSR will require a shift to solid fuels in the future, and the depletion of solid fuels in some of the East European countries will pose a further constraint. As already noted in this session, the proposed emphasis on solid fuels will be hampered also by the remoteness of new resources, especially in the Asian USSR. These problems of depletion and increasing distance to solid fuel supplies are leading to growing emphasis on nuclear energy in regions poorly endowed with fossil fuels.

The structural problems involve essentially the need for expanding electrical generating capacity for use during peak load periods in the principal areas of demand. The large coal-fired steam-electric units and nuclear reactors being installed are designed for supplying the continuous demand portion known as base load and are not suitable for quick start-up required to meet the additional demand for electricity during peak periods. Several types of generating capacity have the characteristics needed for peak load service. They include relatively large oil-fired and gas-fired steam-electric units utilizing moderate steam pressures and temperatures (in contrast to the higher steam conditions used by large, modern base-load units), gas turbine generating units of increasingly large size, hydroelectric capacity and so-called pumped storage installations, which pump water to a high storage reservoir when surplus electricity is available at times of low demand and use the stored water to generate additional electricity at times of peak demand. Since oil-fired power generation is becoming increasingly constrained and hydroelectric power potential is limited in many of the East European countries or has already been largely developed, as in parts of the European USSR, CMEA electric power planners are looking to an expansion of gas turbine and pumped storage capacity. An additional approach to meeting peak period demand is the increasing use of interconnections between power supply systems. Such system interties are particularly effective across time-zone boundaries where blocks of electricity can be shunted back and forth over short distances in accordance with the sequence of peak demand.

Power-system interconnections are becoming necessary not only over short distances to meet changing peak demand but also over very long distances to supplement the electricity supply available for base load. Such long-distance transmission, requiring the use of an extra high voltage technology, is being made necessary by the growing spatial discrepancy between nontransportable energy sources, such as the hydroelectric capacity and the strip-mined low-grade coals of the Asian USSR, and the centers of electricity demand in the European USSR. Two such extra high voltage lines, a 1,500 KV DC line and 1,150 KV AC line, have long been projected in the Soviet Union, but have been delayed by development problems. They are once again scheduled for construction during the new five-year plan (1981-85).[3]

The supply and demand of electrical energy in the CMEA economies in the 1980s can be discussed in terms of three macro-regions with distinctive characteristics: (1) the East European member countries of CMEA; (2) European USSR, including the Urals; (3) Siberia. These regions can be viewed as the principal regions of electrical energy supply and demand, with the flow of electricity moving generally from east to west, as is also true of fossil fuels. Two additional regions of the USSR — Central Asia and the Far East — are still isolated, self-contained electrical supply and demand regins.[4] The Soviet five-year plan (1981-85) calls for a 500 KV intertie between the Central Asian and North Kazakhstan-Siberian power systems, but that transmission line will have too limited a capacity for the transfer of large blocks of electricity. Three member countries of CMEA— Mongolia, Vietnam and Cuba—are minor, isolated elements in the electrical energy system of CMEA, although Mongolia has been receiving small transfers of electricity from Siberia over a 220 KV line since 1977.[5] Generating capacity and electricity production trends in the CMEA countries appear in Table 1.

TABLE 1
Electrical Capacity and Production in CMEA Countries
(capacity* in thousand MW; production in billion KWH)

	1970		1975		1979		1980
	Capacity	Output	Capacity	Output	Capacity	Output	Output
U S S R	166	741	218	1039	256	1239	1295
European USSR	117	547	158	752	184	902	
Siberia**	36	139	42	204	49	230	
Others	13	55	18	83	23	107	
EASTERN EUROPE	52	247	74	340	90	405	419
Poland	14	65	20	97	25	118	121
East Germany	13	68	17	85	19	97	99
Czechoslovakia	11	45	14	59	17	68	73
Rumania	7.4	35	12	54	15	65	67
Bulgaria	4.1	20	7.1	25	8.1	33	35
Hungary	2.8	15	4.3	21	5.8	25	24
OTHERS							
Cuba	1.3	4.9	1.4	6.6	2.2	9.5	
Vietnam				2.4		3.9	
Mongolia		0.6		0.9		1.2	

Notes: *Capacity as of end of year.
       *West and East Siberia plus North Kazakhstan

Source: Central Intelligence Agency, *Handbook of Economic Statistics 1980*
        (ER 80-10452), October 1980, pp. 133, 134.
        1980 output from plan fulfillment reports of the respective countries.
        USSR breakdown estimated by author.

The table suggests that rates of growth of electric power production were remarkably uniform in all three macroregions of the CMEA area, with the Siberian-North Kazakhstan region, the European USSR and the East European bloc all averaging about 65% growth during the 1970's. This situation is likely to change in the future as the projected large-capacity transmission lines are installed and the electricity generating advantages of the Siberian-North Kazakhstan source region come into play.

Although the long-term prospects of energy flows from east to west within the CMEA economies will depend on a wide range of possible technological innovations, such as more efficient transmission of natural gas in chilled or even liquefied form, the construction of coal slurry pipelines and the potential of superconductivity in long-distance electrical transmission lines, a medium-term strategy appears to be emerging among

Soviet planners and has received considerable attention in the Soviet literature.[6] The strategy is based on comparative costs of delivered electric power in three demand regions—Siberia, the Urals and Central Russia—from the following alternative sources of supply: (1) East Siberian hydroelectric power; (2) mineside power stations in the Kansk-Achinsk lignite basin; (3) mineside power stations in the Ekibastuz coal basin; (4) power generation using long-haul Kuznetsk coal; (5) power generation using pipeline gas from West Siberia; (6) nuclear power.

The East Siberian hydroelectric potential, centered on the Angara and Yenisey rivers, is the easternmost source region and has been under development since the 1950s. By the end of 1980, a total of 17,300 MW of capacity had been installed, including some of the world's largest hydroelectric stations:Krasnoyarsk (6,000 MW), Bratsk (4,500 MW), Ust'-Ilimsk (3,600 MW), Sayan (3,200 MW out of a designed 6,400 MW). The ultimate plan, into the 21st century, is to develop 60,000 MW of capacity. Unlike the hydroelectric capacity in the western high-demand regions, the Siberian stations serve base-load functions; they operate at high availability, with an average of 4,500 hours or more of yearly use out of a theoretical maximum of 8,760 hours a year. (In the European USSR, where hydroelectric capacity performs mainly peaking functions, availability in the Ukraine, for example, was 2,800 to 3,000 hours in the late 1970s.) The low-cost hydroelectric power has attracted aluminum reduction plants, which insure fairly regular demand for electricity. The future outlook is for continued development both of hydroelectric capacity and of high electricity users like aluminum and other power-intensive industries. The Siberian hydro stations are situated too far to the east to contribute electricity to the western regions of the USSR, and the use of Siberian hydroelectric power is considered economical only within the Siberian demand area.

According to present design calculations, electricity generated by mine-mouth power stations in the Kansk-Achinsk lignite basin would be the lowest-cost power source of any of those considered in the Soviet strategy. The Kansk-Achinsk lignite is not transportable, for both technical and economic reasons, and is therefore viewed as a base for a major mineside power generating complex. Grandiose plans for the development of Kansk-Achinsk envisage 300 million tons of strip-mine capacity and as many as eight huge electric generating stations of 6,400 MW each. The new five-year plan 1981-85 calls for completion of the first stage of a 55-million-ton strip mine and the start of power generation at the first station. Like Siberian hydroelectric power, the lignite-based Kansk-Achinsk electricity is expected to attract power-intensive industries and, because of distance, is not considered to be an economical source of energy for the western regions. The growing Siberian power demand would thus be met both by the Kansk-Achinsk mine-mouth lignite-fired plants and the East Siberian hydro stations. With Kansk-Achinsk base-load capacity in place, the hydroelectric stations would be used increasingly for peak-load service.

The most immediate eastern source of electricity for the western regions is likely to be the electric power generating complex now being developed at the Ekibastuz coal basin in northeast Kazakhstan. The development of the Ekibastuz basin, which yields a high-ash subbituminous coal, begin around 1950 and reached an annual output of 67 million metric tons in 1980, for shipment to power stations within Kazakhstan, West Siberia and as far west as the Urals. The capacity of the Soviet rail system has become a limiting factor in the expansion of long-haul Ekibastuz coal, with up to 3,000 carloads a day being moved. Further expansion of coal mining at Ekibastuz will be associated with the construction of a series of mine-mouth power stations and the westward extra high voltage transmission of electricity. Four generating stations of 4,000 MW each are projected at Ekibastuz. The first two 500 MW generating units at the No. 1 station began operation in 1980, and two more generators were installed in 1981. About 7,000 to 8,000 MW is expected to be installed by the mid-1980s, and the entire 16,000 MW by the end of the decade. Most of this additional capacity is to be transmitted westward by two extra-high-voltage lines, a 1,500 KV DC line to the Tambov area of Central Russia and a 1,150 KV AC line to Chelyabinsk in the Urals.[7] A crucial condition for success in this project is close coordination and timely completion of generating capacity and transmission lines. For example, the 1,500 KV DC line, after many years of delay, was finally started in 1980. The 2,415 km line calls for the construction of 5,000 pylons, each 32 meters high.[8] It is designed to transmit 6,000 KW of electricity, or about 40 billion KWH a year. The five-year plan 1981-85 calls for the completion of the first stages of the two transmission lines. Ultimately the Ekibastuz power complex is also to be connected eastward by a 1,150 KV AC intertie via the Kuznetsk Basin with the projected Kansk-Achinsk generating stations. According to Soviet design calculations, Ekibastuz power would be the most cost-effective source of electricity for the Urals over the proposed 1,150 KV AC line, but not for Central Russia. The long-term strategy calls for the use of Ekibastuz power in Central Russia only as a supplementary supply if nuclear power turns out to be inadequate to cover the projected base-load requirements in the European USSR.

A second projected source of electricity for the western regions is a gas-fired power complex at Surgut in the West Siberian oilfields. This complex is planned to burn natural gas from the more northerly gas fields in West Siberia. The generating capacity of the Surgut complex is projected at 15,000 MW and would consist of three stations. The first, equipped with 200 MW units, reached its designed capacity of 2,400 MW in December 1980;[9] it has been the principal source of electric power for the West Siberian oilfields. The second station, to be equipped with 800 MW generating units, is scheduled to start operation by 1985 under the new five-year plan, and the third station is projected to use 1,200 MW units (a prototype 1,200 MW unit went into operation in December 1980 at the Kostroma station in Central Russia[10]).[11] Power from the Surgut stations would ultimately be transmitted to Sverdlovsk, in the Urals, over a 1,150 KV AC line. Over the long term, gas-fired Surgut power stations are being viewed as one of the cost-effective sources of electricity for the Urals, in addition to the transmission of power from Ekibastuz and the use of long-haul Kuznetsk coal in Urals-based power stations.

According to present cost calculations, electric power generated by Urals stations burning Kuznetsk coal would actually be somewhat cheaper than the transmission of electricity from the Surgut complex (1.02 kopecks per KWH compared with 1.08[6]). But expansion of the use of Kuznetsk coal will be constrained over the long term both by the resource base and by rail-transport limitations. Out of a current Kuznetsk Basin coal production of 150 million tons a year, more than one-third is being shipped to the Urals and beyond to Central Russia. These shipments of 50 million tons or more impose a tremendous strain on the rail lines leading westward from the Kuznetsk Basin toward the European USSR, and they are among the most heavily used coal-hauling routes in the Soviet Union.[12] Most of these hauls consist of coking coal, which is essential for the iron and steel industry in the European USSR and cannot be replaced. The long-term Soviet energy strategy is therefore designed to develop alternative sources for long-haul Kuznetsk steam coal in the Urals and Central Russia by such devices as Ekibastuz mine-mouth power stations and West Siberian natural gas.

On a pure cost basis, gas-fired power stations in Central Russia would also be one of the most cost-effective energy sources for the European USSR, according to Soviet projections. But incremental expansion of gas-fired power generation in the western regions is constrained by the low efficiency of the present pipeline-transmission technology for natural gas and by the need for converting part of the present oil-fired power stations in the European USSR to natural gas. This leaves nuclear energy as the sole major source of incremental base-load generating capacity in the European USSR as well as in Eastern Europe.

TABLE 2
Electrical Capacity and Output of Nuclear Stations in USSR
(capacity* in thousand MW; production in billion KWH)

	1970	1975 Plan	1975 Actual	1980 Plan	1980 Actual	1985 Plan
Capacity	0.9	8.1	4.7	18.4	12.6	36-37
Output	3.5	25	20.2	80	(73)	220/225

(*)Capacity as of end of year.

Note: The figures relate to utility stations under the Ministry of Electric Power USSR and do not include experimental stations or weapons-oriented military stations.

Source: Dienes and Shabad, *The Soviet Energy System,* 1979, p. 153; *Soviet Geography,* September 1981, pp. 446-448.

Nuclear Power Generation
SOVIET UNION

Although the Soviet Union received electricity from a small nuclear power reactor as early as 1954, it was slow to develop nuclear energy as a significant element of the electric power economy. By 1970, when the European Community had installed 6,700 MW of nuclear generating capacity and the United States 6,000 MW, the Soviet Union had only 900 MW of civilian capacity, not counting a reported "Siberian" weapons-oriented facility with 600 MW. The delay in proceeding to large-scale nuclear energy development appears to have resulted from several reasons: the apparently plentiful supply of fossil fuels in the 1960s and the cost advantage of fossil fuel fired power; indecision as to optimal reactor types, and the lack of reactor manufacturing capacity. By the early 1970s, awareness of the increasing tightness and the rising world price of oil supplies, a decision on optimal reactor types and plans for the development of reactor-making capacity laid the basis for more intensive nuclear power development. Progress has been slowed by a variety of problems, and ambitious plans were underfulfilled, but the policy was clear and the development of an increasingly large nuclear energy capacity appears to be only a matter of time, both in the European USSR and in Eastern Europe.[13]

In the Soviet Union, reactor capacity additions during the 1971-75 plan were projected at 7,200 MW, but only about 3,000 MW was actually completed; during the 1976-80 period, 13,700 MW was to be added, but only 7,900 MW began commercial operation, with an additional 1,000 MW (Leningrad-4) achieving criticality by the end of 1980. (Table 2).

In 1980, nuclear power generation in the Soviet Union was about 73 billion KWH, or 5% of total electricity production. Hydroelectricity accounted for about 14%, fossil-fuel fired thermal power for 80%. The nuclear capacity additions announced for the 1981-85 plan period are again highly ambitious, amounting to 23,000-24,000 MW, or an average of 5,000 MW a year. Such a high rate of nuclear capacity installation has not yet been achieved. But if the new five-year plan were to be fulfilled, nuclear power generation is planned to pull even with hydroelectricity by 1985, each accounting for 14 to 15% of the projected power production level of 1,555 billion KWH.

The Soviet strategy of nuclear power development now focuses on large stations employing two basic reactor types: the VVER, a pressurized-water reactor, and the RMBK, a graphite-moderated, water-cooled channel-type (or pressure-tube) reactor. In the meantime, development is being pressed in the field of breeders, which are viewed as the next generation of reactors in the Soviet economy. With few exceptions, the nuclear power capacity is being concentrated in the industrial and population heartland of the European USSR between the Volga valley and the western border. The principal exceptions are the Kola station in the far north of European Russia; the Beloyarskiy station in the Urals (where a 600 MW breeder went into operation in 1980); the smaller Shevchenko breeder on the east shore of the Caspian Sea (used in part for seawater distillation), and the Armenian station in Transcaucasia.

The installed capacity at the large nuclear power stations in the European USSR as of the end of 1981 was as follows: The Leningrad station at Sosnovyy Bor reached its designed capacity of 4,000 MW; the Chernobyl' station at Pripyat' in the Ukraine was at 3,000 MW, half of the ultimate design; the Novovoronezhskiy station south of Voronezh had 2,500 MW in operation; the Kursk station at Kurchatov had 2,000 MW installed, half of the ultimate capacity, and the Rovno station at Kuznetsovsk in the Ukraine had 880 MW, with an additional 4,000 MW yet to be installed in the middle and late 1980's.

Aside from continued expansion of existing stations, the new five-year plan 1981-85 calls for the start of commercial operation at the following sites: the South Ukraine station at Konstantinovka, Zaporozh'ye station at Energodar, Crimean station at Aktash, and the Khmel'nitskiy station, all in the Ukraine; the Rostov station at Volgodonsk; the Balakovo station on the Volga; the Kalinin station at Udomlya, the Smolensk station at Desnogorsk, and the Ignalina station at Snieckus in Lithuania.

Many of these nuclear station sites are being located near populated areas, reflecting confidence with regard to radiation hazards. A Soviet article in 1979[14] recommending remote sites in unpopulated areas because of the limited "ecological capacity" in the European USSR aroused attention in the West as a possible harbinger of Soviet policy change. But the article appears to have dealt with very long-term issues, beyond the year 2000, and has little relevance for near-term planning. In fact, a Soviet policy decision to proceed with the construction of nuclear central heating plants for urban areas will require the siting of steam-generating reactors even closer to populated areas than power-oriented nuclear stations. The first nuclear steam-heat plants are to be built at Novovoronezhskiy, for the city of Voronezh; at Gor'kiy; and near Odessa.[15]

Reactor-manufacturing capacity is likely to remain a bottleneck until the new Atommash reactor plant at Volgodonsk reaches its designed capacity of making eight 1,000 MW nuclear reactors a year. The first manufacturing capacity, of 3,000 MW a year, went into operation in late 1978, and was expanded to 4,000 MW in late 1979.[16] The first 1,000 MW reactor was delivered by Atommash in 1981. Other nuclear equipment manufacturers are at Khar'kov and in the Leningrad area (at Kolpino and at the Elektrosila and Metallic Plant in Leningrad proper). Under the CMEA long-term target program, which provides for the installation of 37,000 MW of nuclear generating capacity in Eastern Europe in 1981-90, nuclear equipment will also be manufactured in Eastern Europe, for example, by the Skoda Works in Czechoslovakia.

The nuclear power centers in the European USSR, according to long-term plans, are to be interconnected by a 750 KV grid, allowing for larger intersystems transfers of electricity than the present 500 KV intersystems connections. The projected 750 KV grid would form a ring running from Leningrad through the Central Russian nuclear stations of Kalinin, Smolensk, Kursk, Novovoronezhskiy, the Ukrainian stations of Zaporozh'ye, Konstantinovka, Chernobyl' and Khmel'nitskiy, north through Belorussia. to the Lithuanian station of Ignalina, and back to Leningrad.[17] This basic 750 KV ring would be connected with some of the outlying nuclear centers in the Volga valley and, most important, would serve for the transfer of electricity between the power systems of the European USSR and the power systems of Eastern Europe.

The boundary between the USSR and its East European allies is eminently suited for transfers of electricity to help cover peak demand periods. The time difference between Eastern Europe and the western regions of the USSR is two hours, a difference maintained hours from April 1 to October 1 under the new system of double summer time that went into effect in the Soviet Union in 1981.[18] This unusual time difference across a time-zone boundary makes it possible to cover peak loads in Eastern Europe by shunting additional power from the Soviet Union and reversing the flow during peak periods on the Soviet side. The proposed system of 750 KV lines would have a transmission capacity of up to 2,000 MW, or 12 billion KWH a year.

Even before the start of development of the 750 KV lines, there was a steady increase in electricity exports from the western regions of the Soviet Union to Eastern Europe over a system of interties of up to 400 KV. These exports amounted to 12 billion KWH by 1978, going mainly to Bulgaria (4.5 billion) and to Hungary (4.4 billion), the two countries most heavily dependent on Soviet electricity transfers.[19] The first 750 KV link ,completed in late 1978, connected the Ukrainian power system with Albertirsa in Hungary.[20] The overall length of 1,595 km of this intertie, which starts in the Donets Basin, makes it one of the longest extra high voltage transmission systems. In the first year of operation, it raised Soviet exports by 2 billion KWH, with an increment of 1.6 billion for Hungary and the rest shunted through Hungary to Czechoslovakia. The Chernobyl' nuclear power station was connected to the 750 KV intertie in 1980,[21] thus providing the first Soviet nuclear input into the East European power system.

Such nuclear inputs are expected to become the pattern of the future as more 750 KV interties are completed between nuclear stations in the western regions of the Soviet Union and its East European allies. The next such project involves joint construction of the Khmel'nitskiy nuclear station in the western Ukraine and the export of half of its 4,000 MW capacity to Eastern Europe over a 750 KV intertie to Rzeszow in Poland. Of the ultimate Soviet export of 12 billion KWH over this line (equivalent to all Soviet electricity exports in 1978), 50% would go to Poland, 30% to Czechoslovakia and 20% to Hungary. The 377 km transmission line and the first 1,000 MW unit at Khmel'nitskiy are scheduled to go into operation in 1984.

Future 750KV interties are envisaged between the South Ukraine nuclear station at Konstantinovka and Rumania and Bulgaria (700 km) and between the Ignalina nuclear station in Lithuania and Poland and East Germany.

EAST EUROPE

Over the long term, nuclear-based electricity transfers from the western border regions of the Soviet Union to Eastern Europe are expected to complement the proposed expansion of nuclear generating capacity in Eastern Europe itself. The 10-year goal of 37,000 MW of new capacity envisaged in the CMEA target program is likely to be overly ambitious, judging from the past performance and from the fact that the five-year plan 1981-85 of the Soviet Union itself calls for additions of 23,000 to 24,000 MW, suggesting a 10-year program of perhaps 70,000 MW of new nuclear generating capacity by 1990. Capacity additions in the USSR are likely to be several times greater than those in Eastern Europe, so that a more reasonable 10-year goal for Eastern Europe would appear to be additions of 4,000 MW, distributed as follows: East Germany, 1,800 MW (Griefswald and Rheinsberg), Czechoslovakia, 900 MW (Jaslovske Bohunice) and 1,320 MW (Kozlodui). Future sites that have been announced, in addition to the proposed expansion of present sites, are: Magdeburg-Stendal in East Germany; Dokuvany, Mahovce and Milovice in Czechoslovakia; Zarnowiec in Poland; Paks in Hungary; Cernavoda in Rumania as well as Cienfuegos in Cuba. Most of these proposed reactors will be of the VVER 440 MW type, with VVER 1,000 MW reactors beginning to come into play toward the end of the decade.

In view of the limited impact of nuclear power thus far and the restricted potential for hydroelectricity, most East European electricity generation is likely to continue to be based on solid fuels at least until the end of the present century. But there are significant structural differences among countries.

In Poland, the characteristic trend has been for newly developed lignite to replace the high-value Upper Silesian hard coal under power station boilers. Starting with the old Turoszow lignite basin in the southwest corner of Poland, on the Czechoslovak-East German border, mine-mouth power stations were developed in the Konin-Turke lignite basis and in the Belchatow basin, with future prospects in the Lublin basin and the Scinawa basin in Lower Silesia. More than 95% of all Polish electricity is based on solid fuels (two-thirds hard coal, one third lignite), with hydroelectricity contributing only around 2% and some peak-load service is provided by pumped storage stations. Pending the completion of the 750 KV intertie from the Khmel'nitskiy nuclear station in the Ukraine and Rzeszow, cross-border transfers have been negligible (several hundred million KWH out of a national power generation of 121 billion KWH in 1980).

In East Germany, with virtually no hard coal resources, lignite has been traditionally the basic fuel source, accounting for more than 80% of all electricity generation. The principal mine-mouth power complexes are in the Lower Lusatian lignite basin. Nuclear power contributes about 5% of the electricity, and hydro power is negligible, with pumped storage capacity continuing to be developed for peaking service. East Germany exchanges electricity with both Poland and Czechoslovakia to cover peak loads, but net transfers are small.

Czechoslovakia, too, relies mainly on lignite, mine mainly in the North Bohemian basin around Most, and to a lesser extent at Sokolov, to the southwest. Hydroelectricity is somewhat more significant (5% of power generation) and the impact of nuclear energy is beginning to make itself felt. Imports of electricity also play a more important role in Czechoslovakia; in addition to direct transfers from the Soviet Union over a 400 KV line, Czechoslovakia is benefiting indirectly from the 750 KV intertie between the USSR and Hungary, and will similarly receive a share of the electricity transferred over the projected 750 KV intertie from the USSR to Poland.

Unlike the three northern countries in Eastern Europe, Hungary is heavily dependent on electricity transfers from the Soviet Union. Even before the completion of the 750 KV intertie, Soviet transfers accounted for 15% of Hungarian demand. Furthermore, because of a poor solid fuels base, Hungary has been deriving a larger share of its power generation from oil and gas fired stations, using fuels imported from the Soviet Union. In the mid-1970s, only about one-half of all Hungarian electricity demand was met by stations burning domestic solid fuels.

In Rumania, the electric power supply has been largely independent of Soviet assistance thus far, pending realization of the projected 750 KV intertie from the South Ukraine station. The fuel pattern of power stations in Rumania differs substantially from that of the other Eastern European countries because of Rumania's domestic hydrocarbon resources. Natural gas has been consistently an important fuel, accounting for about 60% of thermal power, with growing use of lignite replacing increasingly scarce oil supplies. The joint construction of the Iron Gates hydroelectric project with Yugoslavia makes hydro power a far more important contributor to Rumania's electricity supplies (about 16%) than elsewhere in Eastern Europe.

Bulgaria, like Hungary, is again heavily dependent on Soviet energy supplies of all forms. Low-calorific domestic lignite is burned in mine-mouth stations of the East Maritsa and Bobov Dol Basins. Other fossil fuel stations burn imported Donets Basin steam coal (shipped by water across the Black Sea) and Soviet oil and gas. Both nuclear power (15%) and hydroelectricity (9%) make substantial contributions, as does a net electricity transfer from the USSR over the existing 400 KV transmission line (13% of Bulgarian demand).

Notes

1. I. D. Kozlov. *Energeticheskoye khozyaystvo stran SEV: Problemy i perspektivy sotrudnichestva* (The Power Economy of the CMEA Countries: Problems and Prospects of Cooperation). (Moscow: Nauka, 1980), p. 13.

128   Theodore Shabad

2. *Elektroenergetika yevropeyskikh stran-chlenov SEV* (Electric Power in the European Member Countries of CMEA), edited by P.S. Neporozhnyy. (Moscow: Energiya, 1978), p. 110.
3. *Pravda,* Dec. 2, 1980.
4. *Soviet Geography*, April 1979, p. 266.
5. *Soviet Geography*, June 1978, p. 431.
6. A. Troitskiy, *Elektricheskiye Stantsii*, 1978, No. 12, pp. 11-14; A. Troitskiy, *Planovoye Khozyaystvo*, 1979, No. 2; *Soviet Geography*, March 1979, pp. 188-189.
7. *Soviet Geography*, March 1980, pp. 187-190, with map of Ekibastuz power grid, p. 191.
8. *Stroitel'naya Gazeta,* Dec. 12, 1980.
9. *Stroitel'naya Gazeta*, Dec. 21, 1980.
10. *Sotsialisticheskaya Industriya,* Dec. 23, 1980.
11. *Izvestiya,* Jan. 1, 1981; *Soviet Geography*, March 1979, pp. 189-190.
12. Leslie Dienes and Theodore Shabad. *The Soviet Energy System.* (New York: John Wiley, 1979), pp. 113-114.
13. For recent reviews of the nuclear power situation, see: Jochen Bethkenhagen, "Die Energiepolitik der UdSSR im Rahmen der weltwirtschaftlichen Entwicklung: Die Rolle der Kernenergie," paper prepared for the Second World Congress for Soviet and East European Studies in Garmisch-Partenkirchen, 1980; M. Messengiesser, "Die Atomenergiepolitik der UdSSR," *Osteuropa,* 1980, No. 11, pp. 1207-1219; *Kernenergiepolitik der Länder des RGW* (conference report), edited by Arnold Buchholz. Cologne: Bundesinstitut für ostwissenschaftliche und internationale Studien, October 1979.
14. N. Dollezhal' and Yu. Koryakin. "Nuclear power: achievements and problems," *Kommunist,* 1979, No. 14, pp. 19-28.
15. *Soviet Geography*, May 1980, p. 326; March 1981.
16. *Soviet Geography*, February 1979, pp. 126-127; *Stroitel'naya Gazeta*, Dec. 19, 1979.
17. Kozlov, *op. cit.,* p. 36.
18. *Soviet Geography*, February 1981, pp. 120-122.
19. Theodore Shabad, "Soviet Regional Policy and CMEA Integration," in: Paul Marer and John Michael Montias (eds.). *East European Integration and East-West Trade.* (Bloomington: Indiana University Press, 1980), pp. 223-244; reference to pp. 231-233.
20. *Soviet Geography*, December 1978, p. 744.
21. *Gudok,* Aug. 1, 1980.

A Note on the Cost of Soviet Oil

Peter Wiles

The terms of trade, more strictly called the net barter terms of trade, is not always the best concept with which to judge a country's economic position. As the relation of two market prices, it omits costs, and especially the cost of exports. A country benefits or loses in foreign trade by the quantity of imports it can get for a given cost of exports, the so-called single-factor terms of trade. If export prices rise *pari passu* with export costs, there is no gain or loss on this side—but of course we do not care what it costs the foreigner to make our imports; his prices alone are interesting.

In discussing Soviet oil, and indeed the oil crisis in general, there has been far too little talk of costs, and too much of the quantity produced. The USSR is not Saudi Arabia, producing at a few cents a barrel and restricting output so that marginal cost actually falls—or rises-over time much less than it would have without the restriction. The USSR restricts output no more than the UK; indeed it is precisely Saudi restrictions that force both countries to produce more at a marginal cost about ten times higher[1]. This factor constitutes the oil crisis, which would otherwise not exist at all.

What is the effect of this on the Soviet economy? The USSR must, for political reasons, maintain or increase output. This means, in practice, bringing new wells on stream under very unfavorable climatic and geological conditions; i.e. at rising long-run marginal cost (lrmc). Our first question is, can she have suffered more from the rising lrmc than she has gained from the rising price?—and our answer is, surely not. Our second question is, do our estimates of lrmc support the CIA's views on Soviet oil production and cost? Our answer is, not yet but shortly.

With reference to the Yom Kippur price rises, USSR belongs to an intermediate category in a fourfold classification:

i) The main OPEC countries themselves are cheap[2] producers and big exporters, who however restrict output; so they do not open up expensive new wells. They have unreservedly gained.

ii) Countries without oil are "pure importers" and do not have oil costs, only compensating export costs or increased foreign aid. They have unreservedly lost.

iii) My intermediate categories are the ones that must open up expensive new wells. The third category is "non-OPEC exporters": USSR, China, Norway, Mexico. It is clear that Norway would be better off buying Saudi oil at $2 per barrel (1972 prices) than digging it up for home use at, say, $8 off-shore unless her export profits with the world price at $11 in terms of 1972) compensated her. Her exports are so large that they probably do. USSR, though relatively a small exporter, has her marginal fields mainly onshore, so happens also to be a gainer by reason of her low lrmc.

iv)   A similar category is the "partial importers"; notably the UK, USA, Romania. These suffer both from the high OPEC prices and from the high cost of their new (often offshore) wells; but less from the latter if they are rational (since they must allow for the political and economic risks attending importation).

In mining, the law of diminishing returns cannot be relied upon in the short or medium run. We all know where agricultural land is and roughly what it will produce. Every extension of the plough encounters, technology being constant, diminishing returns, because we have already exploited the better land. The law gives us even a chronological order for an optimum investment program.[3] But not so in extractive industries. Geological prospecting is a very chancy business, notably in the USA, where once the new East Texas field produced more cheaply than the average existing well (Adelman 1972, p. 43). But this is probably not at present true of the USSR; prospecting has not uncovered cheap fields recently. It might seem from the official cost data that the new fields of Western Siberia were cheap, but that very large area is not divided in those statistics into its separate fields. The really new ones are the northerly ones, and they are very expensive. But how expensive, exactly? Surely they are better than the North Sea?[4]

Our concept of lrmc is fraught with difficulties. (a) Once a field is on stream it can be manipulated in many ways that are quite expensive. Also a field can be revived, with new techniques. Notably, we may or may not reinject water in order to keep the pressure up. In at least 70% of cases the Russians do just this. All this might seem to give rise to alternative definitions of "marginal", but no, since if we are rational the marginal cost per ton of oil from the manipulation of an old field should be the same as from a new field. (b) But what is the cost of a new field? All dry wells drilled should be pro-rated amongst new wells on stream; their cost is an important part of lrmc as we have defined it. Most dry wells escape the Soviet cost concept (Campbell, passim). (c) It is paradoxically possible in extractive industries for marginal to be below average cost, whilst the latter rises! This is because the marginal concept is ordinarily defined so that the costs of intramarginal units remain constant. But in oil, old wells necessarily go out of service taking their perhaps lower costs with them: it is then enough that new wells have higher costs than wells dropping out, while the great mass of wells has still higher costs—the average still rises. Such could, with minor changes, be the case in Table II.

We now estimate Soviet Irmc. Our knowledge of Soviet oil costs is far from bad, particularly since Robert Campbell has collected it all! First we select for Table II the only consecutive recent years for which we have all-Union average costs by the limited Soviet accountancy described. In Table I we give a preliminary and an adjusted estimate for the volume of new "production", and one of the "production" dropping out year by year. The Soviet sources call this not "wells" but "capacity", and measure it by output not bore-holes. It is inconceivable that "capacity" should mean wells alone, since the percentage of active new wells is about 2 every year (Campbell, 1976, Table 10), while that of the new active "capacity" is 15-20; it includes the revitalisation of old wells. We apply our concept of Irmc to "capacity" since the data for new wells are insufficient.

In Table I columns (i) and (ii) are interpolated from the five-yearly figures at the bottom, so as to make a smooth annual progression. This initial interpolation is expectedly inaccurate, so that column (iv), in which each year's output is the previous year's in column (iii) + column (i) - column (ii), does not exactly correspond to the actual data in column (iii). In column (v) these deviations are loaded onto column (i) alone, on the assumption that dropping out is more likely to be a smooth series than commissioning.[5]

Table I
Capacity dropped and added in Soviet oil (mn. tons)

	(i)	(ii)	(iii)	(iv)	(v)
	capacity		output		
	added	subtracted	actual[b]	deduced[c]	(i) adjusted[d]
1960			147.9		
1	28.6	9.2	166.1	167.3	27.4
2	29.6	10.5	186.2	185.2	30.6
3	30.7	12.0	206.1	204.9	31.9
4	31.8	13.5	223.6	224.4	31.0
5	33.3	14.8	242.9	242.1	34.1
6	35.3	17.5	265.1	260.9	39.5
7	39.0	20.2	288.1	283.9	43.2
8	43.9	22.9	309.2	309.1	44.0
9	49.3	25.7	328.4	332.8	44.9
1970	55.5	28.7	353.0	355.2	53.3
1	62.5	33.5	377.1	382.0	57.6
2	70.0	40.5	400.4	406.6	63.8
3	79.0	50.0	429.0	429.4	78.6
4[e]	?91.0	?61.5	458.8	458.5	?91.3
5[e]	?104.5	?75.5	491.0	487.8	?107.7
6			520.0		
7			546.0		
8			572.0		
9					
1961-5	154.0[a]	60.0[a]			155.0
1966-70	223.0[a]	115.0[a]			224.9
1971-5	407.0[a]	261.0[a]			398.3

a. Sundry Soviet statements in 1974 (Campbell 1976, p. 30)
b. Campbell 1976, p. 27; this is the normal series and it includes a little gas condensate, rising to 1.5% of the total.
c. E. g. 167.3 = 147.9 + 28.6 - 9.2
d. E.g. 166.1 = 147.9 + 27.4 - 9.2
e. These years are less accurate since they were only forecasts.

We now apply the quantities of added and dropped capacity to the average cost date so as to develop a series for lrmc.

Table II
An estimation of long-run marginal cost, excl. exploratory wells.

	output, av. cost, mn. tons R per ton	last year's cost		cost of capacity dropping out	cost of new capacity	lrmc, R per ton
1968	309.2 × 4.17[a]					
9	328.4 × 4.23[b]	=	309.2 x 4.17	− 25.7 x 3.80[c]	+ 44.9L[d]	4.39
1970	353.0 × 4.29[a]	=	328.4 x 4.23	− 28.7 x 3.80	+ 53.3L	4.39
1	377.1 × 4.37[a]	=	353.0 x 4.29	− 33.5 x 3.80	+ 57.6L	4.52

a. Campbell 1976, Table XII.
b. Interpolated.
c. The 1960 cost plus 50 kopeks for the new finder's fee: see Campbell 1976, p. 35
d. L means lrmc.

Thus the annual rise in lrmc, 1965-71, was 1.5%, while average cost rose 1.6%. Such figures can have no exact value, but they indicate that lrmc = ac up to 1973. Even then, however, it is very important that the finder's fee was said to be much too low and not heavily enough allocated to new wells (Campbell, in correspondence).

We have however a good deal of information on the cost of an exploratory well. This was extremely stable up to 1972:

TABLE III

	exploratory wells completed	average depth in meters[b]	"estimate" cost of drilling such wells Rpm.	total meters drilled, thou.	total cost, Rmn.	Cost per well (R. thou)
1965	2165	2195	148.7	5565	828	382
6	2163	2423	159.6	5648	901	417
7	2240	2447	162.8	5802	945	422
8	2006	2571	185.5	5111	948	473
9	1793	2655	230.7	4924	1136	634
1970	1711	2691	238.8	5746	1229	718
1	1661	2686	253.2	5250	1329	800
2	1673	2622	259.4	5138	1333	797
3				5223		

Our data for development wells are less complete, but these two years give an indication:

1965	2738	1647	65.54	5151	338	123
1970	3600	1769	84.8	6744	572	159

a. Campbell 1976, p. 17
b. This column does not coincide with the fourth divided by the first, and must, as Campbell explains (1976, pp. 17-18), have a different definition.

Three main factors intervene between the cost of an exploratory well and the lrmc of a ton of oil: (i) the cost of a development well; (ii) the cost of transporting oil from the well-head and storing it locally and (iii) the amount of oil coming out of a new well. (i) we know - above. (ii) excludes the long-distance pipe-line, as for instances Umanski: (1965 and 1970) makes clear—all our costs concern oil-mining (neftedobyvayushchaya promyshlennost'). For (iii) Campbell (in private correspondence) provides these numbers:

TABLE IV
Output per new well, tons per day

1972	88.5 (West Siberia only)[a]
1976-80	93[b]
1980	71.1[c]
1981-85	38[b]
1985	15-20[c]

a. Campbell 1976 p. 27
b. Lalyants 1980
c. Filanovski 1980

Performance per well was evidently rising until 1972 at least (Campbell, *ibid.*). There appear to be no older figures for the flow from the new wells. The life-time of a new Soviet well might be sixteen years, but the total flow from a new well might be six times the initial annual flow on average.[6]

We now proceed according to the formula:

$$\text{lrmc} = \frac{(2/3 \times \text{cost of an}) (\text{exploratory well}) + (1 \times \text{cost of a new}) (\text{development well})}{\text{Life-time flow from a new development well}} + \text{other costs (i.e. current operation and transport to nearby storage)}$$

where the weights of 2/3 and 1 are loosely derived from Table III; development wells cost a quarter as much as exploratory ones, as in 1970; and the amortisation of development wells was 30%[7] of the cost of oil in Soviet accountancy in 1972.

We then guess increases in the various costs as below to arrive at these Irmcs in constant rubles of 1972, this time including exploratory wells:

TABLE V

The Irmc of Soviet oil including exploration

1972 $\dfrac{0.92 \times 797,000}{88.5 \times 365 \times 6} + 3.1^8 = R6.9$

1980 $\dfrac{0.92 \times 1,600,000}{71.1 \times 365 \times 6} + 4.0^9 = R13.5$

1985 $\dfrac{0.92 \times 2,400,000}{17.5 \times 365 \times 6} + 4.9^{10} = R62.5$

But the "world" price today is about \$200 per ton; or about 130 foreign-trade rubles; which is possibly 117 domestic rubles.[11] Or to put it another way allot to oil a shadow export price of 96.4 current domestic rubles (R125-145 per ton of conventional fuel) already in 1980 (Vainshtein et al.,p. 22). It remains, therefore, well worth Soviet while to produce oil for home consumption or for export through existing long-distance pipe-lines.

But will the immense cost of new pipe-lines put the issue in balance in 1985? Just how "immense" is this cost, to which honor is so frequently paid—but without quantification? I have no conceptual objection to the inclusion of pipe-lines. When we have estimated extraction costs we have not finished with the law of diminishing returns. If the new fields are further away than the old ones from the main centers of consumption or ports of export there will be extra transport costs due to the mere distance covered. But in addition if the climate is inhospitable the expense of laying pipe-lines increases greatly. Moreover the infrastructure serving the labor force will have to be bigger and it will cost more per unit to build.[12] All these factors weigh on the new Soviet oil-fields; but are they important and can we estimate them?

Ninety-five percent of crude oil moves by pipe. If refined products are also put into pipes in the next ten years that is technical progress within non-extractive industry. It may be expensive, but it is not part of our subject. Ushakov and Borisenko (1980, p. 117) tell us that the average cost of transportation was 0.94 kopeks per 10 ton-km in 1976. Let the new oil from the northern part of Western Siberia be the only marginal oil, as is evident from the regional breakdown in Shabad 1981, Table 1. Then it will have to travel about 2,000 km. The northerly 1000 km are by far the most expensive to build, so put the cost of transportation by them at 1.90 kopeks per 10 ton-km in 1980. Then 2,000 ton-km is R3, and this is marginal transportation cost. If our guess is anything like correct, this sum pales into insignificance when compared with future drilling costs. Also (inGicquiau's artivlr), it is smaller than in previous Five Year Plan, judging by the total expenditure volumes.[13]

Not allowing for transport, we have direct, but not very good, evidence from a Soviet source that lrmc remains quite low. Vainshtein *et al.* (1978 pp. 22-3), clearly lobbying for Western Siberia, present a model with two absolutely different shadow prices for oil users in 1975: R17.9-20.0 per ton c.i.f. Centre, North East and the Ukraine, R71.4-96.2 per ton f.o.b. frontier for export. Compare this with the world price of R117 (domestic) above. They do not justify this distinction, but say that their domestic price is minimal! Their export price is probably somewhat inflated by being loaded with the extra profitability of the imports that foreign exchange is spent on.

But these matters are less important for us here than the rate of growth they foresee for their domestic shadow prices:

"In 1980 and the following decade the increase in the shadow prices (*zamykayushchie otsenk*), strictly cut-off valuations) of oil and natural gas in the main regions of consumption is prognosticated at 15-20% per standard ton, and at the end of the period they will still be growing. The growth of the shadow prices of oil and gas is predicated on the fact that the effectiveness of these resources for other branches of the national economy is now more clearly understood.[14] There is also some (*neskol'ko*) growth in the cost of production because exploitation will spread to deposits with less favorable territorial location, geological and climatic conditions. The share of the northern parts of Western Siberia in the mining of oil and gas will grow, accounting for almost all the increase. Pipe-lines will become longer. Technical progress in the mining and transportation of gas during the current five-year plan and the middle-range future, constrain but do not remove these factors."

This is not even the language of 10% annual increases in lrmc, but we must allow for the authors' "lobbying" bias.

We can now at least answer the first question we set ourselves on at the beginning: has the USSR actually benefited from Yom Kippur 1973? We scale down domestic consumption to a constant 100, so as to isolate the pure effects of the price and cost revolution. The small quantities exported are valued at lrmc, the rest of production at the assumed average cost of the infra-marginal output. The whole treatment is exceedingly schematic (prices in domestic rubles of 1972):

	1972	1980
consumed, tons	100	100
imported, tons[b]	0	0
import price	—	—
produced for home use, tons	100	100
lrac excl. pipe-lines	5[a]	10[a]
exported, tons[b]	17	17
lrmc excl. pipe-lines	7	14

	1972		1980
export price	13	CMEA	51.1[c]
		other	71.5[c]
cost of imports and production			
for home use	500		1000
profit on exports	102		804
net total cost of oil	398		196

[a]These averages are not to be found in our previous workings. They are guesses, and they include the cost of exploratory wells sunk in the past.

[b]In the proportions to home consumption that actually obtain; with one half of exports going to CMEA.

[c]The CMEA price is the "world" price minus 40% as in 1979 (CEPII 1980).

It can be seen that Yom Kippur did not leave the USSR wailing. But one of our most schematic assumptions was that in the Soviet mind the high Irmc is "loaded" on to exports alone. According to strict rational marginalism the least important output should be so loaded, and some exports are more important to the Kremlin than some home uses. I do not doubt however that this is a small category. Allowing for it would make no different to the "net total cost" line.

So the USSR was a very low-cost producer, and remains a low-cost one. And now how does the CIA's pessimism look? This pessimism is based on engineering considerations: on difficulties that arose because equipment was lacking. My relative optimism[15] is based on longer-run considerations.

With a short enough time-horizon the marginal cost of everything is infinite, because technical bottlenecks are insuperable. I suggest that the CIA are quite nearly right over a very brief period, but that in five years the economic prognosis will win out, even though Irmc including pipe-lines will probably rather exceed price. However, while more favorable than the "engineering" prognosis mine is far from brilliant. Provided that Soviet decisions on new oil are made "rationally" and no new lucky field is struck, there will not be much more of it. A far more probable alternative is, of course, that they will not be made rationally. Lrmc will not be calculated properly, since nowhere outside these pages is the cost of exploratory drilling properly allocated, and even if it were Marxism forbids serious attention to marginal concepts. In another extractive industry, agriculture, no marginalism has ever deterred Soviet planners from subsidising very expensive, extra-marginal state farms. There will, then, be over-production, and the Soviet economy will suffer from it a little; but there will be more oil, since marginal cost will be high but not prohibitive.

If the Russians had a rational depletion policy, would it make a difference in their behavior? It is genuinely helpful to spell out what such a policy would be in extremely abstract terms in order, first, to know exactly what "rational" is.[16] We assume that:
   i)   A depleted mineral stock is of course limited and does not deteriorate in the ground (e.g. a well once proved can be capped); but also and

above all it is already a "proved reserve", and there is nothing unknown and nothing unowned in the whole world.

ii) Demand may rise or fall with income, but its future course is known. This means inter alia that technical progress in other fields is known.

iii) There is a fixed rate (r) at which the future is discounted by the planner or the market.

iv) There is no technical progress in the production of the given mineral, and marginal cost does not vary with the quantity extracted.

Our job is now to allocate extraction over the years "rationally". First, a world near-monopolist of the mineral will maximise his profits when he has fixed the prices each year to his satisfaction. In order to do this he must manipulate annual extraction against the known demand of (ii). So:

v) Let the elasticity of demand also be known.

vi) Then in a total time horizon of two years the monopolist maximises

$$(p_1 - c)q_1 + \frac{(p_2 - c)q_2}{1 + r}$$

where p is price, q quantity, c marginal cost, and $q_1 + q_2$ is the total depletable stock. He achieves maximum profit when he cannot "rationally" postpone or advance extraction by one tonne:

vii) $\Delta q (p_1 - c) = \Delta \frac{q(p_2 - c)}{1 + r}$; or, generalising:

viii) $$p_1 = \frac{p_2}{1 + r} = \frac{p_3}{(1 + r)^2}$$

A small competitor, administering his stock quietly under the shadow of the monopolist, will, under condition (vi):

ix) Extract everything in the particular year that the monopolists's prices make best for him. But if he also faces diminishing returns, c will grow over time as the remnants of his stock become more difficult to extract, and he manipulates output until:

x) $$(p_1 - c_1) = \frac{(p_2 - c_2)}{1 + r}$$. Note that:

xi) $p_1 = c_1$ is not a necessary condition: rather is it a limiting condition to a range where $p_1 > c_1$. This is because of the necessary intrusion of the future (the right-hand side of x) into considerations of current production. It is the fundamental peculiarity of the economics of extractive industries, that one cannot simply hire more current inputs at will, even if at an enhanced price and with lower productivity. The basic current input is ex hypothesi irreproducible, so that it cannot be hired in extra quantities and its use constitutes disinvestment.

xii) An excess of price over marginal cost is thus compatible with equilibrium, indeed if condition (i) holds in its full rigor it is necessary for rationality. Equilibrium is when marginal profits are equal over time (discounted).[17] If we allow technical progress within the industry (see iv) we postpone extraction and strengthen this essential point. But if prospecting is currently very successful we weaken it, indeed negate it.

We have now all we need for the analysis of Soviet oil policy in an OPEC-dominated world. But the reader may wish to know what would happen if, retaining (i-vi), we abolished the monopoly and handed over the wells or mines to many competitors. The short answer is that some producers would take a short-run view and raise the extraction rate; and that this would depress current prices and induce other competitors to take the view that $p_1 < \frac{p_2}{1 + r}$. So these would depress their extraction rate, and the course of events would not be very different from what the monopolist had determined. The vast success of the OPEC monopoly is due to the false-hood of condition (i): had it been true, prices would already in 1973 have been higher than what the cartel has made them. The OPEC monopoly is a medium-term affair which other discoveries and of course technical progress will moderate. Its price is limited precisely by the continued action of both forms of competition.

It may well be, however, that in a few years time the "natural" price of oil will have caught up with the OPEC price. In that case, what OPEC will have done is preserve until the end of the consumption of oil by humanity its own low-cost oil, and place the burden of high costs on this generation. Thus oil will have been produced now at high cost and comparatively low price by non-Arabs, and in the future by Arabs, at low cost and comparatively high price.

What does this analysis tell us about the Soviet case? First, the USSR should abide by the principle of item (xii), and *not* produce up to where marginal cost = price. This would be marked reversal of current policies in all fields of extractive industry and indeed elsewhere: the Marxist refusal to distinguish average from marginal cost leads to the cross-subsidisation of very expensive marginal fields. But it is, if our figures are correct, what is actually happening! And it is not absolutely without precedent: Stalin exported no oil, though its marginal cost was then very low. Rather, like a Sheikh before his time, he hoarded it in the ground against an oilless day. No doubt in so doing he used no rate of futurity discount and gave no thought to the intertemporal equalization of the marginal rate of profit; and no doubt he overdid it. But in effect Stalin followed the principle in (xii). Nevertheless at this stage in our knowledge of the subject all plausible values for r and perhaps too the marginal rate of profit are within our margin of error.

These workings for the lrmc of oil have now been exposed at two conferences and survived.[18] I am therefore emboldened almost to believe them, and to recommend not only that they be elaborated and refined, but also that similar work be done on gas and coal. As to gas, investment has recently been switched out of oil into gas (as came out in the discussion on Stern's paper), so in the new climate of comparatively rational economic thinking it is reasonable to suppose that Irmc in equivalent tons is somewhat lower in gas.

This is a less persuasive argument in the case of coal, a traditional industry with a habit of internal cross-subsidisation and a much less mobile labor-force. It is easily possible that there exist mines with very high Irmc indeed,[19] and that they will be tolerated as they always have been. But there is an additional element to be expected in Irmc from now on: the abandonment of Saturday working. Not much of the Polish events, surely, will influence the conduct of economic affairs in other Communist countries, and it would be hard to name a nationality, unless it be Lithuania, that is likely to be inspired to imitate the events themselves. But the abandonment of Saturday working in mines is a specially protected, non-renegotiable element, likely to survive even a Soviet invasion. And the effect of this on other Communist miners may well be great: the contagion of occupations is quite as likely as the contagion of nationalities.

The formal working-time loss could rise, of course, to 16%, but the production loss would be less, since absenteeism would fall and productivity rise. The improved labor conditions would surely not attract more people, but simply contribute to staunching the outflow. the Irmc of a whole new mine would be raised by the requirements of more capital and a longer length of life.

In conclusion I remark that altogether too little has been said about labor conditions in the fuel industries at this conference. Oil workers making a fast ruble on the permafrost, in necessarily temporary accommodation and far from their wives and homes, are mobile. They require indeed high wages, frequent leaves and a good bar; but they will go where they are told. Coal miners, except say in Vorkuta, live in narrow and settled communities. So it is customary in all societies to pay them to go on doing at a loss what they once did at a great profit.

Notes

1. c f. footnotes 2, 4, 11.
2. Costs were about 20 cents a barrel in 1966 (Adelman 1972 p. 76). It is difficult to imagine that they have been doubled in real terms by 1980. I am guessing 80 cents at 1980 prices.
3. Provided that the rate of futurity discount is negative and that technical progress will affect exploitation costs on good and bad fields in about equal proportions.
4. In the USA offshore drilling is six times as dear as onshore (Abs. 1978 p. 766). In the North Sea itself the British Government allowed companies $8-10 a barrel after taxes and royalties in 1980. Pure operating costs and depreciation were $1.50-3.75, and as usual the amortisation of exploratory wells is a problem. Let us assume that $1 was "abnormal" profit. Then "cost was $7-9, and may be equated in this case with Irmc. (Business sources).
5. Plausible as this is, it is not borne out by an equivalent U.S. series: Larue 1979, pp. 210-1.

6. Campbell, correspondence in 1980; cf. Campbell 1967 p. 139. The actual numbers were set by myself. The figure of sixteen was confirmed by Scalan (conversation at the conference). Western practice is to hurry things less and to get more out in total. Of course individual wells differ very greatly.

7. Amortisation as a whole was 36.3% of the Soviet cost concept in 1973 (N.Kh. 1973 p. 249). The portion of this that applies to things other than development wells is only known for gas and oil taken together: $\frac{20.5}{27.5}$ in 1968 (Umanski 1976 p. 18). The figure in the text is rounded upwards from 27% to 30% on the grounds that Soviet amortisation rates are always too low.

8. This is (100%-30%) of R4.4 per ton as in Table II; i.e. we take out exploitative drilling.

9. In 1973 cost including the amortisation of development wells increased by 2.6%, in 1974 by 3.4%, in 1975 by 3.0% (N.Kh. 1975 p. 229). Moreover, in these years development drilling did not increase as a percentage of costs (N.Kh. annually until 1975 incl.). So I treat these increases as representing also "other costs", and extrapolate them at 3.5% p.a.

10. Guessed.

11. Vladimir Treml (1980 p. 187) arrives at 0.9 domestic to 1.0 foreign-trade in 1976. These numbers yield $6.5 per bbl in 1980.

12. The direct wages and the infrastructure serving the pumps and drills are already in our accountancy. The wages are scattered all over Table V, and the productive infrastructure in the figures 3.1, 4.0, 4.9. The cost of transporting people and things to the well-head is also already included.

13. See Gicquiau's article in this volume. M. Gicquiau has been very helpful to me in this calculation.

14. This phrase is very obscure. I believe it to mean: "We have set a minimum domestic consumption price as high as we dare, but bureaucratic opinion will gradually thaw, and the price will edge upwards."

15. If "optimism" is the right word! It may be of interest to know that I began this contribution in the confidence that economics would confirm the CIA (1977), and have been forced by deeper research into a partial volte-face.

16. cf. Richardson 1975 ch. 3.

17. Such profits are a Ricardian "absolute rent". Once again its all in Marshall! Cf. Marshall 1946 p. 438: "A Royalty is not a rent, though often so called. For, except when mines, quarries, etc., are practically inexhaustible, the excess of their income over their direct outgoings has to be regarded, in part at least, as the price got by the sale of stored-up goods — stored up by nature indeed, but now treated as private property; and therefore the marginal supply price of minerals includes a royalty in addition to the marginal expenses of working the mine."

18. Not without the correction of a substantial error by the author after the conference.

19. The short-run marginal cost, of exploiting the last seams of an old mine, will be still higher.

REFERENCES

Aldeman, Morris A.	*The World Petroleum Market*, Baltimore 1972.
Campbell, Robert W.	*The Economics of Soviet Oil and Gas*, Baltimore, 1968.
	Trends in the Soviet Oil and Gas Industry, Baltimore 1976.
CEPII (Paris)	"Les Prolongements de la "Crise de l'Energie" vers les Pays de l'Est," November 1980.
CIA	Prospects for Soviet Oil Production, ER-77-10270, April 1977.

CIA

Prospects for Soviet Oil Production, a Supplemental Analysis, ER-10425, July 1977.

Filanovski

in *Planovoye Khozyaistvo* 3/1980

Lalyants,

in *Sotsialisticheskaya Industriya*, 21 May 1980.

Marshall, Alfred

Principles of Economics, eighth ed., London 1920/1946

Shabad, Theodore

in *Soviet Geography*, April 1981

Richardson, Harry W.,

Economic Aspects of the Energy Crisis, Lexington Mass., 1975.

Treml, Vladimir

in Egon Neuberger and Laura Tyson eds., *The Impact of International Economic Disturbances on the Soviet Union and Eastern Europe*, Pergamon 1980.

Umanski, Lev M.,

Rezervy povyshenia rentabl'nosti v neftedobyvayushchei promyshlenmosti, Moscow 1970

Vainshtein, B., Khaitun, A. and Sokolov, N.,

in *Voprosy Ekonomiki* 10/1978.

Ushakov, S.S. and Borisenko, T.M.,

Ekonomika transporta topliva i energii, Moscow 1980.

Les Transports d'énergie dans le Caem. Problèmes et perspectives.

Hervé Gicquiau

Plus que jamais, les stratégies soviétique et est-européennes de l'énergie vont être confrontées, dans la décennie 1980-1990, à la capacité de fonctionnement et d'évolution des systèmes de transport. L'accroissement prévu des productions énergetiques et par voie de conséquence de leur trafic, l'apparition de nouveaux flux et l'accent mis sur l'exportation vont nécessiter des structures, infrastructures, techniques et méthodes nouvelles que les pays européens du CAEM et principalement les plus vivement concernés, l'URSS et la Pologne, ne semblent pas a priori en mesure de mettre en place ou en application avec plus de bonheur qu'ils ne l'ont fait jusqu'à présent.

I — Le Transport des combustibles solides et liquides par rail et voies fluviales

Le développement encore relativement faible du transport fluvial dans les pays d'Europe orientale et l'inégalité du trafic par voies d'eau selon les régions soviétiques, n'ont pas permis jusqu'à présent de combiner harmonieusement ce mode de transport bon marché avec la voie ferrée. Cette double circonstance, a pour conséquence de laisser à cette dernière l'essentiel du fardeau que représente le transport des combustibles solides auxquels s'ajoutent des tonnages élevés de pétrole brut et surtout de produits pétroliers que le réseau, insuffisamment ramifie d'oléoducs, s'avère incapable d'absorber.

1. Le transport par voies d'eau demeure un système d'appoint.

L'exploitation insuffisante des potentialités du réseau fluvial de l'Europe centrale est un défi au bon sens, surtout si l'on sait que la Pologne et la RDA notamment, qui ont le réseau navigable le plus dense et dans les cas de la Pologne, de gros debits de combustibles à assurer, ont recours au transport fluvial de façon presque marginale.

En 1978 il assure en Pologne 0,6% du trafic total (maritime compris) et 1% du transport de la production de charbon[1] et, surtout, représente à peine 2% du trafic ferroviaire ; pou la RDA on a respectivement 1,5% et 2%[2]. La Tchécoslovaquie, dont le trafic par voies fluviales représente environ 5% du trafic ferroviaire n'a réalisé en 1979 que 4,1% de son trafic de combustibles solides par celles-ci (3,5 millions de tonnes contre 85 millions de tonnes)[3], malgré un tonnage supplémentaire de 750 000 tonnes en un an.

L'affaiblissement de la part du trafic fluvial est régulier depuis 1960 dans toute l'Europe centrale et en valeur absolue le trafic n'augmente depuis 1970 que de 20 à 30% selon les pays. Il n'est pas nécessaire de repérer dans ces données ce qui revient en propre aux combustibles solides et aux produits pétroliers pour se convaincre du faible intérêt accordé au transport fluvial et du soutien insignifiant qu'il apporte au chemin de fer dans le transport lourd. Il est vrai que l'état des fleuves d'Europe centrale permet rarement le passage de barges de plus de 750 tonnes, car la profondeur nécessaire de 2,5 mètres n'est pas assurée sur toute la longueur des voies principales. Des travaux importants sont en cours ou en projet: construction et modernisation d'écluses, de bassins d'eau, modernisation des voies et des ports afin de permettre une augmentation des charges et la navigation de jour et de nuit en toutes saisons. Un plan a long terme (1990) prévoit l'aménagement par la Pologne, de la Vistule (avec le futur port charbonnier de Tychy d'une capacité de 18 millions de tonnes en 1990), de l'Oder, et sourtout d'un canal entre Vistule et Oder (pour le passage de 50 millions de tonnes de charbon par an)[4]. Mais les principaux de ces travaux ont été considérablement ralentis depuis ces dernières années faute d'investissements suffisants (diminution de près de la moitié en 1979 par rapport à 1978).

Des travaux entrepris sur l'Elbe en territoire tchécoslovaque permettent déjà l'approvisionnement en charbon de centrales électriques (Chvaletice et Opatovice) par barges de 1 250 tonnes (8 millions de tonnes par an prevues)[5]. D'autres projets nationaux et interrégionaux seront réalisés dans la décennie. Si toutefois on ne doit pas attendre un changement notable de la part des voies d'eau dans le trafic général, ie est plausible que certaines de ces réalisations si elles sont menées à bien, pourront alléger quelque peu la contrainte du transport combustibles solides et liquides qui pèse sur la voie ferrée.

Le reséau fluvial de l'URSS quoique plus difficile à exploiter (durée limitée de navigation) assure une part plus importante du trafic — marchandises total (227 milliards de T./km en 1980 et 250,2 milliards de T./km prévues en 1981[6]), environ 4%. Cependant à l'examen il apparaît que pour les deux tiers du tonnage le transport fluvial soviétique est consacré à l'acheminement de matériaux de construction (avec 30% tonnage supplémentaire en 4 ans): en effet ces materiaux requierent moins de dépenses matérielles, financières et de travail que le charbon par exemple, et favorisent ainsi l'élévation des indicateurs des organismes de transport fluvial[7]. Par contre les produits énergétiques ne représentent que moins de 20% du fret des matériaux de construction et de plus, leur tonnage transporté, qui avait augmenté entre 1970 et 1979 de 18% pour le pétrole et produits pétroliers et 40% pour le charbon et coke, est demeuré stable depuis 1975. Même en Ukraine où le réseau se prêterait facilement aux expéditions charbonnières du Donbass, en 1978 les voies d'eau ont recu un tonnage de 5,4 millions de tonnes de charbon et coke soit 11% seulement du tonnage total[8]. D'autre part le transport par voies d'eau, de pétrole et produits pétroliers (39,2 millions de tonnes) et du charbon et coke (24,7 millions de tonnes)[9] représente respectivement moins de 10% et 3,4% du tonnage supporté par le chemin de fer. La tendance à la stagnation depuis plusieurs annees ne semble pas pouvoir au cours de la décennie 1981-1990 subir des modifications profondes; au mieux l'accroissement du tonnage sera-t-il parallele a celui de la production de ces mêmes produits.

On ne peut trop tenir compte d'engagements comme ceux exprimés pour 1981[10] selon lesquels, cette annee il est prévu une forte augmentation du tonnage de charbon transporté par voies d'eau (qui serait supérieure donc à l'accroissement prévu de 5,9% du tonnage et 10,9% du trafic de toutes les marchandises?)

Quelques éléments positifs pourraient donner du crédit à une évolution semblable sur plusieurs années:

- prolongement de la durée de navigation (expérience en cours avec brise-glace sur la Volga et le Dnepr;
- aménagements de voies: par exemple sur le Dnepr au passage du Dneproges, pourra doubler dans quelques années le trafic du charbon;
- on prévoit de réaliser quelques aménagements portuaires importants, par exemple la creation sur la Kama (à Kambarka) d'un complexe de transbordement du charbon sibérien du rail à la voie d'eau;
- augmentation de la capacité de charge des péniches pétrolières (jusqu'à 9 000 tonnes) des vracquiers (4 500 tonnes) et emploi de remorqueurs-pousseurs de 450 à 2 000 CV[11];
- la création en 1978 de commissions d'oblast' pour la coordination de l'activité des divers types de transport . . .

Cependant les obstacles actuels ne pourront être surmontés en URSS sans une politique plus rigoureuse pour l'ensemble du transport fluvial:

- d'abord soumettre ce transport à la tutelle d'un organe unique;
- développer les transports mixtes rail-voies d'eau (augmentation obtenue de 30% seulement en 10 ans pour les marchandises en vrac);
- adapter les voies d'eau à l'absorption des flux de pétrole et produits pétroliers de l'Oural, des régions de la Volga, du Nord-Caucase, du Kazakhstan vers les entreprises du centre, de la Volga et du Nord-Ouest, et les flux de charbons du Kuznets et de Karaganda vers les centrales thermiques de Russie centrale, Nord-Ouest et Ukraine;
- améliorer l'exploitation des matériels de transport et développer leur construction (surtout pour les convois fluviaux);

- développer l'infrastructure et les équipements portuaires: l'insuffisance ou même l'absence de quais dans les centrales électriques et les entreprises utilisatrices est un frein actuellement particulièrement important.
- Enfin, oeuvre de longue haleine, développer et maintenir en exploitation le réseau navigable et principalement dans les régions orientales[12].

2. La voie ferrée assujettie aux combustibles solides et liquides.

L'importance, en URSS, des chemins de fer dans le transport de combustibles tient en quelques chiffres: le charbon est évacué et distribué à plus de 90% par rail et représente environ 18% du trafic ferroviaire (et 20% du volume ainsi transporté[13]. Quant au pétrole et produits pétroliers dont le rail supporte un tonnage équivalent à 67% de celui qui incombe aux oleoducs, ils constituent actuellement quelque 13% du trafic ferroviaire (et 11% du tonnage de marchandises); ainsi ces deux types de produits énergétiques constituent au total près du tiers du trafic enregistré par la voie ferrée. C'est dire s'ils sont pour celle-ci un poste essentiel dont l'évolution commande en grande partie le comportement; en revanche l'acheminement satisfaisant des produits énergétiques solides et liquides est étroitement dépendant de la voie ferrée, dont les éventuelles difficultés conjoncturelles ou structurelles peuvent avoir des conséquences très sérieuses pour l'économie du pays.

On peut en dire autant du charbon et des chemins de fer de Pologne puisque dans ce pays le rail (voies ferrées de norme standard) reçoit 87% de la production houillère, ce qui constitue 38% du volume de marchandises transportées par chemin de fer[14]. En RDA la charge es encore assez importante[15] pour qu'un accroissement continu de la production et des importations de ces produits influe sur le fonctionnement des chemins de fer.

Pour la décennie 1980-1990 l'accroissement de la production et des livraisons des produits énérgetiques dans la zone devrait conduire à une progression du trafic de ces produits (malgré le développement du transport par tubes) qui se manifestera essentiellement sur la voie ferrée.

La Pologne prévoyait (mais avant les événements que l'on sait) d'accroître en dix ans (1980-1990) le trafic ferroviaire de charbon de 24,8% (17% de 1980 à 1985) et de pétrole et produits pétroliers de 39% (tout en réduisant quelque peu la part de ces produits dans la structure des marchandises)[16]. La Roumanie, qui en 1979 eut à traiter 32,7 millions de tonnes de charbon et lignite, prévoit dans son programme énérgetique à long terme pour les mêmes postes 85 millions de tonnes en 1985, ce qui imposerait une croissance moyenne annuelle du trafic ferroviaire sans doute superieure a celle de 5,5% observee de 1971 a 1978 (4,4% 1976-78)[17] meme si l'on doit tenir compte du fait que ces combustibles ne forment que 9% environ du volume transporté par rail[17].

Les objectifs charbonniers du plan quinquennal soviétique 1981-1985 ont de quoi inquiéter les responsables du transport ferroviaire puisque pour une extraction de charbons et lignites de 770-800 millions de tonnes, le trafic de ces produits pourrait à notre avis connaitre une croissance de l'ordre de 23% par rapport à 1979 (derniere annee connue du trafic charbonnier) (le plan quinquennal prévoit 14-15% pour l'ensemble des marchandises donc 17,5-18,5 entre 1979 et 1985). Et effet, alors qu'entre 1975 et 1979 la production a augmenté de 2,4% le trafic s'est accru de 18% du fait de l'allongement moyen des trajets (développement de l'exploitation des gisements de la partie asiatique de l'URSS)[18].

Le supplément de la production (sur l'hypothèse basse de 770 millions de tonnes, soit par rapport à 1979, 52 millions de tonnes en plus) qui proviendra en grande partie de Sibérie-Kazakhstan pourrait, semble-t-il, engendrer à lui seul en 1985 un trafic de 130 milliards de T./km environ, soit un total de l'ordre de 720 milliards d T./km. Cependant le trafic pourrait être moindre si les charbons et lignites sont utilisés abondamment dans les nouvelles centrales des bassins d'Ekibastuz et Kansk-Achinsk dont la création a justement pour but d'éviter un tel trafic On se gardera d'une quelconque estimation pour la période 1985-1990 car bien des hypothèques pèsent déjà sur les possibilités d'extraction en 1985 de 770 millions de tonnes de combustibles; on ne doit pas oublier que le plan quinquennal 1976-1980 prévoyait (loi d'octobre 1976) une production de 805 millions de tonnes de charbons en 1980 (au lieu de 716 obtenues).

Cette constatation pourrait, à tort peut-on penser, rassurer les cheminots soviétiques, puisque c'est à cet insuccès des mineurs qu'ils ont dû de répondre tant bien que mal à la demande de transport de combustibles solides, et plutôt mal que bien si l'on se réfère aux nombreuses critiques de toute origine.

La situation du transport ferroviaire des combustibles liquides en URSS pourrait être moins tendue. Le trafic n'a augmenté que d'un quart de 1970 a 1979 (encore doit-on préciser que la présentation des statistiques soviétiques ne permet pas de faire la différence entre pétrole brut, produits raffinés combustibles et produits raffines pour la chimie). Comme le volume transporté a augmenté pour cette période de 34,6% (et la production de près de 70%) on peut penser que la moindre croissance du trafic s'explique par une réduction, certaine, du transport du brut et par conséquent l'accroissement du volume transporté provient de l'augmentation normale des chargements à la raffinerie mais sur des itinéraires relativement stables (flux et longueur). C'est pour ces raisons que l'on peut envisager pour la décennie une croissance du trafic par rail de ces produits plus faible, le taux dépendant largement du rythme de création des conduites actuellement mal développées, de produits raffinés.

3. Des difficultés matérielles persistantes malgré une diversification des remèdes possibles.

L'augmentation du trafic n'est pas une fin en soi ni un sujet de satisfaction. Elle devient une lourde sujétion si le trafic augmente à un rythme plus rapide que celui de la croissance économique puisque les dépenses de transport s'avèrent ainsi excessives. C'est pourquoi les autorités soviétiques souhaitant une croissance plus modérée du trafic ferroviaire, avaient prévu pour celui-ci une augmentation de 7,7% en 1976-1980 (30% en 1971-1975). La croissance modérée de l'économie, inférieure aux prévisions, est certes responsable de ce résultat mais elle ne saurait masquer une réelle insatisfaction de la demande de transport par rail pour les combustibles solides et liquides. Ce sont les causes de cette insatisfaction que nous nous proposons de répertorier ainsi que les moyens d'y remédier. Précisons qu'on ne retiendra que les problèmes et solutions spécifiques des produits qui nous intéressent ici.

3.1 L'encombrement des réseaux et les mesures envisagées ou préconisées pour y remédier.

C'est une situation générale en URSS et dans plusieurs secteurs de l'Europe orientale mais les lignes indiquées comme les plus encombrées sont justement celles sur lesquelles pèsent l'évacuation des charbons siberiens et silésiens, des lignites du bassin de Bohême du Nord et l'expédition des produits pétroliers à partir des grands centres de raffinage (région de la Volga, Bakou, Omsk)[19]. Or les itinéraires charbonniers auront néanmoins à supporter d'ici 1990 un accroissement de charge qui sera par exemple de plus de 100% pour les lignes Sibérie - Oural.

Le transport des combustibles sur la voie d'eau est comme on l'a vu, la principale mesure adoptée par la Tchécoslovaquie; mais les grands projets polonais du même ordre seront probablement reportés; l'investissement polonais pourrait être engagé préférentiellement dans la modernisation prévue des lignes ferroviaes au départ de la Silésie (dont la ligne ''charbon'' jusqu'a Gdynia), au détriment de la ligne ''soufre-acier (frontièr de l'URSS-Katowice), dans la construction de laquelle le gouvernement Gierek avait engagé son prestige, et qui devait dans le sens Katowice-URSS fournir des combustibles aux régions traversées ainsi qu'à l'URSS.

En URSS il est possible que des lignes nouvelles (sur les 3 600 km prévus par le XI-e plan) soient réalisées en priorité dans le secteur le plus critique, Sibérie occidentale—Oural-sud, pour décharger partiellement le Transsibérien, ainsi qu'une ligne vers Kuybyshev[20], et des bretelles vers les centrales thermiques. On préconise aussi la construction d'une ligne Kuzbass—région de la Volga (Belovo-Kuybyshev, 3 000 km)[21] spécialisée dans le transport de combustibles solides. Quant au BAM, au fur et à mesure de l'avancement de sa construction, laquelle s'étendra vraisemblablement jusqu'aux dernières années de la décennie, il dechargera certains tronçons du Transsibérien du fret pétrolier vers les régions extrême-orientales, en prenant en charge, en relais avec des oléoducs, 25 millions de tonnes/an de pétrole brut de Sibérie occidentale dont 20 seraient destinées au Japon; il sera par ailleurs l'artère principale d'évacuation des charbons du bassin de Yakoutie du sud essentiellement vers les ports du Pacifique[22]. Mais ce sont là des oeuvres de longue haleine qui, quoi qu'il en soit, ne pourront avoir d'effect global avant 1990.

D'autre part des spécialistes soviétiques estiment prioritaire pour désengorger les voies, de développer (quadrupler) les voies de service, dont la construction à pris du retard, les allonger comme en Occident a 1 700-2 500 mètres, ce qui réduirait leur encombrement critique (14,5 wagons par km; + 35% en 9 ans) qui déborde quasiment sur la voie principale, et de plus réaménager les gares de triage pour recevoir les convois lourds[23]. Avec d'autres aménagements de la voie ferrée tels que l'emploi systématique de rails lourds sur les grands itinéraires, l'installation accrue des systèmes automatiques de régulation et bien sûr, les progrès dans l'électrification, on a là un catalogue de mesures concernant l'infrastructure qui pourraient temporairement compenser en URSS les insuffisances du reseau. Comme on le verra plus loin c'est affaire de choix de l'investissement.

On ne peut passer sous silence les possibilités futures du transport de charbon par tubes[24] même si cette technologie séduisante n'est pas maitrisee en URSS à l'échelle industrielle (y compris les problèmes annexes de déshydratation de la pulpe de charbon et rejet des eaux usées). Deux petites conduites de 10 km sont utilisées avec plus ou moins de bonheur dans le Kuzbass; un carboduc de 250 km doit être prêt vers 1984 pour l'évacuation de 4,3 millions de tonnes de charbon par an. On pourrait dans l'avenir faire l'économie de voies ferrées nouvelles sur les flux charbonniers sibériens. L'intérêt économique est théoriquement assuré (selon les études comparatives d'investissements et coûts d'exploitation entre voie ferrée et carboduc) il reste à résoudre les problèmes techniques.

3.2 L'améloiration de l'organisation du transport ferroviaire.

Il devient impératif de décharger la voie ferrée des transferts superflu de produits énérgetiques et donc d'éliminer les transports irrationnels. Une commission auprès du Gosplan a pour but de rationaliser les expéditions de marchandises mais elle a peu de moyens de contrôle et de décision. Il existe aussi un document, commun au Gosplan, Gossnab, ministère des voies de communication, datant de 1969 et prévoyant de faire cesser certains transports, mais il semble avoir eu peu d'effets. Le Kuzbass continue à expédier vers la Russie d'Europe son charbon tandis que des produits de qualité assez semblable vont du Donbass vers Gor'ky, Yaroslavl', etc. ou encore du Kuzbass vers Arkhangel'sk et la Carélie, régions voisines du bassin de la Pechora. Il y a deux raisons à ce comportement[25]: la houille du Kuzbass est 2,5 fois meilleur marché; le tarif ferroviaire "très longues distances" a été supprimé, ce qui dans le cas de l'exemple Kuzbass-Pechora, rend le charbon sibérien, tout compte fait, plus rentable pour l'utilisateur. On tiendrait avec le rétar blissement de ce tarif un moyen de dissuasion efficace.

Par contre il sera difficile de réduire les transports répétés de charbon, liés à l'enrichissement de celui-ci: chaque année 110 millions de tonnes[26] sont expédiées par trains vers les fabriques de traitement. Il s'agit là de problèmes sectoriels dont les chemins de fer n'ont pas à connaitre.

Autre forme de transport irrationnel est celle de pétrole brut et produits pétroliers par rail; si pour le petrole le tonnage est modéré, par contre l'essence, le kérosène, la mazout sont envoyés vers les dépôts essentiellement par wagons-citernes. Des conduites devront être construites dans un proche avenir par exemple pour libérer les chemins de fer de la région de Kuybyshev et les voies ferrées de Sibérie, Kazakhstan, régions européennes du sud. Selon les avis autorisés[27] on ne pourra éviter de réduire le transport par rail de ces produits sur les distances très courtes; depuis 1975 ce volume s'est accru de 20%; ainsi jusqu'a 100 km on transporte plus de 30 millions de tonnes, 15 millions de tonnes à 50 km. Or le tube dans ces conditions et ces régions (Bakou, Gor'ky, Ufa, etc.) n'est pratiquement jamais utilise, alors qu'il est le seul remede approprie.

On ne s'etendra pas sur les difficultes relatives a la mauvaise gestion du materiel rouland (temps morts excessifs, vitesse de rotation du parc de wagons de marchandises semblable en 1980 a celle de 1979 malgre 11,2% d'acceleration prevue).[28]

3.3 Les problèmes industriels du matériel de transport ferroviaire.

Depuis quelques années la presse soviétique insiste largement sur les soucis causés aux transporteurs par le matériel roulant qu'ils doivent utiliser. On sait que la quantité et la qualité des wagons de tout type sont loin de répondre à la demande. C'est actuellement l'un des problèmes industriels les plus sérieux. L'usure rapide d'un materiel de mauvaise qualité employé intensivement et sans précautions n'est pas compensée par l'aménagement, trop lent, des entreprises productrices. On ne peut espérer un rétablissement de la situation (à défaut par l'importation) avant quelques années. De plus le transport lourd, qui est une des solutions les plus acceptables pour élever la capacité d'écoulement des grandes lignes, nécessite la mise en production de wagons ouverts (pour le charbon) et wagons-citernes á 8 essieux, à gabarit augmenté, avec capacité de charge de 125 tonnes (permettant un accroissement de 40% du poids de charbon transporté)[29]. Mais là encore des intérêts divergents entre ministère constructeur et transporteurs frienent cette évolution attendue.

Bien d'autres administrations industrielles devront également se mobiliser pour fournir correctement les secteurs "transport" des entreprises comme les organisations ferroviaires, en matériels de toute sorte (matériels de manutention, équipements de transport par bandes convoyeuses, etc.) dont les déficiences et le déficit ont des conséquences nullement mineures sur l'écoulement du trafic et l'excès du recours au rail.

D'ailleurs la modernisation (renouvellement et modèles plus performants) du matériel roulant est une préoccupation dans tous les autres pays du CAEM. La Pologne pour la seule année 1980 prévoyait de mettre en service 6 000 wagons à charbon et 1 630 citernes[30], la Hongrie développant largement son parc de wagons-citernes en 1976-1980. Les Tchèques quant à eux admettent que l'extension des capacités de transport des combustibles se développe moins vite que les besoins.

3.4 Les problèmes inhérents aux combustibles transportés

En URSS, il faut envisager l'accroissement à fonds perdus du volume des charbons transportés du fait:

• du maintien de la pratique de l'enrichissement de produits bruts dans les centrales électriques. L'enrichissement sur les lieux de l'extraction éviterait de transporter 20-25 millions de tonnes/an de roches stériles.

• de l'élévation du degré d'humidité et de la teneur en cendres[31] des combustibles. L'humidité excessive et la présence des stériles requièrent 200 000 unités-wagons supplémentaires par an[32].

Il faut aussi tenir compte des problèmes posés par le gel du charbon dans les wagons, ce qui, tant que des solutions efficaces ne seront pas généralisées, pour ameliorer le déchargement, continuera à ralentir la rotation des wagons. Et on ne peut négliger non plus les pertes de combustible dans les opérations de transport. Pour le charbon (pertes en cours de trajet et du fait de stockage prolongé) elles peuvent actuellement atteindre en URSS annuellement 7 à 8 millions de tonnes (% de la production soviétique) et en Pologne 0,5% du tonnage de fret. Solution proposée pour réduire les pertes en wagons: films plastiques et compactage; mais produits et équipements pour ce faire sont encore au stade de l'experimentation. On s'étonnera aussi de l'existence et de l'ampleur de pertes de produits pétroliers (essentiellement du fait des chemins de fer soviétiques): 2 millions de tonnes par an[33].

4. De la stagnation à la réduction de l'investissement.

On ne peut manquer d'établir une corrélation entre les difficultés qu'éprouvent les chemins de fer et la stagnation de la part qui leur est allouée dans l'investissement national. L'observation de la situation polonaise et soviétique est significative.

La Pologne, malgré une réduction en valeur absolue des investissements dans les transports entre 1975 et 1979 d'environ 9%[34], avait maintenu l'investissement ferroviaire au niveau précédent. Les révisions inévitables de la politique générale de l'investissement, toucheront, dit-on, les grands projets ferroviaires et fluviaux non absolument essentiels, mais l'impossibilité à moyen terme de tenir les objectifs de la production houillère pourrait éviter à la situation du transport de combustibles d'empirer.

Pour les autres pays d'Europe centrale l'information sur l'investissement par types de transport est trop fragmentaire et l'on s'en tiendra aux quelques aperçus de réalisations mentionnées dans les rubriques précédentes.

Les difficultés observées dans les chemins de fer soviétiques s'expliquent largement par la faiblesse de l'investissement[35]. Celui-ci demeure stable par rapport à l'investissement total (2,7%) mais se réduit régulièrement dans l'investissement affecté aux transports (moins du quart). Et ceci malgré une extension régulière du réseau et surtout malgré l'engagement depuis 1974 de la construction du BAM. Or le coût de construction du kilomètre de cette voie (longue de 3 145 km au total) est évalué à 3 millions de roubles[36] ce qui pourrait expliquer que le coût moyen de construction d'un kilomètre de voie ferrée en URSS soit passé de 357 000 roubles à la fin du IXème quinquennat à 555 000 roubles[37] au cours des années 1976-1978, et laisse à penser qu'il s'élèvera dans les prochaines années puisque les tronçons à venir du BAM, les plus difficiles et les plus coûteux, exigeront une dépense encore supérieure. Il est alors évident, ce qui est confirmé de source soviétique[37], que tout ceci s'est fait et se fera au détriment des dépenses de mise à 2 voies de ligues à voie unique et de la construction de voies de service, de l'électrification des lignes et de l'introduction de l'automatique. Sans une forte augmentation de l'allocation annuelle, du fait des coûts croissants (BAM mais aussi couts généraux de modernisation, équipements, etc. qui tous augmentent régulièrement), l'investissement disponible dans les prochaines années pour les opérations susceptibles d'éliminer les difficultés mentionnées sera encore proportionnellement plus faible qu'il ne l'a été depuis le milieu des années 70.

Il reste donc à imaginer que ces difficultés pourront s'affaiblir sans un effort financier particulier par la seule "exploitation des réserves", ce qui n'est pas totalement impossible vu leur nature; encore faudrait-il que les autorités aient les moyens d'incitation indispensable.

II — Le transport d'Energie électrique

Si l'on admet que les difficultés que connaissent l'exploitation houillère et le transport ferroviaire dans les pays du CAEM et principalement en URSS ont une influence directe sur l'utilisation des capacités électriques, et que d'autre part ces capacités demeurent insuffisantes à assurer la satisfaction de la demande en électricité, il apparait que le système de transport d'électricite peut tenir un rôle actif important pour, sinon débloquer une situation tendue dans le domaine de la production d'énergie électrique, du moins favoriser par les moyens qui lui sont propres une détente dans le secteur de la consommation.

Dans le cas du CAEM, du fait des possibilités offertes par l'étendue territoriale de la zone et les énormes ressources d'énergie primaire de l'URSS, les moyens d'action specifiques du systeme de transport d'electricite peuvent s'integrer pleinement dans la strategie energetique du bloc.

Ajoutons que le rôle du transport d'électricité dans le CAEM semble assez bien défini pour la nouvelle décennie puisque les principales options l'ont été elles-mêmes explicitement et implicitement ces dernières années et qu'elles ont déjà reçu un début d'application.

Les conditions climatiques des dernières années et principalement de l'hiver 1978-1979 ont mis en lumière les difficultés d'une fourniture régulière d'énergie électrique dans tous les pays du CAEM, d'ailleurs largement relatées dans leurs presses nationales[38]. Les coupures de courant sont devenues fréquentes, même en été, avec perturbations sérieuses, notamment de l'appareil productif. Certains pays d'Europe Centrale (Bulgarie, Roumanie et sans doute Pologne) ont dû prendre des mesures pour réduire la demande. Ces difficultés sont imputables en priorité à l'approvisionnement défectueux des centrales en combustibles, et à un accroissement de la production d'électricité plus fort que celui des capacités des centrales. Pour ce dernier point il s'agit d'une tendance ancienne mais qui ''contribue à diminuer les réserves dans les systèmes énergétiques à espacer les réparations de l'equipement et à utiliser plus fréquemment des groupes électriques peu productifs''[39] avec tous les risques accrus au fil des ans que cela implique. De plus les lignes de transport du courant et stations de transformation fonctionnent en surcharge d'autant plus que persiste (en URSS) une certaine disproportion entre la construction des lignes et celle des capacités de génération[40].

Les systèmes de transport d'electricité doivent être en mesure par leur organisation et leur développement technique de faire face aux difficultés temporaires des installations de production (incidents techniques, demande accrue des heures de point), de favoriser l'économie de capacités de production et la réduction des pertes d'énergie qu'ils transportent et distribuent.

1. L'interconnexion des réseaux: des perspectives intéressantes pour tous.

C'est le fondement de la stratégie de l'électricité du CAEM. L'interconnexion se développe à la fois à l'intérieur de l'URSS, dans les pays européens du CAEM et entre l'URSS et ces derniers. Elle doit permettre à terme, en vue d'un fonctionnement en parallèle, la liaison entre les systèmes énergétiques régionaux soviétiques et européens. Par voie de conséquence elle nécessite le développement des moyens de transport, c'est-à-dire des lignes électrifiées.

Déjà l'URSS a réalisé pour l'établissement de son Réseau Unifié[41] la majeure partie des interconnexions de ses systèmes régionaux puisque à la fin de 1980, neuf réseaux régionaux regroupent une capacité installée de 211 500 MW (au début de 1980) soit 82% de la capacité totale de l'URSS (et 88% de sa production)[42]. Ainsi à la fin de 1980 le Réseau Unifié couvrait un territoire d'environ 10 millions de km2 s'étendant sur 3 000 km du nord au sud et 7 000 mk d'est en ouest. Comme le rattachement des réseaux d'Asie Centrale et d'Extrême-Orient est prévu pour la fin de la décennie actuelle, tout le territoire soviétique, sauf l'oblast' de Magadan et la Kamtchatka sera couvert par un Réseau à direction unifiée et centralisée en mesure de gérer la production électrique au mieux de la demande avec une marge de manoeuvre (puissance et liaisons) dès á présent largement accrue par le rattachement du réseau sibérien et de ses centrales géantes.

Dupuis 1962 le développement progressif de l'interconnexion des réseaux des pays européens du CAEM (système MIR) a permis à ces pays de disposer théoriquement en 1980 d'une capacité de production de 150 000 MW.

La liaison des systèmes nationaux était réalisee jusqu'en 1978 par 21 lignes à haute tension (7 de 440 KV et 14 de 220 KV)[43] qui permettent des echanges mutuels d'électricité, URSS comprise de 25 Md. de KWh/an. Cependant "MIR" n'était rattaché au réseau soviétique que par l'intermédiaire d'une ligne du réseau d'Ukraine Occidentale. Une interconnexion plus poussée des réseaux nationaux d'Europe Centrale par l'achèvement ou le développement de lignes de 400 KV serait en cours. Elle devient nécessaire en particulier pour absorber et répartir les échanges accrus envisagés dès à présent à l'interiéur du CAEM, à la suite de nouvelles liaisons achevées ou prévues avec le réseau soviétique[44].

En effet depuis 1979 la première partie d'une ligne de 750 KV longue de 1 600 Km relie le Réseau Unifié d'URSS au système Mir, entre Vinnitsa (Ukraine) et Albertirsa (Hongrie). La Hongrie qui est le principal réalisateur et client de cette ligne (avec Tchécoslovaquie et RDA) aura prochainement de ce fait la possibilité de doubler ses importations d'électricité d'URSS (déjà 7,5 Md. de kWh en 1980 au lieu de 4,5 en 1978 soit 20% de sa consommation totale)[45]. Cette ligne permettra aux pays concernés d'économiser la production d'une centrale de 1 580 MW[46].

Deux autres lignes de transmission en 750 KV sont en projet et devraient être réalisées semble-t-il avant 1985; l'une (400 km) reliera la centrale nucléaire de Khmel'nitsky (Ukraine) à la sous-station de Rzeszow en Pologne), l'autre la centrale nucléaire de Konstantinovka (Ukraine) à Dobrudja (Bulgarie) via Macin (Roumaine). Le CAEM recevra la moitié de la production de ces deux centrales. Ainsi la première centrale fournira à la Pologne, la Hongrie et la Tchécoslovaquie 12 Md. kWh/an en 1990[47].

Nous n'oublierons pas de mentionner la création en cours, d'une ligne (220 KV) de transmission entre le réseau soviétique et le réseau (110 KV et 220 KV) de la Mongolie, qui permettra à ce pays de recevoir de la centrale thermique de Gusinoozersk (bassin houiller de Bruiatie) 500 millions de kWh/an[48].

Avant même d'observer les facteurs susceptibles d'influencer le développement du réseau CAEM ou du Réseau Unifié de l'URSS, on peut déjà fournir quelques éléments d'appréciation de la procédure d'interconnexion.

L'union des réseaux des divers pays s'est révélée jusqu'à présent positive même s'il apparaît des difficultés découlant de la spécificité des reseaux nationaux (le fonctionnement en parallèle appelle en particulier des dépenses supplémentaires pour les réseaux)[49], mais plus elle se développera plus elle deviendra économiquement intéressante. Les avantages de l'interconnexion peuvent se résumer ainsi:

- Possibilité d'augmenter la capacité unitaire des groupes et centrales à connecter (avec l'inconvénient néanmoins que le plus grand délai de de mise en route en cas de difficultés sur le réseau sera plus difficile-ment compensé par des turbines à gaz puisque l'URSS a un retard d'équipement de ces matériels).

* diminution de la capacité installée: du fait de la différenciation des maxima de charge, notamment si l'on peut tenir compte de fuseaux horaires très différents; de même sur un territoire étendu il est facile de s'adapter aux variations d'hydraulicité.

L'interconnexion permet au Réseau unifié soviétique de réduire actuellement ses besoins en puissance installée de 3-3,5% (5-6% en été) de la charge maximale, ce qui en 1979 fournit un gain de 12 millions de KW. Et selon des études soviétiques, la capacité de réserve obtenue après l'établissement définitif du REU sera diminuée de 35 millions de KW, ce qui représente un nombre impressionnant de centrales à ne pas construire[50].

Cette circonstance est d'autant plus favorable que la création des très grandes centrales et l'augmentation du volume de travaux de modernisation d'équipements usés imposent par souci de sécurité d'élever la capacité maximale de resérve du REU à 15-17%, au lieu de 13% actuellement[51]. Sans l'union des réseaux la capacité installée bloquée serait donc encore proportionnellement plus élevée.

* mise à disposition de puissances considérables si les lignes de transmission s'y prêtent: hydroélectricité sibérienne, centrales thermiques sur les combustibles abondants de Sibérie et Kazakhstan, à des coûts moindres.

* l'avantage ultime de l'interconnexion des réseaux demeure la garantie d'assistance en cas d'incidents et une sécurité d'approvisionnement dont ont justement grand besoin les pays socialistes d'Europe Centrale.

2. Lignes de transmission nouvelles, projets grandioses et leurs motivations

La réalisation de reseaux interconnectés (CAEM et REU) ne peut être effectuée sans une augmentation des capacités de transport à l'intérieur et entre les reséaux, donc sans l'adaptation des lignes électriques à ces capacités. Comme ces réseaux reçoivent la production de nouvelles centrales à capacité unitaire en accroissement constant et comme ces centrales ne sont pas implantées en général près des centres de consommation, il est prévisible[52] que la longueur des lignes de transport de la production des grandes centrales atteindra au cours des prochaines années, 100 à 300 km dans la partie européenne de l'URSS, et dans certains cas, 500 km; dans la partie asiatique les distances seront de 200 à 500 km.

Pour que les lignes électriques puissent absorber cette puissance accrue et avec des pertes de courant acceptables, le passage à des tensions supérieures s'impose. C'est pourquoi les tensions du courant alternatif de 750 KV (puis en combinaison avec le 1 150 KV) vont devenir l'élément principal du réseau soviétique et comme on l'a vu de l'interconnexion entre celui-ci et les pays d'Europe Centrale. La construction des lignes de 750 KV coûte 30% de moins que l'équivalent de capacité en 330 KV et le coût annuel d'exploitation se réduit également de 10-20%[53]. Il semble donc que la priorite sera accordée d'ici 1990 au développement d'un réseau de 750 KV dans l'ouest de la partie européenne de l'URSS (Nord-Ouest, Sud, et partiellement Centre avec Moscou) recevant et transmettant la puissance des grandes centrales nucléaires prévues.

L'imprécision des projets 750 KV surtout pour 1985-1990 ne permet pas de chiffrer la longueur des lignes de cette tension à construire, sinon approximativement entre 4 000 et 5 000 km sur le territoire soviétique[54]. Dans les autres pays européens du CAEM, on peut escompter la réalisation de quelque 2 500 km de lignes en 750 KV si, aux projets déjà mentionnés, s'ajoutent des liaisons de transit ou d'interconnexion avec des pays d'Europe Occidentale (notamment l'Autriche et à travers la Tchécoslovaquie). En URSS les lignes et les réseaux de 330 KV acquerront une fonction de distribution, comme le deviendront progressivement les lignes de 500 KV qui jusqu'à présent sont utilisées pour la formation de réseaux. Ce sont des lignes de cette tension qui alimenteront la voie ferrée du BAM, et les centres pétroliers et gaziers de l'oblast; de Tyumen' (dont la ligne Surgut — Urengoy en voie d'achèvement).

L'interconnexion des reséaux sibériens avec le REU, l'étendue des distances, l'extension des capacitiés de production électrique au-delà de l'Oural et l'importance unitaire de ces capacités ont incité les Soviétiques à prévoir l'utilisation de la tension de 1 150 KV, palier supérieur du 750 KV[55]. Les lignes de 1 150 KV "garantissent par rapport à celles de 500 KV à plusieurs circuits une réduction de coût de transmission d'énergie de 5 à 15%"[56]. Elles permettront d'alimenter avantageusement des régions grandes consommatrices, en électricité bon marché tout en leur assurant une fourniture stable aux heures de pointe. Le projet de, la ligne Ekibastuz—Oural (et régions avoisinantes) répond au double objectif suivant: éviter le transport par rail de dizaines de millions de tonnes de combustibles énergétiques et permettre à l'Oural de bénéficier le soir du décalage horaire des centrales thermiques futures du bassin houiller de l'Ekibastuz. Cette ligne doit être réalisée au cours du quinquennat 1981-1985 avec en premier lieu la ligne expérimentale-industrielle Itat (bassin de Kansk-Achinsk)—Novokuznetsk (272 km) (prévue initialement pour 1980) qui constituera le premier maillon de la ligne future Réseau de Sibérie -Kazakhstan Nord - Oural. Ultérieurement des lignes de 1 150 KV seraient construites entre le réseau d'Oural et les régions de la Volga et le Centre de la Russie. Malgré les difficultés techniques certaines de l'établissement de tensions aussi élévees pour la première fois dans la pratique mondiale, il existe des projets plus ambitieux encore portant sur des tensions de 1 800 KV pour l'interconnexion des réseaux 750 KV et 1 150 KV mais nul doute qu'il ne s'agisse là de visions à trés long terme.

Les projets de création de lignes de grande longueur à *courant continu* correspondent à la mise en place d'un véritable pont énergétique entre la Sibérie et le Kazakhstan d'une part, avec leurs énormes réserves combustibles et le Centre de la Russie; ils apparaissent par là même comme un prétexte supplémentaire d'exploitation de ces charbons et lignites.

L'envoi de l'électricité en courant continu ne répond pas à une demand particulière de ce type de courant (celui-ci ne représente que le 1/5 de la consommation dans le bilan électrique,[57] pour l'électrolyse, l'électrochimie, les moteurs à vitesses variables, etc.) mais bien plutôt à la possibilité de transmettre à grande distance de grandes masses d'électricité sans pertes excessives. Une première ligne de 1 500 KV sera en partie ("I-ère tranche" dit-on) réalisée au cours du XIème quinquennat. L'ensemble de la ligne Ekibastuz-Centre (Tambov) s'étendra sur 2 414 km avec une capacité de 6 000 MW (le courant alternatif de 1 150 KV pour 6 000 MW n'est pas utilisable pour plus de 1 200 km); elle pourra fournir annuellement aux régions centrales environ 36 milliards de kWh (au point de réception) pour 42 Md de kWh au point de départ. Les avantages du courant continu sur l'alternatif ne sont pas négligeables dans le cas précis de liaisons de 2 500-3 500 km entre les régions asiatiques et européennes. Les pertes sont moindres (car le continu ne change pas de direction), on peut varier les échanges de puissance dans les réseaux car des appareillages peuvent réguler la transmission de puissance; enfin les lignes ne nécessitent que 2 conducteurs (d'où économie de métal non-ferreux de 1/3 par rapport au courant alternatif triphasé), donc pylônes plus légers. Le principal inconvénient consiste dans la nécessité d'avoir 2 sous-stations supplémentaires (aux 2 extrêmités de la ligne).

Si rien d'irrémédiable ne vient entraver la mise en oeuvre de la première ligne de 1 500 KV, d'autres devront être construites au-delà de 1990 en tension plus élevée depuis le bassin de Kansk-Achinsk (Itat-Sud: 2 250 KV, 13 000 MW sur 3 500-4 500 km et Itat-Centre: 2 500 KV, 40 000 MW)[58].

Mais d'ici là et dès maintenant les Soviétiques auront à résoudre des problèmes techniques nombreux, pour la réalisation des lignes de très haute tension, qu'il s'agisse du courant alternatif ou du courant continu, et ceci malgré le fait que le transport d'électricité fasse partie du tres petit groupe du très petit groupe des domaines techniques et industriels où l'URSS se place au premier plan mondial. De nombreux équipements électrotechniques encore non appliqués dans le monde devront être créés, produits, et exploités à grande échelle et dans les conditions climatiques de l'URSS; c'est principalement le cas des stations de transformation, des isolateurs et des installations de compensation (celles-ci ne sont pas adaptées encore à une exploitation satisfaisante sur 750 KV). Au-delà de 750 KV des interrogations demeurent sur la régulation de la tension, la détermination de la section optimale des conducteurs, les solutions pour réduire les pertes en couronne, sans oublier les nuisances éventuelles du champ électrique de très haute tension dont le monde scientifique débat sans conclusions.

Quoi qu'il en soit, les lignes de très haute tension programmées pour le XIème et le XIIème quinquennat n'obtiendront leur plein effet qu'au-delà de ces périodes. Seront-elles en mesure de justifier les investissements très éléves qu'elles auront provoqués? Il faut savoir que les projets de ces lignes géantes datent de 35-40 ans et que jusqu'à ces dernières années du moins les investissements nécessaires avaient été sous-évalués de 2-3 fois; aussi au moment de s'engager dans leur réalisation, il faut tenir compte de la concurrence par les coûts, de construction des centrales nucléaires. De plus pour qu'une ligne (ou groupe de lignes) à courant continu fournisse une aide sensible aux régions manquant d'énergie, cette aide devrait s'élever au moins à 10-15 et même 15-20% de leur consommation, sinon l'intérêt économique de cette ligne serait nul[59]. Or selon les calculs les plus optimistes les régions asiatiques de l'URSS n'enverront d'ici la fin du siècle, pas plus de 5-7% de l'électricité consommée dans les régions de réception[60].

En effet pour une production prévue de 1 550-1 600 Md. de kWh en 1985 et de quelque 2 200 Md. de kWh en 1990, à cette dates les ¾ soit 1 650 Md. de kWh seront consommes dans les regions d'Oural et Europe. La ligne en 1 500 KV prévue fournira 40-42 Md. de kWh/an (pertes non déduites); pour couvrir avant la fin du siècle 10-15% des besoins indiqués il faudrait créer au moins 3 lignes supplémentaires de 2 500 KV (d'environ chacune 80 Md. de kWh). En outre de telles lignes, selon les spécialistes, ne se justifieraient pas plus pour le soutien des réseaux en période de pointe[59]. La concurrence du nucléaire, les difficultés techniques et écologiques semblent devoir limiter les ambitions concernant le pont énergétique est-ouest au seul programme déjà fixé (ligne de 1 500 KV en courant continu d'ici 1990).

Tous ces brillants projets ne doivent pas faire oublier les préoccupations relatives à la modernisation et au développement des autres réseaux et surtout ne pas monopoliser les efforts.

3. Modernisation des réseaux et adaptation aux besoins des utilisateurs.

L'accroissement prévu et souhaité de l'utilisation de l'électricité dans l'agriculture (et les régions rurales) portera sa consommation en 1985 à 170-180 Md. de kWh; en fin 1980 on attendait un résultat de 110 Md. de kWh pour cette même année (au lieu de 130 Md. de kWh prévu initialement)[61]. Les régions rurales du fait de l'organisation de la production de leur énergie ont toujours été particulièrement défavorisées dans leurs relations avec les grands réseaux. A défaut d'informations plus récentes on peut déjà se représenter la tâche probable pour la décennie par les objectifs qui avaient été envisagés pour 1976-1980: construire dans les campagnes 130 000 km de lignes 35 à 110 KV et 890 000 km de lignes 0,4 à 20 KV (dont 200 000 km pour remplacer les lignes trop anciennes)[62]. Si l'on observe que depuis 1970 chaque quinquennat doit étendre de 1/3 son réseau rural (y compris les remplacements nécessaires) ce sont environ 2 millions de km de lignes de basse tension qui devront être installées dans ces seules régions pour satisfaire l'accroissement de la consommation. A quoi il faudra ajouter le doublement probable des lignes urbaines de distribution (0,4 à 20 KV) par rapport à 1975 (un million de km)[62].

Nous nous garderons bien d'extrapoler les réalisations soviétiques sur 10 ans pour les lignes haute tension de 35 à 500 KV, l'évolution des réseaux et les changements de fonction des diverses tensions ne permettent pas d'avancer des pourcentages à partir des kilometrages actuels.

Dans les autres pays du CAEM on peut s'attendre également à des développements accélérés des lignes de tout type. Le cas de la Tchécoslovaquie pourrait être exemplaire pour les autres pays, dont les problèmes sont sensiblement les mêmes. Selon un responsable de ce secteur[63], si l'on considère que de 1976 à 1990 tous les indicateurs électriques (production, capacités, etc.) auront doublé, il faudra, du fait de la modernisation et du remplacement de l'équipement construire d'ici 1990, 100 000 km de lignes électriques (ainsi que la capacité de transformation adéquate) soit 50% des réalisations effectuées depuis plus de 40 ans; si l'on y ajoute les équipements modernes de contrôle et régulation, l'investissement annuel ne sera pas inférieur à 2,5 Md. de couronnes[64] soit 1,7% de l'investissement total du pays en 1978, et peut-être 1,5% vers 1985 si l'on admet un ralentissement continu de la croissance annuelle de ce denier. Parallèlement à la construction ou reconstruction des lignes, tous les pays devront moderniser les équipements. C'est le gage d'une réduction des pertes sur les réseaux. En URSS on ne parvient pas à diminuer sensiblement les pertes d'électricité au cours de la transmission et de la distribution. Elles s'établissaient ainsi (% par rapport à l'envoi dans les réseaux)[65]:

1965: 8,4 - 1970: 9,0 - 1975: 9,0 - 1980 (prévision): 8,6.

Les causes les plus marquantes seraient outre l'augmentation des distances (depuis les centrales hydroélectriques principalement), l'augmentation de la charge des liaisons inter-réseaux, le retard dans certaines régions du développement des réseaux 35-110 KV, le fonctionnement en parallèle de réseaux de tensions différentes, et enfin cause peut-être la plus importante ''le retard de la mise en service d'installations de compensation (compensateurs synchrones, batteries de condensateurs et transformateurs réglables sous la charge[66]''). Le seul fait d'améliorer le dégre de compensation de 50% pourrait réduire les pertes sur tous les réseaux de 15-20%[67] (c'est-à-dire ramener la perte enregistrée a environ 7,5%) et de plus améliorerait considérablement la qualité de l'électricité délivrée aux utilisateurs.

Le quinquennat 1981-1985 ainsi que le suivant va donc être une période de consolidation des réseaux soviétiques et CAEM et de leur intégration plus poussée[68], mais à sens unique; ce sera aussi pour le transport d'électricité une période qui sera riche en informations sur les options techniques de l'horizon 2000[69].

III — Le transport par tubes

La publicité donnée aussi bien en URSS qu'à l'ouest aux réalisations et projets soviétiques en matière de conduites d'hydrocarbures dénote l'importance pour l'URSS de ce secteur de transport dans le contexte énergétique de la décennie.

Les connotations de politique internationale jointes aux besions du CAEM sont telles, que le transport des hydrocarbures soviétiques ne se pose pas en termes habituels de transport. Mais il faut bien préciser qu'il s'agit dorénavant du transport de gaz plus que de celui du pétrole.

On doit donc classer l'exploitation et le développement du réseau de gazoducs dans la catégorie des activités prioritaires et à ce titre s'attendre à lui voir accorder les soins tout particuliers—et la surveillance—du pouvoir. Pour mener à bien les tâches qui commencent à se préciser, pour les 10 prochaines années, nul doute que l'effort financier et technique, devra être exceptionnel, à la mesure des problèmes soulevés.

1. Les oléoducs.

Malgré un résultat inférieur en 1976-1980 aux objectifs planifiés[70] l'extension du réseau soviétique d'oléoducs, qui transporte 95% de pétrole brut[71] ne souleve pas d'interrogations aussi nombreuses que celles posées par les gazoducs comme on le verra ci-après. Les contraintes techniques de transport du pétrole sont relativement moins fortes (tubes, pression, etc.) et de plus il n'existe pas encore d'oléoducs dans les régions de permafrost. Cependant malgré l'accroissement prévu de l'extraction d'ici 1990 et un déplacement vers la Sibérie occidentale des principales sources de cet accroissement il semblait possible de limiter la construction des grandes conduites de pétrole brut à 2 500 km tous les trois ans selon une estimation soviétique[72]. Cependant une information récente[73] sur les objectifs du XIeme quinquennal mentionne la création nécessaire de 11 500 km d'oléoducs de brut, ce qui accroît de façon importante l'estimation précédente et donc l'investissement, car dans le kilométrage indiqué il est peu probable que les conduites de diamètre moyen de type dérivations et raccordements avec les conduites principales représentent plus du tiers environ des constructions. Un programme quinquennal d'au moins 7 000 km de grandes conduites représente donc encore une lourde charge en travail et en coûts de création puisque pour ce dernier point on peut avancer une prévision d'investissement direct dans les conduites de l'ordre de 5 milliards de roubles, et de 6 milliards en y ajoutant les conduites secondaires. Et on ne peut exclure, sauf engagement d'éventuelles grandes exploitations nouvelles, la reconduction d'un programme semblable pour le XIIème quinquennal.

Notons que l'allongement du réseau d'oléoducs augmente le volume des travau de remplacement de sections linéaires de conduites défectueuses[74] ce qui nécessite sinon l'importation de tubes occidentaux supplémentaires, du moins l'emploi de tubes de fabrication soviétique produits en quantité insuffisante. Le vieillissement prématuré de la plupart des tubes devra être considéré avec de plus en plus d'attention dans les prévisions futures. Le problème se pose d'ailleurs encore plus vivement pour les gazoducs.

D'autre part un effort important semble devoir être consacré aux conduites de produits de raffineries, système de transport trop longtemps négligé; en prévoyant 6 500 km mouveaux d'ici 1985 on s'efforcera donc de compenser le retard. En 1976 ce réseau spécialisé s'étendait sur 10 200 km[75] (6 700 km en 1970 et 10 000 km en 1975). Il y a tout lieu de penser que la progression a été faible depuis 1976, malgré l'objectif—non réalisé—de 3 500 km. Aucune information ne nous permet de chiffrer l'investissement à réaliser pour ces conduites, qui toutefois ne devrait pas être supérieur à 1 milliard de roubles. La rentabilité de ces constructions serait incontestable pour l'économie des transports soviétiques puisque les chemins de fer qui transportent 40% du total de ces produits[76] le font à un coût triple de celui obtenu avec des conduites[77].

La réalisation du programme de ces conduites n'est cependant nullement assurée, l'insignifiance des travaux effectués ces dernières années confirme que ce type de conduites n'est pas encore considéré, à en croire les Soviétiques, comme un moyen de transport d'utilisation courante. Elles sont pourtant la seule solution possible pour décharger les chemins de fer d'un fardeau superflu.

En Europe Centrale aucun projet notable ne peut être envisagé pour le réseau d'oléoducs. L'exploitation nominale de 'Druzhba'' ne dépende que du bon vouloir de l'URSS à approvisionner ses alliés en pétrole brut et l'utilisation du récent oléoduc "Adria" prévue pour fournir 10 millions de tonnes par an de pétrole du Moyen-Orient, par moitié à la Hongrie et la Tchécoslovaquie, est un problème de politique économique et non plus de transport. L'ère des grandes réalisations d'oléoducs semble donc être achevée.

2. Les gazoducs soviétiques

2.1 Hypothèses d'un programme de 10 ans

La mise en exploitation accéleréé des gisements de gaz de Sibérie occidentale pose avant tout un problème de transport et avec une acuité autrement plus grande que celle ressentie lors de l'essor du pétrole sibérien dans les années 70.

L'accroissement de la production soviétique de gaz pour le XIème et peut-être le XIIème quinquennat repose entièrement sur ces gisements. L'oblast' de Tyumen', où l'on devait extraire en 1980, 162 milliards de m3 de gaz[78], se voit fixer pour 1985 un objectif de 330-370 milliards de m3[79] avec un développement proche de 500 milliards de m3 en 1990[80]. Le transport de telles quantités de gaz impose la création d'un réseau complet de conduites de grand diamètre à partir de gisements situés toujours plus au nord (Yamburg, et surtout Kharasavey dans la péninsule de Yamal). Selon "le schéma de développement" établi en 1977 pour 1990,[81] les 3 directions de transport du gaz de cette région seraient les suivantes:
Nord-ouest: Urengoy - Nadym - Punga - Minsk - frontière soviétique
Centrale: Medvezh'ye - Nadym - Punga - Kazan' - centre de la Russie

Sud: Urengoy - Surgut - Chelyabinsk - Ufa - Kuybyshev.

Ajoutons que l'exploitation des gisements de la péninsule de Yamal nécessitera de les raccorder à l'une de ces grandes artères.

La situation de plus en plus excentrique des nouveaux gisements accroît assez sensiblement leur éloignement des régions réceptrices par rapport à des gisements tels que ceux de Medvezh'ye et Urengoy. Mais le facteur d'éloignement est surtout important par le fait que l'accroissement de la fourniture de gaz sibérien vers l'ouest et le centre va augmenter de facon considérable la distance moyenne du transport, et donc les coûts; celle-ci qui dépasse déjà 1 500 km (917 km en 1970) sera vraisemblablement dés 1985 surpérieure à 2 000 km. Et les coûts de transport du gaz, qui entre 1970 et 1976 ont augmenté en URSS de 67%[81] (33,67 roubles pour 10 000 m3 de gaz transporté en 1976 et selon des previsions, au moins 40 roubles en 1980)[83] ont plus que doublé entre 1970 et 1980, ne pourront éviter de refléter l'évolution des conditions de transport, même si les améliorations techniques envisagées permettent un rendement plus élevé. L'amortissement qui représente déjà plus de la moitié des coûts de transport, pèsera de plus en plus lourdement sur ceux-ci puisque le programme du gaz sibérien se fonde principalement sur la création d'un kilométrage impressionnant de gazoducs.

Depuis déjà quelques années des spécialistes soviétiques avaient donné l'échelle des projets de transport du gaz sibérien. En 1978 Yu. Bokserman[84] préconisait la construction de 10 gazoducs de grand diamètre (1 420 mm pour pression de 75 atm.) s'étendant sur 30 000 km pour acheminer 300 milliards de m3 de gaz par an. En 1980 O.M. Ivantsov[85] indiquait: "plus de 30 000 km". En janvier 1981 la Pravda[86] mentionnait le besoin dès 1985 de 6 ou 7 gazoducs nouveaux en plus des 4 existants (en 1981 le 5ème, Urengoy-Moscou, 2 800 km).

D'après les trois variantes possibles d'extraction de gaz (ce qui suppose de retrancher environ 6% pour obtenir le gaz expédié dans la conduite et 16% pour avoir le volume de gaz transporté, ainsi qu'il ressort des données fournies par O.M. Ivantsov) on obtient 3 variantes de volume de gaz à expédier de Sibérie occidentale. On retiendra pour base l'extraction de 160 milliards de m3 en 1980 (soit environ 150 milliards de m3 de gaz expédié) ce qui n'a pas été confirmé mais correspond au plan, lequel pour l'ensemble de l'URSS fut réalisé:

Extraction	Gaz expédié	Gaz transporté[80]	Expéditions supplémentaires 1980
1980: 160 Md. de m3, soit:	150 Md. de m3		
a) 1985: 330 Md. de m3, soit:	310 Md. de m3	275 Md. de m3	160 Md. de m3
b) 1985: 370 Md. de m3, soit:	348 Md. de m3	310 Md. de m3	198 Md. de m3
c) 1990: 500 Md. de m3, soit:	470 Md. de m3	410 Md. de m3	320 Md. de m3

Les conduites actuelles de 1 420 mm de diamétre peuvent débiter à la pression de 75 atm., 25-30 milliards de m3 de gaz par an ou plus de 40 Md. de m3 si le gaz est refroidi; avec une pressoin de 100 atm., prévue pour

1982-1983 (et peut-être 120 atm. avant la fin de la décennie) on peut expédier 45 Md. de m3 de gaz non refroidi, mais les tubes adéquats, multi-couches, ne seront probablement pas produits par l'URSS en quantité suffisante avant le XIIème quinquennat[87], ni achetés en Occident. Si nous retenons les deux hypothèses "a" et "c", la construction des gazoducs pourrait s'effectuer ainsi (en admettant que la capacité des tubes sera optimale comme indiqué ci-dessus et que la productivité nominale soit rapidement obtenue):

● Hypothèse "a": expédition de 160 Md. de m3 de plus gu'en 1980: La construction de 5 gazoducs (1 420 mm - 75 atm.) de 3 000 km de longueur moyenne chacun ne suffirait pas à permettre le débit de 160 Md. de m3 sauf si l'un d'eux au moins transporte du gaz réfrigéré. Cependant si l'une de ces conduites sert a là réalisation éventuelle du projet de fourniture de 40-45 Md. de m3 par an de gaz marchand à l'Europe occidentale à partir de 1985, il faudra expédier 43-48 Md. de m3 (du fait des consommations intermédiaires) d'un gaz préalablement refroidi afin d'obtenir cette productivité dans une seule conduite et donc extraire pour celle-ci 48-53 Md. de m3. Dans ce cas 5 gazoducs conviendraient.
Longueur totale possible des 5 gazoducs à construire en 1981-1985: 15 000 km. Tonnage de tubes nécessaire: plus de 10 millions de tonnes[88]. Cependant pour nous maintenir en accord avec la revue spécialisée des conduites d'hydrocarbures[73], source la plus récente, nous nous tiendrons in fine à son chiffre prévisionnel de 16 600 km de gazoducs (sibériens) pour 1985.

● Hypothèse "c": expédition de 320 Md. de m3 de plus qu'en 1980, soit 160 Md. de m3 supplémentaires par rapport à 1985 (hypothèse "a"). Si l'on admet la possibilité de réaliser au moins un tube multi-couches qui recevra 45 Md. de m3, il faut 4 autres conduites de type classique, puisque la production soviétique en multi-couches sera encore peu élevée. L'expédition de gaz réfrigéré pourrait réduire au moins d'une unité les gazoducs à réaliser. Retenons le principe de 5 conduites pour rester en accord avec le chiffre avancé par les spécialistes et responsables soviétiques, de 10 gazoducs à construire en 10 ans.

Les deux hypothèses sont en fait optimales puisqu'elles reposent sur l'obtention de parametres tels que la généralisation d'une pression de 75 atm. permettant de fournir un débit annuel moyen de 28-29 Md. de m3 très tôt après la mise en service, ou bien l'éventuelle réalisation d'une tube multi-couches ou l'éxpedition de gaz réfrigéré. La construction de 10 gazoducs d'un longueur totale minimale d'environ 33 000 km signifie l'emploi de 22 millions de tonnes ou plus de tubes de haute qualité. Dans les 3 entreprises soviétiques susceptibles de produire des tubes de *gazoducs* de grand diamètre, la production totale en 1985 pourrait etre de l'ordre de 3,5 millions de tonnes, mais d'ici la au moins il faudra importer probablement plus de la moitié des tubes nécessaires aux programmes annuels, moins par réelle insuffisance de ces tubes que par souci de qualité et fiabilité élevées du fait des conditions techniques et naturelles sévères auxquelles ils seront soumis. L'URSS importe chaque année environ 1,5 million de tonnes de tubes qui sont utilisés désormais presque exclusivement par les gazoducs. La production nationale est employée à notre avis principalement dans les conduites (gazoducs et oléoducs) les moins vulnérables et pour le remplacement des tubes détériorés. Le recours systématique aux importations semble satisfaire les Soviétiques, ce qui corrobore l'impression que le développement des entreprises de tubes de grand diamètre est loin d'être encouragé autant qu'on pourrait le penser.

Il va de soi que les gazoducs sibériens ne devront pas accaparer toute l'attention dans les travaux concernant les gazoducs dits de longue distance. L'objectif pour ces gazoducs étant de 32 000 km[73] en 1985, il reste environ 16 000 km qui peuvent être répartis ainsi:

- pose de conduites de raccordement (tubes de 529-820 mm de diamètre) sur une longueur supérieure à la croissance moyenne annuelle observée de 1 000 km[89] puisque le volume de gaz transporté étant plus important qu'auparavant, il faudra le répartir dans de nombreuses directions secondaires, de même que l'on devra établir plusieurs conduites vers des centrales thermiques utilisant dorénavant le gaz (au lieu du mazout). La construction en 10 ans de 20 000 km de ces conduites secondaires (et 10 000 km d'ici 1985) semble être une estimation raisonnable.
- des gazoducs devront aussi être créés pour l'évacuation du gaz par exemple de gisements nouveaux prenant le relais de gisements épuisés dans les grandes régions gazéifères (Asie Centrale en particulier) même si on peut s'étonner de l'importance du kilo-mètrage quinquennal (5 500 km en 1981-1985) qui découle de cette répartition. On ne peut pourtant proposer pour explication le fait que chaque année il devra être remplacé une longueur considérable de tubes hors d'usage. Ainsi dans certaines sections de gazoducs, "lors de la remise en état des protections d'isolation, il faut remplacer jusqu'à 60% des tubes (pour une durée générale d'exploitation de ces sections de 7-10 ans)" proportion plusieurs fois supérieure à celle des oléoducs exploités de 25 à 35 ans[90]. On peut s'attendre à ce qu'entre 1980 et 1990 il faille consacrer quelques millions de tonnes de tubes pour assurer l'exploitation de gazoducs déjà anciens constitués de tubes de fabrication soviétique mal protégés contre la corrosion, notamment les tubes de diamètre élevé les plus vulnérables.

A partir de l'objectif 1981-1985 et du contenu possible du programme, on peut estimer que les travaux du XIIème quinquennat seront de même importance, puisque la demande de transport augmentera dans les mêmes conditions et proportions. C'est pourquoi en résumé la tâche décennale pourrait se résumer ainsi, selon une approximation très large:

	1980-1990	Tonnage de tubes (millions de tonnes)
Tubes de 1 420 mm de diamètre (km)	33 000	22
Autres tubes de grand diamètre (km)	11 000	5,5
Tubes de diamètre moyen (km)	20 000	5,0

Il faudra également utiliser plusieurs millions de tonnes de tubes de remplacement de sections détériorées. De même au cours de la décennie il faudra commencer à reconstruire un nombre croissant de stations de compression (dont la période d'amortissement est fixée à 17 ans). Enfin l'extension du réseau de gazoducs devra s'accompagner de la création de plusieurs réservoirs souterrains de grande capacité.

2.2 Les conditions de la réalisation de ce programme.

La longueur des gazoducs longue distance posés en 1976-80 serait de 31 000 km[91] (le plan quinquennal prévoyait 35 000 km), portant ainsi le réseau à 130 000 km environ. On ne peut comparer valablement ce résultat avec l'objectif de 1985, de plus de 16 000 km à créer d'ici la fin de 1985 sur l'axe est-ouest, car ces conduites seront constituées de tubes de 1 420 mm de diametre alors qu'en 1976-80 il en fut posé moitié moins de ce type[92], et que les conditions naturelles et techniques sont cette fois difficiles pour une plus grande partie des conduites, ce qui se répercutera sur le coût et la durée des travaux. L'allongement de la durée de construction des gazoducs depuis 1975 étant causé le plus souvent par le relief, le climat, la nature des terrains et le plus grand diamètre des tubes, il sera difficile de renverser cette tendance. L'exemple du gazoduc Urengoy-Chelyabinsk (1 500 km) posé en un an, est encore unique. Sa réalisation a bénéficié d'une méthode nouvelle de soudage et d'ancrage des tubes dans le sol, ce qui a considérablement élevé la productivité; de plus, l'organisme constructeur, au lieu d'organiser le travail par succession des activités des diverses équipes spécialisées, les réalise de front par "sections complexes" avec un gain de temps important[93]. Il semble utile d'insister sur des facteurs précis susceptibles d'influencer dans un sens ou dans l'autre le déroulement du programme.

Les Soviétiques auront d'abord à résoudre le problème de transport de matériaux et matériels vers les régions démunies des infrastructures même les plus sommaires; la création d'un réseau minimal de routes revêtues, même à prix élevé (500 000-600 000 roubles le km) est une première nécessité. L'acheminement des tubes par mer et rivières, plus rapide et plus économique, a reçu un début d'application. Peu d'améliorations sont à prévoir d'ici longtemps pour répondre aux besions de tous les transports dans les régions nord-orientales; c'est là un goulet d'étranglement de première importance. Or l'accélération de la construction, condition sine qua non, ne peut être obtenue sans la poursuite des travaux pendant toute l'année et donc pendant l'été, saison où les régions concernées sont impraticables (marécages, terrains gorgés d'eau). Aussi, outre les moyens de transport adéquats, on manquera des matériels (à faible pressoin au sol avec chenilles résine-métal) capables de se mouvoir sur ces sols et de les travailler (excavateurs, poseurs de tubes, etc.). Dans ce domaine tout reste à faire. Dans le même ordre d'idée, l'emploi de matériels et équipements adaptés aux températures extrêmes du nord ne semble pas pouvoir se developper de façon satisfaisante (10% du parc de machines actuellement) et pourtant le problème n'est pas nouveau puisque la Sibérie occidentale est exploitée dupuis 15 ans, et il touche tous les domaines d'activité, sans que des mesures appropriées aient connu un début d'application notable. D'ailleurs les matériels spécialisés ne sont pas les seuls en cause. Contrairement à ce qu'on pourrait penser, la mécanisation de l'ensemble des opérations sur les chantiers de gazoducs (ou autres chantiers prioritaires comme le BAM) n'est pas sensiblement plus poussée qu'ailleurs. Ceci n'est pas sans inquiéter les responsables de l'industrie du gaz puisque, à la réalisation de travaux aussi contraignants que la pose des gazoducs 'nordiques", devra correspondre l'emploi impératif d'une gamme complète de matériels libérant les hommes de tâches insurmontables. Le manque de main-d'oeuvre déjà déploré sur ces chantiers et qui sera de plus en plus prononcé, ne pourra être compensé qu'à cette condition et aussi au prix d'une transformation radicale du monde de vie proposé aux travailleurs.

Les Soviétiques attendent beaucoup de l'industrialisation de la construction des gazoducs. Des améliorations sont prévisibles à ce titre dans la durée de la construction. En premier lieu la généralisation de la méthode modulaire, c'est-à-dire la réalisation et la livraison par l'industrie de sous-ensembles d'équipements, aurait un heureux effet sur l'installation essentiellement des stations de pompage et de compression; la mise en place par exemple d'une station de compression pourrait s'effectuer en 9-10 mois au lieu de 14-15 en moyenne actuellement[94]. Or il est bien connu que de nombreux gazoducs soviétiques dont la partie linéaire est posée, attendent longtemps l'installation de stations de compression pour commencer à fonctionner et plus souvent pour atteindre leur capacité nominale.

Pour les tubes on s'oriente progressivement vers un traitement de protection dans l'entreprise même de production ou dans des fabriques implantées dans les grandes zones d'utilisation; cette méthode qui, dit-on, sera appliquée à tous les tubes à la fin du XIème quinquennat, permettrait d'élever de 25% le rythme du "flux technologique"; de plus elle garantit incontestablement une meilleure qualité de l'opération (plus de $1\frac{1}{3}$ des détériorations des tubes est provoqué par la corrosion); mentionnons encore l'amélioration technique que représente le soudage électrique par contact que les Soviétiques utilisent avec leur système "Sever"; ici encore les gains de temps et de productivité (5 à 10 fois superieure) deviendraient importants si cette technique était employée sur une grande échelle (quand les difficultés d'alimentation électrique seront éliminées).

Il existe aussi un risque que l'accélération de la pose des conduites s'effectue au détriment de la qualité des diverses opérations[95], d'autant plus que nombre de solutions techniques envisagées sont loin d'être éprouvées. Car au-delà de la construction des gazoducs c'est la fiabilité de leur exploitation qui est en cause.

Malgré les quelques éléments positifs énumérés on ne peut s'illusionner sur les chances de succès du programme des gazoducs— qui est d'ailleurs un programme minimum pour répondre au développement de l'extraction. Les Soviétiques eux-mêmes ne sous-estiment pas l'extrême difficulté de la tâche. La charge écrasant dévolue au XIème quinquennat sera vraisemblablement reportée partiellement sur le quinquennat suivant, au cours duquel, malgré des possibilites techniques accrues, il sera difficile d'atteindre l'objectif final d'évacuation du gaz en 1990. L'importance des difficultés matérielles de l'entreprise est corroborée par le ministre de la construction pour les industries gazière et pétrolière[96], puisque en chiffrant à 1 milliard de roubles le coût de 1 000 km de gazoduc sibérien (de 1 420 mm), il fournit un élément supplémentaire d'appréciation de ces difficultés. Certes le ministre, en adoptant un ton dramatique et en ne lésinant pas sur les grands chiffres, semble vouloir dégager sa responsabilité future aux yeux de ses lecteurs et à ceux du Gosplan (auquel appartient la revue où il s'est exprimé). C'est pourquoi on ne peut prendre pour argent comptant cette affirmation du coût de construction, d'autant plus qu'un autre expert l'avait évalué en 1978 également[97] à 730 000-830 000 roubles au km. L'une et l'autre estimation valent, nous semble-t-il, pour les sections de gazoducs des régions sibériennes ou nord-européennes, soit environ moins de la moitié du parcours total. Cependant, prenant en considération l'augmentation inévitable des coûts en 5 et 10 ans du fait d'achat de tubes et autres équipements occidentaux et des pertes et dépenses supplémentaires de tout ordre que les constructeurs devront supporter, on peut admettre des maintenant l'estimation la plus élevée d'un million de roubles par km de gazoduc longue distance (et 1 420 mm de diamètre). En l'appliquant aux hypothèses et objectifs énoncés plus haut, l'investissement gazoducs serait alors égal à 33 milliards de roubles pour 33 00 km à réaliser pendant la décennie. On y ajoutera au moins 8 milliards de roubles pour les autres réalisations (non compris la "rénovation" anticipée de certains gazoducs)[98], et la reconstruction des stations de compression, soit un total de 41 milliards de roubles d'investissements, c'est-à-dire plus de 4 milliards de roubles par an et en considérant que ce chiffrage ne comprend pas la création des infrastructures sociales industrielles et autres.

Il faut remarquer que l'investissement—gazoducs s'était elevé à 6,17 Md. de roubles en 1971-75 (plan: 5 Md. de roubles)[98] et qu'en 1976-80 il était prévu 10 Md. de roubles[99]; le dépassement des devis en 1971-75 n'appelle pas nécessairement semblable supposition pour 1976-80. L'investissement—gazoducs et stockage comptait pour 61,3% de l'investissement dans l'industrie soviétique du gaz en 1975 et il y a tout lieu de penser que ce pourcentage· ne fait que progresser. Enfin en 1976-80, l'investissement—gazoducs moyen annuel de 2 milliards de roubles représentait environ 11% de l'investissement total dans le "complexe combustibles—énergie" de l'URSS.[100]

Malgré la stabilité du poste oléoducs, l'investissement futur dans les conduites d'hydrocarbures semble disproportionné. Il s'élèvera à plus de 55 Md. de roubles pour 10 ans (14 pour les oléoducs, 41 pour les gazoducs); il aurait ainsi représenté en 1976-80 près du tiers des dépenses réalisées pour l'énergie et les combustibles, ce qui aurait été insupportable. Mais les faits pourraient d'eux-mêmes décider de la situation. Il est pratiquement exclu que les Soviétiques puissent construire dans les prochaines années, les gazoducs au rythme indiqué, ce qui diminuera d'autant l'investissement nécessaire, et ce qui renforce aussi leur intérêt pour la participation matérielle et financièr maximale des Occidentaux dans un éventuel gazoduc "européen"— ainsi que leur assistance technique accrue sous des formes diverses: fourniture de tubes, de stations de compression, d'équipements de génie civil, etc.

Mais le problème est politique, tout comme le fut récemment celui de la fourniture de gaz iranien par le gazoduc "Igat-2" abandonné en cours de construction.

A défaut de grands projets fermes dans l'immédiat, les pays d'Europe centrale poursuivent l'achèvement de leur réseau de liaisons avec l'URSS. C'est la Bulgarie qui complète le gazoduc qui lui permettra de doubler vers 1985 son approvisionnement depuis les réservoirs d'Ukraine (Shebelinka)—soit 5,8 Md. de m3 par an. C'est soutout la Tchécoslovaquie, territoire de passage des grandes conduites internationales (Transit 1 et 2, Soyuz), où se poursuit la construction du gazoduc "Consortium", afin de porter la capacité de gaz en transit à 53 md. de m3 en 1984[101], et d'importantes capacités de stockage souterrain (3 Md. de m3 vers 1985)[102].

Quoi qu'il en soit, il apparaît en définitive que désormais, et plus que dans la décennie précédente, le transport du gaz sibérien sera une affaire commune à tout le continent européen où ne sera pas, tant il est vrai, ainsi que le soulignait la Pravda[103] "qu'un plus fort accroissement de l'extraction du gaz (de la région de Tyumen') dépend non pas de la disponibilité de ressources, mais de la possibilite de transporter ce gaz."

Conclusion

L'attention accordée par les Soviétiques aux problèmes énergétiques mondiaux privilégie assurément le pétrole et le gaz naturel. Leur attitude—c'est-à-dire les décisions pour la décennie nouvelle—à l'égard des moyens de transport d'énergie le confirme.

La possession de l'atout politique des hydrocarbures, le souci de l'autosuffisance du CAEM ou au moins de la sécurité des approvisionnements, méritent les plus grands efforts matériels et financiers, sans que l'on soit assuré de la rentabilité des opérations; mais celle-ci est-elle en l'occurence une préoccupation majeure?

En comparaison, le transport des charbons et lignites, problème d'importance plus nationale qu'internationale, est donc traité par les pays du CAEM selon leurs conceptions, besoins, et possibilités propres. On peut s'étonner ainsi que l'URSS, malgré un transfert progressif vers les combustibles solides et les difficultés de plus en plus grandes rencontrées par la voie ferrée, n'envisage pas de développer son réseau conformément aux nouveaux besoins. Car l'expédition vers l'ouest et le centre de l'énergie des charbons sibériens sous forme d'électricité n'est nullement garantie ni justifiée.

Il est donc clair que la priorité dans le transport accordée aux hydrocarbures devra se pratiquer à un prix si élevé que l'économie soviétique n'aura pas les moyens de répondre à de telles exigences; mais de plus, la désorganisation des autres systèmes de transport, privés des investissements indispensables, ira en s'aggravant, touchant tous les secteurs d'activité, avec cet effet de boule de neige qui ne doit rien aux hivers soviétiques.

Notes

1. Przeglad Komunikacyjny, 2, 1980, p. 49-52.
2. Statisticheskiy ezhegodnik Chlenov SEV, 1979, p. 322-326.
3. Statistická Rocenka ČSSR, 1980.
4. Przeglad Komunikacyjny. op. cit.
5. En 1976 le charbon représentait 14% des marchandises transportées par voies d'eau en RDA, 27% en Tchécoslovaquie, et environ plus de la moitié en Pologne. M. Kahn - T. Globokar. "Les transports fluviaux en URSS et en Europe orientale". Courrier des Pays de l'Est, No. 220, 1978, p. 16.
6. Rechnoy Transport, 1. 1981, p. 1-2.
7. Planovoe Khozyaystvo, 7. 1980, p. 96.
8. D'après Narodnoe Khozyaystvo Ukrainskoy SSR. 1978, p. 175.
9. Narodnoe Khozyaystvo SSSR v 1979, p. 331.
10. Rechnoy Transport, op. cit.
11. Exportations soviétiques. 3. 1980. - Des vracquiers fluviaux de 10 000 tonnes, sur le modéle "Volga-Don", à coque renforcée pour navigation prolongée, seront construits au cours de XIème quinquennat. Pravda, 10.11. 1980, p. 1.
12. On ne connait pas le montant de l'investissement dans le transport fluvial; l'accroissement prévu de 50 millions de roubles en 1981 (selon Rechnoy Transport, op. cit.) pourrait permettre, si l'on prend arbitrairement 5% d'augmentation, d'estimer l'investissement annuel à environ 1 milliard de roubles, soit 0,7% de l'investissement soviétique annuel officiel dans l'économie (à comparer avec la part des chemins de fer: 2,7%).
13. Précisons que l'on a retenu dans ce chiffre que le seul charbon (donc sans le coke) D'après Narodnoe Khozyaystvo, 1979, p. 324-325.
14. Przeglad Komunikacyjny, op. cit.
15. En 1978: charbon et coke: 28,8% et pétrole et produits pétroliers 8% du volume transporté par rail. Statistisches Jahrbuch DDR. 1979, p. 199.
16. D'après Eksploatacia Kolei. 1. 1980, p. 4-7.
17. Anuarul Statistic al R.S. Romînia, 1979, p. 444-447.

18. D'après Narodnoe Khozyaystvo SSSR, 1979, p. 171 et 324-325.

La longueur moyenne du trajet pour le charbon qui était de 691 km en 1970 a atteint 750 km en 1978 et de 1976 à 1979 elle a augmenté de 103 km, ce qui a occasionné des frais supplémentaires de 180 millions de roubles; les chemins de fer ont ainsi accru leur trafic de 75,5 milliards de T. km. Ekonomitcheskaya Gazeta. 36. 1980, p. 15.

19. Au milieu de 1980, plus de 9 millions de tonnes de charbon étaient en souffrance dans le Kuzbass, soit un tonnage très supérieur aux normes. Pravda, 22.7. 1980, p. 1.

20. Anzhero-Barzas et Achinsk — ligne de Sibérie moyenne. Selon I. G. Pavlovskiy: "Problemy i perspektivy razvitiya transporta". Moscou, 1981, p. 85.

21. Akademiya Nauk SSSR. Sibirskoe otdelenie. "Ocherki ekonomiki Sibiri". Novosibirsk 1980, p. 311.

22. A. Michaud. "La voie ferreé Baykal-Amur: ambitions et perspectives d'un grand projet sibérien". Thèse ue doctorat. Université de Paris III. 1981, p. 76. Dès 1980, le BAM devait charger 3 millions de tonnes de charbon.

23. Pravda, 9.12.1980, p. 3. Les pays du CAEM prévoient d'élever la capacité de charge des trains en Europe centrale jusqu'à 4 000-4 800 tonnes sur plusieurs lignes. Commerce extérieur tchécoslovaque, 8. 1980, p. 3.

24. Planovoe Khozyaystvo, 10. 1977, 11. 1978, 8. 1980. Pravda, 31.6.1980. Ugol' 10. 1980, p. 19.

25. Ekonomicheskaya Gazeta, 36. 1980, p. 15.

26. Voprosy ekonomiki, 7. 1980, p. 51.

27. Izvestiya, 25.5.1980, p. 2.

28. Pravda, 13.11.1980, p. 1.

29. I. G. Pavlovskiy, op. cit. p. 104.

30. Eksploatacia kolei, 2. 1980, p. 37-42.

31. La teneur en cendres augmenterait de 2 a 4% dans un proche avenir pour la plupart des charbons soviétiques. Pravda, 10.11.1980, p. 2.
Pour cette raison il est donc peu souhabtable, car peu économique, d'expédier vers le centre de la Russie les combustibles de l'Ekibastuz et Kansk-Achinsk.

32. Pravda, 31.3.1980, p. 2.

33. EKO. 9. 1980, p. 115.

34. D'après Rocznik Statystyczny, 1980. Warszawa, p. 289.

35. G. Wild. "Le transport ferroviaire sovietique en 1970-1980." CEPII. Paris, mai 1979.

36. D'après V.L. Mote. "Problems of regional development in the BAM service area", p. 7. IIème congrès mondial d'etudes soviétiques et est-européennes. Garmisch-Partenkirchen, octobre 1980.

37. N.N. Barkov. F.P. Mulyukin. "Planirovanie i effektivnost' kapital'nykh vlozheniy na zheleznodorozhnom transporte."Moscou, 1980, p. 28. Ces auteurs indiquent que les investissements dans les chemins de fer en 1976-1980 devaient s'élever à près de 15 milliards de roubles, compte non tenu des travaux du BAM (p. 21). Ils indiquent (p. 23) que les investissements en 1976-1977 pour les nouvelles lignes (y compris le BAM) representaient 43,3% de l'investissement ferroviaire (au lieu de 26,5% en 1971-1975 et 27,7% en 1966-1970).

38. RFE-RL, 26.11.1979. Pravda, 15.7. 1980.

39. Pravda, 20.11.1980.

40. Pravda, 26 mai 1980. Sotsialisticheskaya Industriya, 12.7.1980.

41. C'est à partir de 1972 et du fait de l'interconnexion du reséau européen, de celui du nord-Kazakhstan et de certains reséaux de Sibérie occidentale, que le système prend le nom de Réseau Unifié d'URSS.

42. Elektricheskie Stantsii, 12. 1980, p. 4.

43. Sodruzhestvo Stran-chlenov SEV, Moscou, 1980, p. 195.

44. L'URSS est reliée au réseau du CAEM par 9 lignes haute tension dont une de 750 KV, 4 de 400 KV et 3 de 220 KV. De même devait s'achever vers 1980 la liaison par une ligne de courant continu du REU soviétique au réseau de la Finlande et donc au réseau scandinave "Nordel".

45. Bulletin hebdomadaire hongrois, 30.1.1979.
46. Ekonomicheskoe sotrudnichestvo stran-chlenov SEV, 3. 1979.
47. Voprosy ekonomiki, 10. 1980, p. 100.
48. Energetika SSSR v 1976-1980 godakh. Moscou, 1977, p. 195.
49. Elektroenergetika evropeyskikh stran-chlenov SEV, Moscou 1978, p. 191.
50. D.G. Zhimerin. "Problemy razvitiya energetiki, Moscou, 1978, p. 283.
51. Elektricheskie Stantsii, 12. 1980, p. 65.
52. L. L. Peterson. Colloque franco-soviétique sur l'énergie. Moscou, novembre 1980.
53. Colloque franco-soviétique, op. cit.
    Les lignes de 750 KV existantes ou en construction sont constituées de 4 conducteurs;
    l'on prévoit de réaliser des lignes à 5 conducteurs dont les expérimentations soviétiques
    laisseraient prévoir de meilleurs indicateurs économiques. (Elektr. Stantsii, 7. 1980, p.
    41).
54. Les prévisions pour 1980 sur la longueur des lignes étaient de 300 km. pour 1 150 KV, 3
    000 km pour 750-800 KV, 28 550 km. pour 400-500 KV, 26 000 km. pour 330 KV et le
    total des lignes haute tension (35 à 1 150 KV) devait s'élever à 793 000 km. D. G.
    Zhimerin op. cit. p. 223. On peut comparer ces chiffres avec les estimations founies en
    1960: 1 millions de km en 1975 et 1,5 million de km. en 1980 (Planovoe Khoz. 3. 1960).
    En fait les résultats attendus pour 1980 sont les suivants:
    lignes de 750 KV: 2 500 km.; 400-500 KV: 25 000 km.; 330 KV: 23000 km (Elektr.Stantsii,
    12. 1980, p. 64.
55. Les lignes de 1 150 KV ont une capacité de charge 4 000-6 000 MW par circuit sur
    1 200-2 000 km, alors que pour les lignes de 750 KV le rapport s'établit à 1 800-2 000 MW
    par circuit sur 800-1 500 km.
56. Colloque franco-soviétique sur l'énergie, op. cit.
57. D.G. Zhimerin, op. cit. p. 239.
58. D.G. Zhimerin, op. cit. p. 246.
59. "Toplivno-energeticheskiy kompleks Sibiri". Akademiya Nauk SSSR. Sibirskoe
    otdelenie, Novosibirsk, 1978, p. 198 à 200.
60. V. A. Pyl'skiy. "Shagi sovetskoy energetiki" in Novoe v zhizni, nauke, tekhnike. Izd.
    "Znaniya", Moscou, 7. 1980, p. 34.
61. Elektrotekhnika. 12. 1980, p. 5.
62. Energetika SSSR v 1976-1980 godakh, Moscou, 1977, p. 160 et 163.
63. Planovane Hospodarstvi, 4. 1978.
64. A titre d'information fragmentaire, indiquons que la RDA étendra son réseau de 110
    KV, de 24 000 km en 1977 à 34 000 km en 1990. Energietechnik. vol. 29, n⁰ 9, septembre
    1979, p. 337-341.
65. EKO, 9. 1980, p. 127.
66. Pravda, 20.11.1980, p. 2.
67. Energetika SSSR v 1976-1980 godakh. op. cit. p. 183.
68. Dans le cadre du développement de l'automatisation, signalons la création en cours du
    Système Automatique de Régulation du régime de fréquence et des surpintensités, de
    la première tranche du système central de coordination du REU, etc.
69. Les Sovietiques ont' espoir d'être en mesure d'utiliser industriellement des câbles sur-
    aconducteurs avant 1990. Une ligne experimentale de 1 km de longueur devait être
    réalisée au cours de la période 1976-1980. Ces câbles permettent, on le sait, d'eviter
    pratiquement toute perte d'electricite dans le transport.
70. Plan 1976-1980: création de 18 500 km d'oleoducs (dont 3 500 pour les produits
    pétroliers) afin de porter le réseau à 75 100 km à la fin de 1980; on attendait un total, en
    fait, de 69 700 km, soit la construction de 2 600 km par an. D'apres B. Shcherbina. Plan.
    Khoz. 3. 1980, p. 5, et Narodnoe Khoz. SSSR 1979, p. 334.
71. Neftyanoe Khozyaystvo, 11. 1980, p. 4.
72. S.S. Ushakov. T.M. Borisenko. "Ekonomika transporta topliva i energii" Moscou, 1980
    in Ch. Beaucourt. "La politique pétrolière soviétique dans le monde". CEPII, octobre
    1980, p. 30, note 5.

73. Stroitel'stvo truboprovodov, 2. 1981, p. 3.
74. Ainsi l'oléoduc Uzen'-Gur'ev (nord-est de la mer Caspienne) construit il y a 5 ans sans protection électrochimique, dans des sols salés, est actuellement hors d'usage. Pravda, 3.10.1980, p. 3.
75. L. Dienes. Th. Shabad. The Soviet Energy System. J. Wiley and Sons. (New York), p. 62, selon des sources sovietiques.
76. Izvestiya, 24.5.1980, p. 2.
77. Les conduites de produits pétroliers seront développées entre les raffineries et les dépôts d'hydrocarbures et entre raffineries et centrales électriques. Pour ces dernières, l'approvisionnement en mazout, quand il est réalisé par tubes, s'effectue dans des conduites ne dépassant pas actuellement 32 km; aussi prévoit-on de construire "quelques" conduites à mazout (diamètre: 250 mm) de 70 à 200 km de longueur, de 3-6 millions de tonnes/an de capacité chacune d'un mazout chauffé à 80°, pour un coût de 250 000-290 000 R.km. J.A. Skovorodnikov. Colloque franco-soviétique. op. cit.
78. Pravda, 24.8.1980, p. 2.
79. Pravda, 27.1.1981, p. 2.
80. Selon O.M. Ivantsov, chef de département technique du Minneftegazstroy, en 1985 il faudra transporter 275 milliards de m3 de gaz depuis la Sibérie occidentale et 410 milliards de m3 en 1990. Colloque franco-soviétique pour l'enérgie. Moscou, 1980. L'objectif planifié pour 1981 est de 175,4 Md. de m3 (Gazovaya Prom. 1. 1981)
81. Ekonomicheskaya Gazeta, 9. 1979, p. 6.
82. D'aprés I. Ya. Furman. "Ekonomika magistral'nogo transporta gaza". "Nedra". Moscou, 1978, p. 78 et 82. Les dépenses totales de transport de gaz s'élevaient à 948,5 millions de roubles en 1976; en 1980 on peut les estimer à près de 1,6 milliard de roubles (pour environ 390 milliards de m3 de gaz transporté et non pas 435 Md. de m3 de gaz extrait).
83. D'après une étude dans "Ekonomika gazovoy promyshlennosti". 2. 1980, p. 30.
84. Yu. Bokserman. Plan. Khoz. 11. 1978, p. 19.
85. O.M. Ivantsov. Ibid.
86. Pravda, 27.1.1981, p. 2.
87. Les pays occidentaux ne jugent pas utile de produire ce type de tubes et d'employer une telle pression, alors que l'URSS, à la fois pour appliquer une pression plus élevée et pour assurer la fiabilité des conduites, commence à fabriquer des tubes multi-couches. L'usine de Khartsyzsk devait en produire 50 000 tonnes en 1980 et à Vyksa un atelier d'une capacité de 1 million de tonnes/an devait être construit en 1976-1980 (première tranche de 250 000 tonnes/an prévue pour 1979); en fait c'est seulement au cours de l'actuel quinquennat que sera construit l'atelier.
88. Yu. Bokserman. op. cit. p. 19. L'auteur indique "environ 20 millions de tonnes de tubes de grand diamètre pour 30 000 km", soit 666 tonnes au km.
89. I. Ya. Furman. op. cit. p. 51.
90. Stroitel'stvo truboprovodov. 10.1980, p. 10.
91. Stroit. trub. 9. 1980, p. 11. Le réseau des gazoducs "longue distance" ("Magistral'nye") pourrait se répartir ainsi: 98 400 pour les grandes conduites, 28 000 km de dérivations et raccordements et 5 000 km de gazoducs locaux. Estimations d'après les données pour 1976 fournies par I. Ya. Furman. op. cit. p. 51.
92. L'emploi de ces tubes dans les régions inondées ou marécageuses (Sibérie occidentale et nord de la Russie d'Europe) est source d'invonvénients d'ocdre technique: contarct plus étendu avec des sols non fixés, d'où déformations amplifiées dans les sections courbes sous l'action de la pression et de la température. A la fin de 1975 il existait 3 600 km de conduites de 1 420 mm de diamètre et 4 400 km en 1976; il etait prévu d'en poser sur 10 200 km en 1976-1980 (selon I. Yu. Furman, op. cit. p. 72 et 80) Or il en aurait été construit en 1976-1980, 11 000 km (Stroit. trub. 2. 1981, p. 2) ce qui semble excessif du fait que le plan total de gazoducs ne fut pas realise; 11 000 km pourraient représenter plutôt, semble-t-il, la longueur totale de ces conduites à la fin de 1980 et par conséquent une création de 7 600 km au cours des 5 dernières années.

93. Pravda, 24.8.1980, p. 2.
94. Stroit. trub. 6. 1980, p. 18.
95. La coordination des travaux est rarement assurée. Très fréquemment la partie linéaire des gazoducs, une fois posée, ne bénéficie qu'avec retard de la création des indispensables systèmes de protection électrochimique contre la corrosion. Les tubes exposés ainsi à l'action de certains sols sont corrodés quelques années après leur pose. L'absence de cohérence dans la réalisation des gazoducs se remarque aussi dans le décalage dans le temps entre la réception de la partie linéaire et celle des stations de compression et capacités de stockage, ce qui a été reconnu comme une des causes principales de sous-utilisation de la capacité normative des nouvelles conduites.
96. Plan. Khoz. 3. 1980, p. 5.
97. Yu. Bokserman. Plan. Khoz. 11. 1980, p. 19.
98. En 1975 l'investissement-gazoducs comprenait notamment les nouvelles réalisations pour 93,1% et la reconstruction et l'extension pour 4,0%. Selon Ekonomika gazovoy promyshlennosti, 4. 1977, p. 6. Il serait logique de penser que l'investissement comprend les coûts de rénovation anticipée. D'autre part en 1971-75, les investissements dans le stockage souterrain ont constitué 2,0-2,5% de l'investissement-gazoducs réalisé. (ibid. p. 4).
99. I. Ya. Furman. op. cit. p. 67.
100. Le complexe combustibles-énergie de l'URSS a reçu un investissement de 18 milliards de roubles/an au cours du Xème quinquennat. Ugol', 11. 1980, p. 15.
101. Svet Hospodarstvi, 28.8.1980.
102. Rude Pravo, 10.1.1981, p. 1.
103. Pravda, 24.8. 1980, p. 2

Energy and East-West Relations*
Tyrus W. Cobb

New York Times columnist James Reston noted in 1979 the two major issues facing American foreign policy-makers are questions relating to energy and national security and the direction of Soviet military power and policy[1]. In fact these two broad policy concerns are not quite so distinct. They coalesce to form a single major security issue for American policy planners in the 1980's in which questions of Soviet strategic doctrine and COMECON energy trade with the West will be interwoven on our national security agenda. This "energy/security" framework encompasses several specific foreign policy issues, including growing OECD energy dependence on foreign sources, the economic burden of petrodollar transfers, security of energy supplies, the use of exports as a foreign policy instrument, Alliance cohesion, the "detente" relationship with the Communist world, and the development of a comprehensive policy package for dealing with the Soviet Union.

This paper will attempt to make the case for the integration of commercial and economic potential as an integral part of American policy toward the USSR in the narrowest sense and, in a broader context, as a feature of an Alliance strategy for dealing with the Socialist Camp. In developing this thesis I will first survey recent trends in the global energy market, the prospects for energy production and demand in both the United States and the Soviet Union, and the energy future of their respective Allies. Energy as a factor in Soviet-American relations will be examined in a historical perspective and current levels of East-West trade delineated, specifically in energy-related raw materials and equipment. The impact of energy trade with the Soviet Union on Alliance cohesion will be analyzed and the potential for Western cooperation or conflict presented. Questions of "energy leverage", both Soviet and American, will be evaluated in terms of the national security potential represented

*This paper does not necessarily represent the views of the U.S. Government or the United States Military Academy.

175

represented by technology and credit transfers to the East and exports of energy to the West. Finally, recent Soviet proposals for a high-level energy conference and Brezhnev's suggestions for a comprehensive Persian Gulf security zone will be examined. The paper will conclude with a proposal directed toward the integration of commercial and foreign policy concerns in a national security policy framework.

International Energy Trends

The global energy market has been in a state of constant change since the 1973 Yom Kippur War. The conflict, which led to a partial oil embargo and a four-fold jump in petroleum prices, gradually shifted the terms of trade away from the major consuming countries to the advantage of the oil exporters. Questions of energy availability, access to fuel resources, and the price at which the supplies are traded have become central concerns of government officials in the West in the last decade. Recycling of petrodollar holdings of the OPEC countries is now a major politico-economic issue as the current accounts deficits of the industrialized West mount and the balance of payments surpluses of the oil exporters surge. The toppling of the pro-Western regime of the Shah of Iran in 1978, the rise of Islamic fundamentalism, increased Soviet penetration of the area and a perceptible deterioration in Saudi Arabian relations with the United States have generated concerns over the security of oil supplies emanating from the resource-rich Persian Gulf area.

International energy flows in this decade will continue to be dominated by sales of crude oil and petroleum products. Oil accounts for approximately 50% of the world's energy consumption; however, over 80% of the energy that is traded internationally is accounted for by the export of oil. The major consuming countries have made some progress in reducing oil consumption since 1973 through intensive conservation measures and the limited substitution of other sources in place of petroleum. An increased utilization of coal, construction of nuclear energy facilities, and the development of synthetic and renewable (solar, fission) sources are planned as a further means of reducing our dependence on petroleum. However, these alternatives are bogged down in questions of safety, environmental damage, and the economic wisdom of the massive initial investment required. The shift away from oil will be a long and difficult process with few significant substitution and conservation efforts capable of making an impact before 1990. The dominant role of the hydrocarbons, especially oil, in world energy usage will continue.

Petroleum supplies to the world market are likely to decline more rapidly than demand can be reduced. A recent International Energy Agency study anticipates a shortfall of between 2.1 and 3.7 million barrels a day by 1985 and a gap of 5.7-8.6 mb/d by 1990[2]. Although past projections of energy supply and demand have been extremely inaccurate,[3] the probability of supply shortfalls generated by policy-driven and resource depletion production downturns, considered against even moderate increases in demand projected under low economic growth scenarios, should be anticipated. This will result in continued upward pressures on the price petroleum trades for on the world market and a greater potential for the major oil exporters to use their petroleum exports for political objectives.

One of the most important characteristics of the world oil market in this decade is the growing constriction in the number of countries capable of exporting oil in this decade. Production downturns will lead many of the traditional oil suppliers to leave the market. The Middle East, which enjoys a very favorable export-to-production ratio as the chart below demonstrates, will serve as the focus of energy trade. But more precisely the nexus of oil exports will increasingly focus on the Persian Gulf Region, where five countries—Saudi Arabia, Kuwait, Iraq, Iran, and the United Arab Emirates—account for fully 75% of OPEC productive capacity.[4] The total exports of these five countries plus fellow Persian Gulf state Qatar exceeded 20 mb/d in 1979, a figure that represents about 2/3 of the oil entering the world market prior to the Iraq-Iran war. These exports satisfied 75% of Japan's imports, 60% of West Europe's, and 35% of U.S. purchases from abroad. As the chart #2 illustrates the Persian Gulf region possesses 2/3 of world proven oil reserves (80% of OPEC's) and this potential, viewed against minimal domestic requirements and supply constraints in other parts of the world, demonstrates the dominant role this area will play in global energy transfers.

Chart 1
REGIONAL OIL PRODUCTION, CONSUMPTION AND EXPORTS: 1979

Region	Production	Consumption	Exports/ Imports
Middle East	21.1	1.7	19.4
West Europe	1.8	14.3	− 12.5
United States	9.7	17.8	− 8.1
Japan	Negl.	5.2	− 5.2
China	2.2	1.9	0.3
USSR	11.4	8.3	3.1
East Europe	0.4	2.4	− 2.0

(All figures represent million b/d of oil)

Toward a COMECON Energy Crunch?

In April of 1980, CIA director Stansfield Turner forecasted that the USSR would become a net importer of oil by 1981.[5] The ramifications of the world's leading oil producer, and currently number two exporter, suddenly joining the competition for scarce resources are ominous. A deteriorating energy situation in the USSR would impact severely on the Soviet Union's domestic politico-economic growth and would have major repercussions on her foreign and defense policies as well.

Energy production in the USSR to date has been a bright spot in an otherwise dismal economic picture. The USSR is the world's number one producer of oil, will soon take over the top spot in natural gas, and leads the world in coal output. The Soviet Union is not only self-sufficient in energy, it has become a leading exporter of fuels. Moscow exports about 22% of its oil output, with two-thirds of that export destined for East Europe (about 1.8 mb/d in 1980) and most of the rest to the OECD countries for badly-needed hard currency. Natural gas sales, marginal to date, will accelerate rapidly after 1985.

In this decade the Soviet energy system will face increasing stress.[6] Demand growth will outpace incremental increases in production, costs of exploration, production, and transportation will increase tremendously, and requirements for advanced technology in the extraction and distribution of energy resources will multiply. Soviet technology is inadequate for the demands of the 1980's. In the petroleum field the USSR will need advanced seismic equipment for exploratory drilling, drilling rigs to probe into the deeper depths at which oil will be found in the future and for exploration in the off-shore areas, better drill bits, submersible pumps and gas lift and fluid lift equipment. To improve the production and distribution of natural gas the Soviets will need wide-diameter pipelines, compressors and geophysical exploratory equipment. Imported technology could also help in other areas, such as coal excavators and slurry pipelines. Another major deficiency will be credits and capital, considerable quantities of which are needed to overcome the urgent Soviet requirement for investment that a stagnating economy cannot provide.

Brezhnev has given credence to the somber appraisals of the Soviet energy future published in the West, declaring energy a major priority issue in the current five-year plan period. The Soviet energy prospectus is analyzed at length in other papers presented in this volume, so I will not belabor the obvious. In brief, however, it appears to me that the Soviet planning targets in this Five-Year plan period are quite ambitious. Oil production is slated for a slight rise above the 12 mb/d present level and gas production is targeted for a 45% increase over 1980's performance, and both targets are optimistic to say the least. Coal production will continue its dismal performance to date and much of that output will be the cheaper lignite coals of Siberia which must be transported great distances.[7] An alternative development could be the conversion of the brown coal to electricity on the spot and which would then be distributed great distances over extra-high voltage lines (2250 KV) to consuming centers—a technological marvel if it can be done.[8] Finally, Soviet planners expect a surge in nuclear power production in the European regions, but the targets are likely to be underfilled by at least 30% due to the current slow pace of the construction program of the nuclear plant components.

Even assuming that the Soviet Union reaches its planned targets for energy production for 1985, the leadership faces a major dilemma. The USSR currently exports oil and gas to the industrial countries of the West, sales that generate over 50% of its hard-currency earnings. In view of Moscow's extensive debt to the West, these sales are vital and must be maintained so that the Soviet Union can import grain and technology. Without these purchases the Soviet standard of living would deteriorate and overall economic growth would be severely hampered. Exports to East Europe account for the lion's share of Soviet sales abroad, but to restrict these deliveries would force the Bloc countries to a greater dependence on the world market and thereby loosen the Kremlin's hold on East Europe. Perhaps even more important than these two centers of demand are the domestic requirements where continued increases in energy supplies are a prerequisite for the achievement of sustained economic growth.[9]

While the situation in the USSR presents difficulties, the other COMECON countries are immersed in the depths of an energy quagmire. Eastern Europe is substantially less endowed with energy resources than the Soviet Union. With the exception of Romania, none of the Bloc countries have significant oil or gas reserves. East European energy production is centered primarily on coal, which accounts for 80% of their total energy production, 40% of which is mined in Poland. The East European countries as a whole are dependent on external sources for approximately 25% of their energy requirements, but must import 80% of their petroleum and 40% of their natural gas consumption.

In the 1980's the USSR, which traditionally has covered most of the Bloc petroleum shortfall at very favorable prices, has indicated that deliveries will not be increased over 1980 levels. East Europe will be paying world prices in hard currency to OPEC producers to satisfy a growing percentage of their energy requirements. However, since the East European countries will find it difficult to generate exports to hard currency areas to cover these purchases, imports may have to be curtailed. The likely result is reduced economic growth which in turn could lead to social unrest and political instability.

Even under the most optimistic scenario the USSR will not be able to simultaneously satisfy domestic demand, meet East European requirements, and provide sufficient volumes to the export sector needed to generate hard currency earnings to offset grain and technology imports. Considered as a whole the COMECON countries will probably become net importers of petroleum by 1985. This energy dilemma will exacerbate an existing hard-currency crisis. The Bloc countries as a whole are deeply in debt to the West, an estimated $77 billion at the end of 1980, up from $70 billion the year before and $58.5 billion in 1978.[10] The limits of Western credit would seem to have been reached, indicating a probable reduction of purchases from abroad for all of the Bloc countries.

The net result of import reductions from the West and decreased provisions of energy to Soviet domestic (industrial) consumers will combine to hamper the prospects for economic growth in this decade. Reductions in energy deliveries to East Europe will weaken Soviet leverage over the Bloc and possibly lead to political instability. Loss of the lucrative hard currency earning exports will force the USSR to attempt to secure supplies of feedgrains and high technology by persuasion and coercion. At this juncture it is difficult to predict the route the Kremlin will pursue, but we should not dismiss the possibility that these economic difficulties could persuade the leadership to follow a more conciliatory line in international politics, particularly if it were made clear that such a shift in national security policy were a prerequisite to increased economic intercourse with the West. Finally, the OECD countries must take cognizance of the likelihood that the decline in the rate of growth of COMECON energy production will result in fewer supplies reaching the world market, an upward pressure on world oil prices, greater political leverage for the remaining oil exporters, and a potential for superpower confrontation over access to energy resources.

The Western Energy Crisis: America and her Allies at the Brink

American energy consumption has been growing at a steady 5-6% rate annually and today our per-capita energy use is six times the world average. With only 6% of the population we account for 16% of total world energy production, but consume 34% of the output. The USA was self-sufficient in its energy balance until 1950 and was still 90% self-reliant until 1970, but in the last decade that figure has dropped to 80%. Domestic crude oil production peaked in 1970 and consumption of natural gas has exceeded the discovery of new reserves since 1968. Coal production remains at 1940 levels, nuclear power development is beset by a host of environmental, safety, and cost considerations, and synthetic fuels are unlikely to make a significant contribution to the energy balance until the 1990's.

The United States now imports about one-half of its oil requirements. That figure is likely to increase in this decade despite intensive conservation and substitution efforts, due to rapidly declining level of proven reserves. The USA has come to rely more and more on the Arab oil exporters, but has managed to maintain a commendable diversification in its suppliers. As chart #3 demonstrates, no one country provides the U.S. with more than 19% of its oil imports. The USA is still the world's leading producer of natural gas, but declining reserves will soon force the USA to look increasingly to foreign suppliers.

While the American energy picture is discouraging, that facing many of the Allies is even bleaker. Only a few of the OECD countries today are energy self-sufficient and most are heavily dependent on foreign suppliers to satisfy their requirements. The situation is especially tight in the oil sector where most of the countries import over 75% of their needs and the sources of these supplies are concentrated in the Persian Gulf area.

Japan, for example, imports 88% of its energy, including all of its oil. West Germany buys abroad all but 5% of its oil and these imports account for just over half of the FRG's total energy requirements. France has a similar oil import dependence at 95%, but purchases fully 75% of all energy from abroad. The United Kingdom and Norway have provided a bright respite in this otherwise strained picture as the North Sea oil production has brought both countries to energy self-sufficiency, at least temporarily. As a whole the OECD countries today import about 2/3 of their petroleum requirements and these purchases account for approximately half of their total energy demand.

As noted earlier the IEA forecases an oil shortfall of up to 6 million barrels a day by 1985. Representatives of the IEA countries and France pledged at Venice (1980) to initiate an intensive campaign designed to reduce the Allied dependence on oil, specifically to decrease oil's contribution to the energy balance from 53% today to 40% in 1990. The means to achieve this end were intensive conservation measures, increased attempts to improve energy efficiency (over the 1:1 previously accepted ratio between energy production and GNP growth), building more nuclear power stations, and, especially, by doubling the use of coal.[12]

If this ambitious proposal is implemented, West Europe and Japan should be able to sharply reduce overall oil consumption and hold imports constant. However, imports of natural gas are likely to expand five-fold in the next two decades, emanating primarily from the Middle East and the USSR, and coal imports will expand four times in the same period.

By way of review the international energy outlook and the prognosis for the Allies' future energy balances are not encouraging. Reduced petroleum supplies will be delivered to the world market and the number of nations capable of exporting significant quantities will also decrease, leaving the Persian Gulf region to plan an even more critical role than it has today. The deteriorating energy situation in the COMECON countries will cause a further tightening in the global petroleum market, although Soviet exports of natural gas will begin to take up some of the slack by the second half of this decade. In the interim, however, the danger of conflict over access to oil supplies between the "Socialist and Capitalist Camps" will increase. Finally, the growing dependence of the Allies on energy imports in the face of a tighter global market will strain traditional bonds and possibly lead to increased divisiveness over foreign policy issues, particularly the issue of relations with the Soviet Union.

EAST-WEST ENERGY RELATIONS: THE ALLIANCE DIVERGES

In the last ten years the Western Alliance has experienced a number of wrenching problems that have challenged the viability of both the formal and informal bonds between the industrialized democracies. This trend toward disintegration of unanimity is probably no more evident than it is with respect to energy trade with the Soviet Union and the question of establishing a common commercial policy toward the Eastern bloc. This section will contrast the impasse that has developed in Soviet-American trade, which evolved following a promising start at the beginning of the last decade, with the flourishing commercial relationship that has developed between the other· Western nations and the COMECON countries.

Energy and the Soviet-American Relationship in Perspective

Trade between the United States and the Soviet Union has never approached a level where these sales have had a significant macro-impact on either economy. One is struck, in fact, by the surprisingly small volume of goods involved in US-USSR trade, a level that is far below what might be expected to occur between the two nations whose combined GNP's constitute 40% of the world's total output. Still, despite the relatively small trade turnover between the two superpowers, the importance of these sales should not be underestimated. For the Soviet Union the purchases have meant the opportunity to secure items critical to plan success, especially feedgrains and high technology manufactures. To the United States the commercial importance of the bilateral trade has been minimal, but the political significance of the exports as a means of reflecting American policy toward the USSR has transcended the low volume of the sales.

The Soviet Union appears to be gradually abandoning its earlier trade philosophy. In an attempt to achieve self-sufficiency in the economic arena in the Stalin era the Kremlin utilized the foreign trade sector as a means of solving particular "bottlenecks" in the economy, trading sufficient raw materials to cover the cost of purchases of certain high-technology products. More recently the USSR seems to have moved perceptively away from Stalin's demand for economic autarchy and entered the world market on the basis of economic calculations. However, the Soviet Union certainly has not allowed its economy to respond solely to the dictates of international comparative advantage, preferring to view foreign trade primarily as a useful foreign policy tool.

Indeed, while the volume of the USSR's trade turnover has certainly grown impressively, partially due to higher domestic prices, the foreign trade sector remains an instrument of state policy. Its primary task is to secure goods from abroad that are urgently needed to shore up the stagnating economy. In many respects the search for a "technological infusion" from the West represents a last-gasp attempt to avoid instituting the far-reaching economic reforms and structural modifications urgently required to revitalize the Soviet system.[13] In this sense the expansion of East-West trade in the 1970's is best explained as a concerted effort to secure a technological "quick-fix" and the commodities the USSR is simply unable to produce in sufficient quantities. Foreign trade temporarily alleviates the necessity of revamping the economically regressive but politically useful "command economy".

In the late 1960's the Soviet Union turned to the foreign trade sector to fulfill a national security imperative—obtaining high-technology goods and agricultural products from the West, particularly from the largest capitalist power, the USA. At this same time American policy-makers were conducting a review of their post-war commercial attitude, a reappraisal toward the USSR that brought a termination of a "denial" trade policy and the active promotion of greater economic intercourse with the Soviets. In 1949 the United States had adopted a policy of overtly seeking to retard the economic growth of Soviet power, an attitude embodied in both the Export Control Act (ECA) of that year and the establishment in cooperation with the Allies of a Coordinating Committee (COCOM) tasked with administering multilateral trade restrictions.

As the "Era of Detente" blossomed the USA reversed its stance and eliminated most of the controls on trade with the USSR. The 1969 ECA, in fact, was designed to promote trade in general and with the Communist countries in particular. The Act terminated most of the export restrictions, although goods with potential military application were still under embargo. Expanded trade would not only alleviate American balance of payments problems, provide a spur to economic growth, and improve our access to a greater range of raw materials, but could be instrumental in mitigating aggressive Soviet behavior in the international political arena. Mark Miller has indicated that a further objective of enhanced trade relations was that we anticipated a siphoning of resources away from the defense sector in the USSR, more attention devoted to consumer goods, and ultimately, the "enmeshing of the Soviet Union in a web of economic interdependencies with the capitalist world" leading to behavior more conducive to global cooperation.[14]

In the euphoria generated by the Nixon-Brezhnev meeting in 1972 the USA and the USSR signed two agreements in the energy field. The 1973 "Atomic Energy Agreement" pledging cooperation in the production of electricity from nuclear fuels and the 1974 overall "Energy Agreement" covering numerous areas of energy information and research exchanges were promulgated with high expectations. The American objectives were to bring about a further relaxation of tensions and to enhance access to information, facilities, and specialists. The Soviets appeared to be primarily interested in obtaining sophisticated technology and "know-how" from the U.S.

None of the 17 projects initiated under the Agreements, with the possible exception of the MHD program, has exhibited any forward movement.[15] The American side has been especially disappointed in the Soviet failure to provide data required by the energy information and forecasting aspects of the agreements. These statistics are needed in order to permit a better understanding of the future Soviet impact on world energy markets, to engage Soviet experts on energy economics and to discuss the security implications involved in shifting global energy patterns. Although the agreements have not been terminated there is little of substance occurring today under this rubic of energy cooperation.

The Soviet Union clearly had greater expectations for energy cooperative ventures with the West. Of particular interest to Moscow was the acquisition of credits, capital, and manufactures that might alleviate anticipated or emerging problems in the energy sector. On a macro scale the Kremlin hoped to entice the West into participating in a series of mammoth energy schemes designed to exploit Siberian resources. Moscow especially sought advanced energy equipment, such as deep seismic exploration equipment, secondary and tertiary recovery methods, wide-diameter pipelines, and computerized information-processing equipment. The Soviet proposals were designed to secure Western financing (repaid over long terms at very favorable rates or by compensation from future energy production), the transfer of technology and know-how, and access to Western-style managerial expertise.

In retrospect some of the Soviet proposals for energy cooperation are astounding in their scope. At the heart of the cooperative schemes lay a desire to establish an all-European energy complex with the USSR as the resource base, a complex which would be rapidly developed with the assistance of Western credits, capital, and technology.[16] The Soviet Union raised the possibility of several joint ventures involving West European, Japanese, and American participation. The two most well-known were the "Yakutia" LNG project and the "North Star" proposal. The "Yakutia" scheme focused on East Siberia and envisioned a consortium of American and Japanese companies developing the region's gas potential with a portion of the output destined for Japan and the U.S. West coast. "North Star" called for the cooperation of the United States and some West European partners in exploiting the West Siberian fields, with gas shiped as LNG to Europe and the American East Coast.[17]

For a myriad of reasons none of these projects has gotten off the ground. Economic and political issues were raised on both sides of the fence. The Soviets exhibited some hesitancy in accepting a Western presence as well as a reluctance to export Siberian fuels that might alleviate the Western energy crisis. On the other side the United States and her Allies have been dubious of the economic viability of the projects themselves, wary of the huge initial investment required, reluctant to offer the highly attractive financing preferred by the USSR, concerned over the hard currency debt possessed by the Eastern Bloc that casts a shadow over their ability to repay the loans, and worried about the long break between investment and return. The "compensation" agreements, calling as they do for massive initial investments from the West in return for a share of the production in the future, create a dependency on Soviet whims to adhere to the agreement.[18]

These ambitious projects are in limbo now and there is little prospect for their immediate revival, although contemporary schemes such as the West Siberian pipeline project now set to go forward certainly can be regarded as "Son of North Star". The earlier schemes floundered when Japan and the European partners were unwilling to commit themselves to these cooperative ventures without the security protection that the participation of the USA implied. Further, the financing requirements were so extensive that these projects could not be undertaken without government guarantees and encouragement. Although initially this was a realistic prospect, the American side placed limits on the level of its potential involvement with the Jackson-Vanik and Stevenson restrictions on credits and guarantees.[19]

A genuine commitment to these massive schemes could only have come after the United States developed its own coherent, long-range national energy policy and a clear position with respect to Soviet-American energy cooperation. Neither of these were present, and as detente began to fade these energy projects went into a state of limbo.

In the last few years the United States has shifted away from an active promotion of trade with the Soviet Union towards a policy of selective denial and the increasing tendency to use exports as an instrument of national security policy. The change in attitude was driven by several factors, including the disappointment over the Soviet failure to reallocate resources away from the defense sector, the rapid expansion and modernization of the Soviet armed forces, human rights violations in the USSR and a reluctance to permit emigration by repressed minorities, and a growing Soviet assertiveness in the Third World.

According to former National Security Council official Sam Huntington, the Carter Administration began to consider the potential represented by American exports to the USSR as a foreign policy tool soon after the 1976 election. In the controversial Presidential Decision #18 (PD-18) document, the President, according to Huntington, declared that.[20]

> ... the United States must take advantage of its economic
> strength and technological superiority to encourage Soviet
> cooperation in resolving conflicts, reducing tensions, and
> achieving adequately verifiable arms control agreements.

Huntington's thesis received considerable publicity following an address delivered at West Point in June of 1978, calling for increased discretion for the President in promoting or impeding trade with the Soviets.[21] Huntington argued that Congressional restrictions such as Jackson Vanik and Stevenson Amendments only tied the President's hands and prevented him from fully utilizing the "carrot" aspect of the American trade potential. On the other hand, he noted, the Executive must have the authority to place export controls on deliveries to the Soviets when Soviet actions or policies were inimical to U.S. interests.

The controversy over the integration of national security and trade policies erupted within the U.S. government. Although the President had the authority by virtue of the 1969 Export Control Act to "use export controls to the extent necessary to further significantly the foreign policy of the U.S.", there was little unanimity over the wisdom of utilizing such restrictions to punish the USSR. The Commerce and State Departments, in particular, questioned the "growing tendency for the United States to deny trade as a political gesture" as Commerce Secretary Juanita Kreps phrased it.[22] The effect of trade embargoes was further hampered by the demonstrated unwillingness of America's Allies to accord the same importance to Soviet activities, or to impede trade which was of considerably greater importance to them than it was to the United States.

The revision of American trade policy, in particular the perception that exports which could enhance the Soviet capability to exploit their energy resources could be politically useful, came in the wake of some rather pessimistic assessments of the USSR's energy prospectus published by the CIA (or vice-versa as some critics have alleged!) These studies forecast severe difficulties for the Soviets in the extraction and distribution of its fossil-fuel resources, particularly in the petroleum sector.[23] The CIA focused attention on the Soviet inability to build sufficient wide-diameter gas pipelines, to exploit oil reserves located at greater depths and in extremely inhospitable climes, and to locate potential hydrocarbon fields that could offset the expected decline in the most prolific deposits. The idea that the Soviet Union would be turning to the West for assistance in the form of technology, investment, and credits in order to successfully develop its energy potential raised the prospect of the USSR being vulnerable to "linkage politics."

When Moscow decided to try dissidents Anatoli Shcharansky and Alexander Ginzburg for spying in the summer of 1978, a new impetus was given to the forces arguing for the implementation of export restrictions. The President initially decided to cancel approval to Dresser Industries to export a drill bit plant to the USSR, but reversed this decision in September. The decision was made against the insistence of senior NSC officials and the Defense and State Departments, but with the support of State, Commerce, and influential business circles.

The issue lay dormant until the Soviet invasion of Afghanistan in late 1979. An angry President Carter quickly issued an executive order suspending any new high technology (and grain) sales to the USSR and in February, 1980, officially prohibited American companies from selling the Soviet Union the technology and expertise that would permit them to produce their own equipment. This "presumption of denial" on technology, however, did not apply to end-products; i.e., the equipment for use in energy exploitation and distribution could be exported but the technology to produce this equipment could not.[24] The utility of the trade restrictions will be examined later in this paper following a look at Soviet trade with other OECD nations and the vulnerability of the USSR to commercial disruptions.

Shifting Patterns of East-West Trade: Contrasts in Western Commercial Policies Toward the USSR

While the United States has imposed several economic and political limitations on trade with the Soviet Union the Allies have been generally less inclined to invoke trade restrictions. As a consequence Soviet trade turnover with the other OECD countries has expanded much faster than it has with the United States.

As noted earlier American trade with the USSR has been far below what might be expected from the two largest economic powers. Neither the USSR nor the USA is a major trading nation (trade turnover as a percentage of GNP being the measure) and their economic intercourse only accounts for 1% of total U.S. foreign trade and 5% of the Soviet Union's. In the five-year period following the consecration of detente in 1972 trade turnover accelerated 400%. Following a drastic dip in 1977 trade again jumped in 1978 by 50% and another 32% over the previous year in 1979. Trade figures are incomplete for 1980 but the post-Afghanistan imposition of export controls will certainly lead to a dramatic falling off in this trade.

The graph (Chart 4) below demonstrates the pattern of Soviet-American trade over the last decade. As the chart indicates, the export of agricultural products, principally feedgrains, have dominated American exports to the USSR, with energy related products a minor contributor. Imports from the Soviet Union have been dispersed rather evenly, with manufactured goods accounting for about a third of the sales. Moscow exported only limited quantities of oil to the United States, none after 1978. The terms of trade have clearly benefitted the United States which has sold the USSR roughly seven times the dollar amount of the goods which it has purchased from the Soviets.[25]

While Soviet-American trade has clearly languished in the last five years trade between the OECD countries and the Socialist camp has flourished. As Chart 5 shows there has been a constant upward swing in trade turnover between the Socialist countries and the developed Western nations (less the USA). The European Community plus Japan now accounts for 60% of total Soviet imports. Ironically, the two leading exporters to the USSR in 1978 were the United States and Germany, each accounting for 20% of all exports to the USSR.

There are, however, some rather significant elements of divergence in the nature of the trade that is conducted by the United States with the Soviet Union and that of the other OECD countries with the USSR. First, the Allies have a more even trade balance with Moscow, importing just 9% less than they export, in contrast to Washington's highly favorably balance with the USSR. More importantly, the main feature (prior to 1980) of the American commercial relationship with the USSR was the domination of the trade turnover by American sales of feedgrains and the virtual absence of energy purchases from the Soviet Union. The non-U.S. industrialized countries, in contrast, provide the USSR with manufactured goods primarily and receive significant amounts of energy supplies in turn. Three-fourths of the Soviet Union's exports to the industrialized West are composed of fuel supplies and crude materials, with energy deliveries alone representing 60% of the total export value in 1979.

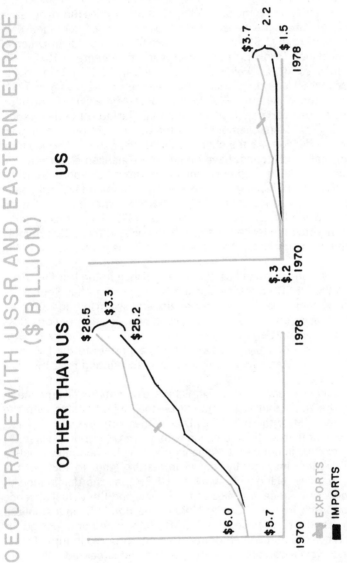

OECD TRADE WITH USSR AND EASTERN EUROPE
($ BILLION)

US

OTHER THAN US

EXPORTS
IMPORTS

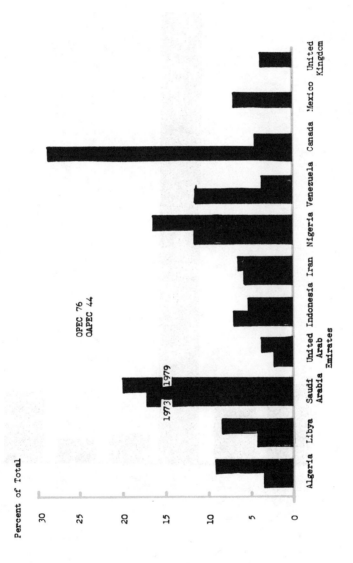

UNITED STATES: CRUDE OIL IMPORTS BY SOURCE

Percent of Total

OPEC 76
OAPEC 44

1973   1979

Algeria   Libya   Saudi   United   Indonesia   Iran   Nigeria   Venezuela   Canada   Mexico   United
                  Arabia   Arab   Kingdom
                           Emirates

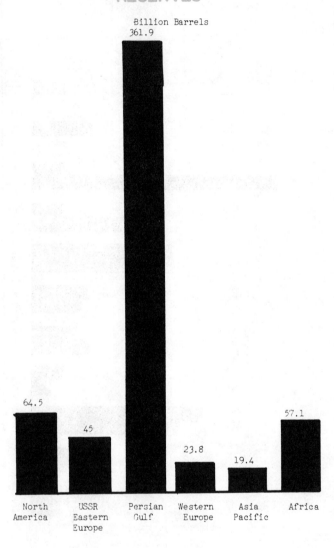

OIL LOCATION OF WORLD PROVEN
RESERVES

Billion Barrels
361.9

64.5

45

23.8

19.4

57.1

| North America | USSR Eastern Europe | Persian Gulf | Western Europe | Asia Pacific | Africa |

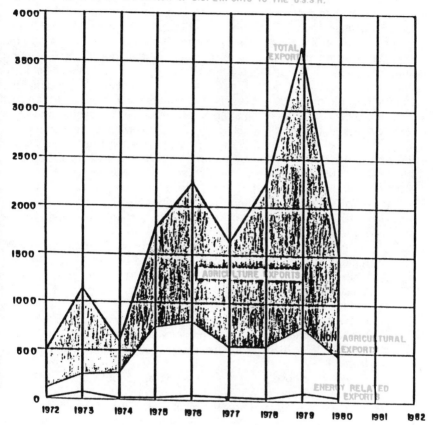

ENERGY AS A PORTION OF U.S. EXPORTS TO THE U.S.S.R.

According to the International Energy Agency the USSR now exports about one million barrels of oil a day to West Europe, about 7½% of the region's consumption.[26] West Germany depended on the USSR for 8% of its petroleum, France 5%, Italy 4%, and Greece over 12%. With the expected decline in Soviet oil production in this decade and surging domestic and East European requirements, these scales should begin to turn down. However, exports of natural gas are expected to expand rapidly, especially in the mid 1980's following the probable completion of the West Siberian pipeline. Europe was able to supply 97% of its own gas requirements in 1970 but only 86% by 1978, and imports will continue to account for a growing share.[27] By 1985 some one-third of the EEC's gas demand might have to be met by imports, a figure that could rise to 80% by the year 2000.[28] Increasingly the Soviet Union will be viewed as an attractive supplier of this gas.

Exports of energy extraction and distribution equipment from the non-U.S. OECD countries have accounted for a substantial share of the sales. As a recent Congressional study summarized.[29]

> . . . while the issue of technology transfer to Communist nations is a matter of controversy in the United States, such debate is virtually nonexistant in Japan and most West European countries . . . For a variety of reasons, America's European and Japanese allies do not necessarily share its concern over the economic and security problems raised by the trade and technology transfer to Eastern Europe, the USSR, and the People's Republic of China (PRC).

West Germany, whose foreign trade accounts for 30% of its GNP, has tended to promote exports without much concern over their destination. Indeed, trade has been limited only marginally by political factors and would probably be even greater today if the Eastern Bloc had the financial capability to expand this volume. Today the FRG is the largest single supplier of technology to the Soviet Union accounting for one-third of all Russian high-technology imports.[30] France maintains a similar "laissez-faire" attitude toward technology sales to the Soviet Union, and like Germany, has actively promoted the sale of sophisticated energy-related equipment. In Japan export controls reflect purely economic concerns, and although Tokyo participates in the COCOM machinery, national security or human rights considerations have not affected trade. However, the Japanese have been reluctant to get involved in any of the Soviet-proposed joint developments projects in Siberia for fear of the political or strategic leverage that could accrue to the USSR.

The Soviet Union has consistently played on the theme that the Western Alliance has been split over the trade embargo and that such attempts are doomed to failure. Referring to the American "denial policy", one Soviet commentator noted.[31]

Everyone knows the ignominous end of that farce. The realistically minded business circles and governments of a number of West European countries disagreed with the notorious 'NATO Embargo' in the interests of developing mutually advantageous businesslike cooperation with the USSR and the other socialist community countries.

The Soviet observers have an obvious political axe to grind, but their comments should not be dismissed lightly. The divergence of views between the United States and its allies over the issue of commercial relations with the USSR reflects the reality of international energy trends, particularly the increasing dependence of the Western industrialized democracies on energy imports. It further mirrors the differing appraisals of the seriousness of Soviet initiatives in the Third World and the question of Moscow's ultimate intentions manifested in the rapid modernization and expansion of its military power. However, Allied policy on East-West energy approaches is only one of a number of issues that will impact on the national security policy of the United States and other Western democracies. In the final section of this paper I will delineate a range of energy-related issues that will need to be addressed in the 1980's, and offer some proposals that might serve as a preliminary step toward the solution of these problems.

ENERGY AND THE EAST-WEST RELATIONSHIP: ISSUES FOR THE EIGHTIES

Energy issues have been raised in a national security context before, but the emergent trends in the international energy market will accord growing importance to these problems and demand the increased attention of our foreign-policy decision-makers. Questions of technology transfer and the security of energy supplies have already generated considerable concern. While these familiar issues will persist in this decade they will be augmented by a series of energy-related national security problems that have as yet not aroused great interest. This section will look at the policy implications of a series of these issues, including the debate over the application of Western economic leverage on the Eastern Bloc, the less-discussed opposite side of that question dealing with the potential for Soviet economic leverage based primarily on the USSR's energy exports, the implications of energy policies on Alliance cohesion (East and West), and the significance of Brezhnev's proposals for the convening of two "energy summits" dealing with the guarantee of Persian Gulf security and the call for an all-European "High Level Energy Conference".

Economic Leverage and Western "Linkage Politics"

The United States and most of the Western industrialized democracies have traditionally rejected the notion of utilizing a country's economic potential as a means of furthering the narrow interests of the state. Such a "mercantilist" approach runs counter to the "liberal" form of political economy characteristic of most of the developed countries. Still, the imperatives of foreign and defense policies have in the past led to a periodic inclusion of economic power as an instrument of national security policy, although long-term programs integrating commercial and security concerns are rare. The desirability of employing economic capabilities in a security matrix has been given new impetus recently as the United States searches for more effective instruments to employ in its competitive relationship with the Soviet Union.

Economic leverage is generally viewed in a pejorative context as a means of "punishing" an adversary, but this instrument has often been employed in a positive vein by rewarding "good behavior" with access to our commercial and financial capabilities. As noted earlier in this paper the United States has followed both paths in its dealings with the Soviet Union, pursuing a "denial" policy akin to economic warfare until the late 1960's in which we overtly attempted to impede Soviet economic growth, followed by a shift to the use of our economic largesse to integrate the USSR in a "web of interdependencies." Which direction the USA should pursue in the 1980's is the subject of intense debate in the country today and the question of the transfer of energy-related technology to the USSR has emerged as the focal point of the dispute.

This paper is not the place to raise anew the whole debate over technology transfer. The literature is prolific on the subject[32] and the issue received considerable attention at the 1976 NATO Conference on "East-West Technological Cooperation".[33] I will simply attempt at this point to review the essence of the argument, stressing the energy-related questions involved. The key sub-issues are first the normative aspect, "Should We Attempt to Employ Energy Leverage Against the Soviets?"; secondly, "Is the USSR Vulnerable to Economic Persuasion?"; and finally, "Can Linkage Politics Actually Work?" Assuming American technological and financial assistance could have a significant impact on Soviet energy development should the U.S. government restrict or encourage such participation? On the other hand the argument could be made that this assistance could be instrumental in stabilizing world energy markets, promoting East-West interdependence, and mitigating potential Soviet aggressive behavior. A counterpoint would stress that the U.S. should not attempt to promote the economic viability of an archaic and hostile social system and should actively work to impede Soviet economic growth.

Opponents of controls on exports (except for distinctly military-related goods) argue that the basic interests of the United States are better served by the promotion of long-term cooperation. Trade between the U.S. and the USSR is beneficial to both sides: the USA could alleviate its balance of payments deficit by the export of grain surpluses and high-technology manufactures and the USSR could sell fuel to the energy-starved West in order to gain badly-needed hard currency. Such a relationship is in consonance with the American desire to enhance exports in general and promotes the long-term certainty essential for profitable business relationships. At any rate, they indicate, economic sanctions could achieve their objectives only in a situation where the USSR was highly dependent on American exports or if the controls were universally applied   virtually an impossible event given the Allied unwillingness to share Washington's inclination to view economic power as a security instrument. Thus, application of sanctions will merely place the Americans outside of a lucrative marketplace, raise costs to the USSR but not enough to cause any fundamental policy changes, and fuse any divisions within the Soviet leadership that might exist as the Politburo "rallies around the flag."[34]

Specifically, with respect to the energy trade, this argument contends that the United States has a direct interest in the Soviets succeeding in Siberia. Maintaining a high level of oil production in the USSR will insure a diversification of suppliers on the world market, alleviate the upward pressure on global petroleum prices, and serve as a moderating force on Soviet agressiveness by giving the Kremlin the prospect of gaining substantial rewards from the export of energy supplies; that is, a stake in the system.[35] Finally, there is a danger that the Soviets will meet their oil production plans no matter where they have to find the petroleum. As Giovanni Agnelli surmises in a recent *Foreign Affairs* article.[36]

> Any policy that seeks to reduce the Soviet Union's access
> to energy at home practically invites the Red Army to the
> Persian Gulf and constitutes an added danger to our
> security and our welfare.

Proponents of exercising restrictions on American trade with the USSR are of two minds, one group positing that no economic intercourse at all should be permitted with the United States' major adversary (complete denial) while another coterie of national security specialists calls for the selective use of export controls to serve political objectives. The first school contends that America must question the utility of transferring technology that could create a more formidable contender in world politics. They would argue that the USA has no interest in attempting to solve the contradictions inherent in the Soviet system and the Communists simply ought to be left to wallow in their own economic morass. America, by denying the USSR the means of postponing significant economic reform, can accelerate the process of change in the Soviet Union, although it is not clear that such a shift would necessarily lead to liberalization and reform. Further, any assistance given to the Soviets today not only alleviates the necessity of implementing reform, but precludes the necessity of reallocating resources away from the defense sector toward the solving of their energy crisis. This argument also holds that there are particular dangers in assisting the USSR in the energy arena. Continued high levels of Soviet energy production promotes the capability of the USSR to continue current levels of exports to Eastern Europe and thereby retain a major means of leverage over the Bloc. Further, Soviet proposals for joint economic ventures discussed earlier involve extensive Western investment and technology transfer at the front end with the tenuous promise of repayment sometime in the future by a share of the production. These "compensation" deals create a vested interest in Soviet benevolence and foster dependencies on the USSR for energy deliveries, since turning the spigot off or down would have significant impacts on industrial productivity.

Proponents of the selective application of controls argue against unlimited participation in Soviet energy development, but in favor of governmental oversight of foreign involvement and the promotion of private and public assistance when certain political conditions have been met. This argument relies heavily on the assumption that American involvement in Soviet economic development is perceived in Moscow as highly desirable and necessary. If this is the case, then the sophisticated application of export controls and financial assistance would persuade the USSR to moderate its aggressive foreign policy behavior and mitigate its repressive internal policies. Successful employment of this technique depends not only on Soviet vulnerability but on the capability of the American government to implement and conduct such a sophisticated policy package and the cooperation of alternative suppliers.

On the first point, that of Soviet dependence on American technology transfers and financial aid, the evidence is mixed. Although the question is often phrased in the context of "technology transfer", referring to the export of the knowledge required to design or implement a technical process or to utilize the system transferred, the definition is too narrow for the purposes of this paper. Economic leverage questions must include not only the technology transfer process, but the sale of end-use products, managerial expertise, and financial assistance.

Imports of Western technology into the Soviet Union have never been high and the overall impact on the economy has been minor. Still, Anthony Sutton has argued that the most important factor in the development of the Soviet economy has been the absorption of Western technology and skills.[37] Herb Levine and Donald Green support this conclusion, pointing out that while the macroeconomic magnitude of these transfers have been minor, exports of machinery to the USSR have played a prominent role in past Soviet economic development.[38] Their general conclusions are that crash purchases of Western manufactures have played a critical role in eliminating bottlenecks in the Soviet economy and have served to enhance factor productivity in certain key industries, such as chemicals. As Mark Miller concludes:[39]

> To recapitulate, the Soviet investment in Western technology is rather small, and the total impact on the Soviet economy is modest. At the same time, the effect of

Western technology on certain sectors has been substantial, raising both productivity and the quality of output. From this it can be concluded that in the Soviet schema, Western technology serves as a "Quick fix" for those industries that are most critical to the technological progress and basic strength of the Soviet economy.

In the 1970's the Soviets sought such a "quick-fix" to solve endemic problems in energy exploitation and distribution. They sought to alleviate, in particular, the bottlenecks that were developing in the secondary recovery of oil, the removal of water from petroleum fields, the short life and low quality of their drill bits, the lack of wide-diameter pipelines and compressors for use in transporting natural gas, the absence of reliable seismic equipment for locating new reserves, and the inability to drill off-shore or at great depths. The purchase of Western technology appears to have made a significant contribution to recent Soviet plan success in the energy sector, with the submersible pumps alone contributing as much as an extra one mb/d of oil themselves.[40] Former CIA Director Stansfield Turner testified that the Soviets will continue to require substantial imports of steel products (particularly large diameter pipeline for oil and gas distribution) and a "wide range of oil and gas technology".[41] The leading American expert on the Soviet energy system, Robert Campbell, agrees, and in his testimony to Congress last year concluded:[42]

In short, it is my belief that extensive import of Western equipment could seriously assist the USSR to break the bottlenecks that interfere with solving its energy stringency. I further believe that the USSR can obtain savings and other benefits from using this technology that would far exceed what it costs a world market prices. Our ability to provide or deny technology constitutes a significant leverage for us to use on the Soviet Union.

Campbell, it should be noted, does not advocate linkage politics in the context of economic warfare. He adds, in fact, that it is very much in the interest of USA that the Soviets continue to provide significant quantities of energy to the world market. Further, he stresses that USSR is not going to collapse in the absence of such technology. However, Campbell concludes, they can save time and resources by getting the technology from the West and such transfers are highly valued by Moscow.[43]

While I am substantial agreement with Professor Campbell, I would add that such potential leverage could only be effectively implemented if two other conditions were present. Since energy-related transfers of technology and products from the United States represent such a minor aspect of the total Soviet import package, not to mention a miniscule fraction of overall GNP, denial of these exports alone will only cause irritations in the Soviet hierarchy, not a reevaluation of policy. Therefore, to make an impact on the Kremlin, the controls should not be limited to energy products and knowhow, but include all U.S. experts (especially grain) and the provision of financial assistance. Secondly, since there are few technologies today that the United States produces that are unavailable from alternative sources export controls can only be effective in an Alliance context.

Equally important as energy technology to Soviet planners in achieving plan success is the acquisition of agricultural products, particularly feedgrains. Although the American grain embargo imposed after the invasion of Afghanistan suffered from many "leaks" and the refusal of some friendly nations to support the U.S. sanctions, the Soviets have had to scramble to obtain replacement supplies. No doubt that most of the grain can be purchased from other sources, but with the Americans providing 60% of the world's grain exports the USA is clearly the preferred place of purchase. Evasion of sanctions can be accomplished, but for the Soviets last year it was an expensive and time-consuming process.[44] It appears that another bleak harvest forecast for 1981 leads credence to the belief that the Soviets will be back in the world grain market again this year. To lift the grain embargo now without any positive change by the Kremlin would reduce any incentive for Moscow to modify its aggressive behavior in the international arena and impair what little leverage we have over the Soviet Union today. At a time of impending leadership change in the Kremlin it would be unwise to signal that we are prepared to return to a "business as usual" relationship.[45]

American and other Western financial power may be just as significant as technology and grain. As noted earlier in this paper, the Soviet energy development schemes are based on the assumption that massive capital investments, credits, and favorable repayment terms will be proferred by Western partners. At a time when the Communist Bloc is $71 billion in debt to the West the limits of financial assistance may seem to have been stretched. However, the Soviets recognize the necessity of continuing to strive to secure additional investment help from the West if the energy exploitation schemes, particularly the big Siberian ventures, are to be undertaken. A policy that integrated technology and grain sales with the financial strength of this country would have the best chance of influencing Soviet behavior.[46]

We should not be under any illusion that even a total integration of our commercial strength into a national security framework will keep the Soviets from pursuing what they consider to be their vital national interests. For example, the Kremlin probably viewed the collapse of the Afghan regime that seemed imminent in late 1979 as a genuine national security concern. Regardless of what conceivable response the West might make the Soviet leadership probably would have been willing to accept the "punishment" rather than see a country bordering on the USSR and located close to the critical Persian Gulf region fall into the "energy camp." In the past there have been certain unreasonable expectations generated by an inflated evaluation of the importance of our commercial contribution to the USSR. What a commercial policy as an integral part of our national security strategy could do, however, is to give our policy-makers the capability of responding to Soviet adventurism and repressive domestic actions at an appropriate level.

We must have the ability to respond flexibly to Moscow's initiatives, using our economic strength as a means of demonstrating displeasure when necessary but also capable of promoting positive developments in Soviet internal and foreign policies. This is the "carrot and stick" approach suggested by Prof. Huntington, whereby Washington and, hopefully, its Allies can persuade Soviet planners to consider the broad consequences of their actions in their strategic calculations. To forego this critical element of our national capabilities is to limit policy-makers to responding with rhetoric or military power. In terms of the contemporary military balance characterized by strategic "essential equivalence", conventional Soviet superiority in Central Europe, and a growing power projection capability possessed by Moscow, it is difficult to expect words or saber-rattling to be effective policy tools. By the same token there is no room for ambitious claims for such an integrated approach: the Soviet leadership is not going to chart its every move in fear of the retribution of American power or adjust each policy in order to gain some commercial advantage. It does suggest, however, that such a policy carried out comprehensively and subtly will cause the Soviets to consider the value of Western commercial cooperation into their strategic calculations.

And there is the rub. To be effective such a policy package would have to reflect a unanimity of opinion in influential American business and government circles, be administered in a flexible and highly sophisticated manner, and be implemented in an Alliance context. The experimentation with the application of export controls in the past few years does not lend itself to expansive claims with respect to these preconditions for success. The Alliance problem will be dealt with shortly, but a prerequisite for the successful use of controls and rewards is a demonstrated effective American capability to conduct these measures.[47]

Bureaucratic feuding in the U.S. government and a lack of high-level interest have impaired the effectiveness of the controls. Even where there have been strict sanctions imposed against the export of goods, the Soviet Bloc has managed to obtain many items by purchases from "Front Companies" and from U.S. firms seeking to evade the controls.[48] Leakage of technology through the Allies has also been pervasive and probably uncontrollable. In the American political system there is no clear opinion on the wisdom of implementing controls, with the opposition led by private firms with explicit interest in Soviet contracts,[49] and this division over policy has extended to the various government bureaucracies as well. The export control system itself is beset by administrative delays and a shortage of professionals on the strategic trade controls staffs.[50] The whole process has been impaired by the diffusion of responsibility for the formulation and implementation of controls, and, most importantly, by the absence of a well-defined, coherent commercial policy as an integral component of a comprehensive policy toward the Soviet Union.

And the Future Question of Soviet Leverage

While considerable attention has been directed to the question of Western leverage on the Soviet Union, the real issue by the end of this decade may very well be the degree of economic influence the USSR will be able to exercise over the capitalist world. This may seem to be a conclusion at odds with most of the evidence suggested in this paper earlier. The review of Soviet economic prospects painted a bleak picture—a stagnating rate of growth, poor labor and capital productivity, a living standard abysmal for a major industrialized country, and even the likelihood of an energy crunch on the horizon.

The issue of Soviet leverage is a real one that must be addressed even though it will not become a reality much before 1990. The Kremlin's future ability to exercise such influence lies in a combination of power manifested by the possession of "debtor leverage", probable domination of many strategic minerals markets, and what ironically may be a plethora of energy riches!

The debt question is quite interesting. At present the Soviet Bloc is in debt to the West for $77 billion, 80% of which is held by West Europe. Today the financial health of the USSR and its Allies, especially Poland, is quite important to several banking firms who have a vested interest in the maintenance of a relationship that does not endanger their extensive investments. There have been suggestions that if the United States were to impose further trade restrictions, the USSR would begin to default on its loan payments.[51] Thus far the Soviets have not attempted to play on whatever debtor leverage they have in view of the continuing requirements for more capital and credits. However, the overexposure of Western financial institutions in the Soviet Bloc could be utilized by the COMECON countries in the future, particularly by playing one creditor against another.

Another potential for future Soviet economic influence is the fact that the USSR is the most self-sufficient industrial power in terms of strategic minerals and, in fact, is a major supplier of precious metals to the West. It provides all of the West's palladium, is the world's second largest exporter of gold, and is a major supplier of chrome, manganese, titanium, and platinum. By itself this strategic minerals wealth is not threatening since there is a diversity of suppliers available for many of the items. In the future, the possession of these critical minerals in conjunction with energy fuels could leave the USSR as the world's primary resource base.

The real interesting potential, however, lies in the distant energy prospectus of the USSR. There is disagreement over the extent of the Soviet energy dilemma today, but most observers (including the Soviets) find that the USSR will not be able to continue to simultaneously satisfy all the claimants on its energy production. This situation, given the failure of Soviet planners to identify and begin exploitation on any new supergiant oil field, will continue through this decade. After 1990, however, it may be quite a different story.

Most estimates of global petroleum exhaustion predict a depletion of presently economically recoverable proved oil reserves by the year 2005, or sooner if growth rates are not curbed. The Economic Commission for Europe (ECE) in a 1978 reassessment of economically recoverable fossil fuels accords the USSR an unusually prestigious position. According to the ECE the Soviet Union currently possesses 15% of the world's proven coal reserves, 12% of the oil, and 37% of global natural gas reserves.[52] What is even more significant is that while most of the regions of the world have probably identified the vast percentage of what will ever be "proved" (except for off-shore deposits), the USSR has only begun to tap its potential riches.

Studies by geologists indicate that West Siberia in particular is potentially the world's richest reservoir of hydrocarbon reserves.[53] Others have indicated that as many as 50 giant fields will ultimately be identified there. The Southern Komi area, Krasnoyarsk, Central Siberia, and off-shore regions (particularly in the Arctic) are equally promising. An article in *Leningradskaya Pravda* early in 1981 confirms this optimism, indicating that "the main oil discoveries in West Siberia will be made in the future". "Nature has hidden her riches", the article continues, but leaves no doubt that the geological structure promises enormous riches.[54] And while the long-range oil picture is bright, that for natural gas, with the USSR holding 35% of the world's reserves, will begin paying dividends even sooner.

Thus after 1990 the West will increasingly feel the pressure to respond to Soviet coercive and persuasive measures. When one considers the potential power represented by this future energy and mineral wealth and the growing dependence of Western nations on Soviet deliveries, coupled with the capabilities inherent in the rapidly-expanding Soviet military machine, the combination is indeed impressive. What would happen if the Kremlin ever got its act together, rationalized the archaic command economy, instituted political and economic reforms designed to reinvigorate popular support and initiative, and brought in a younger generation of leaders prepared to exploit the strategic and economic power of the USSR?

Energy in the Alliance: A Factor for Cohesion or Disintegration?

The potential for leverage in the future represented by Soviet energy deliveries was suggested early in 1981 when natural gas distribution from the USSR to West Germany and Austria were curtailed. Although the cutbacks had no apparent political manifestation and was the result of supply difficulties, the shortages raised again the wisdom of increasing European dependence on Soviet gas deliveries. As of late 1981, a consortium of West European industries and credit institutions had completed its negotiations with the Soviets over the construction of a 3,000 mile pipeline from West Siberia to the Western border of the USSR. Construction of the line will enable the Soviet Union to increase gas deliveries to Europe 300% by 1985 if construction were to begin today. The pipeline project will be a test case for Allied energy policy toward the USSR and the forum and manner in which the project is debated will be reflective of unity or disunity in the Western nations.

The energy issue will introduce additional strains between America and her Allies. Doubts over the reliability of the U.S. commitment to defend Europe, allied disinterest in participating in sanctions against Iran and the Soviet Union following the hostage seizure and the invasion of Afghanistan, differences over policy approaches to the Arab-Israeli dispute, North-South relations, and defense burden-sharing have led to an erosion of unity within the Allied camp. In this decade the issues that will appear on the Allied discussion agendas will increasingly deal with energy problems—the degree of dependence on Soviet exports that can be tolerated, transfer of technology to the COMECON countries, Persian Gulf security, and competition for increasingly scarce oil supplies.

International energy trends would seem to portend increasing dissension within the Alliance. As noted earlier the United States, Japan, and West Europe imported over 90% of the oil traded internationally in 1979. With domestic production declining and demand holding constant or increasing, considered against the reduction in oil availability in this decade, the Allies are going to be in growing competition for scarce resources. Although the International Energy Agency has devised an emergency import-sharing program to be initiated in case of a sudden downturn in supplies, the efficiency of the plan has not been tested. Dissension amongst the Allies in 1973 over American landing rights in Europe needed to support Israel in the Mid-East War and the scramble that ensued in 1978-79 as the major importers engaged in panic buying to insure their own supplies following the fall of the Shah are not good precedents for the import-sharing program.

The Europeans and Japanese are disturbed over the huge American energy appetite, where 6% of the world's population consumes 28% of the energy produced on earth and buys 23% of the oil traded internationally. These countries have also questioned the U.S. commitment to energy reduction, citing the significant rise in oil imports following the 1973 Mid-East War (while the Europeans' import levels held steady) and the absence of a coherent long-range national energy program.

The United States, on the other hand, would counter that the Allies have come to depend on oil to meet too great a percentage of their energy requirements (e.g., Japan 73%, the USA 50%) and now consume fully ¾ of all the oil in the world market. The Allies have also failed to diversify their sources of supply, as has the United States, leaving themselves overexposed to the Persian Gulf (74% of Japan's, 72% of France's oil imports). Finally, the United States has shown some exasperation with its friends over the lukewarm support given to American initiatives designed to improve Persian Gulf security and the willingness to conduct a "business-as-usual" energy relationship with the USSR after the Afghanistan invasion.

American public opinion has been somewhat perplexed by the failure of the Allies to demonstrate greater concern over Soviet ambitions in the Persian Gulf region and the challenge posed by the emergence of radical Arab states, especially considering the relatively minor U.S. dependence on Gulf oil and the heavy European and Japanese stake there. While American defense experts ponder the necessity of developing a "Rapid Deployment Force" that can be quickly dispatched to the region, the Allies seem to be taking a "hands off" perspective.[55] This has given rise to unfair comments that our friends are either hoping that the United States will carry out the unpleasant security tasks or that a policy of appeasement is appropriate due to the heavy import dependence.

I say unfair since there has been some Allied movement in this direction. Already the French maintain one of the largest naval presences in the Indian Ocean, the West Germans have indicated a willingness to offset American efforts in the Gulf area by reinforcing the Central European contribution, and Britain has given vociferous support to America's tough stance. Still, there is no clearly delineated common analysis of the situation that exists in the Persian Gulf region today, much less a unified plan of action. A European newspaper, commenting on what it perceives to be a self-deceiving reticence to treat the Gulf security issue seriously, notes:[56]

> The hole in south-west Asia will either be plugged by American military power or will remain unplugged — in which case some hidden hand, it is presumed, will arrange for the two thirds of Europe's oil which comes from the Gulf to keep flowing peacefully out of the Strait of Hormuz.

The issue of the manner in which the Allies should deal with the USSR on energy-related problems is a microcosm of a larger split over the interpretation given to the broader question of how to deal with the Soviets across-the-board. The United States tends to view the Soviet-American relationship as the focal point of the East-West competition. With less to lose from a deterioration in these relations, the Americans are more prone to advocate harsher policies in response to Soviet misbehavior; as the major military power in the Western Alliance system it treats the growth in Soviet military power with greater concern. The Europeans and Japanese, whose trade with the USSR is quite important and who have a greater stake in such issues as exchanges, tend to interpret Moscow's actions more benignly and exhibit a greater reluctance to treat Soviet international initiatives as threatening.

The split among the Allies in energy trade policy vis-a-vis the USSR essentially reflects the differing stakes the nations involved perceive. For Europe and Japan energy trade with the USSR represents a rational diversification of their import suppliers and a means of recycling petrodollars since the Soviet Union (unlike the Arabs) will be purchasing manufactures in return. Outstanding Western loans, the vast majority of which are held in Europe, also stifles any tendency to adopt sanctions against the Soviet Union. Trade with the USSR in general contributes heavily to overall economic growth, and a cutoff of this exchange could result in a severe cut in employment.[57] Added to this is the European (particularly German) interest in maintaining a detente relationship that insures greater human contacts.

West European countries already obtain a significant portion of their energy supplies from the Soviet Union, including 5% of the FRG's oil imports, 7% for Italy, and 5% for France. While the oil trade will slacken soon, gas dependency will grow rapidly upon completion of the proposed Siberian pipeline project. Security planners are voicing concerns over the growing dependency, but in economic terms the exchanges with the USSR are viewed with enthusiasm. Germany, for example, has begun to experience current account deficits for the first time since the War and the Soviet market offers a very lucrative potential for the export of sophisticated manufactures. For the Europeans, or the Japanese who are involved in similar negotiations with the USSR, questions of strategic energy dependency and economic sanctions will not carry the same urgency that is generated in this country. They will likely oppose American efforts to impose limits on technology transfer or investment, arguing that such an embargo would cause more harm than good. They can also be expected to downplay the security aspects of the growing energy dependency on the USSR, pointing out that since they are so reliant on foreign countries for these supplies anyway, it really doesn't matter if the USSR, Libya, or Iran is doing the exporting.

It may be naive in the extreme to believe that under these circumstances some sort of unified Allied energy policy, particularly with respect to dealing with the USSR, could be effected. Still, the prospect of the Western Allies transferring technology, highly-sophisticated products, and financial assistance and then patiently waiting for the compensation to come in the forms of energy deliveries down the line, sould raise security concerns on the part of even the most jaundiced observer. Although it might be argued that a reverse dependency also exists in the Soviet need to earn hard currency from the sales, waiting out an interruption of monetary flows will be much easier to accept than a cut-off of energy deliveries in the winter. While this situation might not cause a desire to back down from a direct threat, it could lead to a greater tolerance of Soviet aggression in other areas.

The establishment of a multilateral energy policy within the Alliance has been initiated with the common pledges agreed upon at Venice. A strategy for dealing with future energy disruptions has been adopted by the International Energy Agency. These initial steps are welcome, and, hopefully, they will serve as the foundation upon which a comprehensive Allied energy policy could be developed. Reaching agreement on the wisdom or practicality of multilateral trade sanctions may not be a feasible goal and any attempt to develop a coherent Western energy relationship with the COMECON countries may also be doomed to failure. However, we should not prejudge this outcome. These issues should be raised in an appropriate forum representing the industrialized democracies of the West, where both the economic and security aspects of future energy issues can be discussed.

The Brezhnev Initiatives: Persian Gulf Security Proposals and the High-Level Energy Talks

The USSR has let it be known that major decisions regarding energy and national security in this decade must include the Soviet Union as a major participant. Brezhnev's proposals to guarantee access to and the distribution of oil supplies located in the Persian Gulf region and his long-stated demand for the convening of an all-European High Level Energy Conference are two of the most visible programs emanating from the Kremlin. The proposals are intended to cast the USSR as the major force seeking to establish a rational foundation for the solving of global energy stringencies and to insure that the international community realizes that no decision can be taken without consideration of the Soviet interest in the resolution of the issues. In the first instance it is Soviet military power that provides the USSR with its entree to play a pivotal role in Persian Gulf security considerations; in the second it is the prospect of the Siberian resource base serving as the foundation for European and broader energy cooperation.

The Soviet proposals with respect to the Persian Gulf surfaced in 1980 with Moscow's UN initiatives, which were ostensibly designed to lead to an agreement limiting the level of military presence and activity in the region, followed up by vociferous support for suggestions from the littoral states to declare the area a "zone of peace". General Secretary Brezhnev formalized the Soviet position in a speech to the Indian Parliament last December, proposing that no military forces or nuclear weapons be deployed in the region, an abandonment of any attempts to form military alliances in the area, to respect the sovereign rights of the regional powers, and not to "raise any obstacles or pose threats to normal trade exchanges and to the use of sea lanes linking the states of that area with other countries".[58]

The Brezhnev suggestions appear quite reasonable on first glance and contain many proposals that are quite acceptable. The thrust of the Persian Gulf guarantees however, are designed to force recognition of the USSR as a major powerbroker for the region and to limit a potential Western presence. Read carefully, the points Chairman Brezhnev raises would eliminate Western nuclear forces in the area, but does not affect the Soviet capabilities only 300 miles away. The proposals would ignore the Soviet presence in Afghanistan as an unrelated issue to be judged on the basis of Soviet national security considerations. The suggestions which would forbid the basing of non-regional forces in the area or regional ties with other states is an explicit recognition of the Soviet inability to make inroads in the region. In effect, the Soviet proposals are designed to rectify Moscow's largely unsuccessful diplomatic overtures to the Arab States. Finally, the prohibition against basing recognizes the USSR's traditional proclivity to remain self-sustaining in distant operations, but would neutralize Western attempts to offset their geographic liabilities by permanently stationing forces in the area.[59]

While Brezhnev's points are energy-related, the proposals are based on long-standing Soviet objectives toward the region. The Kremlin views the area as the weakest link in a loosely-coordinated Western-Chinese attempt to "contain" the USSR. This ring of "anti-Soviet states" could be breached by the establishment of Soviet client states in the area, through the neutralization of the region, by the prevention of a Western presence in the Indian Ocean littoral, or possibly by a Soviet land link to the seas. The latter would satiate the yearning for a "window to the South" and establish a warm water port on the lower flank, but this is an unlikely possibility unless Iran disintegrates or some such similar radical change occurs. The Kremlin also views the region as important from the standpoint of the possibility of an Islamic infection spreading to its 50 million Muslims and as the land area which sits astride the major sea line of communication linking Western Russia with the Far East.

The energy attractiveness of the region is of more recent origin. The Soviet Union recognizes the importance of the Gulf to the West and desires to be in a position to coerce the oil-importing Western nations or at least to exercise influence over the direction of petroleum shipments. Coupled with this "denial" aspect of Soviet policy is a desire, in view of the coming COMECON energy crunch, to exploit the region's energy supplies for use at home. However, the USSR undoubtedly recognizes the difficulties that would be involved in a seizure of the oil fields—the likelihood of local sabotage, the problem of securing long distance supply lines, producing and transporting oil from the Gulf, and probable Western opposition. Thus the goal of gaining a position from which energy distribution can be influenced is primary; the objective of securing Gulf oil for export to the USSR probably is one that is not treated seriously unless the political conditions in the region should deteriorate sufficiently to present opportunities.

Brezhnev's original suggestions for an all-European "High Level Energy Conference" in 1975 followed the establishment of the International Energy Agency (1974) and the energy crisis in the West that emanated after the Yom Kippur War (1973). The proposals had little of substance, but seemed to be aimed at the establishment of the Soviet Union as a reliable energy supplier for Europe in the wake of the Arab oil embargo and the sabotaging of the effectiveness of the IEA. The proposals designed to convene such a conference were originally forwarded when Brezhnev floated a whole series of suggestions for high-visibility meetings of great pomp and splendor that signified nothing more than the consecration of the Soviet achievement of superpower (economic and military) status. The energy conference was part and parcel of the Kremlin's repeated demands for the convocation of a European security conference, a world conference of communist parties, summit meetings with Americas and other Western nations, and the signing of a strategic arms limitations agreement.

The high-level energy conference was not simply a propaganda device, cut also reflected the ambitious Soviet proposals for massive joint projects designed to exploit the resources of the USSR. One Soviet energy expert, Konstantin Ananichev, indicated last year that the COMECON countries were still interested in seeking a way of uniting the power systems of Eastern and Western Europe.[60] The Soviets ultimately hope to renew the prospect of joint projects that would establish Siberia as the basis of an all-European (and Japan) energy system, detach West Europe and Tokyo from American influence, and leave Moscow in a position of deciding the allocation of energy supplies. More ambitious aspects of the Soviet suggestions have envisioned the inclusion of the Middle East in this energy scheme, leaving the USSR playing the multiple roles of supplier, transporter, and strategic arbitrator.

The Soviet Union has presented the West with a series of proposals that integrate Moscow's energy and foreign policies into a coherent, attractive package that masks the underlying objectives. The proposals are designed to obscure the threat to Western access to secure energy supplies and to play on growing OECD import dependencies. There will still be a tendency in the West, given the economic attractiveness of the Soviet politico-economic proposals, to avoid harsh appraisals of Moscow's intentions and to rationalize the Kremlin's forward posture in the global arena as reflective of legitimate Soviet interests.

By Way of Conclusion

The trends are clear. The international energy situation in this decade will be characterized by diminishing supplies, level or growing demand, and a diminution of nations capable of exporting energy resources to the global market. The focus of energy consumption, especially in international transactions, will remain on the hydrocarbons,, especially oil. The major importers of petroleum are and will continue to be the Western industrialized democracies, traditionally allied nations who will see their bonds severely tested by a potential scramble for scarce energy supplies in this decade.

The Soviet Union will suffer an energy dilemma in the 1980's when it can no longer simultaneously satisfy its own domestic demand, export to East Europe in sufficient quantities to prevent stagnating economic growth, and sell on the world market to earn the hard currency to purchase grain and technology it badly needs. The Western nations have potential leverage available to them in the form of their technology, sophisticated manufactures, grain, and financing to "leverage" the USSR, but accomplishing such a "linkage" will be difficult to achieve given Allied diversity and conflicting approaches to a number of security and foreign policy issues.

The "leverage" situation may reverse by the mid-1990's when the Soviet Union begins to develop its enormous energy potential. Coupled with its steadily expanding military power, the establishment of the USSR as a major supplier of the energy requirements of the industrialized democracies will give the Kremlin a powerful calling card in international politics. Although this writer does not wish to suggest a Soviet plot to orchestrate all of its potential in a master plot designed to subdue the West in the next few years, we should not ignore the cumulative effect represented by the rapid modernization and expansion of the Soviet armed forces, the suggestions for the establishment of an All-European and Japanese energy system based in Siberia, and the proposals for a series of political conferences aimed at consecrating the key role the Soviets wish to play in global energy politics.

Countering the Soviet gambit will require a sophisticated Western response. As a starting point it demands the ability of the industrialized democracies to withstand energy embargoes by the establishment of real strategic energy reserves and the maintenance of a surge capacity. It requires the implementation of genuine national energy targets designed to reduce the Alliance's collective dependence on imports and cooperation in the case of sudden supply disruptions or shifts in global energy distribution patterns. The establishment of a common position with respect to dealing with the USSR may be too difficult to achieve at the present time, but continuing discussions regarding technology transfer, long-range energy ventures, and supply dependency on the Soviet Union must be conducted. Only on such a careful basis can a mutually advantageous energy cooperative relationship be developed with the USSR.

Notes

1. Reston sees the two fundamental and most urgent problems in the world as first, the economic and financial crisis aggravated by the supply and price of oil, and second, a military and strategic crisis with the Soviet Union, (the *New York Times*, 9 December 1979, p. E21.)
2. International Energy Agency forecasts (Paris, April, 1980). The IEA estimates assume OPEC production will increase slightly, internal consumption will double, and non-IEA demand will grow. Thus the amount of oil available to the IEA countries will decline from 23.8 mb/d at present to 19.4 mb/d in 1990.
3. For example, the Central Intelligence Agency forecast in April of 1977 that OPEC oil production would reach 43-48 mb/d by 1985, but three years later had scaled that prediction down to a range of 36-38 mb/d. The demand side of the equation had been adjusted downward also, reflecting the failure of most forecasts to anticipate the degree of energy savings that could be implemented. The Exxon Corporation's

estimates as reflected in the annual *World Energy Outlook* were also substantially downgraded. The December, 1980, report predicts that world oil production will reach 53 mb/d by 1990, compared to an expectation of 60 mb/d forecast in the 1979 report (not including the centrally planned economies).

4. Persian Gulf production could be substantially increased over present levels if policy demanded such upturns in output. The ratio of proved to probable reserves in Saudi Arabia is 50:1 and production could theoretically rise as high as 14 mb/d by the late 1980's, compared to 9.5 mb/d at the end of 1980. Kuwait could sustain its production rate of 2 mb/d of oil for over 50 years, Iraq has some geologically promising regions not yet explored, Iran (assuming the existence of a national government dedicated to expanding production) could easily climb back to its high of 6 mb/d, compared to 1.5 mb/d as of this writing, but it is doubtful that such a commitment will be made.

5. Don Oberdorfer's report in the *Washington Post*, (23 April 1980, p. 34) indicated that Adm. Turner predicted that the Communist countries as a group will go from net exporters of oil to net importers "within the next several years". The *New York Times* report indicated that the CIA Director saw this import status coming by 1981.

6. For a more complete discussion of the Soviet energy forecast, see Tyrus W. Cobb, "The Soviet Energy Dilemma", *ORBIS*, 2, Summer, 1979, pp. 353-385. A comprehensive analysis of the USSR's resource base and energy policies is found in Leslie Dienes and Theodore Shabad, *The Soviet Energy System: Resource Use and Policies* (Winston and Sons, Washington, D.C., 1979). For Soviet perspective see, A.M. Nekrasova and M.G. Pervukhina, *Energetika SSSR v 1976-1980 godakh* (The Energy System of the USSR in the Years 1976-1980, "Energiya" Press, Moscow, 1977) and S.L. Pruzner, A.N. Elatopol'skii, and A.M. Nekrasov, *Ekonomika energetiki SSSR* (The Economics of the Energy System of the USSR), "Vyshaya Shkola" Press, Moscow, 1978.

7. Official policy has been to keep the transport of coal to a minimum, concentrating instead on locating processing plants close to coal deposits. An intensive program was initiated in the 1960's to exploit local fuel resources fully, generally by constructing large power stations at the coal fields and encouraging the immigration of power-intensive industries to those sites. Soviet officials now hope to restrict the shipment of coal to semicoke or hard coal sent to the western part of the country, burning the cheap brown coals near the extraction sites. For a further discussion see CIA, *USSR: Coal Industry Problems and Prospects* (ER 80-10154, March, 1980) and William J. Kelly and Hugh L. Shaffer, "Soviet Options for the Utilization of Siberian Coal", paper presented at the Midwest Economics Association meeting, March 27-29, 1980, (Battelle Memorial Institute, Ohio State Univ.).

8. The conversion of Siberian fuels into electricity for direct transmission to major demand centers has been a long-standing Soviet goal. The idea of a unified power system transmitting electricity over great distances and fueled by the abundant brown coal and hydropower resource potential of Siberia is receiving intensive study. To date the Soviets have not overcome the technical problems involved with power loss over distance and the enormous investment required; the Soviet dream of an inexpensive and efficient method of transporting Siberian resources has not been practically implemented.

9. The importance of energy in the economic development of any society is generally recognized, but perhaps nowhere more so than in the Soviet Union. Energy – and especially electrical power has been viewed as the basic lever in the development of regional production complexes. In the Soviet Union the correlation between economic development and energy consumption has been very close, similar to the 1:1 ratio experienced in the West until 1973. However, in the last decade the industrialized democracies have achieved some remarkable efficiencies and the ratio has been reduced to .6:1 as a unit increase in energy production now results in much greater improvements in GNP growth. The USSR has already reaped the savings inherent in the switch to hydrocarbons and in the future problems such as the growing dependence on poorer quality fuels, more difficult accessibility of supplies, and what

two experts call the "worsening of their (fuels) location and, primarily, the geological conditions of extraction" will inhibit any improvement in the energy:GNP ratio. See A. Makarov and L. Melent'yev, "Issledovaniya Perspektivnoi Struktury Toplivno-Energeticheskova Balanca SSSR: Osnovy Zon Strany" (Research into the Future Structure of the Fuel and Energy Balance of the USSR and Basic Zones of the Country) (Unpublished paper, Moscow, 1980), p. 14. For a complete discussion comparing historical energy and national income growth rates, see S. Yatrov, "The Fuel-Energy Complex", *Ekonomicheskaya Gazeta* (-10, March, 1980). Yatrov, in a more optimistic analysis than the other report noted here, finds a "coefficient of elasticity" of .84 over the last two decades.

10. The Soviet Bloc's debt to the West and Japan is discussed in *Business Week,* February, 1981 ("Polish Debt: A Game of Chicken"), p. 86. Two studies by the U.S. Department of Commerce analyze this problem in some depth. See "Communist Country Hard Currency Debt in Perspective" (July, 1980)) and "Projected CEMA Hard Currency Debt Levels Under Selected Trade Growth Assumptions" (July 7, 1980), both by the International Trade Administration.

11. The Persian Gulf countries today account for 30% of U.S. oil imports, but that share will grow in this decade. Three African countries, Algeria, Libya, and Nigeria, provide about 40% of the total. Mexico's provisions are becoming increasingly important, while Canada has relinquished its former pivotal role and Indonesia has also declined.

12. The results of the Venice summit are reported in the *New York Times*, June, 24, 1980, "Text of the Venice Economic Summit", p. 7. The energy strategy that evolved at Venice was formulated in a May, 1980, meeting of the International Energy Agency. An assessment of the IEA program and the Venice summit is provided in Paul Lewis, "Europe Blends Diplomacy, Economics in Fuel Strategy", the *New York Times*, 29 June 1980.

13. For a Western perspective see Wolfgang Leonhard, "The Domestic Politics of the New Soviet Policy", *Foreign Affairs*, October, 1973, who asserts that the detente policy developed by the Soviet Union was largely driven by the necessity to obtain technology from the West needed to salvage a deteriorating economy. Leonhard argues that such a transfer was seen as an attempt to avoid undertaking serious structural modifications in the economy and summarizes that the Kremlin realized such a massive technological infusion could only be secure in an atmosphere of detente. A Soviet view, largely focusing on the exchange of technology as a means of American politico-economic expansion into the affairs of foreign countries is provided in I.E. Artem'iev, *Amerikanskii kapitalizm i peredacha tekhnologii* (American Capitalism and the Transfer of Technology) Nauka Press, Moscow, 1980, especially the last chapter which argues for the development of "scientific-technical ties on an equal and mutually advantageous basis".

14. Mark E. Miller, "The Role of Western Technology in Soviet Strategy", *ORBIS*, Fall, 1978, p. 540. A U.S. State Department summary of "US-Soviet Economic Relations" (GIST, Bureau of Public Affairs, July, 1977) reflected this viewpoint, pointing out that "Increased trade with the USSR benefits the US through higher employment an improved balance of trade, and access to valuable raw materials. It also increases contact between our two peoples; gives the USSR an incentive to relax its traditional isolation and play a more normal role in the world eocnomy; and adds an element of stability to our political relations".

15. The U.S. Department of Energy, Office of Technical Cooperation, provides a semi-annual report on the US-USSR Agreements on Energy and Atomic Energy to the State Department. These reports reflect the conclusion that there have been few programmatic benefits to the U.S. under the exchanges, except possibly for the MHD work. The major complaints are that the U.S. participants are accorded usually only a "walk through" look at facilities, technical information is often dated and of poor quality, and particularly, energy forecasting information has not been forthcoming.

16. An example of the ambitious scope of these early Soviet proposals is N.N. Nekrasov, "Energetics and Natural Resources", paper presented at an international economics

conference in Vienna, November, 1974, in which he argues for a three-stage development of a unified European energy system. Since the USSR "commands big reserves of fuel and energy resources" which could be used to satisfy a part of West Europe's energy appetite, such a partnership would be mutually beneficial. Of course, he notes that basic to such development is the fact that ". . . the future exploitation of Siberian deposits requires large capital investments" (p. 14.)

17.   An optimistic interpretation of the Siberian development schemes is provided by one of the American participants in James P. Lister, "Siberia and the Soviet Far East: Development Policies and the Yakutia Gas Project", the El Paso LNG Company, prepared for the 1979 NATO Colloquium.

18.   The Soviets have indicated that they prefer compensation agreements whereby the Western investment is repaid through the delivery of a portion of future output. Such a transaction minimizes hard currency transfers and alleviates the Soviet debt burden. However, this arrangement leaves the investor in a dependent situation on the supplier, in effect creating a situation where the involved Western firms and nations will perceive a vested interest in maintaining stable relations and may tend to "overlook" minor transgressions. Of course, it can be argued that the USSR, needing hard currency as it does, will be reluctant to interrupt deliveries because of the loss of revenues. However, a hard-currency disruption would be easier to absorb than would a temporary cutoff of energy deliveries in mid-winter.

19.   The Stevenson Amendment places a $40-million limit on energy-related development assisted by the Ex-ImBank and the Jackson-Vanik Trade Reform Act ties increases in outstanding Soviet debt and MFN status to Moscow's emigration policies.

20.   Samuel P. Huntington, "Trade, Technology and Leverage", *Foreign Policy*, #32, Fall, 1978, p. 64.

21.   Huntington's address is reprinted in the Final Report of the West Point Senior Conference, *Integrating National Security and Trade Policy: The United States and the Soviet Union*, June, 1978, pp. 17-27.

22.   As quoted in Richard Burt, "Carter Aides Favor Ban on Oil Equipment for Soviet", the *New York Times*, 27 June 1978, p. 3.

23.   The reports that focused on Soviet energy were the CIA's two 1977 studies, *Prospects for Soviet Oil Production* (Washington, DC, April, 1977) and *Prospects for Soviet Oil Production: A Supplementary Analysis* (ER-77-10425, June, 1977). The most controversial report was the Agency's *The International Energy Situation: Outlook to 1985* (CIA-ER-77-10240U, April, 1977). Critics have alleged that the pessimistic analysis of Soviet energy prospects was instrumental in gaining support for President Carter's national energy plan introduced that year. The CIA noted that if the Soviets expected to increase economic growth at the rate they probably desired, the COMECON countries as a whole could wind up importing as much as 4.5 mb/d of oil by 1984.

24.   The early 1980 revisions are reported in Steve Rattner, "Trade as a US Weapon", the *New York Times*, 8 January 1980, p. D5 and Richard Burt, "U.S. Curbs Technology for Soviet" the *New York Times*, 19 March 1980, p. D1.

25.   Less than 5% of US exports are destined for Communist countries, about half of these to the Soviet Union. The United States purchases only about 1% of its imports from the Socialist Bloc, the USSR accounting for a third of that or .4% of all American purchases from abroad. The major American trading partners were the OECD nations (62%), followed by the LDC's (33%) on the export side, with just over half of its imports coming from the developed countries and 44% from the LDCs (half of that from OPEC). For the Soviet Union, trade turnover with other Socialist countries accounted for about 58% of the total and the OECD countries represented 31%. Just over 1% of Soviet exports were destined for the American marketplace, but 5½% of Moscow's imports came from the USA.

26.   The IEA figures are reported in Eric Morgenthaler, "Europe-Soviet Energy Trade Grows", the *Wall Street Journal*, 25 June 1980.

27.   "Gas Seen Holding Europe Market Share", the *Oil and Gas Journal*, 4 February 1980, pp. 28-30.

28. See the *Petroleum Intelligence Weekly,* 16 June 1980, p. 8, "EEC Getting Uneasy About Outlook for Gas Supplies".

29. U.S. Congress, Office of Technology Assessment, *Technology and East-West Trade,* project directed by Dr. Ronnie Goldberg, (U.S. Government Printing Office, Washington, 1979), p. 173. This OTA study is one of the most comprehensive analyses of the issues surrounding East-West Trade in general and the technology transfer debate in particular.

30. *Ibid.,* p. 180. The FRG exports a wide range of technologies to the USSR, including machine tools and petrochemical plants. The most visible of the FRG's activities has been the giant steel complex being constructed near Kursk by a consortium of West German firms, the largest single transaction in the history of East-West trade to date.

31. COL E. Kuzin, "About a CIA Fraud", printed in *Sovetskaya Litva,* 17 June 1980, translated in FBIS-SOV-147, 29 June 1980, p. A4. The author continues to point to the significant Soviet oil and gas sales and the fact that coal and gas from the USSR ". . . were for a number of countries a substantial factor in surmounting the difficulties of the energy crisis".

32. See, in addition to the OTA study, *An Analysis of Export controls of U.S. Technology — A DOD Perspective,* by the Pentagon office of DDR&E, [Washington, February, 1976]; J. Fred Busy, "Technology Transfer and East-West Trade", *International Security,* Winter, 1980/81, pp. 132-152; *International Transfer of Technology: An Agenda of National Security Issues*; by the Congressional Research Service for the Committee on International Relations, U.S. House of Representatives (February 13, 1978); Phillip Hanson, "The Import of Western Technology", in Brown and Kaser (eds), *The Soviet Union Since Khrushchev* (MacMillan, London, 1975); and Anthony Sutton's volume #3 of his comprehensive survey, *Western Technology and Soviet Economic Development, 1945-1965. (Sanford, 1970).*

33. *Colloquium on "East-West Technological Co-Operation"* Main findings published by the NATO Directorate of Economic Affairs, 1976. (Brussels)

34. For an analysis that tends to be highly critical of the possibilities inherent in using trade as an instrument of security policy, see Ann Crittenden, *"Warfare: Trade as a Weapon",* New York *Times,* 13 January 1980, p. 1, Section 3.

35. Two articles that argue in favor of the promotion of trade between East and West and that argue the thesis that the potential benefits of Western involvement in Soviet energy exploitation is warranted, are William Greider, "U.S. Should Help Russia Alleviate Its Oil Crisis", *Washington Post,* 13 August 1978, and William Verity, chairman of the ARMCO Steel Corporation, "Taking Politics Out of Trade with the Soviet", the *New York Times,* 2 January 1979.

36. Giovanni Agnelli, "East-West Trade: A European View", *Foreign Affairs,* Summer, 1980. Agnelli argues that the Western countries made a major mistake in not accepting the Soviet proposals of the 1970's, particularly in the field of LNG ventures, designed to exploit the Siberian resources through joint East-West cooperation.

37. Anthony Sutton, *Western Technology . . .,* op. cit., as quoted in Miller, "The Role of Western Technology in Soviet Strategy", *op. cit.,* p. 554.

38. Green and Levine indicate that end-product transfers to the Soviet Union contributed no more than 1% to overall economic growth, perhaps 2-3 times that for growth in heavy industry. See Donald W. Green and Herbert S. Levine, "Macro-economic Evidence of the Value of Machinery Imports to the Soviet Union", in John Thomas and Ursula Kruse-Vaucienne, (eds), *Soviet Science and Technology* (Washington, DC, National Science Foundation, 1977). Green and Levine point out that those sectors of the economy which employ Western technology the greatest, especially the machine building and chemical sectors, have experienced significant productivity increases.

39. Miller, *op. cit.,* p. 549.

40. American submersible pumps were much more efficient than the comparable Soviet products. Major problems with the domestic pumps were metal fatigue, precision of manufacture, and susceptibility to wear. The CIA *Supplementary Analysis (op. cit.)* in 1977 noted that these pumps increased fluid lift capacity to permit a rise in oil output of

at least 1 mb/d (p. 29). By the end of 1977 over 1200 of the pumps, which were available only from the United States, were shipped to the USSR. The requirement for the pump stems from the water-injection program by which the Soviets attempted to obtain a higher initial level of production, but the injected water later breaks through the oil-bearing formations into the producing wells. Expensive pumps must then be installed in order to produce the large volumes of water and oil. These pumps did temporarily stabilize production in the Urals-Volga region. Prior to 1971 submersible pumps were embargoed by the United States.

41. Adm. Stansfield Turner, Director of the CIA, testimony to the Joint Economic Committee of the U.S. Congress, in *Allocation of Resources in the Soviet Union and China — 1979* (JEC, U.S. Congress, Washington, 1980), p. 19.

42. Robert W. Campbell, "U.S. Technology and Soviet Energy", testimony to the U.S. Senate Committee on Banking, Housing, and Urban Affairs, *U.S. Embargo of Food and Technology to the Soviet Union* U.S. Government Printing Office, 1980), p. 220.

43. *Ibid.,* pp. 220-221.

44. President Carter indicated that we fully realized that the withholding of grain would not force the Soviet Union out of Afghanistan, but that the embargo would put the USSR on notice that they will "suffer" in the future from similar actions. The State Department estimated that the grain embargo would deny the Soviets 8-9 million metric tons of the 36 MMT of grain they expected to import in 1980. See U.S. Department of State, "U.S. Partial Embargo on Grain Sales to the USSR", *GIST* (Bureau of Public Affairs), September, 1980.

45. Stephen Rosenfeld argues that "Every time a Soviet family sits down to dinner, the evidence of the Kremlin's failure is on the table." ("It's Our Grain Deal"), the *Washington Post,* 6 February 1981, p. 15. The perspective of a former Carter official on the embargo is found in Steven Larrabee, "The Grain Embargo: II", the *New York Times,* 10 February, 1981, p. 23.

46. Part of the problem in evaluating the success of trade controls is that the public has been led to expect significant returns, such as a Soviet pullout from Afghanistan as soon as the technology and grain embargoes were imposed. The limited leverage effect of this 1980 action should not be misconstrued. The embargoes caused the USSR delays in time, considerable expense, and severe embarrassment. As such they will not prevent the Soviets from responding to their perceived national interests, but will not restrain them in certain areas. In the past leverage has been crudely or unconsciously applied, but still with some significant results. In the early 1970's the USSR made important concessions over Berlin leading to a 4-Power Agreement there, largely as a gesture to further a detente relationship that would accelerate technology transfers. Another example was the increased Jewish emigration in the mid-1970's, a practice that the Kremlin clearly accepted as a necessary concession in order to entice American involvement in the Siberian energy schemes. Only when the USA demanded that the Soviets publicly submit to the leverage, thus to suffer a "loss of face", and agree to the Congressionally-imposed restrictions, did they renege.

47. Soviet officials frequently remind the West of the divergence between the Allies over the imposition of export controls and the internal differences of opinion that exist in this country on the issue. For example, a recent issue of *SShA*, the official journal of the Institute for the Study of the USA and Canada, carried an interview with Robert Schmidt, executive vice president of the Control Data Corporation, who indicated that there "is no clear agreement" in the U.S. regarding export controls against items destined for the USSR. Schmidt indicates that ". . . it is extremely important to remove the obstacles impeding the normal development of trade and technological exchange between our countries". ("Remove Obstacles to Trade", *SShA*, #6, June, 1979, p. 80).

48. For example see "Eastern Bloc Evades Technology Embargo", *SCIENCE,* 23 January 1981, pp. 364-368.

49. For a "pro-trade perspective", see the articles by David Rockefeller of Chase Manhattan, Donald Kendall of Pepsico, and C. Williams Verity of ARMCO, Inc., in the

May, 1979, issue of *The American Review of East-West Trade*, the Journal of the US-USSR Trade and Economic Council.

50. A complete review of the administration of export controls is found in the testimony of LTC Jim Golden before the U.S. House of Representatives Committee on Foreign Affairs, 14 March, 1979. Golden, who chaired an interagency task force charged with a review of the procedures and mechanisms involved in the inter-agency export control process, indicates that the review procedures are unnecessarily slow and cumbersome. He recommends that the participating departments consider the addition of more professionals on strategic controls staffs and increasing the number of licensing officers.

51. "Can the Russians Retaliate on Trade?" *Business Week*, 11 February 1980, p. 46.

52. Economic Commission for Europe, *New Issues Affecting the Energy Economy of the ECE Region in the Medium and Long Term* (United Nations, New York, 1978), p. 13.

53. See Peter R. Odell, "Soviet Energy Policy: Some Resource Base and Geo-Political Considerations", in Robert Jensen, ed., *Soviet Energy Policy And the Hydrocarbons: Comments and a Rejoinder* (Association of American Geographers, February, 1979). Odell notes that "The geological situation in the Soviet Union indicates a high probability of at least several sets of discoveries of the same order of magnitude of these (North Sea, Mexico and Alaska) recent western world developments" (p. 15).

54. Interview with Stanislav Maltsev, Director of a West Siberian Oil Institute, "My Country is Wide", *Leningradskaya Pravda*, 8 January 1981, p. 1, translated in FBIS-SOV-012, 19 January 1981, p. S1.

55. Zbigniew Brzezinski, former Assistant to the President for National Security Affairs, remarked in January in an address to French Institute of International Relations in Paris that American actions to shape a regional security framework have been unilateral. "What is needed", Brzezinski stated, "is a multilateral response, involving not just the affected states, but our European and Asian allies whose dependence on Persian Gulf oil is even heavier than our own". Dr. Brzezinski indicated that allied support need "not be purely military or purely local", but that it is necessary for our friends to demonstrate tangible support.

56. "Push Comes to Shove", the *Economist*, 3 January 1981, p. 7.

57. For example, some estimates of the impact of a sudden cutoff of West German trade with the USSR claim that as many as 300,000 jobs would be lost in the FRG.

58. The Brezhnev proposals are summarized in "Exceprts From Soviet Leader's Speech to Parliament in New Delhi", the *New York Times*, 11 December 1980, p. A12. The Soviet suggestions were initially broached in February of 1980 by TASS commentator N. Portugalov who asked that guarantees for Persian Gulf security be included on the upcoming CSCE agenda.

59. A complete analysis of the Soviet President's concepts is found in Radio Liberty report RL 475/80 by Bruce Porter. "Brezhnev's Proposals on Persian Gulf Security" (11 December 1980).

60. Interview with Konstantin Ananichev, delegate to the 1980 World Energy Congress held in Munich, reported by TASS and reprinted in FBIS-SOV-175, 8 September 1980, p. CC8. Ananichev stated that "Many problems of energy would find more successful solutions should an all-European energy conference be convened".

CMEA Trade and Cooperation with the Third World in the Energy Sector[1]

John B. Hannigan and
Carl H. McMillan

Energy—almost exclusively petroleum and natural gas—played a central role in the intensification of CMEA-Third World relations in the 1970s.[2] Given its abundant resources, the Soviet Union developed its energy relations with the Third World along lines rather different from those pursued by its East European allies. This paper examines the nature and scope of CMEA-Third World energy relations, tracing their course over the decade. The analysis shows that, by the end of the 1970s, the CMEA countries found themselves increasingly constrained in their ability to pursue energy policy objectives in the Third World. The nature of the policy dilemma faced at the outset of the 1980s, and the more limited options open to the CMEA countries in the new decade, are outlined in a concluding section.

The Policy and Institutional Framework for Relations in the 1970s

In this period, CMEA relations with the Third World were pursued within the framework of policies directed, since the mid-1960s, to the creation of more organic links with the developing economies. Policy emphasis had shifted away from grandiose, isolated aid projects, and from a few, politically preferred countries in the Third World, to development of more diversified relations, with a broader spectrum of partners, and based on firmer economic foundations of "mutual interest".[3]

These more pragmatic approaches were motivated by the real need of the CMEA countries to gain increased access to Third World sources of raw materials, especially fuels and energy, and at the same time to find profitable outlets for the products of industries developed in the "extensive" phase of their planned development. The rapid growth of CMEA-Third World trade over the decade (Table 1) served as a result to reinforce its traditional structure, with manufactures, in 1977, constituting 70% of CMEA exports to the Third World and primary products comprising 90% of CMEA imports from the developing countries.[4]

More intensive economic ties would create a more solid basis on which to promote Soviet bloc political interests in the Third World. By providing developing countries with a more effective alternative to Western trade, technology and capital, they would also serve to restrict Western influence. Richard Lowenthal, among others, has stressed the geo-political aspects of these economic approaches, and has viewed them as forming a strategy which he has dubbed "counter-imperialism".[5]

New policies required new instruments. To the traditional modes of trade and aid, the CMEA countries added new, more direct and more permanent forms of involvement in Third World economies, in the nature of long-term, industrial cooperation arrangements and even equity investments. The preferred form of industrial cooperation has been the "compensation" agreement, whereby credits granted to finance capital equipment and technical assistance for specific projects in the developing countries are repaid in kind, through deliveries of all or part of the resulting output, typically raw materials. These agreements have on occasion been institutionalized in the form of joint venture companies linking Comecon and Third World enterprises. In support of these various activities, Comecon organizations have also established marketing companies, engineering firms, transport agencies and banks in the developing countries.[6] Sometimes Western firms have participated in these projects and activities.[7]

CMEA-Third World relations have been conducted primarily on a bilateral basis; and multilateral agreements and projects have been comparatively rare.[8] These relations have been conducted in the 1970s against the background of changing payments policies and practices, to which developments in the energy sector have contributed. Long-term, bilateral clearing agreements traditionally provided the mechanism for settlements in trade between CMEA members and developing countries. Given consistent CMEA surpluses in this trade (Table 1), bilateral clearing agreements have also provided a channel for low-interest credits to many Third World countries.

Since the early 1970s, there has been an important shift away from bilateral clearing towards hard-currency settlements in East-South trade. The United Nations has estimated that trade between the Comecon Seven and the developing countries, conducted under clearing agreements, fell from 77% in 1965 to 57% in 1975, with a consequent, proportional rise in

TABLE 1
CMEA Trade with the "Developing Market Economies" (DMEs)*
(in mln. current $US)

Year	Exports to DMEs				Imports from DMEs				Trade Balance		
	CMEA Seven		USSR	CMEA Six	CMEA Seven		USSR	CMEA Six	CMEA Seven	USSR	CMEA Six
	$	as % of world exports to Third World			$	as % of total imports of CMEA Seven					
1970	2456	4.4%	2036	420	2099	7.3%	1173	926	357	863	-506
1972	3834	5.5%	2427	1407	2584	6.1%	1392	1192	1250	1035	215
1974	7420	4.4%	4478	2942	5832	9.3%	2955	2877	1588	1523	65
1975	8312	4.2%	4588	3724	6802	8.2%	3663	3139	1510	925	585
1976	8720	4.1%	4958	3762	7148	8.2%	3453	3695	1572	1505	67
1977	12059	4.7%	7250	4809	7421	7.7%	3436	3985	4638	3814	824
1978	13628	4.6%	8370	5258	7638	6.9%	3229	4409	5990	5141	849
1979	15599	4.4%	9634	5965	9289	7.3%	4532	4757	6310	5102	1208

* This is a U.N. Classification which includes Cuba. We have adjusted U.N.   figures for trade of "Developing
Market Economies" by subtracting Cuban trade.

Sources: U.N., Statistical Yearbook, various years   and U.N., Monthly Bulletin of Statistics, various issues.

TABLE 2

CMEA Trade with the Developing Market Economies (DMEs) In Mineral Fuels and Related Materials (SITC, Revised. 3)*

(in mln. current $US)

	SITC-3 Exports to DMEs						SITC-3 Imports from DMEs					
	CMEA-7		USSR		CMEA-6		CMEA-7		USSR		CMEA-6	
Year	$	as % of total CMEA exports to DMEs	$	as % of total USSR exports to DMEs	$	as % of total CMEA-6 exports to DMEs	$	as % of total CMEA-7 imports from DMEs	$	as % of total USSR imports from DMEs	$	as % of total CMEA-6 imports from DMEs
1970	110	4.4%	75	3.7%	35	6.3%	60	2.1%	30	1.7%	30	2.8%
1972	130	3.4%	100	4.1%	30	1.9%	270	9.3%	125	7.6%	145	11.4%
1974	560	7.5%	480	10.7%	80	2.5%	1130	16.3%	490	12.6%	640	21.1%
1975	615	7.4%	485	10.6%	130	3.2%	1760	19.3%	700	12.3%	1060	30.7%
1976	650	7.5%	490	9.9%	160	3.9%	2240	23.6%	820	15.0%	1420	35.3%
1977	840	7.0%	650	9.0%	190	3.7%	2100	20.5%	840	14.2%	1260	29.2%
1978	745	5.5%	590	7.0%	155	2.8%	2150	19.3%	870	13.4%	1280	27.5%

- 5 -

*SITC, Revised, 3 consists almost entirely of energy products. Its main subgroups are coal, coke and briquettes; petroleum and petroleum products; natural and manufacgred gas; and electric energy.

Source: U.N., Statistical Yearbook, various years, U.N. Monthly Bulletin of Statistics, July 1980, and Vneshniaia Torgovlia SSSR: Statisticheskii Sbornik, various years. Soviet oil exports to Cuba have been subtracted from U.N. figures on CMEA trade with the DMEs.

trade under convertible currency agreements.[9] By 1979 intergovernmental clearing agreements remained in effect with only two important energy-exporting countries, Algeria and Syria, and then only between those countries and the Soviet Union. In their weakened position, vis-à-vis the newly rich, energy-exporting countries, CMEA members are increasingly faced with the prospect of settling their energy-import bills (Table 2) in convertible currencies, at current world prices.

It is important to distinguish between inter-governmental clearing agreements and more narrowly focused payments arrangements, such as compensation deals, barter and switch transactions and re-export agreements. The latter may take place within the framework of bilateral clearing agreements or exist independently of them. In either case, they have typically involved the extension of low-interest credits by the CMEA countries to finance exports of machinery, equipment and related services (including personnel training) to Third World development projects. Available data indicate that the Middle East (especially Egypt, Syria, Iran and Iraq) has been the recipient of more than half of such credits, with the development of the energy sectors of their economies a principal aim.[10] With rapidly rising energy prices and mounting pressure for hard currency settlements, however, barter and compensation agreements have become increasingly difficult to negotiate in the energy sector.

The trends in trade and payments noted above, as well as the growing, direct involvement of CMEA member-countries in the economies of the Third World, have brought CMEA-Third World relations closer in structure and in form to North-South relations. These trends have served to undermine the long-standing ideological claim of the Comecon countries to a common cause with the Third World against the "neo-colonial exploitation" of the Western industrial countries. In particular, the developing countries have been locked into the same role, as importers of manufactures and exporters of primary products, in relations with the socialist countries that they have deplored in their relations with the capitalist West. The Comecon countries have accordingly found themselves increasingly challenged by the developing countries in the dialogue on the New International Economic Order, through which the Third World has sought to restructure its external relations in order to provide the impetus and scope for its more rapid economic development.[11]

Soviet Oil Exports

In the mid to late 1950s and throughout the 1960s, the Soviet Union rapidly increased the volume of its oil exports, including those to developing countries. Competition between the USSR and the major Western oil companies contributed to the creation of state-owned oil companies in several importing countries (India and Ceylon, for example) to process and distribute Soviet oil. By causing a decline in price, Soviet exports contributed to the formation of OPEC in 1960.[12] This Soviet oil "offensive", as it was labelled at the time by many Western observers, caused much anxiety in the West about potential disruptions to the world oil market and fears of Communist penetration into Third World countries. Although political factors undoubtedly had a role to play in Soviet oil export policy, by the beginning of the 1970s, it was felt in most quarters that the Western reaction to the Soviet oil "offensive" was generally exaggerated.[13] In the 1970s, while too marginal to compete seriously with OPEC exports, Soviet oil exports nevertheless substantially benefited from the OPEC-administered price increases.

The volume of Soviet oil exports to the Third World is estimated to have increased by more than 60 percent during the 1970s (Table 3). After declining from 3.7 to 2.9 million metric tons (mmt) between 1971-73, Soviet oil (crude and products) exports to the Third World rose to 4.5 mmt in 1976, the last year when figures were published by the USSR on the volume of its oil exports and imports. If Soviet official data on the annual value of exports to the Third World after 1976 are deflated by index numbers based upon the average OPEC crude oil sales price, then an approximate measure of the volume of Soviet oil exports in 1977-79 can be obtained.[14] These calculations, presented in the final columns of Table 3, put the 1979 volume of Soviet oil exports to the Third World at 6.1 mmt.

Almost all the growth in oil exports resulted from increased deliveries to India. Together with Turkey and Morocco, India accounted in 1979 for almost 90 percent of Soviet oil exports to the Third World.[15]

The share of the Third World in total Soviet oil exports remained small. Over the 1970s, this share fluctuated between 2.5 and 4 percent. The estimated rise in this share from 2.8 percent in 1978 to 4.0 percent in 1979 is particularly noteworthy because the volume and share of Soviet oil exports to western industrialized countries fell in this period.[16]

Soviet oil deliveries have been concentrated more and more in certain countries strategically located on its southern flank. This was largely the result of the expansion of exports to India and the renewal of oil exports to Turkey in 1978. The Soviet Union also added two regular customers in Southwest Asia—Bangladesh and Nepal. Meanwhile, it ceased exporting oil to three countries in Africa—Egypt, Ghana and Somalia.

Elsewhere, the USSR began exporting significant quantities of oil to Brazil in 1974. Brazil discontinued these imports at some point in 1978, but recent reports indicate that Brazil signed a new contract in October 1980 to renew its imports of Soviet oil at a rate of 20,000 barrels/day (b/d) (1 mmt per year).

In several of these Third World countries Soviet oil exports account for a predominant share of total oil consumption. The countries which have a high dependence on Soviet oil imports (over 25 percent of their total liquid fuel consumption supplied by Soviet oil) are Afghanistan (30-50%), Cyprus (40%), Guinea (30%), Morocco (25%), and Nepal (70-80%). Ghana and Somalia also had a very high dependence on Soviet oil in the early to

TABLE 3
Soviet Oil (Crude & Product) Exports to the Third World
1970-79 (by country, volume ('000 metric tons) and value '000 rubles)

Country	1970 Volume	1970 Value	1971 Volume	1971 Value	1972 Volume	1972 Value	1973 Volume	1973 Value	1974 Volume	1974 Value	1975 Volume	1975 Value	1976 Volume	1976 Value	1977 Volume	1977 Value	1978 Volume	1978 Value	1979 Volume	1979 Value
Asia																				
Afghanistan	141	5293	147	5513	157	5221	165	4885	193	5852	149	12900	149	14307	n.a.	18635	n.a.	23436	n.a.	39442
Bangladesh	-	-	-	-	35	594	48	983	173	11915	167	12936	95	8103	n.a.	6872	n.a.	5732	n.a.	12281
Cyprus	135	1355	204	2662	128	1786	122	1675	106	5535	206	9237	257	13188	n.a.	13202	n.a.	12749	n.a.	16616
India	252	4315	473	9830	379	7062	477	10782	1009	66462	1207	93585	1113	98002	n.a.	191035	n.a.	220097	n.a.	403174
Nepal	-	-	-	-	-	-	-	-	18	1230	59	4280	77	6269	n.a.	1695	n.a.	6481	n.a.	9799
Syria	47	936	-	-	-	149	36	1056	51	3911	2	766	385	28840	n.a.	7341	n.a.	7799	n.a.	1790
Turkey	185	3821	70	1979	-	-	-	-	-	-	-	-	-	-	-	-	n.a.	4406	n.a.	172009
Sub-Total	760	15720	894	19984	699	14812	848	19381	1550	94905	1790	133704	2076	168709	n.a.	238780	n.a.	280700	n.a.	655111
Africa																				
Egypt	1638	25704	1604	31841	1442	26178	352	9712	229	17526	231	18992	226	20284	n.a.	18459	n.a.	395	-	-
Ghana	515	5183	598	8671	625	8803	614	9080	309	24376	144	9442	250	16185	n.a.	10914	-	2801	-	-
Guinea	61	1769	77	2079	66	1895	85	2442	82	6786	62	4673	81	7350	n.a.	8369	n.a.	8840	n.a.	15246
Morocco	699	7691	868	12108	934	13398	943	13522	647	45192	649	38213	665	42720	n.a.	47468	n.a.	44599	n.a.	54027
Somalia	59	1393	73	1698	66	1879	75	1928	113	4301	118	8570	136	8831	n.a.	10056	n.a.	n.a.	n.a.	n.a.
Sub-Total	2972	41740	3214	56397	3133	52153	2069	36684	1380	98181	1204	79890	1358	95370	n.a.	95266	n.a.	56635	n.a.	69273
South America																				
Brazil	-	-	-	-	-	-	-	-	1233	79237	1475	88724	1071	70291	n.a.	95597		19091	-	-
Total, of above	3732	57460	4108	76381	3832	66965	2917	56065	4163	272323	4469	302318	4505	334370	5311[e]	429643	4366[e]	356426	6138[e]	724384
(as a % of total Soviet oil exports)	3.9%		3.9%		3.6%		2.5%		3.6%		3.4%		3.0%		3.5%[e]		2.8%[e]		4.0%[e]	

[e] estimate

[1] Based on official Soviet trade statistics, we assume that the totals given represent close to 100 percent of Soviet oil exports to the Third World. There have been occasional, ad hoc shipments to other Third World countries (Liberia, Nigeria, Senegal, Sudan, Yemen Arab Republic), but only in small quantities.

Sources: Vneshniaia Torgovlia SSSR: Statisticheskii sbornik, various years. The volume estimates for 1977-79 are from U.S. National Foreign Assessment Center, International Energy Statistical Review. (ER IESR).

mid-1970s. In comparison, the largest Third World importer of Soviet oil, India, relies on Soviet oil imports for less than 10 percent of its liquid fuels consumption.

As noted earlier, Soviet oil exports to developing countries have often been made within the framework of bilateral clearing agreements. With the gradual disappearance of bilateral clearing, however, the Soviet Union has recently concluded oil barter deals of a much more specific nature. In June 1978, a three-year agreement was signed with Turkey to exchange one to three million tons of Soviet oil for wheat and metals.[17] In 1979 and 1980, the USSR concluded oil-for-grain barter agreements with India. Although the Soviet intention was to receive primarily wheat in exchange, India has so far shipped only rice. In 1979, 600,000 metric tons of crude oil were shipped under the first barter agreement.[18] The 1980 shipments are less certain, but it has been reported that the USSR designated for delivery to India, in exchange for rice, 200,000 tons of Iraqi crude on its own account, plus 500,000 tons of Soviet petroleum products.[19] There have been scattered, recent reports of negotiations for barter deals with Morocco and Brazil, but the specifics are unknown.

Thanks principally to price increases, oil exports accounted, in the mid-1970s, for an increasingly important share of the value of Soviet-Third World trade. Table 2 indicates the dominant Soviet role in CMEA exports to the Third World of "mineral fuels and related materials" (SITC 3) within which oil has typically accounted for upwards of 85%. The share of energy in Soviet exports to the Third World rose from under 4% to more than 10% between 1970 and 1975, with most of the rise coincident with the 1973 jump in the world price of crude oil. This share fell to 7% in 1978; but increased significantly in 1979 with the escalating world market price for oil, and the rise in the volume of Soviet oil exports to the Third World (Table 3).

Several major points emerge from the analysis. While Soviet oil dominates CMEA energy exports to the Third World, the volume of Soviet oil exports is comparatively small (6.1 mmt in 1979). Moreover, exports are concentrated in a few Third World countries, with the largest share going to India, and there is little evidence of diversification over the 1970s. Several Third World countries are nevertheless highly dependent on imports of Soviet oil to meet their domestic requirements. If India is excluded, the volume of Soviet oil exports to the Third World did not increase over the decade. On the other hand, with rapid increases in price, oil exports have assumed a more important share (12% in 1979) of the total value of Soviet exports to the Third World.

CMEA Oil Imports from the Third World

The shift to hydrocarbons in Eastern Europe's fuels-energy balances had led by the late 1960s to heavy dependence on imports from the Soviet Union.[20] At this time only small quantities of oil were imported from outside the CMEA.[21] Encouraged by the USSR, which was concerned about the terms of its trade with Eastern Europe and the increasing burden on its resources, the East European countries sought to increase their imports of, still relatively cheap, Middle Eastern crude. The diversification of oil imports continued to motivate the expansion of Eastern Europe's relations with the OAPEC countries and Iran throughout the 1970s.[22]

The rising importance of OAPEC and Iran in CMEA crude oil imports at the beginning of the 1970s is apparent from the data presented in Table 4. What is particularly noticeable is the exceptionally high increase in the volume of imports from OAPEC and Iran between 1970 and 1972. In this short period, CMEA crude oil imports from OAPEC and Iran jumped almost three-fold, from 6.1 million metric tons to 17.0 million metric tons; and the share of OAPEC and Iran in total CMEA crude oil imports increased accordingly. For the CMEA Six (Eastern Europe), this share rose from 9.3 percent in 1970 to 17.5 percent in 1972. Iran and Iraq became the two major suppliers. In 1972, these two countries together supplied about 60 percent (10.3 million tons) of the CMEA's total crude oil imports from outside the region.

After the 1973-74 oil price hikes, the upward trend was reversed, and there was a contraction of crude oil imports from OAPEC and Iran. The magnitude of these imports and their share in the total volume of crude oil imports by the Six declined (columns 1 and 4, Table 4) at this time. In addition to the negative impact of higher prices on the volume of imports, transportation problems caused by the closure of the Suez Canal disrupted imports from some Gulf suppliers.

The lower level of crude oil imports from OAPEC and Iran proved to be more an aberration than a new trend. After 1975, under new CMEA pricing arrangements, the price of Soviet oil deliveries to Eastern Europe began to catch up with the world price.[23] The reduction in the differential between the two prices caused the Six to look once again to extra-regional sources. By 1976-77, the CMEA had increased its imports from Middle Eastern suppliers, to 21.7 mmt in 1976 and 20.8 mmt in 1977. In 1978, according to Vanous's figures, these imports jumped to 29.4 mmt. The Six East European members accounted for 70 percent of these imports. Iran and Iraq remained the predominant suppliers, providing 69 percent of the CMEA Seven's total crude imports from extra-regional sources in 1976, 76 percent in 1977, and 67 percent in 1978. Algeria, Libya and Syria were the other major suppliers.

It is apparent, from analysis of the data presented in Table 4, that the Six have turned to extra-CMEA sources of crude oil to varying degrees. Romania is the most exceptional, relying on OAPEC and Iran for almost all of its imports between 1970-78. Romanian crude oil imports from these sources increased steadily and significantly over the 1970s, from 1.3 mmt in 1970 to 12.9 mmt in 1978.[24] Only in 1979 and 1980 did Romania finally turn to the USSR and begin to import Soviet crude oil in quantities of any significance.[25]

TABLE 4
CMEA Imports of Crude Oil

Country	Year	Imports of crude oil from OAPEC + Iran				Imports of Soviet crude oil	
		thousand metric tons					
		Total OAPEC + Iran	Iran	Iraq	as a % of total crude oil imports	thousand metric tons	as a % of total crude oil imports
Bulgaria	1970	930	250	60	16.4%	4750	83.6%
	1972	1920	40	200	23.2%	6370	76.8%
	1974	1620	140	800	13.7%	10220	86.3%
	1976	820	420	-	7.1%	10690	92.9%
	1977	900	380	150	7.7%	10860	92.3%
	1978	1340	740	80	10.5%	11400	89.5%
Czechoslovakia	1970	-	-	-	0.0%	9400	100%
	1972	330	330	-	2.6%	12240	97.4%
	1974	210	-	210	1.4%	14660	98.6%
	1976	760	-	240	4.4%	16320	95.6%
	1977	1340	1090	250	7.3%	16980	92.7%
	1978	870	170	150	4.7%	17710	95.3%
GDR	1970	1070	150	-	10.3%	9280	89.7%
	1972	3530	2970	370	23.8%	11330	76.2%
	1974	2290	220	1760	13.9%	14140	86.1%
	1976	1840	-	1580	10.2%	16200	89.8%
	1977	1400	-	1070	7.4%	17470	91.8%
	1978	2170	-	1060	10.9%	17700	89.1%
Hungary	1970	400	130	-	9.2%	3950	90.8%
	1972	860	100	520	14.2%	5200	85.8%
	1974	630	-	580	9.2%	6190	90.8%
	1976	1060	260	800	12.1%	7720	87.9%
	1977	920	120	730	10.8%	7620	89.2%
	1978	1470	130	1340	14.7%	8500	85.3%
Poland	1970	-	-	-	0.0%	7000	100%
	1972	-	-	-	0.0%	9700	100%
	1974	260	200	60	2.5%	10320	97.5%
	1976	3280	-	-	21.7%	11820	78.3%
	1977	1360	400	-	8.3%	13440	82.0%
	1978	1930	780	1150	11.5%	13500	80.6%
Romania	1970	1290	820	410	100%	-	0.0%
	1972	2870	1750	300	100%	-	0.0%
	1974	4540	3100	1250	100%	-	0.0%
	1976	8160	3700	2810	96.3%	-	0.0%
	1977	8490	3870	2200	96.0%	-	0.0%
	1978	12940	2710	5180	100%	-	0.0%
USSR	1970	2510	-	-	100%	-	-
	1972	7450	-	4080	95.5%	-	-
	1974	4400	-	3410	100%	-	-
	1976	6430	-	5930	100%	-	-
	1977	6360	-	5870	96.7%	-	-
	1978	8710	-	6340	100%	-	-
CMEA-6	1970	3690	1200	410	9.7%	34380	90.3%
	1972	9510	5150	1190	17.5%	44840	82.5%
	1974	9550	3520	3650	14.7%	55530	85.3%
	1976	15920	3960	5430	20.2%	62750	79.5%
	1977	14410	5860	4400	17.4%	66370	80.1%
	1978	20720	4530	8960	22.8%	68810	75.7%

<u>Sources:</u> Trade data for 1970-77, except those for Bulgaria, are from U.N., <u>World Energy Supplies</u>. Statistics on Bulgarian imports, and all data for 1978, are from J. Vañous, "The Changing Role of Iran, Iraq and Libya in the CMEA Strategy for Imports of Fuels", Discussion Paper 80-13, Department of Economics, University of British Columbia, Vancouver, Canada, May 1980, pp. 16-17.

Year-by-year fluctuations in both the volume of crude oil imports from OAPEC and Iran and their share in total crude oil imports of individual countries, also attest to changing import strategies. To illustrate, the 1973-74 escalation in world oil prices forced the GDR and Bulgaria to cut back their imports of non-Soviet crude oil. Prior to the price hikes, these two countries were the leading importers of crude oil from OAPEC and Iran after Romania. In 1972, imports from these sources accounted for 23 percent of both countries' total crude oil imports. Since 1973, Bulgaria and the GDR have held non-Soviet crude oil imports to levels below that of 1972. In 1978, the share of these imports in total crude oil imports was about 11 percent in Bulgaria and the GDR.[26]

The other East European countries increased their crude oil imports from OAPEC and Iran after 1974. With the exception of Romania, levels of imports fluctuated widely, however. For example, in 1976 Poland imported more crude oil from OAPEC and Iran (3.3 mmt) than any other East European country except Romania, but then cut these imports by almost 2 mmt the following year; in 1977, Czechoslovakia almost doubled its imports, to a level almost as high as any of the other Six except Romania, only to cut back the next year; and in 1978, Hungary increased its imports by 60 percent over the preceding year.

The ups and downs recorded in crude oil imports from OAPEC and Iran are in marked contrast to the steady rise in Eastern Europe's crude oil imports from the Soviet Union. With the exception of Romania, demand for crude oil from non-Soviet suppliers has been determined by the marginal requirements of any country in a given year, limited by its current balance-of-payments position. In addition, fluctuations often mirrored the commencement and termination of short-term barter agreements.

Disruptions in supply from East Europe's two major, non-Soviet suppliers, Iran and Iraq, caused by the Islamic revolution in Iran and by the Iran-Iraq war, had a sharp, adverse impact on the volume of CMEA crude oil imports in 1979-80. Iranian authorities suspended oil barter deals with East European countries in 1979. In early 1980, Romania and Bulgaria took up an offer to purchase Iranian crude at world market prices, but deliveries (45,000 b/d to Romania and 40,000 b/d to Bulgaria) ceased with the outbreak of the Iran-Iraq war. Exports of Iraqi crude (about 200,000 b/d to the CMEA Six) were also cut back severely within a week of the start of the war, as the major Iraqi pipeline to the Mediterranean and some tanker terminals on the Gulf were badly damaged. The sharp rise in the world market price of crude oil which resulted from these events dictated a decline in the overall volume of extra—CMEA imports of crude oil by the East European countries after 1979.

In the case of the Soviet Union, major agreements with several Arab countries led to an increase in Soviet crude oil imports from OAPEC sources in the 1970s (Table 4). Although these imports rose from 2.5 mmt in 1970 to 8.7 mmt in 1978, the climb was not steady. Soviet imports appear to have been especially affected by the events of 1973-74. In 1973, Soviet imports of crude oil had reached a level of 13.2 mmt; but in the following year, the volume fell off sharply to 4.4 mmt.[27]

In contrast to those of the Six, Soviet crude oil "imports" from the OAPEC countries are not motivated by inability to meet internal requirements from domestic output. They are apparently imports on account only, for direct re-export; and there is no clear evidence that any oil is actually imported for Soviet domestic use. Before 1973, there may have been some price advantage to oil imports, at least to serve the southern areas of the USSR, but subsequent OPEC price hikes have no doubt served to erode, if not eliminate, any such advantage.[28]

Purchases of oil from OAPEC have been a convenient means of reducing the Soviet Union's trade surplus with these countries, while supplementing, and rendering more flexible, its petroleum export capabilities. Middle Eastern and North African suppliers are well situated sources of re-exportable crude with which to supplement deliveries of oil to the Soviet Union's traditional customers in Asia, Western Europe and even Eastern Europe. The problem of sourcing became more pressing as Soviet oil production began to shift, in the early 1970s, to more easterly and northerly locations, further from markets in both Western and Eastern Europe. Egypt, Algeria and Libya are particularly well placed for Soviet re-export of North African crude oil to West European buyers, especially Italy and France. Iraq— with its pipelines from northern oil fields (Kirkuk) to the Mediterranean, and with the Soviet-assisted development of southern oil fields (North Rumailah) and associated pipeline to the port of Fao on the Persian Gulf—provided a source of supply for Soviet customers in Western and Eastern Europe, and in Asia. Although re-exports of crude oil on Soviet account are difficult to trace, it has been reported that the Soviet Union has supplied India, Japan and Eastern Europe with Iraqi crude, and Greece with Libyan crude.

To reduce transport costs of shipping Soviet crude oil to Cuba, the Soviet Union entered into an unusual swap arrangement with Venezuela whereby Cuba would receive Venezuelan crude; while Spain, Venezuela's traditional customer, would receive an equivalent amount of Soviet crude oil.[29] The original two-year agreement signed with Venezuela in October 1976 was extended in October 1978. These transactions are not readily traceable in published Soviet foreign trade statistics.[30]

The payment arrangements for CMEA oil imports from OAPEC and Iran changed over the course of the 1970s. In the late 1960s and early 1970s, barter agreements were concluded between Bulgaria and Libya, the GDR and Iraq, Romania and Iran, and the USSR and Iraq. All were medium- to long-term arrangements, and specified annual deliveries of crude oil in exchange for a variety of products from the CMEA country. Imports of crude oil by the CMEA countries were also designated within the framework of bilateral clearing arrangements; and in the case of the USSR were, as noted, a convenient way of balancing trade with an energy-exporting Third World partner.

The CMEA Seven employed the compensation format heavily in their energy relations with Iraq. Between 1969-73, they extended credits to Iraq totalling some $900 million, approximately half this amount by the USSR. The credits from Czechoslovakia, Hungary, Romania and the USSR were to cover the purchase of material, equipment and technical services from these countries specifically for the development of Iraq's oil industry. Czechoslovakia's Technoexport constructed the 3.5 million tons/year Basrah oil refinery; Romania supplied drilling rigs, refining facilities and technical assistance in drilling and exploration; the USSR and Hungary participated in the development of the North Rumailah oil field in southern Iraq; and the USSR further assisted in the construction of the 1.5 million tons/year Mosul oil refinery, and an oil products pipeline between Basrah and Baghdad. All of these credits were to be repaid in Iraqi crude from Kirkuk and Rumailah fields, delivered to both Mediterranean and Gulf ports.

It appears likely, given the nature and timing of involvement by individual member-countries, that the CMEA-assisted development of Iraq's oil industry was co-ordinated among the participating CMEA countries. If credits and assistance were indeed co-ordinated, it is also likely that shipments of Iraqi crude to CMEA countries were harmonized. The Soviet Union could then have easily redirected Iraqi crude on its account to East European customers.

Since 1974, there have been no major compensation agreements concluded by CMEA countries for the import of Iraqi crude although Czechoslovakia, Hungary and the Soviet Union continue to assist, on a non-compensatory, contractual basis, in the development of Iraq's oil industry. In addition, medium- to long-term barter deals have become almost impossible to negotiate with OAPEC and Iran generally. Given these developments, and the continued rise in their hard-currency debt, the CMEA countries now have little alternative but to increase their hard-currency earnings from exports of goods and services in order to pay for any imports of crude oil from OAPEC and Iran.

In an attempt to raise hard-currency revenues, the CMEA countries are bidding on major capital projects, including technical assistance as well as supplies of capital equipment in the Third World. The energy sector is one important area of activity. While the Soviet Union plays the most prominent part in this regard, several East European countries have also been active. Outside Iraq, some of the more recent CMEA-assisted projects in Third World countries' oil and gas industries include the following:

(1) the Soviet foreign trade organization (FTO) Tsvetmetpromexport constructed two oil products pipelines in Nigeria (from Warri to Lagos and Lagos to Ilorin) and the El Braga-Misurata Natural Gas Pipeline in Libya;

(2) the Soviet FTOs Soyuzzagrangaz and Neftechimpromexport were to construct one section of the IGAT-II natural gas pipeline in Iran; and the Polish firm Energopol was to help with construction on another section of the same pipeline;[31]

(3) Technoexport of Czechoslovakia, in cooperation with an Austrian firm, built an oil refinery in Syria;

(4) Romania constructed an oil refinery in Karachi, Pakistan, and is presently building the Zarqa oil refinery and associated crude oil pipeline in Jordan, and a gas liquefaction plant in Syria;

(5) the USSR has built a second oil refinery in Ethiopia, and an oil products line linking this new refinery with the older, Soviet-built Assab refinery;

(6) Hungarian geologists from the Hungarian Oil and Gas Trust have explored for oil in India, Libya and Algeria; Romania has conducted oil exploration activity in Syria; and the USSR has assisted numerous Third World countries in oil exploration, including Afghanistan, Algeria, Angola, Ethiopia, India, Jordan, Libya and Syria.

There is, however, an important constraint on the extent to which this strategy of technical assistance and capital project construction can be employed in the energy sector. While securing hard-currency for energy imports, these foreign projects divert skilled labor and other resources from urgent energy projects in the CMEA countries.[32]

The limitations on the ability of East European countries to increase, or even maintain, imports of OAPEC or Iranian oil in the circumstances we have outlined is sharply illustrated by the failure of Czechoslovakia and Hungary to utilize the "Adria" pipeline, built and in part financed by these two countries (with Yugoslavia) to import crude oil from the Middle East and North Africa. Completed in December 1978, Adria had not, at end-1980, been used to deliver crude oil to the two CMEA partners because of the cancellation of barter agreements and the rise in the price of Middle Eastern oil. To make use of the pipeline, Hungary is reportedly considering the construction of a spur line to the Austrian border. In this way, Austria could import oil from the Mediterranean through Adria, and Hungary would collect transit fees.

Romania's failure to conclude with Kuwait a joint venture arrangement to build an oil refinery in Romania is a further example of the difficulties CMEA countries have met in developing strategies to ensure Middle East oil supplies. The deal originally envisaged construction of an 8 mmt/year oil refinery at the Black Sea port of Constanta, to be supplied with Kuwaiti crude, at world market prices. Equity shares in the refinery were to be apportioned 51:49 between Romania and Kuwait, respectively. Negotiations collapsed in 1978, and despite overtures to Nigeria and Libya, Romania has since been unable to secure a new partner. Meanwhile, Romania proceeded on its own with construction of the refinery, albeit at a smaller capacity, and has had to turn to traditional suppliers, like Iran, for the necessary crude.[33]

Given the difficulties which the CMEA Seven have recently encountered in securing oil from the Arab countries and Iran, the question arises of other possible Third World sources to whom they might turn for imports on favorable terms. Angola, because of its close ties with the Warsaw Pact allies, would seem to offer the most potential in this regard. Prior to the nationalization of its hydrocarbon resources in September 1978, Angolan oil exports of over 7 mmt were directed towards the United States (the Virgin Islands was the largest single importer of Angolan crude oil in 1977 because of its huge Hess oil refinery), Puerto Rico and Western Europe. At present, SONANGOL, the state-owned oil company in Angola, is lifting oil under production-sharing agreements with several, major Western oil companies. Consequently the potential for exports by SONANGOL to Eastern Europe is limited, and probably could not exceed 2-3 mmt. Meanwhile, there is no available evidence of Angolan oil exports to Eastern Europe.

Soviet Imports of Natural Gas[34]

Regional supply considerations have caused the Soviet Union to turn to neighboring countries in the Middle East for additional supplies of natural gas. The compensation format was used to import natural gas from Iran and Afghanistan in order to supplement fuels supplies to the southern Soviet republics in the Transcaucasus and Central Asia. These arrangements predate the beginning of major CMEA oil imports from OAPEC and Iran. In 1963, an agreement was signed for Soviet financial and technical assistance in the development of Afghanistan's Shibarghan natural gas fields, including construction of a pipeline from these fields to the Soviet border for delivery of gas into Central Asia. In 1966, the Soviet Union concluded an agreement with Iran whereby associated gas from oil fields in Khuzistan province would be delivered, in repayment for Soviet credits, to the Soviet border through the IGAT-I pipeline, itself partly constructed by Soviet enterprises.

Both of these agreements were very long-term. Afghanistan agreed to supply the Soviet Union annually with at least 1.5 billion cubic meters (bcm) of natural gas for twenty years, starting in 1966; and Iran committed itself to deliver 6 bcm per year between 1970-73, and 10 bcm annually from 1974, until expiry of the agreement in 1985. Both deals made provision for possible extension of deliveries beyond the year of expiration. Moreover, both were supplemented by additional agreements negotiated in the mid-1970s.

In 1975, the Soviet Union entered a tripartite, "swap" agreement with a West European consortium of gas utilities and Iran, whereby the USSR would take delivery, at the Soviet-Iranian border, of 13.4 bcm of gas per year from the National Iranian Gas company, on consignment for the West European consortium, and then deliver 11 bcm of gas to West German and Austrian borderpoints. Iranian gas deliveries to the Soviet Union would be made via a new pipeline, the IGAT-II, which again was to be built in part by IGAT-II, which again was to be built in part by Soviet construction enterprises. The Iranian gas would actually be consumed in the Transcaucasus, and Soviet gas (apparently from Tyumen or Orenburg) was to have been delivered to Western Europe. This agreement was unilaterally abrogated by Iran in the summer of 1979.

The Soviet Union also agreed in 1975 to undertake, on a turnkey basis, development of new gas fields in Afghanistan, situated 50 km southwest of the original Shibarghan fields. With the commissioning of this field in January 1980, the potential for gas exports to the USSR increased but as no new pipeline was built, the extent of the increase would be limited by existing pipeline capacity. In 1980, Afghan exports were scheduled to be about 16 percent higher than in 1979, rising from 2.15 to 2.5 bcm per year.

Soviet gas imports from Afghanistan and Iran (1967-79), in volume and as a percentage of "apparent gas consumption" in the USSR, are presented in Table 5. Because of disruptions in Iranian gas deliveries, total imports have fallen considerably since 1977. In 1980, total gas imports declined again, as Iran ceased entirely, in February of that year, to export gas to the USSR until it negotiated a higher price. Imports probably accounted for less than 1 percent of the USSR's "apparent gas consumption" in 1980.

TABLE 5
Soviet Imports of Natural Gas

Year	Imports from Afghanistan (bcm)	Imports from Iran (bcm)	Total Imports (bcm)	Apparent USSR Consumption (bcm)	Imports as a % of Apparent USSR Consumption
1967	0.2	– –	0.2	156.4	negl.
1968	1.5	– –	1.5	168.9	0.9%
1969	2.0	– –	2.0	180.5	1.1%
1970	2.6	1.0	3.6	198.2	1.8%
1971	2.5	5.6	8.1	216.0	3.8%
1972	2.8	8.2	11.0	227.4	4.8%
1973	2.7	8.7	11.4	241.0	4.7%
1974	2.8	9.1	11.9	258.5	4.6%
1975	2.8	9.6	12.4	282.4	4.4%
1976	2.1	9.3	11.4	305.9	3.7%
1977	2.9	10.3	13.4	326.5	4.1%
1978	2.1	7.2	9.3	344.1	2.7%
1979	2.2	4.1[e]	6.3	358.4	1.8%

[e]estimate

Sources: Statistics for the years 1960-76 come from *Narodnoe Khoziaistvo SSSR: Statisticheskii eghegodnik*, and *Vneshniaia Torgovlia SSSR: Statisticheskii sbornik*, various years. After 1976, Soviet statistical yearbooks did not report natural gas imports. The source for 1977-79 figures is United States National Foreign Assessment Center, *International Energy Statistical Review*, ER/IESR.

Although even at their height imports from the Middle East represented less than five percent of the Soviet Union's natural gas consumption, they played a significant role in regional supply-demand balances in the

Transcaucasus and, to a lesser degree, in Central Asia. At their peak, in 1977, imports of Iranian gas accounted for approximately 50 percent of all natural gas consumed by boilers and furnaces in the Transcaucasus.[35] The disruption of imports from Iran—including complete cut-offs between December 1978 to April 1979 and from February 1980 to the time of writing (Spring, 1981)—caused serious fuels supply problems in this region. These disruptions in Iranian gas supplies have forced the Soviet Union to schedule construction of a new natural gas pipeline to carry Siberian gas from Novopskov to Kazi-Magomed in Azerbaijan. Planned deliveries to the Transcaucasus through this new line are 9 bcm by 1985 and 15 bcm by 1990.[36]

Although Afghan gas has accounted for a lesser share (10%) of Central Asian gas consumption, it has been important to certain areas, such as the Vakhsh valley of southern Tadzhikistan and Dushanbe. Most importantly though, Afghan gas was piped into the Central Asian gas distribution network, allowing more Soviet gas from the Gazli fields (near Bukhara, Uzbekistan) to be directed northward, to the Urals region and Moscow.

Trends and Prospects

Economic considerations, especially the desire to gain increased access to Third World sources of oil and gas, have shaped Soviet and East European relations with the developing countries over the past decade and a half. By the end of the 1970s, however, CMEA policy objectives in the Third World had run into serious obstacles, most apparent in the energy sector. Important turning points have been reached in major areas of CMEA-Third World energy relations; and the new circumstances which they presage will require new policy approaches by the CMEA countries in the 1980s.

The most important trend in CMEA-Third World energy relations in the 1970s was the attempt by the six East European members to source an increasing share of their crude oil import needs outside the CMEA. While all of the Six shared this objective, they pursued it with varying degrees of intensity and success. In the forefront was Romania, which sought to combine Third World imports with its own substantial domestic production base in order to maintain energy self-sufficiency vis-a-vis the USSR and a more autonomous position within the alliance. Other East European countries, however, Poland and Hungary in particular, also succeeded between 1970 and 1978 in raising the share of extra-CMEA oil in their total oil imports. Two extra-regional sources, Iran and Iraq, accounted for most of Eastern Europe's oil imports. In 1978, CMEA purchases accounted for only some 3 percent of total demand for Middle Eastern oil, however.

A number of factors have served to impede progress towards diversification goals, and have become increasingly obstructive. Diversification policies suffered an initial setback soon after they were launched, with the 1973 jump in the OPEC price. After a period of relative price stability, further price shocks came at the end of the decade. By the beginning of the 1980s, the CMEA countries faced an OPEC price which was twelve times higher than in 1972, together with the prospect of future price rises and general price uncertainty. Following the rapid rise in the world price of oil in 1979-80, the gap between the intra-CMEA price and the world price opened up again, increasing the relative attractiveness of oil imports from the Soviet Union.

The explosion of energy prices contributed to the erosion of soft-currency payments possibilities in CMEA trade with the Third World. By the end of the 1970s, bilateral clearing agreements with energy exporting countries in the Third World all but disappeared, and compensation and barter agreements with these countries had become rare exceptions. The Six faced, as a result, not only a higher oil import bill, but one which had to be settled in convertible currencies.

In addition to the sharp deterioration over the decade in the terms of extra-regional sourcing, diversification goals were increasingly beset by instability of supply. Political developments in the Middle East had served to disrupt flows of oil from those sources on which the CMEA countries had relied the most: Iran and Iraq. These events affected existing, as well as new, contracts. (Bulgaria, Poland and Romania had reached agreements in early 1980 to increase oil imports from Iran and/or Iraq.)

The obstacles which the East European CMEA countries have encountered in their attempts to expand their oil imports from the OAPEC countries and Iran were strikingly illustrated by the inability of Czechoslovakia and Hungary to make use of the new Adria pipeline and the collapse of Romanian negotiations with Kuwait for a joint refinery complex. The limits on extra-regional sourcing were also dramatically demonstrated by Romania's recourse to the USSR for assistance at the end of 1978, marking the beginning of Romania's small, but growing imports of Soviet oil.

Events in the Middle East also disrupted Soviet arrangements for the import of energy from the Third World. Imports of natural gas from Iran and Afghanistan served to supply southern regions of the USSR and to release Siberian gas for export to Eastern or Western Europe. While military occupation of Afghanistan has ensured Soviet access to the Afghan gas fields, these cannot make up for the loss of Iranian gas supplies.[37]

In the circumstances outlined above, increased oil imports from the Third World will depend on the ability of the Six to expand their hard currency revenues substantially. In pursuance of this objective, the CMEA countries will continue to provide material and technical assistance for the development of Third World energy resources. Such assistance is likely to be rendered on a straight commercial basis, rather than in the form of barter or compensation agreements. While there may be some success in earning hard-currency revenues by these means, a recent analysis of the overall competitive performance of CMEA exports on the markets of major energy-exporting countries of the Third World indicates the prospects for CMEA export expansion in this direction to be not very promising.[38] Moreover, there are major supply constraints on the expansion of CMEA exports to these markets: slower rates of economic growth in the CMEA countries, regional commitments, including the need to balance trade with the Soviet Union, and export requirements to reduce payments imbalances with the West, now compounded by the debt service burden.

In these circumstances, the Six have little choice but to operate within the current level of Soviet supplies, which show no signs of increasing much above 1980 levels.[39] The prospect of discovery and exploitation of significant petroleum resources in Eastern Europe seems remote.[40] Any improvement in the situation must then come from the success of conservation measures and from the development of alternative energy sources, especially nuclear power.

In sum, the CMEA Six are not in a position to aggravate the global shortage through substantial increases in their demand for Third World oil. At the same time, increased imports from the Third World cannot realistically be regarded as a means by which Eastern Europe can relax the oil constraint on its economic performance in the 1980s.

Given the stronger Soviet hard-currency balance of payments position, the USSR is better able to finance increased imports of oil from the Third World. We have seen that in the past it has used such purchases to supplement its overall export capabilities. While events in Iraq have served to disrupt Soviet oil re-export operations, the importance of Libya as a supplier has been rising. The USSR might purchase additional quantities of Third World oil for delivery to Eastern Europe, to assist its CMEA partners; and the Adria pipeline could be used for this purpose in supplying Czechoslovakia and Hungary.

We saw that Soviet oil exports to the Third World remained limited and concentrated over the 1970s. Domestic production trends in the Soviet Union make it unlikely that these exports can be much expanded in the next decade. On the contrary, to the extent which they are maintained at past levels, they seem likely to be provided on stricter terms. This does not rule out the careful deployment of oil supplies in specific instances to advance political, as well as economic, goals. The oil-for-grain barter agreements with India concluded in 1979 and 1980 are indicative.

It is ironic that, just when the need of the CMEA countries for extra-regional energy sourcing is greatest — due to the diminishing prospects for production of traditional fuels within the CMEA — their efforts to gain increased access to Third World, especially Middle Eastern, sources of supply should have been blocked by the developments we have outlined. It is unlikely, however, that they will abandon these efforts altogether; and they will no doubt exploit all opportunities, economic and political, both to reestablish links with traditional Third World suppliers and to develop new sources of Third World supply. In this regard, the CMEA countries may be forced to respond more seriously than they have in the past to the claims of the developing countries in the debate on the New International Economic

Order. The collapse, at least temporary, of their diversification policies has meanwhile compelled them to raise the priority of regional development projects and of measures designed to increase the efficiency of energy use within the CMEA.

Footnotes

1. This paper deals with the relations between the Third World and the seven European members of the Council for Mutual Economic Assistance (CMEA or Comecon): Bulgaria, Czechoslovakia, GDR, Hungary, Poland, Romania and the Soviet Union. While forced, by the limits of the paper, to deal with them as a group, we shall make some reference to individual policies and experience, distinguishing Romania, in particular, in this regard. All references to the CMEA (member-states) herein are to the Seven or to the Six (excluding the USSR). We disregard the three newer members of the organization — Cuba, Mongolia, and Vietnam — whose geographic location and level of development might easily lead to their inclusion in the Third World. For statistical purposes we define Third World by the U.N. classification of "developing market economies", which excludes the centrally planned economies in Asia (China, Mongolia, North Korea and Vietnam) and Yugoslavia. We have adjusted for Cuba's trade with the Seven, since Cuba is included by the U.N. among the "developing market economies" in trade reporting. This is necessarily a crude adjustment, as Cuba's trade with the CMEA Seven is conducted at prices which diverge significantly from world market prices. Some of these divergences are partially offsetting; for example, Cuba imports oil from the USSR at below world market price, but exports sugar at a price above it.
2. Apart from a few examples of CMEA exports of coal (Polish exports to Argentina and Brazil, and Soviet exports to Egypt), petroleum and natural gas dominate CMEA-Third World energy relations.
3. These new directions in Soviet policy towards the Third World have been analyzed in E.K. Valkenier, "The USSR and the Third World", *Survey* (Summer 1973), pp. 41-49; E.K. Valkenier, "Soviet Economic Relations with the Developing Nations", in *The Soviet Union and the Developing Nations,* edited by R.E. Kanet, Baltimore: Johns Hopkins University Press, 1974, pp. 215-236; and R. Lowenthal, *Model or Ally? Communist Powers and Developing Countries,* New York: Oxford University Press, 1977.
4. Percentages derived from U.N. trade data.
5. Lowenthal, *op. cit.,* 1977. Valkenier has shown how, more recently, in some Soviet circles, relations with the developing countries are analyzed in the broader context of the integration of the CMEA economies into the world economy, an approach which tends to emphasize the possibilities of cooperation with the West in the Third World. E.K. Valkenier, "The USSR, the Third World and the Global Economy", *Problems of Communism* (July-August 1979), pp. 17-33.
6. For more details on Comecon investments in the Third World, see C.H. McMillan, "Growth of External Investments by the Comecon Countries", *The World Economy,* Vol. 2, No. 3 (September 1979), pp. 363-386.
7. Such projects have been termed "tripartite industrial cooperation". Their present form and extent are described in P. Gutman, "Tripartite Industrial Cooperation and Third Countries", in *European Economic Relations and the Developing Countries,* edited by C.T. Saunders, Vienna-New York: Springer Verlag, forthcoming.
8. A potential mechanism for coordination of bilateral relations with Third World countries exists in the organs of the CMEA; and the CMEA's 1971 Comprehensive Program stressed both the desirability of coordination of member-countries' policies with non-members and the importance of collective approaches to the Third World. One of the major targets of developmental efforts by CMEA member-countries in the energy sector

has been Iraq. In 1975, the CMEA member-countries concluded a collective agreement with Iraq which established a joint commission through which their relations could be more effectively coordinated. (The CMEA-Iraq agreement is described in Iu. P. Zhuravlev, *Mezhdunarodnye sviazi soveta ekonomicheskoi vzaimopomoshchi,* Moskva: Mezhdunarodnye Otnosheniia, 1978, pp. 58ff.) While there is some evidence of coordination of member-countries' involvement in Iraq, it is beyond the scope of this paper to attempt to establish the extent to which the CMEA has served more broadly as a mechanism for the coordination of member policies and activities in the Third World.

9. UNCTAD, *Review of the Present State of Payments between Developing Countries and Socialist Countries of Eastern Europe*m (TD/B/AC.22/2), October 1977, Chp. 1. The complex causes of this trend, as well as the statistical pitfalls in quantifying it, are reviewed in M. Lavigne, *Les Economies Socialistes*, Paris: Armand Colin, 1979, pp. 399-400.

10. M. Lavigne, *op. cit.,* p. 401.

11. The nature of the Third World challenge and the CMEA response to it are outlined in B. Despiney, "Pays Socialistes et Nouvel Ordre Economique International", in *Strategies des Pays Socialistes dans l'Echange International,* edited by M. Lavigne, Paris: Economica, 1980, pp. 103-118.

12. B. DasGupta, "Soviet Oil and the Third World", in *Economic Relations between Socialist Countries and the Third World,* edited by D. Nayyar, New Jersey: Allensheld, Osmun and Co. Publishers, Inc., 1977, pp. 191-197. DasGupta reviews the early history of Soviet-Third World oil relations and links them to the emergence of national policies and institutions in the developing countries.

13. M.A. Adelman, *The World Petroleum Market,* Baltimore: The Johns Hopkins University Press, 1972, p. 201.

14. These index numbers reflect only the changes in average annual prices of crude oil exports by OPEC. Applying this index to Soviet oil exports to the Third World assumes that the price of oil product exports increased in proportion to, and consistently with, crude oil export prices, and that the price of Soviet oil exports to the Third World conformed to world market prices for oil.

15. If India is excluded from the calculation, the estimated 1979 volume of Soviet oil exports to other developing countries is almost equivalent to the 1970 level. At present, India is overwhelmingly the main Third World recipient of Soviet oil exports to the Third World. In 1979, over one-half of the total value of Soviet oil exports to the Third World went to India.

16. All of the shares calculated in Table 3 are based on volume of exports, thus there is no distortion resulting from discrepancies in the price of Soviet oil exports to different regions. The shares of CMEA countries and of the industrialized Western economies in the volume of Soviet oil exports have in recent years (1976-79) been in the vicinity of 55 percent and 40 percent, respectively.

17. *Petroleum Intelligence Weekly,* July 17, 1978, p. 8; and *New York Times,* January 13, 1979, p. 2.

18. *Petroleum Intelligence Weekly,* April 23, 1979, p. 10; and *East-West Trade News,* March 14, 1979, p. 4.

19. *Eastern Europe,* Vol. 9, No. 11, June 12, 1980, p. 12; and *Financial Times,* August 22, 1980, p. 2.

20. At this time, the East European countries relied upon the USSR for about 96 percent of their crude oil imports.

21. Total East European imports of crude oil from extra-regional sources prior to 1969 were in the vicinity of 1 mmt.

22. Organization of Arab Petroleum Exporting Countries (OAPEC) members include Algeria, Bahrein, Egypt, Iraq, Kuwait, Libya, Qatar, Saudi Arabia, Syria and the United Arab Emirates.

23. For an analysis of the post-1975 pricing mechanism and its immediate effect on intra-Comecon raw materials prices, see F. Lemoine, "Les prix des echanges à l'intérieur de

conseil d'aide economique mutuelle'', in *Comecon: Progress and Prospects*, Brussels: NATO Directorate of Economic Affairs, 1977, pp. 135-148.

24. Romanian crude oil imports were refined into products for export primarily to hard-currency markets. Since 1976, Romania has imported, in volume, more crude than tons of oil products it has exported. It is estimated that Romania's crude oil import bill exceeded its petroleum product export earnings in 1977. See P.H. Rogness, "Eastern European Energy Relations with OAPEC and Iran in the 1970s: The Case of Hungary and Romania", unpublished Master's Thesis, Carleton University, 1981. In 1979, Romanian crude oil imports exceeded domestic production.

25. Soviet trade statistics show a small value of exports of "oil and oil products" to Romania in 1978. In 1979, Romania reportedly imported 400,000 metric tons of Soviet crude oil. These imports apparently rose in 1980 to over 1 mmt.

26. It should be noted that the percentages referred to are for crude oil only. If oil products imports are included, the shares change somewhat, because East European countries import oil products from the USSR, but little, if any, from OAPEC and Iran.

27. Iraqi exports to the USSR were cut back from 11.0 mmt in 1973 to 3.4 mmt in 1974. Apparently, this was a politically-motivated move by Iraq, in reaction to Soviet re-exports of Iraqi crude on the spot market, which ultimately went to countries in the West which continued to trade with Israel during the 1973-74 Arab embargo. (See M.I. Goldman, *The Enigma of Soviet Petroleum: Half-Empty or Half-Full?* London: Allen and Unwin, 1980, p. 90.)

28. Pointing out that oil production costs in the Middle East are far below those of the USSR, Campbell has suggested that it would be advantageous for the Soviet Union to divert resources from its own oil and gas industry and invest in the Middle East. R.W. Campbell, *Trends in the Soviet Oil and Gas Industry*, Baltimore: The Johns Hopkins University Press, 1979, p. 81. Subsequent events in the Middle East have of course serioulsy diminished this possibility. Should the Soviet Union import OAPEC oil for domestic use, its Black Sea ports would provide easily accessible points of delivery.

29. The reported annual volume of crude oil thus swapped was 1 mmt.

30. In the *1978 Soviet Foreign Trade Yearbook*, the reported value of Soviet oil exports to Spain in 1978 was 35.3 million rubles. In the *1979 Yearbook*, the 1978 value had been adjusted upwards to 84.9 million rubles. This change may have resulted from the manner in which oil movements under the quadrapartite deal were registered.

31. This pipeline was under construction when a trilateral natural gas "swap" deal, for which the pipeline was being built, was unilaterally abrogated by Iran in the summer of 1979 (see next section). Pipeline construction was consequently stopped. At the present time its status is unknown, although Iranian authorities have indicated on occasion that they intend to use the pipeline for domestic purposes.

32. This problem became apparent within the context of Comecon joint investment projects in the energy sector, such as Orenburg. For details, see J.B. Hannigan and C.H. McMillan, "Joint Investment in Resource Development: Sectoral Approaches to Socialist Integration", in Joint Economic Commiteee, Congress of the United States, (ed.), *East European Economic Assessment*, Washington, D.C.: GPO, 1981, pp. 259-295.

33. The Romanian-Kuwaiti joint venture proposal is analyzed in detail in Rogness, *op. cit.*, 1981.

34. The material for this section is drawn from the authors' "The Soviet Energy Stake in Afghanistan and Iran: Rationale and Risk of Natural Gas Imports", Research Report 16, *East-West Commercial Relations Serier,* Institute of Soviet and East European Studies, Carleton University, 1981.

35. Based upon calculations by Dienes on boiler and furnace fuel consumption by economic region in the USSR. L. Dienes, "The Regional Dimension of Soviet Energy Policy", Discussion Paper No. 13, Association of American Geographers' *Project on Soviet Natural Resources in the World Economy,* August 1979, p. 19.

36. We are indebted to Theodore Shabad for providing us with this information, which was

originally disclosed at the Georgian and Armenian party congresses in January 1981.

37. Afghan production capacity and potential is more limited, and it is less important to the requirements of Soviet Central Asia than was Iranian gas to the Soviet Transcaucasus.

38. R.G. Oechsler and J.A. Martens, "Eastern Europe-OPEC Trade: A Solution to Emerging Energy Problems?", in *East European Economic Assessment*, Joint Economic Committee, Congress of the United States, Washington, D.C.: GPO, 1981, pp. 509-540. In analyzing Eastern Europe's prospects for increased merchandise exports to OPEC, using a sample of eight countries, Oechsler and Martens found Eastern Europe's share of these countries' market for manufactures not only to be very small, but declining.

39. See the statement by Soviet Prime Minister Kosygin at the 34th Session of the CMEA, in June 1980.

40. Renewed exploration efforts have led to announcements of finds by Poland and Romania; while Hungary possesses some reserves which now appear economically justifiable to exploit. None of these prospects appears substantial enough to alter the basic deficit situation in the countries in which they are located.

Planning and Management of Energy R and D in CMEA

Robert W. Campbell

Introduction

In any analysis or forecast of the CMEA energy situation in the 80's issues of R and D performance always intrude. Most of the energy policy options require significant technological changes. Whether it will be possible for the USSR to maintain oil output, for example, depends crucially on improvements in exploration technology and in drilling that will make it possible to get more wells from a given stock of rigs and to reach deeper horizons. Substituting other energy sources such as coal, gas, or nuclear power for oil as its supply tightens requires the creation of new, or the upgrading of old, technologies and equipment for production, processing and transport of the alternate fuels. Conservation involves the design and commercialization of new technologies, such as MHD and other combined cycle approaches intended to reduce the heat rate in electric power generation.

Thus it is very important in projecting CMEA energy development to have some perspective on CMEA experience in innovation in the energy sectors. Out of that concern I have spent several years working on this question, in a study which has now come out as a book.[1] My work has focussed on the USSR, rather than on CMEA generally, but Soviet developments dominate the CMEA energy situation, including its technological aspects. The Eastern European countries are likely to remain heavily dependent on Soviet energy and a very large part of the energy sector technology used in these countries originates in the USSR as well. Nuclear power in Eastern Europe is based on Soviet technology, for example, and indeed electric power

---

[1] *Soviet Energy Technologies: Planning, Policy, Research and Development*, Indiana University Press, 1980. This paper is based largely on that book, and I have accordingly not felt it necessary to provide this paper with the usual detailed documentation. The reader interested in the evidence for the generalizations here can consult the book.

generating equipment in general is mostly developed and produced in the Soviet Union. These countries have developed their own new equipment in such cases as coal mining machinery, oil field equipment, or reversible units for pumped storage. Occasionally equipment developed in the smaller countries has been adopted or copied by the USSR to meet its own needs—e.g., bucket wheel excavators for open mining of coal. On the whole, however, this reverse flow is rather small.

Planning of Energy R and D

In the USSR energy R and D planning, like R and D planning in general, involves a mixture of direction from above and initiative from below. The top-down function of establishing a set of mission-oriented research programs is handled by the State Committee for Science and Technology (GKNT), the Academy of Sciences (ANSSSR), and the State Planning Committee (Gosplan). The first step is the establishment of a list of "problems", and the designation of the ministries and departments responsible for solving each of them. For each of these problems, the most important associated "tasks" are established, and it is these tasks that are actually specified in the Five-Year-Plan document in the form of (1) particular machines and systems of machines to be created and mastered, (2) technological processes to be created and mastered, and (3) improvement of methods of planning, organization, and administration of production. The construction of a list of *problems* seems to be part of the Five-Year-Plan process, and the translation into *tasks* takes place both in the Five-Year-Plan and in the annual plans. This system of designating the problems apparently began with the Eighth Five-Year-Plan, 1966-70.

The choice of R and D problems grows out of forecasts of technological potentials and economic needs, responsibility for which is also assigned to GKNT. A good example of such a forecast is a 14-page chapter in a book by two Gosplan economists[2] outlining a number of energy policy objectives and discussing particular technological means for attaining them, such as the creation of larger boiler-turbine generator sets to cut labor expenditure rates.

For problems which involve cooperation among research and production institutions in several ministries ("complex problems") there are also "coordination plans" worked out by the State Committee. An analysis of the 246 complex problems established for the Eighth Five-Year-Plan, mentions such energy R and D examples as "creation of the production engineering and production of equipment for liquifying natural gas," and "creation of equipment for high speed drilling of deep and superdeep oil and gas wells." The coordination plans are apparently not part of the

[2]Tolkachev, A.S. and I.M. Denisenko (eds.) *Osnovnye napravleniia nauchno-tekhnicheskogo progressa.* M. 1971.

official state plan; rather their function is to see that the various tasks that *are* part of the plan form a coordinated solution in each problem area.

This system has changed somewhat over time: In the Tenth Five-Year-Plan (1976-1980) "programs" replaced "coordination plans." They are supposed to be more explicitly focused than were the plans on end results such as the creation of a prototype, construction of a pilot plant, series production, or commissioning of a commercial production facility embodying the new technology. This shift is still continuing, with a great deal of attention being given to establishing centers of responsibility for each problem, phasing the work, and establishing financing and incentive arrangements that will focus effort on achieving specific development goals.

The set of mission-oriented tasks described here covers only part of all Soviet R and D. The remainder of the national R and D effort consists largely of projects that originate at lower levels. Some may be substantial and important projects, but they are projects of branch or local interest and require less elaborate interdepartmental cooperation.

In recent years, the formulation of R and D goals has grown out of exercises modeling energy options. The first step is to outline a number of energy scenarios based on alternative assumptions about production potentials for various sources, demand, and production and transport cost estimates. A linear programming model is then used to develop a program that will minimize the cost of meeting demand. The features common to all the solutions, such as heavy emphasis on Siberian oil and gas, together with such differences as the cost savings that would flow from rapid nuclear power buildup, suggest some general strategic objectives, in the sense of what resources it is crucial to develop, where the big R and D tasks are, and what technical changes, if achieved, will have large payoffs.

An analogous form of strategic planning takes place at the Ministry level, where R and D goals from above are absorbed and fitted into a larger framework. For the Ministry of the Coal Industry (Minugol') the emphasis in the national program on the goal of developing eastern coal means that it must concern itself with technological improvements in open-pit mining. That goal also implies for the Ministry of Electric Power and Electrification (*Minenergo*) that it must deal with a complex of problems associated with utilizing these low-quality coals in mine-mouth generating plants and transmitting the power to markets in the West.

The responsibility at this second level, however, is not only to translate the rather grossly expressed technological objectives specified from above into more fully specified R and D programs and projects, but also to repeat the whole process of establishing a strategic framework of policy goals and then shaping R and D inputs to achieve these goals. The planners at the level of a ministry must do a great deal to integrate its responsibilities for contributing to the achievement of programs of national importance with the more tactical application of the R and D resources under its control to the large number of other technical improvements important in its own operations. There is obviously a lot of room for bottom-up initiative from the ministerial-level R and D planning organizations as they carry out their role.

The ultimate target of all this planning is the network of R and D organizations in the energy sector which will have to perform the R and D program proposed. These organizations are mainly under the control of the ministries but a significant number of basic research institutes in energy are located in the Academy of Sciences, and there is a non-negligible group within higher educational institutions. In fact these R and D organizations receive the planned tasks, but also have a very important role in shaping the energy R and D plan. There are many indications in the literature, and in conversions I have had with people in these institutes that much of the R and D plan originates with them, and that much of the planning from above consists of trying to fit the proposals from below into a plan with some semblance of coherence.

I will not try to say much about this network of R and D organizations here, though anyone interested in details will find a lot in my book. Still a few generalizations might be made about it as an instrument and resource for creating new energy technology. It is a very large establishment in terms of manpower and expenditures, as large as or larger than, that in the U.S. It exhibits most of the features of the Soviet R and D establishment in general. For instance, financing has traditionally been on an institutional basis rather than on a project basis. This kind of financing and the absence of intimate links to producers tends to make the R and D organizations unresponsive to either the producers or the users of new equipment. They also tend to suffer from inbreeding—they depend heavily on certain respective institutions for their recruits and researchers make lifetime careers in them. There is more duplication and competition among energy R and D organizations than we might expect given the effort to coordinate research activity—one can find numerous instances of parallel development programs in two different institutions. On the whole they are probably undersupplied with experimental facilities. Against the background of what we know about Soviet R and D organizations in general, I would judge that energy R and D organizations tend to be somewhat more effective than the average. Many of the organizational innovations aimed at improving R and D performance have first appeared in the energy sector R and D establishment.

Effectiveness of Energy R and D Efforts.

The important question is how effectively this system works—what biases does it exhibit, what kinds of failures are characteristic, does it have sufficient innovation to its credit? The best way to get at that is to consider some concrete examples of technological levels, the efforts that have been made to deal with them, and the degree of success achieved. This will have to be a very small sample, but I have chosen some cases that are both important in forecasting Soviet energy performance and instructive in showing characteristic distinctive features of Soviet R and D.

Pipelines. One of the most important elements in meeting the future energy needs of the CMEA group is expansion of Siberian gas output, and one of the crucial questions is whether the USSR can manage the tremendous transport task involved in moving very large volumes of gas over the extraordinary distances to the European USSR, Eastern Europe and even Western Europe. Soviet pipelines have traditionally exhibited low productivity. The throughput on a gas pipeline system ought to be more or less proportional to its average cross section. Since the average cross section of the Soviet pipeline in the mid-70's was roughly 1.75 times that of the U.S. system, one would expect it to have had a much higher throughput, but in fact throughput on Soviet gas pipelines was only about two-thirds of that in the U.S. system. Underlying this low productivity are problems with pipe quality (which restricts working pressure and leads to service interruptions); problems with compressor equipment (appropriate models have been developed and produced only with great delays and are unreliable in operation); poor preparation of gas (which leads to fouled lines and low throughputs). A careful study of the development history of compressor equipment shows very great delays in the domestic R and D programs and failure to meet quality specifications. Models of the desired size have been greatly delayed in introduction and there have been several makeshift alterations in strategy to cover for development failures. A great inertia has carried forward old design concepts that were excessively costly, and only belatedly did the Russians attempt to develop an indigenous version of the aviation-type gas turbine unit for pipe-line use. In the end the Soviet pipeline designers have often been forced to give up on domestic efforts and resort to importing compressor equipment from abroad. There has been a similar failure to develop domestic pipe of a quality that would permit operation at high pressures (Soviet pipe has customarily limited Soviet designers to 55 atmospheres versus the 75-100 atmospheres they could attain with foreign pipe) and would avoid the corrosion problems that plague their domestically produced line pipe. So in the end they have also used imported pipe very extensively in the gas pipeline system.

Eastern coal. A second component in the Soviet strategy for meeting future energy needs is expansion of output of the coals of the Kansk-Achinsk and Ekibastuz basins, which can be produced cheaply from open pit mines, but which are very low in quality. They have high ash content (and for Kansk-Achinsk coals—high moisture content) that greatly complicates their transport and combustion. Ekibastuz coal is so low in quality that Minenergo complains that what is shipped to it scarcely differs from what Minugol' dumps on the spoil heap. To absorb these coals into the fuel balance in large quantities will require solution of several clusters of technological problems—creation of equipment for open-pit mines to produce the coal, development of processes to convert it into transportable forms, and introduction of new methods to transport the resulting products. The latter will include use of ultra-high voltage transmission lines to link mine-mouth power plants to markets in the European USSR, and perhaps slurry pipelines to ship raw or processed coal.

In all these areas performance so far has been poor and suggests that there are certain characteristic weaknesses in the system. The USSR has failed badly in producing excavators and haulage vehicles adequate to the scale of eastern strip mines. Case histories of development and introduction of the major excavator models of both the walking dragline type and the mechanical shovel type show very long delays, vacillation and reversals in technological decisions, and what seem to be some spectacular failures. One of the most important explanations seems to be that the customers are in a weak position vis-a-vis the suppliers and the latter, which tend to produce excavating equipment as a sideline, accord it a very low priority. But another factor seems to be that the designers are limited by steel quality. Characteristically the Soviet excavators cannot attain simultaneously the boom length and bucket size of comparable American equipment. For a long time the only truck the industry was able to acquire for hauling coal or overburden in the mine was a 27-ton version of a general dump truck, then a 40-ton model. Development programs for 65- and 75-ton vehicles have dragged on over many years, and scheduled dates for protype production, testing and industrial production are regularly missed. What the industry needs is a 150-200 ton vehicle, and there seems to be nothing encouraging happening in getting such a model produced. To meet the needs of the Neriungri mine in the Far East which is exporting coking coal to Japan, American excavators and Canadian haulage vehicles were imported.

Solid fuel processing has gone through an interesting reversal. R and D on this problem was given a very high priority in the pre-hydrocarbon period in an effort to develop a source of liquid and gaseous fuel, but was then downgraded in the sixties and seventies when it became clear that there was plenty of natural gas and oil to meet these needs. Although some R and D work continued, my reading of the record suggests it was never re-oriented to the new task of processing coal to make it into a transportable fuel. This case is also an instructive example of what I think is a common feature of Soviet R and D. When the need to change direction to make it possible to convert Kansk-Achinsk coal to a transportable fuel was finally recognized, a crash program was started which attempted to telescope the R and D process, moving ahead to an overambitious demonstration plant with too little intermediate testing of ideas, processes and concepts or adaptation of research directions to fit the needs. In all the discussions of this program there is considerable ambiguity as to whether the goal is mainly to salvage liquid components from these brown coals for higher value uses or to produce a transportable fuel for boiler and furnace use.

Electric Power Generation: The greatest successes in Soviet energy R and D have been in the electric power field. The main achievement is a very low expenditure of fuel per KWH generated, as a result of heavy use of cogeneration and supercritical steam parameters. Of the total fuel burned in fossil fired stations more energy is captured and used in the form of heat than in the form of electric power (32.1 MTst and 22.3 MTst respectively in 1980). With this captured heat netted out of total fuel expenditure, the Soviet heat rate for power generation is now about 9,200 BTU per KWH whereas it is more like 10,500 BTU per KWH in the U.S. As another example, the Russians have successfully commercialized two different thermal neutron nuclear power reactors, and are among the leaders in the effort to commercialize the breeder and develop fusion reactors. They have had considerable success in high voltage transmission. On the other hand, careful study of each of these programs shows some characteristic weaknesses. Failure to get phased and co-ordinated development of systems as a whole has been extremely common — the turbo-generator units have been put into production before all the auxiliary equipment needed to make them operate effectively was developed — circulation pumps and control equipment are cases in point. Another common outcome has been design of equipment assuming specifications that were not realized, undercutting the gains that would otherwise have been achieved. Supercritical power generating equipment was designed to operate with steam at 565 °C. but it turned out that steel quality was inadequate for this temperature, and it was subsequently decided to operate all this equipment at 545 °C. Boiler-turbine-generator units have been designed on the basis of a specified heat content for coal but since that specification is not realized in practice, the boilers produce less than the intended steam output and the turbogenerator sets are underutilized.

Cross-sectoral Generalizations

In addition to those specific cases, there are a number of general features that emerge when looking across the whole span of energy R and D efforts. For example, contrary to what I had expected, Soviet R and D has often been willing to gamble resources on speculative efforts that are risky and unlikely to pay off at an early date. Although much of their energy R and D work has involved following well established technological paths, where the experience of other countries has demonstrated the validity of an approach, there are other ares where they have been fairly bold. The USSR has done significant work on tidal power, for example, and on MHD and other combined-cycle approaches for power generation. It has made a significant commitment to developing the breeder reactor and to some unconventional nuclear technologies involving dissociating oxides of nitrogen as a coolant.

My study corroborates a fairly well accepted idea about Soviet R and D, i.e., that it is strongly influenced by a strategic point of view. R and D efforts are likely to get focused on only selected elements in a given situation considered crucial. One of the paradoxes of Soviet behavior is that despite endless emphasis on the "systems approach" in these matters, R and D efforts tend to be concerned with only part of a system. In electric power, attention has been excessively devoted to getting the heat rate down while competing goals get neglected. The R and D establishment has consistently ignored the task of developing peaking equipment, where the goal is to sacrifice some thermal efficiency in order to obtain flexibility and save capital. In the development of equipment for open-pit mines the emphasis has gone mainly to excavators and transport equipment, while such important auxiliary equipment as bulldozers, augers, and shot-hole drilling rigs were neglected. A coal industry commentator says that much of the equipment developed for underground mining tends to be undertaken with little concern for where in the cycle of operations it would be easiest to raise labor productivity.

This feature of the system is probably very relevant to our forecasts for the eighties. For one thing, it is unlikely to be very effective at developing conservation technologies, which are an important alternative to supply solutions to meeting the energy needs of the economy. Potential energy savings are scattered all across the industrial landscape, but this system will neglect all but the most visible possibilities, and ones that get targeted at the top. We can also expect that important innovations are going to continue to founder or be delayed because the necessary work on some subsidiary process gets neglected. For example, I can see the Russians solving the pipe quality problem by one of the routes they are considering, such as multilayer pipe. They are even likely to make a lot of progress on the compressor problem. But these breakthroughs toward better pipeline productivity could be seriously impaired because of neglecting the R and D to improve storage at the using end, or gas preparation at the sending end. They may succeed in turning out nuclear reactors like sausages at Volgodonsk, but find they can't use them effectively because the pumped storage that should go along with the baseload capacity nuclear plants provide doesn't get built because the reversible units don't get developed.

There are bound to be R and D efforts to improve oil refining to guarantee a mix richer in motor fuel and poorer in residuals for boiler and furnace use, and to raise octane ratings to permit higher compression ratios to reduce fuel consumption, but somewhere in that complex of interrelated innovations some won't get made, and there will be an embarrassing breakdown. These disjunctions may involve other spheres of decisionmaking as much as R and D, but one insight this study has provided for me is that R and D is not something separate and unconnected, it is just one of the instruments energy policy-makers must orchestrate into their overall efforts to meet energy needs.

One of the best ways to summarize what I have found in a way to make it useful for speculating about the future is to organize the evidence around the question of "commercialization." Energy R and D, like R and D in general, involves a spectrum of activities. At the one end is basic research on a wide variety of possible solutions to some need, and at the other concrete embodiment in equipment of a working solution and its diffusion in use. Along this spectrum there is reduction of uncertainty, a narrowing of the possible alternatives considered, an increase in the scale of R and D outlays, and an increasing acceptance of givens to which the innovation must conform. R and D management involves the process of movement along this spectrum, and it is useful to ask what is distinctive about the Soviet system's behavior in handling it.

First, the system is perfectly capable of supporting work in novel areas and at the frontier of technological advance, even when the direction chosen has not been validated by foreign experience. Ideas and possibilities that are a long way from realization because they involve basic research or because their potential must be evaluated through a long period of experimentation do get supported. Even organizations we might expect to be biased toward current production tasks have often supported long-shot ideas. Minenergo, for example, has been willing to spend resources on tidal power and to risk prestige and quite large resources on MHD. How is such work protected from the short time horizon that indeed dominates most decision making in the USSR, and pressure to focus on solving immediate production problems? Despite operating with a generally mission-oriented perspective, R and D planners understand well enough that there should be a distinct mission conceived of as building up a scientific-technical backlog of ideas that might be useful at some future time—the so-called *nauchno-tekhnicheskii zadel.* This is reinforced in execution by a kind of institutional decoupling—the designers of the R and D system really do try to set up organizations that can be independent of current production concerns because they have high level protection and independent financing. This is the positive side of phenomenon already noted—the inertia and insensitivity of many R and D organizations that comes from assigned specializations and the prevalence of institutional, rather than project, financing.

Moreover, it is clear that high-level decision makers in the production establishment *are* capable of vision, and *are* willing to accept significant risks in supporting R and D. There are examples of research directions which have received continued and substantial support even though they may be at variance with the general directions of world technological development or have been consciously rejected by decision makers in other countries. Support for the MHD program has continued through the ups and downs this idea has suffered in other countries. The oil industry supported through thick and thin a completely distinct line for improving drilling technology—the turbodrill. In both these cases I believe the explanation must be partly in terms of personal and bureaucratic influence. When a bureaucratic structure or a powerful individual is really convinced and committed to some direction, it will be doggedly pursued despite discouragements or the contrary example of other countries.

On the other hand, centrally imposed strategic views play an important role in energy policy and the R and D efforts that support it. This means that if an idea does not get central attention the system is weak in mechanisms for advancing it to the next stage along the spectrum. It is clear that the high-level decision makers in the energy R and D establishment do not see much hope for geothermal or solar energy, and have kept R and D efforts on these alternatives at starvation levels. The central figures themselves say so; the gas industry which is supposed to explore for and develop geothermal resources has practically organized the effort out of existence; Minenergo has treated power generation from geothermal sources like a stepchild.

I would also like to suggest that the various devices that protect basic and speculative research in the system exact a serious penalty by complicating the problem of moving smoothly from one stage of the science-production cycle to the next. The institutional decoupling that protects speculative and basic research from the attention of officials with short time horizons and production orientations also makes it difficult to accomplish a smooth transition from one stage of the cycle to the next. Everything is either rather speculative research or overhurried movement toward industrial application.

A decision to move ahead on introducing a significant innovation is likely to be made only in response to great pressure-pan outside example, a crucial bottleneck, a sectoral priority that creates a pressing technological need. In the absence of such pressure, R and D work in any area of technology is likely to mark time, with little effort put into intermediate kinds of applied research, such as accumulation of data or research on materials and components, that would provide a foundation for a subsequent decision to commercialize. Once a commitment is made, however, then it is likely to be a crash program, in which stages are telescoped, and attention is given primarily to some components, with little attempt to design the whole technology as an optimized system. A fairly ambitious step upward is likely to be attempted in choosing the scale of the demonstration plant, unit size of equipment, or technical parameters. As a corollary there is a strong preference for going directly to an expensive prototype or demonstration facility as a substitute for additional work on the elements of the new technology to enhance predictability in design. Indeed, the testing of the new technologies is likely to take place using what are intended essentially as commercial designs, to which producers have made heavy commitments, or in facilities that are expensive enough that they must be considered for commercial exploitation. Such an overambitious and premature commitment may well result in large wastes and delays.

The MHD Program

The prototypical illustration of this description is the MHD program, but the development effort for a number of other examples also fit — gas turbine compressors, the creation of each successive generation of power generating equipment, the experience with excavators and trucks. The report of the U.S. nuclear power reactor delegation that visited the USSR in 1974, underlined the preference for "complex or integrated reactor experiments for test purposes, versus the U.S. preference for single purpose tests," and noted that "major plant construction was started without complete designs in hand and without extensive prior proof-testing of all features . . . The Soviets clearly accept risks associated with the price of moving foward with demonstration plant construction."

Solid fuel processing reveals a long history of rather poorly guided effort, followed by the scheduling of an overambitious demonstration effort. Test data and economic evaluations of the processes were based on units handling about 15-20 tons of coal a day. The next two steps, however, are to be a plant of one million tons annual capacity and then one of 24 million tons annual capacity. Because step-up to one million tons was probably premature, Minenergo has subsequently vacillated in pressing ahead with it. Slurry pipelines, geothermal and solar power examplify technologies that have not yet been given the nod, and R and D in those areas pokes along with little indication of exploratory work appropriate to their current status and prospective importance and designed to provide a basis for future decisions about application.

I must admit there is a kind of internal contradictionin the picture I have presented. An ambitious step upward is often moderated by conscious avoidance of developing the new generation as a complete system. To insure against failure the energy equipment' programs we have looked at tend to use auxiliary equipment models that have already been extensively tested in practice. The innovative elements are usually introduced into a fairly conventional environment, and in this way the R and D risk can be limited to the novel elements. In the U-25 MHD plant, everything outside the MHD element itself is quite conventional. The aviation-type turbo compressors the Russians developed for gas pipelines were based on an existing aviation engine, and the task of designing a new model from scratch was rejected. The heavy emphasis on parts commonality evidences the same philosophy applied to individual items of equipment. The 300 MW power generation block was reported to have 65 percent parts commonality with early models, and we find the same emphasis on this principle in the excavator field and in the development of underground mining machinery. This form of incrementalism is a way of easing the commercialization of a new technology at the crucial sticking point—the manufacture of new equipment—by using components already in production. This approach is quite consistent, by the way, with the conclusion of a recent R and D report on military R and D that designs tend to be conservative, with a preference for small incremental changes rather than efforts to create completely new systems with large performance gains.

As another form of insurance, early versions and demonstration facilities are commonly designed with considerable reserves to cope with disappointments and to permit subsequent upgrading in performance. The first 500 KV line was operated originally at 400 KV; only later were experiments made to see if it could operate at 500 KV. The original design for the 1,000 MW RBMK nuclear reactor was so conservative that it is expected that upgrading to a 1,500 MW version can be achieved by intensifying the heat exchange process, without modifying the design of the reactor as a whole. Likewise, in the VVER nuclear reactor, capacity is to be raised by exploiting the technical slack in the original model revealed through operating experience, rather than by extensive redesign. But even with this kind of insurance, Soviet experience in a number of cases—new power generating blocks, especially boiler design, the MHD facility, the nuclear power program, and several of the excavator models, all suggest that in relation to the actual capabilities of the R and D establishment planners decide on big enough steps into the unknown to cause real difficulties.

The R and D approach outlined has some serious disadvantages. U.S. observers of the MHD program seem to agree that the Soviet method is wasteful in fixing too many parameters in advance, and in putting ideas into metal and concrete too soon. Soviet commentators themselves are often highly critical of the failure to do enough intermediate testing as new equipment is being designed and readied for production.

Traditionally it has been the final stages of the R and D cycle—commercialization proper or the introduction of a new technology into practice—that most distinguish Soviet practice from that in other economies. In a market economy one of the main reasons for so much caution in the design and testing phase is the desire of the developer of new equipment that the innovation be competitive and appealing to prospective customers when it is ready to be marketed. Potential users will want to know when it can be delivered; the seller of the equipment must be able to assure buyers about cost and performance. Failure here can mean that a firm's innovation will not win acceptance. The same argument applies to a considerable extent even to the energy R and D programs sponsored or financed by governments rather than profit-making firms. In most market economies any new technologies developed with the stimulus of government financing will still have to meet market tests if they are to be successfully commercialized. Moreover, a technology brought successfully to the commercial stage in a given national context can be wiped out by international competition even if it is technically successful.

In the Soviet setting many of these considerations matter less. User ministries have much more limited motivation and freedom to reject technologies that are not commercially appealing than do firms in a market economy. If the decision from the top is that the new technology is to be developed in variant A rather than variant B then there is enough monopoly in the system for foreclose the subsequent emergence of a truly superior form B to forestall diffusion of A. Considerations of international competitiveness also appear much less forcefully in the USSR, and a different way. Foreign competition is unlikely to supersede a domestically developed technology, except possibly in the form of technology transfer if the domestic program is a flagrant failure. International competitiveness may also influence the fate of the new technology if its development is motivated in part by the hope for foreign sales of the equipment (as in the example of power-generating equipment). This kind of international sensitivity was generally unimportant in the USSR in the past, though it has become more prevalent in recent years. There is now far more frequent resort to technology transfer; the USSR has now had some success and has larger ambitions regarding exports of energy technology. Eastern Europe, which in the past was essentially a captive market for the USSR, is now a much more discriminating comparison shopper in choosing the source of new energy technology.

One way to interpret this difference in Soviet and Western approaches to R and D is to relate it to differences in the kinds of uncertainties that dominate the respective systems. In the United States, R and D program managers work to reduce technological uncertainties by precommercialization forms of R and D, the better to be prepared for acceptance at the commercial stage. In the USSR, the uncertainties imposed by interorganizational unpredictability are the ones that can doom a project, and program managers try to ease these by demanding only conventional inputs from outside the program. At the same time they are much less worried about getting the technology accepted once they have developed it, and so they push ahead with a crash program to deliver it in some form, not worrying that they may later have to do considerable backtracking to cope with defects that energy in practice and that were not thought about enough in the precipitate rush to commercialization.

Conclusion

It might be thought that an in-depth look at past experience in dealing with energy R and D might generate some predictions as to how CMEA energy policy will evolve, how technological considerations will influence outcomes on the big choices confronting energy policymakers in the Socialist world. Such a hope was a part of the inspiration for this study. As my investigation has proceeded, however, that expectation has been disappointed, but it does seem possible to formulate some summary reflections on the general issue of how the peculiarities of R and D in the Soviet-type system are likely to interact with energy policy.

It seems unlikely that the USSR will achieve the kind of dramatic breakthroughs in any given technological area that could tilt the balance of economic advantages decisively one way or the other on any of the major choices. Most Soviet energy R and D programs drag out over long periods, the equipment and facilities that finally emerge from them only partially meet the needs that motivated them. This is inherent in R and D, of course, and might be said about any economy, but I read the Soviet record as more disappointing in this respect than the norm in market economies. In the light of past experience, it just doesn't seem realistic to expect breakthroughs in the technology of coal conversion or in power transmission that would give Kansk-Achinsk coal a dominant place in the solution of the energy deficit in the European USSR. Nor can one expect that the nuclear program, even in the light of its efforts to adapt reactors to permit applications other than power generation, will proceed in accordance with the hopes of its managers to make a dominating contribution to solving that problem. I would be very wary of a line of argument saying that just because it is so clear that exploration holds the key to solving the oil problem, they are bound to focus and achieve a breakthrough there.

By a similar argument, we should not expect that R and D in the energy sector is likely to so influence the structure of relative advantage in energy options as to move the main features of CMEA policy much away from that in the rest of the world. There are and will continue to be many distinctive features in the pattern of production and utilization of energy resources in the USSR and Eastern Europe, but these grow much more out of the nature of the regional resource endowment and demand structure than out of special strengths or predilections in the creation of energy technologies. It is true that Soviet planners have made some major commitments in energy technology that differ from those in the rest of the world, such as the emphasis on the breeder reactor or the dominant place given the turbodrill. But it is still too early for a conclusion that they will succeed in making the breeder an environmentally viable and economic contributor to overall energy supply. And the turbodrill illustrates the phenomenon, fairly common in Soviet energy R and D experience, of pulling back from a distinctive technological line if it runs counter to world technological trends.

From the other side, none of the specific technological weaknesses associated with the various energy policy alternatives are likely to be so insurmountable as to render a given option impossible. The Russians have often dealt with energy R and D failures in the past by importing technology. That is how they compensated in pipelines, in oil exploration, in oil production. The Soviet planners like to think they can handle any R and D problem with their own resources and in the energy sector they more or less cover the waterfront. They originally expected to use domestic compressors on the Bratstvo line, and on the Chelybinsk line. When it was clear that high capacity models would not emerge from the domestic R and D program on schedule, they decided to resort to imported compressor equipment instead. I believe the technological challenges will be such that the USSR will not outgrow its needs for Western technology. There will continue to be a market in energy technology, with the corollary that the West will have this as a lever if it is decided to use it.

Moreover, it is often possible to design around technological bottlenecks. One of the differences in the world view of economists and of others is the economists' sensitivity to the fact that there are always more alternatives than appear to be available at first blush. There are always substitutions and alternatives that make it very short-sighted to draw conclusions about what can and cannot be done. The Russians have often designed around technological limitations, or have overcome technological weaknesses by brute force approaches. They get the gas moved by building excess capacity. If they don't have semi-peaking equipment, they operate equipment optimized for baseload service at low utilization rates. If the R and D people succeed in designing a peaking prime mover, but no generator optimized for peaking use, a decision will be made to use a standard generator. The turbodrill may be very ineffective, but if it proves impossible to turn the R and D programs around to modernize rotary technology, the oil industry can still substitute quantity for productivity within the turbodrill constraint.

What is fascinating about R and D, and what makes it so elusive to analyze from the point of view of making economic choices, is that it expands the range of choice still further. Technological alternatives aren't given, they are created, and the way they are created is through R and D efforts. It does not make much sense to say that the breeder reactor won't work, without specifying the particular technological embodiment of the general physical principle involved. Because R and D in its broadest concept involves the possibility of going back and starting with more fundamental approaches to almost any problem, the range of alternatives at any one place along the continuum of technological possibilities can be increased by shifting the effort backward toward the basic research end of the spectrum.

The following generalization about Soviet energy R and D may be helpful as we try to predict what may happen as Soviet energy policy unfolds. What is distinctive about the Soviet system, what constitutes the real weakness in the R and D process (which is one of the means to be manipulated in any large policy decision area) is its general clumsiness in its movement back and forth along the R and D spectrum—it tends to make commitments too soon, generate too few technological alternatives at each stage, find it difficult to move backward to correct the consequences of miscalculations once commitments are made. This tendency is deeply ingrained in the system, perhaps an inherent feature of its basic organizational properties, and has a pervasive inference on technological advance. An awareness of that tendency is perhaps the best general orientation this study can provide for our continuing effort to evaluate technological potential as we seek to forecast energy policy in the CMEA over the next decade or two.

USSR and East Europe Energy Outlook

Clara Szathmary
Exxon Corporation

The USSR and East Europe produce and consume about 25 per cent of the world's energy. While available information on CMEA energy is not as extensive as it is for other areas, it is sufficient to permit a broad analysis of likely future developments.

Fundamentally affecting the USSR's energy situation is the fact that one-fifth of the Soviet Union's area, which measures some 5,000 miles across, is located above the Arctic Circle; one-half of its territory is under permafrost conditions. The Ural-Volga divides the country into European and Asian Russia: While 80 percent of industry and population is in European Russia, most of the new coal, oil and gas is beyond the dividing line.

Energy Production in the USSR

The USSR is richly endowed with oil, gas and coal resources, but is encountering increasing problems in developing, producing, and transporting them. The historical rate of growth since 1965 of total Soviet energy supplies is slowing down substantially, from about 5 percent in the 1960's to a little better than 2 percent currently.

The USSR is emphasizing nuclear development, including breeder reactors, of which it has three demonstrator units. As a result of a substantial shortfall of development seen in the 1980's, nuclear growth is expected to be slower than USSR plans indicate. Nevertheless, nuclear energy shows the fastest growth, and as seen in the accompanying chart, may contribute 10% of total energy in 2000 compared to about 1% currently.

Growth in coal production has been small since 1965 and growth rates will probably not increase during the 1980's though they may increase during the 1990's, to somewhat below 2 percent per year to 2000. The

The average heat content of coal extracted will fall, however, ,ause most of the increase in production will be brown coal.

The USSR today is the world's largest oil producer. In the 1970's Soviet oil output grew rapidly, at 5.4 per cent a year, and it is still increasing at about 1 per cent annually. But oil production growth rates are slowing down, and one can anticipate a production peak of 12 million barrels/day and then a range of 11-12 million barrels/day perhaps to the year 2000. As a result, oil will account for a declining share of total energy production.

Most of this loss in share will be picked up by gas, which is the one really bright spot in the Soviet energy outlook. Output of gas is expected to grow substantially, at a yearly rate of 5 per cent to 1990, and 3.5 per cent thereafter. Between 1990 and 2000 gas will be the largest contributor to total energy production.

The USSR, with substantial Western technology and equipment inputs, seems to be able to construct the gas pipeline capacity needed. In the decade ahead, the same incremental volumes (about 30 billion cubic meters/year) as achieved in 1975-80, will have to be transported.

The USSR is the only country which is extensively using 56-inch gas pipelines, whose carrying capacity is about 30 billion cubic meters of gas annually; in additon, the USSR has built a 2.5-mile experimental line of multilayer steel pipe which it claims could almost double carrying capacity. In any case, the Soviets have limited capacity to produce 56-inch pipe, so line pipe of this dimension is being imported from West Germany, and other wide-diameter pipe from France, Japan and Sweden.

Energy Demand in the USSR

At these projected levels of oil and gas production, the Soviets will have to adjust energy consumption patterns to accommodate no increase in oil availability and rapidly growing gas supplies. Although end-use data as it is used in the West are not published by the USSR, end-use analysis based primarily on the work of Professors Robert Campbell and Leslie Dienes, as well as on some limited Soviet electricity data showing fuel input to power plants in the USSR, suggests that two-thirds or more of electricity is used by industry. All these figures show that energy use in the USSR differs significantly from that of other industrial nations.

The accompanying diagram shows per cent shares of energy input used by economic sectors in the USSR in 1970 and 1975, as compared with that used in Western Europe in 1975. The big users of energy in the USSR are industrial installations and power generating plants. In 1975 they accounted together for 73 percent of total energy consumed, compared to 55 percent compared to 55 percent in Western Europe. Transportation and residential and commercial use occupy small shares in the USSR, 6 per cent and 9 per cent respectively, compared to 18 per cent for transportation and 20 per cent for residential and commercial use in Western Europe. The category

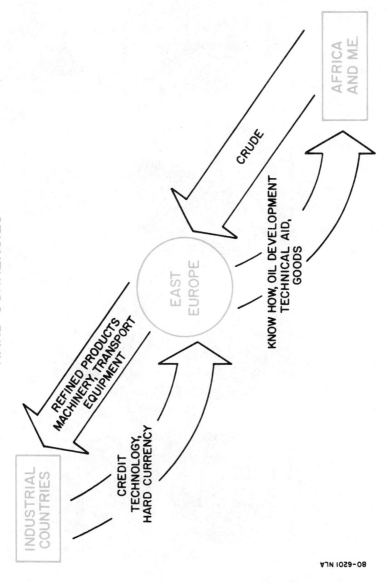

MECHANISMS TO EARN HARD CURRENCIES

AFRICA AND M.E.

CRUDE

EAST EUROPE

KNOW HOW, OIL DEVELOPMENT TECHNICAL AID, GOODS

REFINED PRODUCTS MACHINERY, TRANSPORT EQUIPMENT

INDUSTRIAL COUNTRIES

CREDIT TECHNOLOGY, HARD CURRENCY

80-6201 NLA

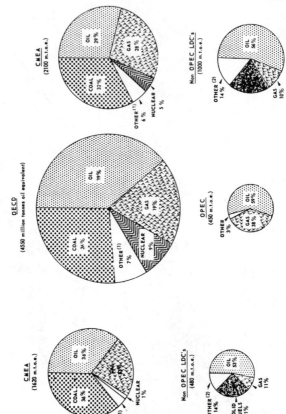

WORLD ENERGY PRODUCTION
1979
BY COUNTRY GROUPS

(DIAGRAM I)

PLAUSIBLE WORLD ENERGY CONSUMPTION
1990
BY COUNTRY GROUPS

(DIAGRAM IV)

OECD
(2500 million tonnes oil equivalent)

COAL 29%
OIL 29%
GAS 26%
NUCLEAR 5%
OTHER (1) 10%

C M E A
(1620 m.t.o.e.)

COAL 36%
OIL 36%
GAS 23%
NUCLEAR 1%
OTHER (1) 4%

O P E C
(1670 m.t.o.e.)

OIL 94%
GAS 5%
OTHER 1%

Non OPEC LDC's
(480 m.t.o.e.)

OIL 53%
GAS 11%
SOLID FUELS 21%
OTHER (2) 14%

OECD
(4550 million tonnes oil equivalent)

OIL 39%
COAL 26%
GAS 19%
NUCLEAR 9%
OTHER (1) 7%

C M E A
(2100 m.t.o.e.)

COAL 32%
OIL 29%
GAS 28%
NUCLEAR 5%
OTHER (1) 6%

O P E C
(450 m.t.o.e.)

OIL 59%
GAS 38%
OTHER 3%

Non OPEC LDC's
(1000 m.t.o.e.)

OIL 56%
GAS 10%
OTHER (2) 14%

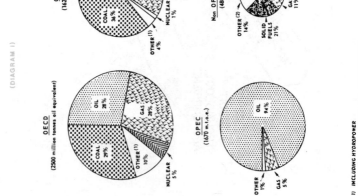

1) *INCLUDING HYDROPOWER*
2) *INCLUDING NUCLEAR, GEOTHERMAL AND HYDROPOWER*

SOURCES : CIA, IEA

1) *INCLUDING HYDROPOWER*
2) *INCLUDING NUCLEAR, GEOTHERMAL AND HYDROPOWER*

SOURCES : IEA, NATO COLLOQUIUM 1981

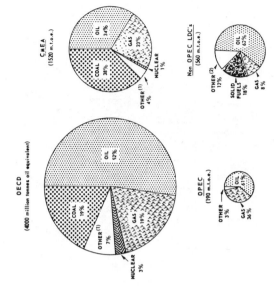

WORLD ENERGY CONSUMPTION
1979
BY COUNTRY GROUPS

(DIAGRAM III)

1) INCLUDING HYDROPOWER
2) INCLUDING NUCLEAR, GEOTHERMAL AND HYDROPOWER
SOURCES : IEA, NATO COLLOQUIUM 1981

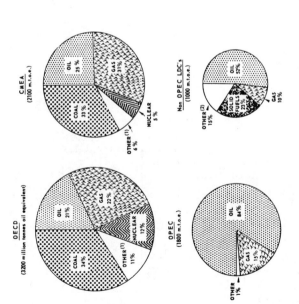

PLAUSIBLE WORLD ENERGY PRODUCTION
1990
BY COUNTRY GROUPS

(DIAGRAM III)

1) INCLUDING HYDROPOWER
2) INCLUDING NUCLEAR, GEOTHERMAL AND HYDROPOWER
SOURCES : IEA, NATO COLLOQUIUM 1981

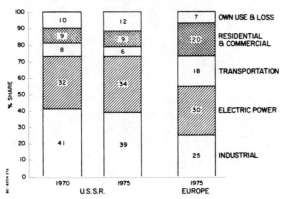

SHARE OF CONSUMING SECTORS OF ENERGY USE
IN THE U.S.S.R. AND EUROPE

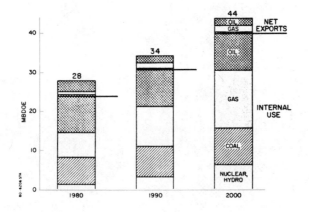

U.S.S.R. DISTRIBUTION OF ENERGY

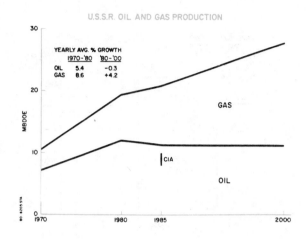

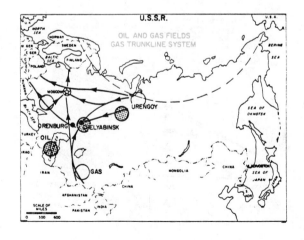

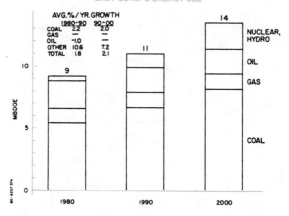

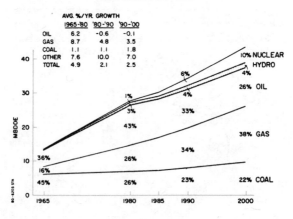

"Own Use and Loss" is higher in the USSR — 12 per cent, compared to 7 per cent in Western Europe.

Part of the electric power generated in the Soviet Union is used to produce both heat for residential/commercial purposes and steam for the industrial sector. This so-called "cogeneration" is significantly higher in the USSR than in Western countries.

With almost three-fourths of the energy consumed by power plants and the industrial sector, the energy outlook in the USSR implies a switching away from oil in these sectors. The Soviets should be able to accomplish this transition, provided they can put the required gas and electricity distribution systems in place. One indication that the switch is occurring is that no more oil-fired power plants are being built. On the other hand, the outlook for oil implies modest growth in the transport sector, but no increase in share of total energy consumed.

As to the distribution of energy use by type of source, the Soviet Union is different from other industrial nations in two major respects: it is in an overall surplus position, and coal still contributes a large portion of total energy consumed. On balance, an increase in gas use coupled with no increase in oil consumption can probably be accommodated, since most increases in energy use will occur in the industrial sector where oil and gas are interchangeable.

The USSR currently exports energy to Eastern Europe and to Western countries, but these exports are relatively small compared to domestic energy consumption. Oil exports to the West for hard-currency earnings will most likely continue in the decade ahead, as they will to Eastern Europe for political reasons. Oil exports to the West, however, will probably decline from 1.2 million barrels/day to 0.5 million barrels/day by 1985, and remain about the same as in the past to Eastern Europe. Gas exports will grow to both areas, and those to the West will probably make up for the lost revenue from declining oil exports. Coal exports are small and should remain relatively unchanged to the end of the century.

The Energy Situation in Eastern Europe

Having examined the energy prospects for the USSR, it is interesting to contrast them with the expected energy-short situation in Eastern Europe. Closely allied to this question is the means by which Eastern Europe obtains hard currency in its economic ties to the West.

Growing indebtedness is forcing Eastern Europe to increase exports of competitive items to the West. Such items are limited, consisting of machinery and transport equipment, food, and small quantities of refined oil products. To remain competitive on Western markets, the East European nations will have to import Western technology, for which they must pay hard currency and also obtain more credit. On the other hand, they have been quite successful in exporting know-how, services, technology, and merchandise to developing countries, sometimes in exchange for crude oil supplies. These supplies are used to supplement East European oil provisions, and some of them are re-exported as refined products to the West for hard currency earnings.

Cheap labor and increasing refining capacity make East European energy product exports profitable, despite tightening oil availability, so exports will probably continue on a modest scale as they have done in 1979 and 1980.

Energy use in Eastern Europe is expected to grow at a very modest rate of 2 per cent throughout the 1980's. Coal will remain the major contributor, providing around 60 per cent of total energy requirements. Since Eastern Europe is almost entirely dependent on imports for oil and gas supplies, use of these two commodities will not significantly increase because domestic production of oil and gas is decreasing. Rumania is the largest oil and gas producer in Eastern Europe, but its output levels are in decline.

Nuclear energy, which with Soviet help is the fastest growing energy source in Eastern Europe, along with additional imports of electricity from the USSR, will ease some of the energy strain in Eastern Europe in the decade ahead. At this stage, it is still not possible to evaluate the potential effects on the East European energy situation of current developments in Poland.

Conclusion

To summarize, predicted energy exports from the USSR and Eastern Europe might be outlined as follows:

Total Net Exports by Fuel:

Oil exports from USSR and E. Europe decrease, reflecting lower USSR exports: combined Soviet and East European oil exports to the West virtually cease to exist by 1985. Gas exports increase, all of the increase coming from the USSR. Coal exports remain steady or increase slightly.

Total Net Exports by Origin:

The USSR remains a net energy exporter, but with gas substituting for oil. Eastern Europe becomes a larger energy importer.

Linkages Between Soviet Energy and Growth Prospects for the 1980s

Joseph Licari

Growth in Soviet energy supplies is expected to slow considerably during the 1980s. Western interest in the emerging Soviet energy plight stems form the impact it will have on both Soviet economic growth and Moscow's ability to remain a major exporter of energy, especially to the West. The purpose of this paper is to integrate Soviet energy issues into broader considerations of economic growth and to suggest the sensitivity of growth prospects to developments in the energy sector.

The linkages between Soviet energy and growth prospects for the 1980s can be examined through a simulation model of the Soviet economy.[1] The model generates a set of internally consistent energy demand, economic growth and foreign trade projections for any given assumptions regarding domestic energy production. This framework is used in the paper to scale the impacts of different energy supply scenarios on growth prospects through 1990.

Growth projections discussed below suggest several conclusions about Soviet growth prospects for the eighties:[2]

a) In the likely case of falling oil production during the 1980s, average GNP growth rates are not likely to exceed 2.5 percent a year during the first half of the decade and 2 percent during the second half.

b) The Soviets could recover some of the growth loss due to declining domestic oil production by importing oil from the West, but oil imports on any sizable scale would hold imports of Western machinery, steel and other industrial goods far below recent levels.

---

[1]For details of the model, see "SOVSIM: A Model of the Soviet Economy," National Foreign Assessment Center (NFAC), ER 79-100001, February 1979.

[2]Earlier projections were given in "Simulations of Soviet Growth Options to 1985," NFAC, ER 79-10131, March 1979.

c) Guidelines for energy production in the 11th Five Year Plan (FYP) for 1981-85 imply no energy constraint on growth through 1985 and an average annual rate of growth of almost four percent. Although not likely to be realized, these optimistic energy expectations would permit oil exports to the West to be as high as a half million barrels per day (mbd) in 1985 compared to roughly one mbd currently.

d) In the absence of continued growth in oil production; there is little short of slashing energy exports to Eastern Europe that Soviet policymakers can do to contain the ensuing negative effects of energy supply trends on economic growth and trade with the West. Some hard currency oil exports could be maintained through 1985 to keep machinery and other industrial imports roughly at recent levels, but this would simply aggravate near-term growth prospects by worsening the domestic oil imbalance.

Key Assumptions and General Methodology

Energy is not the only factor that will limit aggregate Soviet growth over the next decade. Irreversible demographic trends will hold the increment to the Soviet labor force during the eighties to its lowest ten-year level in the postwar period. Investment in the 11th FYP is scheduled, for the first time, to grow more slowly than national income; and as a result, the decline in growth of the stock of plant and equipment will certainly continue. This will occur at a time when the capital intensity of production is rising, in part due to massive investments necessary to exploit Siberian resources. Gains in productivity associated not with new investment but with improvements in organization, management, and work incentives traditionally have been small and are likely to remain so without a comprehensive economic reform.[3]

The shifting energy picture will şimply compound unfavorable trends in other factors influencing overall Soviet growth prospects. This is of course most pronounced in the case of oil (see Table 1). Even the 11th FYP guidelines indicate that Soviet oil production cannot maintain its traditional rapid growth into the eighties. The plan calls for production growth by 1985 of less than one mbd. Even this modest gain is unlikely to be achieved. With rapid depletion of existing reserves, especially outside of West Siberia, with the expected peaking and decline in West Siberian production over the next five years, and with new discoveries falling far short of reserve

---

[3]See Gertrude S. Greenslade, "The Soviet Economy on a Treadmill of Reforms," JEC: Soviet Economy in a Time of Change, 1979, pp. 312-340.

depletions, Soviet oil production in 1985 will probably be in the 10-11 mbd range (midpoint of 10.5 mbd). Unless prospects improve dramatically in the next year or two, a further decline to 7-9 mbd is likely by 1990 (midpoint of 8.0 mbd).

Table 1
Soviet Energy Production

A. Production Levels in Key Years

	1978	1980	1985 Plan*	1985 Assumed	1990 Assumed
Oil (mbd)	9.8	12.0	12.9	10.5	8.0
Coal (mt)	701	716	800	770	845
Gas (bcm)	289	435	640	600	700
Electric Power (bkwhr)	1039	1295	1600	1600	1900

B. Average Annual Growth Rates (percent)

	1971-75	1976-80	1981-85 Plan*	1981-85 Assumed	1986-90 Assumed
Oil	6.8	4.2	1.4	-2.7	-5.3
Coal	2.4	0.4	2.2	1.5	1.9
Gas	7.9	8.5	8.0	6.6	3.1
Electric Power	7.0	4.5	4.3	4.3	3.5

*Plan figures for 1985 are the upper ends of the ranges in the announced 11th FYP guidelines.

While prospects in other fuels are far less bleak, there is no way for the Soviets to compensate fully for the expected loss in oil production with additional production of other fuels. Enormous Soviet gas reserves should allow gas production to expand at a healthy pace throughout the decade. Nonetheless, pipeline and compressor constraints should hold growth rates below levels of the last ten years and below current plan guidelines.[4] Coal output growth expressed in gross tonnage could be better than during the 1976-80 FYP when production almost stagnated, but most of the gain will be in low quality Siberian coal. In terms of total energy content, coal output may rise little during the eighties. Gains in nuclear power generation will help support growth in electric power. However, the bulk of power output represents secondary energy production and the expected slowing of growth in this sector is a reflection of the problems in hydrocarbon fuels.

These energy production assumptions are linked to economic growth prospects in several explicit ways through the simulation model. Energy and capital are assumed to be complements in the description of production

[4]For a discussion of the likely role of imported technology in future Soviet gas expansion see Robert Campbell, "Soviet Technology Imports: The Gas Pipeline Case," February 1981.

relations within the model. Consequently, energy requirements are calculated as a function of the size and structure of the capital stock in each producing sector. The energy intensity of capital is projected from historical trends on energy use and the future size of the capital stock follows from calculations of investment and retirements. Capital utilization depends upon the relationship between this requirement and available energy supplies. The sensitivity of capital utilization to an imbalance between requirements and availabilities varies somewhat by sector based roughly on the relative importance of equipment and structures in the existing stock of capital. The stock of plant and equipment adjusted for utilization affects sector output through a production function that allows some substitution between capital and labor. Since these linkages imply perfect substitution between types of energy at the margin,[5] let capital utilization fall more slowly than energy use, and allow some substitution between capital and labor in the face of reduced capital utilization, they lead to an optimistic projection of output for a given shift in the energy production picture.

This formulation of the linkage between energy and economic growth leads to an energy elasticity of GNP that depends critically on the state of domestic energy balances. If no domestic energy shortages exist, an additional increment in energy can affect output only by increasing the exportable energy surplus, raising machinery imports and eventually increasing the productive capital stock. This process takes several years to complete its cycle and is highly damped by the large existing stocks of capital. On the other hand, if domestic energy shortages exist, an additional increment of energy can affect output immediately by permiting a higher rate of utilization of the existing capital stock. Since part of this incremental output is investment goods, this increment in energy will also have longer-term output effects as well through an increase in productive capital in later years.

A Baseline Projection of Soviet Growth Prospects

The assumptions for primary and secondary energy production in Table 1, when combined with a projection of energy requirements based on the projected size and structure of the Soviet capital stock, indicate energy imbalances during the 1980s. These imbalances restrain potential capital utilization levels and hold GNP growth to trend rates of about 2.5 percent a year for the first half of the decade and somewhat less than 2 percent for

---

[5]Perfect substitution at the margin implies that the total energy available to a particular sector, not the fuel mix, determines capital utilization.

the second.[6] Per capita consumption could grow at around one percent a year during the full period. (Key results for the baseline projection — Case A — and other cases examined below are summarized in Table 2).

Oil shortages begin to emerge in the projection before mid-decade, as the Soviets are unable to adjust the fuel requirements of a relatively static capital stock to a rapidly shifting fuel mix picture. Domestic oil use holds at a little more than 9 mbd through 1985 but falls to 8 mbd by 1990. Smaller but potentially significant imbalances between supplies and requirements for coal, gas and electric power also emerge by 1990 but these shortages were not allowed to constrain projected economic growth. Otherwise, projected GNP growth would have been closer to 2 percent a year through mid-decade and 1.5 percent a year over the later years.[7]

Much of the potential imbalance in the gas sector follows directly from a very large assumed share of gas in new power generation, an assumption which was essential to avoid even further imbalances in oil and coal. Despite the resulting considerable decline in the average share of coal and oil in power generation, the assumed growth of about four percent a year in power output for the decade as a whole still leads to slowly growing oil and coal requirements in the power sector throughout the period. This is simply a particular example of a more general problem — the Soviets will not be able to change the energy characteristics of new plant and equipment fast enough to keep the energy requirements of the total capital stock consistent with the shifting energy supply picture. Hence, imbalances of one kind or another seem unavoidable and adjustments in capital utilization may be the only way to reconcile them during the 1980s.[8]

---

[6]Average annual growth over the 11th FYP — 1981 to 1985 — could be nearer 3 percent because of the depressed base year performance in 1980 when, because of the second straight year of poor crops, GNP grew only 1.4 percent. The projected trend between 1982 and 1985, however, would be around 2.5 percent a year and is more indicative of medium-term growth prospects. Higher-than-trend growth in 1981 would reflect primarily a rebound from depressed 1980 levels, not improved medium-term growth prospects.

[7]These growth projections are based upon mid-range assumptions for oil production of 10.5 mbd in 1985 and 8 mbd in 1990. If instead upper end estimates of 11 mbd in 1985 and 9 mbd in 1990 are used, this additional oil would add only a few tenths of a percentage point to average growth rates over the decade. From another prospective, it would add somewhat less than one percent to the potential level of GNP in 1985 and somewhat more than one percent in 1990. All of the additional oil would be used to meet domestic requirements under our basic assumptions (see Case B, Table 2).

[8]The assumptions for the power sector allow for 20 percent of new electric power generated by hydrocarbon fuels to be generated by oil, compared to the current average of around 30 percent. This reflects the fact that distribution and storage factors will argue against a strict prohibition on construction of new oil-fired power stations. If such a prohibition were feasible and the extra power generation burden was placed on new gas-fired stations, the Soviets would be able to export about a third less gas to the West in 1985 and 1990. At the same time, affordable oil imports from the West also would be down about one-third in those years. While this strategy has no overall impact on domestic energy availability and therefore economic growth, it would be consistent with an autarkic policy designed to reduce the Soviet Union's dependence on foreign trade during a period of increased internal and external political uncertainty.

Table 2

Summary of Soviet Growth Projections

| Variable | A Baseline Level | Variations due to:[1] | | |
		B Higher Oil Output	C Unlimited Western Oil Imports	D 10% more Import Capacity
GNP				
AARG 1982-85 (%)[2]	2.4	+0.2	+0.8	+0.1
AARG 1986-90 (%)	1.8	+0.1	+0.8	Negl
1985 Level				
(B 1970 rubles	627	+5	+18	+2
1990 Level				
(B 1970 rubles)	684	+10	+49	+2
Domestic Oil Output				
1985 (mbd)	10.5	+0.5	0	0
1990 (mbd)	8.0	+1.0	0	0
Domestic Oil Use				
1985 (mbd)	9.1	+0.5	+1.9	+0.2
1990 (mbd)	8.0	+0.9	+5.1	+0.2
Net Hard Currency Oil Exports				
1985 (mbd)	-0.5	Negl	-1.9	-0.2
1990 (mbd)	-0.9	Negl	-5.1	-0.2
Net Oil exports				
1985 (mbd)	1.4	Negl	-1.9	-0.2
1990 (mbd)	0	Negl	-5.1	-0.2
Hard Currency Import capacity				
1985 (B 1980 $)	24	Negl	+27	+2
1990 (B 1980 $)	36	-2	+87	+4
Imports of Western Industrial Goods				
1985 (B 1980 $)	11	0	0	0
1990 (B 1980 $)	11	0	0	0

Variable	A Baseline Level	E Lower Oil Exports to EE	F Fixed Imports of Western Industrial Goods	G 11th FYP Energy Guidelines
GNP				
AARG 1982-85 (%)[2]	2.4	+0.4	-0.2	+0.9
AARG 1986-90 (%)	1.8	Negl	Negl	--
1985 Level				
(B 1970 rubles)	627	+9	-6	+21
1990 Level				
(B 1970 rubles)	684	+5	-5	--

Table 2 (continued)

Summary of Soviet Growth Projections

			Variations due to:[1]	
	A	E	F Fixed Imports of Western Industrial Goods	G
Variable	Baseline Level	Lower Oil Exports to EE		11th FYP Energy Guidelines
Domestic Oil Output				
1985 (mbd)	10.5	0	0	+2.4
1990 (mbd)	8.0	0	0	— —
Domestic Oil Use				
1985 (mbd)	9.1	+1.0	-0.6	+1.3
1990 (mbd)	8.0	+0.5	-0.5	— —
Net Hard Currency				
Oil Exports				
1985 (mbd)	-0.5	Negl	+0.6	+1.1
1990 (mbd)	-0.9	Negl	+0.5	— —
Net Oil exports				
1985 (mbd)	1.4	-1.0	+0.6	+1.1
1990 (mbd)	0	-0.5	+0.5	— —
Hard Currency				
Import capacity				
1985 (B 1980 $)	24	Negl	+2	+9
1990 (B 1980 $)	36	-1	-1	— —
Imports of Western				
Industrial Goods				
1985 (B 1980 $)	11	0	+8	+16
1990 (B 1980 $)	11	0	+8	— —

[1]The difference between the value of the variable under the given conditions and its value in the baseline case.

[2]This figure is the projected four-year trend growth rate between 1982 and 1985 rather than the more conventional five-year average between 1981 and 1985. The depressed performance of the Soviet economy in 1980 leads to a somewhat higher calculated average growth between 1981 and 1985 — up to a half percentage point more — but this difference is not truly indicative of added medium-term growth potential. The difference is really a projected recovery to trend levels in 1981 from below trend actual performance in 1980. The figure in the table is more suggestive of true medium-term trend growth prospects.

Interactions between energy supplies and economic growth will lead to dramatic shifts in Soviet oil trade over the decade. The Soviets could cover part of the potential oil gap by trading-off lower imports of Western equipment and other industrial products for imports of Western oil. Even if Moscow were willing to see these imports of manufactures fall to around half of recent levels, affordable oil imports from the West would be only about a half mbd in 1985, and somewhat less than one mbd in 1990. These levels fall far short of fully closing the oil gap if, as we have assumed, Moscow continues oil exports to other communist countries at around 2 mbd through 1985 and then gradually cuts them to a little below 1 mbd by 1990. In this case, Soviet domestic oil production of 8 mbd in 1990 would be used to cover around two-thirds of domestic oil requirements—the rest would be covered by adjustments in capital utilization after allowing for some substitution between oil, coal and gas—and hard currency imports of about 1 mbd would balance exports to Eastern Europe.

Flat and then falling domestic oil production combined with even somewhat slower growth in domestic oil requirements could bring about substantial changes in Soviet hard currency trade over the decade. The policy choice facing Moscow involves balancing concerns for longer-term growth, which is tied to imports of Western machinery and equipment, against concerns for near-term growth, which could benefit from oil imports when chronic shortages emerge around mid-decade.

The baseline projection assumes that the Soviets will protect grain import claims on hard currency earnings at 20-30 mmt a year, but will allow imports of Western machinery and equipment to deteriorate to about half the recent volume to provide some room for imported oil in the Soviet hard currency balance. These assumptions give the best prospects for Soviet growth during the 1980s, since oil imports to improve utilization of existing capital have a stronger and more immediate impact on output than capital imports to improve output in later years.

Under these assumptions, oil exports to the West could approach zero by 1982 or 83 and the import capacity could fall in real terms for the next few years.[9] The potential for gas exports to the West is very strong, however, and gas earnings would provide the basis for an expanding import capacity through the second half of the decade. Nonetheless, the import capacity would not return to present real levels until 1985 or 86.

Any change in these foreign trade assumptions would make growth prospects for the eighties worse than this projection suggests. For example,

[9]Import capacity equals earnings on commodity trade, gold and arms sales and invisibles, plus net new credits less interest payments. Projections of new credits are tied primarily to Soviet imports of Western equipment.

[10]Remember that the baseline projection also suggested smaller imbalances in coal and gas that were not allowed, however, to limit calculated economic growth during the 1980s.

it is not at all clear that the assumed domestic production levels for gas and oil could be achieved with imports of Western equipment and steel pipe as low as the trade assumptions imply. However, holding oil exports up longer and oil imports down when the transition occurs will improve Moscow's ability to import Western machinery and steel pipe only at the expense of Western oil imports. This would be at a time when they could be important in providing some limited relief from oil shortages, and near-term growth would suffer.

Effects of Different Foreign Trade Assumptions

Linkages between Soviet energy and growth prospects tie heavily to the foreign trade sector. This follows from the large role energy exports play in Soviet trade with both the West and Eastern Europe. When growth is constrained by domestic energy availabilities, maintenance of these exports represents a real opportunity cost to the Soviets in terms of lost near-term growth.

If the Soviets could finance enough Western oil imports to close the gap between oil requirements and domestic supplies that is likely to emerge during the eighties, it would remove the oil constraint on growth (Case C, Table 2).[10] Projections show that hard currency oil imports would have to exceed 2 mbd by 1985 and more than double by 1990. With this additional oil, the gain in growth would be almost a percentage point a year for the whole decade. GNP would exceed expected levels by about 3 percent in 1985 and more than 7 percent in 1990. From another perspective, these hypothetical growth gains are the likely cost of the energy constraint to Soviet growth prospects over the next ten years. That these gains cannot be realized through debt-financed increases in imports of Western oil is seen in the required increments in import capacity and the resulting trend in the debt-service ratio—it would double by 1985 to about one-third, reach 100 percent by 1987/88 and exceed 200 percent by 1990.[11]

If the Soviets did try to use imported Western oil as a stop-gap measure around mid-decade, the debt-service burden would rise too fast for it to become a long-term policy option. After a couple years of large oil imports, Moscow would have to return to exporting oil to the West to keep its hard currency financial position under control. This return to oil exports to the West would come at a time of increasing oil imbalances at home, if domestic oil production falls to the levels we now expect.

---

[11]To the extent that Western lending institutions viewed the Soviet energy problem to be transitional, with a major turnaround likely in the 1990s, Soviet access to Western credit would not be as jeopardized as these high debt-service ratios might suggest. Soviet earnings from arms and gold sales are also substantial and are not included in the standard debt-service ratio of interest and principle repayments to commodity earnings. Including these additional earnings would lower the debt-service ratio by about a quarter of its prior value.

Projections of Soviet hard currency export earnings are admittedly subject to considerable uncertainty. As a basic assumption, we have taken non-energy exports and arms sales to be flat in real terms over the next ten years. Gold sales rise in volume to roughly equal annual gold production by 1983 and hold at that level through 1990; gold prices rise 10 percent a year. Earnings from energy exports depend upon both exportable surpluses derived from energy balances and world prices rising in real terms from 2 to 5 percent a year. If earnings were to be ten percent higher than implied in our baseline growth simulation, this would add about $2 billion to the hard currency import capacity by 1985 and around $4 billion by 1990 (Case D, Table 2). Even if all of this additional import capacity were devoted to financing oil imports, its impact on Soviet growth would be negligible. The reason is that the cost of oil purchased on the world market is likely to grow at a faster pace than other prices during the eighties — our basic assumption is an average annual real price increase of 5 percent. As such, the extra import capacity would translate into only a couple hundred thousand barrels per day of oil or merely two percent or so of domestic oil use.

As problems deepen in the Soviet oil sector over the next few years, the burden of oil exports to Eastern Europe will become increasingly apparent. Soviet exports to communist countries are now running at about 1.9 mbd and, based on Soviet statements, are expected to hold at about that level through 1985. In the absence of any hard information on Soviet intentions after 1985 and in view of probably domestic oil imbalances by then, we have assumed that deliveries to communist countries will be cut back gradually to around one mbd by 1990. A sharper cutback over the decade is always an option open to Moscow if the burden of adjustment to lower Soviet oil production is to be shared differently.

Alternate growth projections assuming a gradual reduction in oil exports to communist countries to about one mbd by 1985 and further to less than a half mbd by 1990 would add less than half of a percentage point to average annual growth rates during the 11th FYP and a negligible amount beyond (Case E, Table 2). The level of Soviet GNP in 1985 and 1990 would be about one percent higher with the oil diverted from export to Eastern Europe than without. However, analysis of the impact of such a Soviet policy on the East European economies shows that it would exacerbate an already dreary growth outlook and could even result in declining per capita output in Czechoslovakia, Hungary and Poland.[12] Obviously, the potential political consequences of these trends sharply constrain Moscow's maneuverability in this area.

A final issue to examine in the linkages between foreign trade, energy and growth is the question of the macroeconomic tradeoff between imports

---

[12]The connection between Soviet and East European energy issues is examined by Robin Watson, "The Outlook for Energy and Economic Growth in Eastern Europe," elsewhere in this Colloquium collection.

of Western oil and industrial goods. The baseline projection of Soviet growth prospects for the eighties assumed that, in the face of oil shortages, Moscow would opt to cut imports of Western equipment and steel back as much as 50 percent below recent levels to provide some room for hard currency oil imports. This trade of less future growth for more present growth leads to a somewhat optimistic growth projection.

If the decision instead were to hold imports of industrial goods flat in real terms, even in the face of oil shortages at home, this policy would result in a 60-70 percent increase over the baseline case in the volume of these commodities imported over the decade (Case F, Table 2). To provide the extra import capacity, oil exports would have to be maintained through 1985, although the level would decline to around one hundred thousand barrels per day by then. There would be room in the hard currency trade balance for limited hard currency oil imports by 1990, but the level of less than a half mbd would leave a very large potential gap.

These policy decisions to maintain imports of Western technology and industrial commodities at the expanse of a worsened domestic energy balance would cost about one-quarter of a percentage point in average annual GNP growth during the 11th FYP. The growth impact during the latter half of the decade would be negligible, but the levels of GNP in both 1985 and 1990 would be a little less than one percent below the levels projected assuming restricted technology imports.

Growth Prospects Seen Through the 11th Five-Year Plan

The recently announced guidelines for the 11th FYP provide an alternate basis upon which Soviet growth prospects can be examined, at least through 1985. As Table 1 shows, the upper ends of guideline ranges for fuels are above levels we judge likely to be achieved. The difference is 7 percent for gas, 4 percent for coal and 23 percent for oil. In the unlikely event that these higher output levels are reached by 1985, they would raise trend growth above the annual 2.5 percent average projected in the base case.

Since the plan figures envision more gas and coal as well as oil, there is the potential under this view for some additional substitution away from oil. This would not only lessen possible domestic oil imbalances but would also help ease the hard currency trade situation through 1985. An alternate optimistic projection of growth prospects can be developed by allowing the increment in coal and gas production above levels assumed in the base case to be substituted for oil in the electric power sector. Not only would this require that no new oil-fired power plants be built, but old ones would have to be converted to gas or coal at the rate of 5-6 percent a year during the 11th FYP.

If these higher energy production levels could be reached and interfuel substitution in the power sector could be accelerated to the maximum rate allowed by the planned fuel production figures, economic growth would not be constrained by energy supplies through 1985 (Case G, Table 2). The GNP trend growth rate would be almost one percentage point above that in the base case—somewhat less than 3.5 percent a year. For the 11th FYP as a whole, annual growth would average somewhat less than 4 percent. In addition, oil exports to the West would fall only slowly under the 11th FYP, still exceeding a half mbd in 1985, and affordable machinery imports over the five year period would almost double. All this could be achieved while fully meeting energy commitments to Eastern Europe.

The growth implications of energy under the 11th FYP guidelines can be rather comforting to the Soviet leadership. If upper-end output levels are achieved, and if substitution can proceed to the maximum extent the fuel mix will allow, then economic prospects over the next five years will be limited by labor, capital and productivity growth, not energy. There would be sufficient oil to maintain sizable exports to the West and finance large imports of Western industrial goods. Furthermore, the implied GNP growth rate of almost 3.5 percent a year would allow consumption, defense and investment claims on output to expand with roughly constant shares. The consumer, in particular, would not have to suffer from an increasing defense burden and per capita consumption would rise at the respectable rate of around 2 percent a year.

The projections in the base case show how vulnerable this rather rosy picture is to shifts in several of the key energy assumptions behind the plan guidelines. Production of coal, gas and especially oil is more likely to fall towards the lower end of the guideline range or below. The resulting lower economic growth will put a heavier burden on the Soviet consumer in the face of continued steady growth in defense spending, and hard currency trade could be forced to undergo a dramatic transformation. The best policy for Moscow may be to hope for the best, but be prepared for something much worse.

The Outlook for Energy and Economic Growth in Eastern Europe

Dr. Robin A. Watson

Introduction

The recent abrupt slowdown in economic growth in Eastern Europe marks the onset of a prolonged period of slowed economic expansion throughout the region. Declining increments in the labor force, sluggish productivity growth, and limited hard currency trade will combine with energy shortages to constrict GNP growth.

This paper assesses the impact of energy supply changes on the outlook for economic growth in each of the six East European countries — Bulgaria, Czechoslovakia, the German Democratic Republic, Hungary, Poland, and Romania. The estimates are developed with the help of an analytical framework that explicitly links energy prospects, hard currency trade, and economic potential. I first review the changes in energy supplies and patterns of use that have occurred in Eastern Europe during the 1970s. This gives a basis for estimating expected energy requirements and the share that can be met in each country with indigenous resources. The remaining energy demand can be met only partially by expected Soviet deliveries; yet balance-of-payments constraints severely restrict the amount of Western oil that can be purchased.

The projections show, therefore, an unavoidable and sizable gap between East European energy requirements and affordable supplies over the next five years. Since energy use will be limited by available supplies, I examine the economic prospects in the region in light of these discrepancies. I also look at the sensitivity of these prospects to any reduction in deliveries of Soviet oil.

In all East European countries impressive economic gains during the 1970s were fueled by rapidly expanding energy supplies. In the decade, energy use grew at annual rates of 6 percent in Bulgaria and Romania, 5 percent in Poland, 4 percent in Hungary and Czechoslovakia, and 2 percent in the GDR. The relation between energy use and economic activity varied, though, among the six countries. In Romania, Poland and the GDR, energy consumption grew less rapidly than GNP. The GDR and to a lesser extent, Poland, shifted from less efficient solid fuels to more efficient gas and oil. In Romania, the slower relative growth in energy use may have reflected extremely high investment rates which brought rapid improvement in the efficiency of the productive capital stock. Energy use grew faster than GNP in the other countries — Czechoslovakia, Bulgaria, and Hungary. In Bulgaria, this is probably due to industrialization and a major shift in the structure of production in one of the least developed European economies. The smaller differences in Hungary and Czechoslovakia have less obvious explanations, although low rates of investment and therefore small improvements in capital efficiency may have been contributing factors.

This growth in the overall use of energy was accompanied by major shifts in the mix of fuels consumed (see Table 1). Between 1970 and 1980, the share of coal in total energy consumption fell from two-thirds to little more than half for Eastern Europe as a whole. At the same time, the share of oil and gas rose from less than one-third to just over 40 percent. The shift from solid fuels was even more pronounced in some countries. In Hungary, for example, coal supplied more than half of domestic energy consumption in 1970 and oil and gas around 40 percent; by 1980, oil and gas accounted for almost two-thirds of the total and coal less than a third.

The broad regional expansion in energy use and shift away from solid fuels was due more to an increase in energy imports, especially from the Soviet Union, than to growth in domestic energy production (see Table 2). In all six countries, domestic energy production as a share of consumption fell during the decade. Romania's case is particularly striking. In 1970, Romanian energy production exceeded domestic use; by 1980, domestic output had fallen short of use, and Romania was a large net energy importer, despite large exports of refined oil products.

Energy imports from the Soviet Union almost doubled during the last ten years, and the share of imports from the communist countries in domestic consumption rose by about one-third. This shift was most pronounced in Bulgaria, Czechoslovakia, the GDR, and Hungary, where the communist-origin import share rose by more than ten percentage points. Oil import dependence is even greater; in 1979 Eastern Europe imported about three-fourths of all the oil it consumed from the USSR. Czechoslovakia received 98 percent of its oil from the Soviet Union, and the GDR, Bulgaria, and Hungary, close to 90 percent.

Hard currency oil imports are substantial only in Romania, where imported Western crude has been used to offset the falling contribution of domestic production to refinery feedstocks. In all other countries, imports from the West are still well below 100,000 barrels per day.

Analytical Approach

Because of the linkages among economic growth, energy, and the balance of payments, prospects for the East European economies have been examined within a quantitative analytical framework that considers all of these factors simultaneously. The framework describes, in a highly aggregated fashion, the links connecting each country's energy requirements and availability, hard currency trade, investment, and economic growth.

GNP is determined in the model by projected employment and active capital stock. The portion of the capital stock that can be used (the "active" part) depends on the ratio of energy availability to energy requirements. I assume that energy and capital are pure complements; as such, the energy requirement is generated by the size of the capital stock. Net additions to capital stock are a function of total investment.

International trade is an alternate source of energy. The capacity of each East European country to import from the West depends on its merchandise export earnings, net earnings from invisibles, borrowing propensity, and the availability of Western credit. Deficits in the net invisibles category, at least for the near term, will exert a significant drag on the import capacity of several of the countries as a result of large debt-service obligations on recent heavy borrowings. To estimate debt-service obligations, I have specified the interest and principal repayments components of debt-service separately. Interest payments depend on total debt and the average interest rate, which varies with the assumed rate available on new borrowings. Principal repayments depend on the repayments obligations on existing debt and the assumed maturity structure of new debt incurred.

Hard currency import capacity not absorbed by debt-service is allocated to two categories: non-energy imports—raw materials, food, and manufactured goods—and energy imports. The portion of import capacity devoted to energy imports is simply the residual left after debt-service obligations have been met and assumed minimum non-energy import requirements have been satisfied.

Table 1

Eastern Europe: Energy Consumption by Fuel Type 1/
(thousand barrels per day)

	Coal		Oil		Gas		Primary Electricity	
	1970	1980	1970	1980	1970	1980	1970	1980
Bulgaria	199 (50.9)	209 (29.4)	174 (44.4)	326 (45.9)	8 (2.0)	100 (14.1)	11 (2.8)	75 (10.6)
Czechoslovakia	848 (74.6)	900 (59.4)	206 (18.1)	391 (25.8)	38 (3.4)	152 (10.0)	44 (3.9)	72 (4.8)
German Democratic Republic	1283 (86.0)	1183 (65.6)	183 (12.3)	381 (21.1)	11 (0.7)	159 (8.8)	14 (1.0)	80 (4.4)
Hungary	229 (53.1)	180 (29.7)	121 (28.0)	220 (36.3)	59 (13.8)	164 (27.1)	22 (5.1)	42 (6.9)
Poland	1366 (82.7)	1924 (76.7)	171 (10.4)	376 (15.0)	104 (6.3)	190 (7.6)	11 (0.7)	18 (0.7)
Romania	168 (19.9)	267 (19.3)	218 (25.8)	420 (30.0)	456 (54.0)	649 (48.9)	2 (0.2)	48 (3.1)
Eastern Europe	4093 (68.8)	4663 (54.7)	1073 (18.0)	2214 (24.8)	676 (11.4)	1414 (16.6)	104 (1.8)	335 (3.9)

1/ The figures in parentheses are percentages.

Source: Energy Supplies in Eastern Europe: A Statistical Compilation, National Foreign Assessment Center, Central Intelligence Agency, ER 79-10624, December 1979.

Table 2

Eastern Europe: The Changing Structure of Energy Supplies

A. Thousand Barrels per Day Crude Oil Equivalent

Energy Production and Trade :	Bulgaria 1970	1980	Czechoslovakia 1970	1980	GDR 1970	1980	Hungary 1970	1980	Poland 1970	1980	Romania 1970	1980	Eastern Europe 1970	1980
Domestic Production	151	181	906	975	1172	1114	277	281	1895	2483	879	1098	5280	6367
Imports from Communist Countries 2/	228	494	324	636	365	632	176	371	232	457	43	141	1368	2622
Imports from non-Communist Countries 2/	19	50	8	16	22	40	8	4	0	62	46	297	102	460
Exports 2/, 3/	-7	-15	-101	-112	-68	-83	-29	-50	-474	-494	-124	-152	-805	-1049
Apparent Consumption	391	710	1136	1515	1491	1803	431	606	1653	2508	844	1384	5946	8400

B. Percent of Energy Consumption 1/

Energy Production and Trade :	Bulgaria 1970	1980	Czechoslovakia 1970	1980	GDR 1970	1980	Hungary 1970	1980	Poland 1970	1980	Romania 1970	1980	Eastern Europe 1970	1980
Domestic Production	38.6	25.5	79.8	64.4	78.6	67.3	64.3	46.4	114.6	99.0	104.2	79.3	88.8	75.8
Imports from Communist Countries 2/	58.3	69.6	28.5	42.0	24.5	35.1	40.1	61.2	14.0	18.2	5.1	10.2	23.0	31.2
Imports from non-Communist Countries 2/	4.9	7.0	0.7	1.1	1.5	2.2	1.9	0.7	0	2.5	5.6	21.5	1.7	5.5
Exports 2/, 3/	-1.8	-2.1	-8.9	-7.4	-4.6	-4.6	-6.7	-8.3	-28.7	-19.7	-14.7	-11.0	-13.5	-12.5
Apparent Consumption	100	100	100	100	100	100	100	100	100	100	100	100	100	100

1. Figures are for apparent energy consumption.
2. Energy trade figures for 1980 are preliminary estimates.
3. Exports are negative entries in these tables because they represent a subtraction from domestic consumption.

Table 3

Eastern Europe: Projected Residual Energy Requirements for 1985
(thousand barrels per day, crude equivalent)

Eastern Europe	Nominal Require- ment	Domestic Produc- tion	Imports from Communist Countries	Total Exports	Net Available	Remaining Require- ment	Imports from Non-Communist Countries in 1980
Bulgaria	9960	6900	2860	1140	8620	1340	470
Bulgaria	770	230	550	10	770	0	50
Czecho- slovakia	1770	1030	690	100	1620	150	20
German Democratic Republic	1870	1240	620	80	1780	90	40
Hungary	700	310	370	50	630	70	10
Poland	3030	3040	490	770	2760	270	60
Romania	1820	1050	140	130	1060	760	290

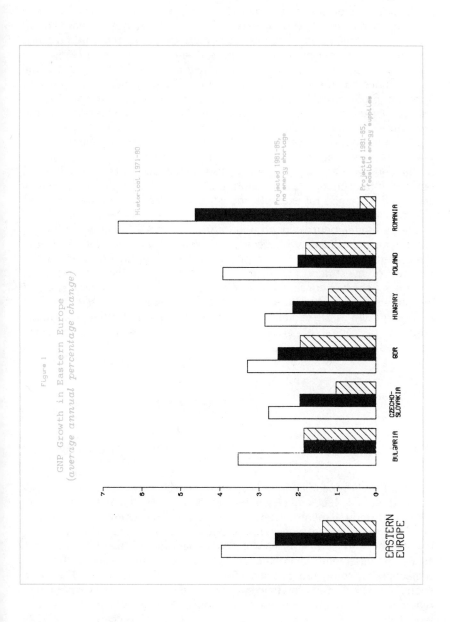

Figure 1

GNP Growth in Eastern Europe
(average annual percentage change)

Projected Energy Requirements

The struggle for greater energy efficiency is hindered by many factors: a lack of management and worker incentives to conserve energy, an unresponsive price system, an inefficient capital stock, and hard currency constraints that limit imports of more efficient Western technology. The conflict between economic development favoring industrial growth and the current need for conservation complicates efforts to stress less energy-intensive production. Furthermore, the recent move back toward greater use of coal and other solid fuels means the fuel mix will be less efficient in the future.

With the possible exception of the GDR, East European conservation measures have been ineffective because they have placed more emphasis on the consumer and government sectors, which account for only 15 to 25 percent of total energy consumption, than on the more important industrial sector. In Romania, for example, industry consumes over 70 percent of all energy used, while only ten percent goes to the consumer sector.

Energy requirements depend upon both the stock of energy-consuming assets and the efficiency of these assets as energy users. Naturally, both the quantity and efficiency of capital assets are critically dependent upon the level of investment. I project a constant real level of investment for all countries, which is consistent with plans to reduce somewhat the share of investment in the allocation of GNP. Requirements estimated from the implied growth of the capital stock and rough trends in the average energy intensity of capital all show substantial reductions in growth when compared with the past decade:

Eastern Europe:
Average Annual Rates of Growth in Energy Requirements
(percent)

	Eastern Europe	Bulgaria	Czecho-slovakia	GDR	Hungary	Poland	Romania
1971-80	3.5	6.2	2.9	1.3	3.5	4.3	5.1
1981-85	2.7	2.0	2.5	0.9	2.9	3.2	4.0

In every East European country I expect noticeably slower growth in energy demand in the 1980s because of slower growth in capital stock and continued improvements in energy efficiency. The regimes are trying to hold down investment and external trade deficits to deal with economic imbalances, and labor supplies will increase less rapidly than they did in the 1970s. Requirements in Poland could grow even more slowly than the projection if current labor problems further constrain investment. Even with such markedly slowed growth in energy demand, however, the total energy requirement to operate all of the fixed capital the region could have by 1985 would exceed 10 million barrels per day, nearly 20 percent above 1979 levels.

While energy requirements will grow more slowly in the 1980s, estimated domestic energy supplies will not keep up with demand. Indeed the rate of growth of domestic production is likely to fall in Romania:

Eastern Europe:
Average Annual Rates of Growth in Domestic Energy Production
(percent)

	Eastern Europe	Bulgaria	Czecho-slovakia	GDR	Hungary	Poland	Romania
1971-80	1.5	1.8	0.7	-0.5	0.1	2.7	2.3
1981-85	2.0	4.9	1.0	0.4	1.7	4.1	-1.0

I expect a sharp decline in Romanian oil production during the next five years as domestic reserves become seriously depleted. Growth in domestic production of gas in Hungary is also expected to slow appreciably. In the cases where I project stronger growth of indigenous energy supplies, most of the gains will come from nuclear power plants. The optimistic projection in Poland depends on a strong rebound in coal production, which is certainly feasible. However, continued labor strife or shorter work schedules have resulted in continued coal shortfalls throughout 1980 and 1981 and this trend could easily continue. On the average, the countries of Eastern Europe would have to import increasing quantities of energy to satisfy their requirements.

Table 3 shows how much of projected total energy requirements can be satisfied through domestic sources and imports from other communist countries. These estimates assume that Moscow holds oil deliveries at current levels through 1985 and increases gas exports by an average 2.5 percent annually—which seems consistent with current Soviet policy. Most of the countries will require substantial amounts of additional energy by 1985 to reach their growth potential, even though potential growth is still much less than recent economic experience. The residual energy needs indicated in Table 3 are equivalent to more than 10 percent of total projected Soviet oil production in 1985 (estimated at 10-11 million b/d).

Bulgaria's enviable position depends on new nuclear power generating capacity and substantially increased deliveries of Soviet gas. Romania, Poland, and Czechoslovakia, on the other hand, seem to face large residual supply requirements by 1985, amounting to 42, 9 and 8 percent, respectively, of total requirements. Romania's position is particularly desperate because her domestic oil reserves are declining rapidly. While Poland's total energy needs could fall short of the projections because of continued slow economic growth, the same negative factors also would likely curtail growth in domestic energy production, especially coal. The gap between requirements and supplies under these conditions probably would not be very different, therefore, than Table 3 suggests.

To fully cover East European energy needs, the USSR would have to increase energy deliveries to Eastern Europe to nearly 3 million barrels per day in 1985 compared with total deliveries of about 1.6 million barrels per day in 1980 — raising Soviet oil exports to Eastern Europe to nearly one third of production. If instead, Moscow were to purchase the additional million barrels per day of oil on the world market, the cost could approach $30 billion (projected 1985 prices). In either case, the burden for the Soviet Union seems unrealistically high. To meet energy requirements completely, most of the countries would need to buy considerably more energy from the West.

How Much Western Oil Can Eastern Europe Afford?

East European prospects for covering future energy shortfalls with purchases on the world market are not promising because the cost of the oil needs I project is so large relative to import capacity. Eastern Europe's limited ability to purchase energy through hard currency trade is a complicated function of each country's export earnings, debt-service obligations, requirements for other hard currency imports, borrowings from Western creditors, and the price of imported energy. Several of the countries are already heavily indebted to the West. Poland's repayment obligations on the existing debt now amount to nearly all of her hard currency earnings, and substantial new financing must be acquired merely to stay afloat. Moreover, none of the countries can expect marked improvement over the near term in their ability to earn hard currency. The ability of Eastern Europe to finance trade deficits through Western credits will be limited both by credit availability and by East European reluctance to become more heavily indebted. The burden of future debt obligations could become especially heavy with the recent rise in interest rates and the trend toward shorter maturities.

If residual energy requirements were fully met by Western oil, total oil imports would have to rise nearly three-fold from the 1980 level — from 480,000 to about 1.3 million barrels per day (Table 3). The projected bill ($15 billion in 1980 prices) would amount to almost half of total hard currency earnings by the region in 1980.

Projections of hard currency debt and debt-service ratios in 1985 that assume Eastern Europe buys all the oil it needs in the West suggest why this option is closed. In all countries except Bulgaria, debt-service would absorb practically all of the export earnings derived from trade with the West, and total debt for the region by 1985 would be six times the present figure of around $50 billion.

Table 4
Eastern Europe: Crude Oil Imports from Non-Communist Countries
(thousand barrels per day)

Requirements	1970	1980¹	Feasible	1985 Requirement
Bulgaria	20	50	—	0
Czechoslovakia	1	20	0	150
German Democratic Republic	20	40	20	90
Hungary	10	10	10	70
Poland	0	60	0	270
Romania	50	300	170	760
TOTAL	110	480	200	1340

¹Preliminary Estimates.

Taking into account a more realistic outlook for growth in hard currency debt and the practical limits in Eastern Europe's ability to cut non-energy imports from the West, I arrive at a much more sober assessment of prospects for Western oil imports (see Table 4). Romanian oil imports, financed mainly by reexport of refined products, would be far less than needed. The likely continuation of the balance of payments crisis in Poland will leave little if any room for oil imports from the West. Oil imports paid for in hard currency could rise for Eastern Europe only if hard currency debt grew much faster than I have projected or if imports of Western equipment and other goods were cut back much more sharply than I have assumed.

These calculations assume that hard currency exports of non-energy goods can be expanded at a real rate of three percent annually by all countries in Eastern Europe. Although modest, this rate is generally higher than the expected growth in domestic output, which means that the export burden on the economies will rise in the future. This rate of growth may also exceed the rate of GNP growth likely in hard currency trading partners. Export growth at the assumed rate, therefore, will take both sacrifice and good luck to achieve.

Energy Shortages in the Early 1980s

Since the countries of Eastern Europe will not be able to rely on imports of Western oil to close their energy gaps in the 1980s, the gaps suggested in Table 4 will have to be closed in other ways. The prospective energy gap for the region as a whole is almost 10 percent in mid-decade (Table 5). In three countries—the GDR, Hungary, and Czechoslovakia—projected energy supplies cover a falling portion of requirements, increasing the energy drag on growth.

The contrasting roles of domestic energy are particularly evident in Poland and Romania. Unprecedentedly rapid growth of Polish coal production could hold the shortfall in Poland within a narrow range because reserves are both extensive and exploitable in this timeframe. However, this would require a sharp turn-around in Poland's domestic political situation.

The expected decline in Romanian oil production will cause a continuing energy imbalance through 1985; Romania's extensive refinery industry will be hard-pressed to operate at anything near capacity.

Bulgaria is counting mainly on her nuclear electrical generating capacity and substantially larger Soviet gas deliveries to increase energy supplies in the 1980s. Hungary, Czechoslovakia and the GDR, in contrast, can hope to have much more nuclear capacity only by the mid-1980s and will not be able to purchase much oil from the West.

Outlook for Economic Growth to 1985

In the analysis energy shortages combine with slow growth in the labor force and investment to curtail sharply East European economic growth prospects for the eighties. Prospective gaps between energy demand and supplies are eliminated by slower growth as energy shortfalls force reduced rates of utilization of the capital stock in 1985 in all countries except Bulgaria. Rough estimates of possible capital utilization ranges from 100 percent in Bulgaria to less than 70 percent in Romania.

GNP in Eastern Europe grew at an average of 4.0 percent per year in 1971-80. The projections reflecting an energy constraint show economic growth from 1981 to 1985 declining to below half this rate (see Figure 1). In Hungary and Czechoslovakia, GNP growth falls to little more than one percent a year under the assumption described above, and in Romania the projected rate drops to little more than zero.

Table 5
Eastern Europe: Projections of Energy Requirements and Availabilities[1]
(thousand barrels per day, oil equivalent)

	1981			1985		
	A Require- ments	B Avail- ability	B as % of A	Require- ments	Avail- ability	B as % of A
Bulgaria	710	710	100	770	770	100
Czechoslovakia	613	1560	97	1770	1610	91
GDR	1810	1770	98	1870	1770	95
Hungary	630	610	97	700	630	90
Poland	2690	2670	99	3030	2970	98
Romania	1570	1180	75	1820	1550	85
Eastern Europe	9023	8500	94	9960	9300	93

[1]Requirements are the quantities of energy necessary to fully utilize existing and projected capital stock. Availabilities are based upon domestic production and net imports, including projections of affordable oil imports from the West.

Prospects calculated for Poland must certainly be viewed as optimistic. While it is impossible to factor the implications of recent Polish events precisely into any framework for looking at growth prospects, the Polish economy will have to rebound very quickly to realize even the very modest growth potential shown in Figure 1.

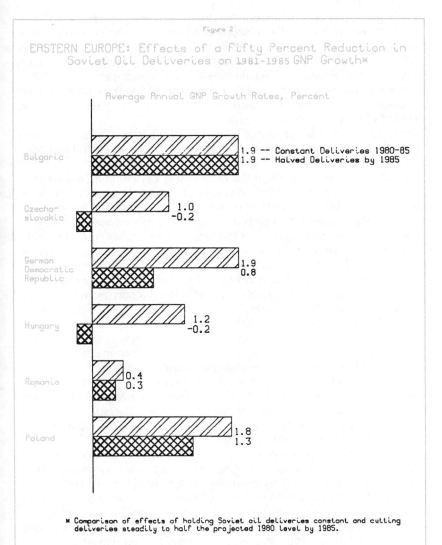

Figure 2

EASTERN EUROPE: Effects of a Fifty Percent Reduction in
Soviet Oil Deliveries on 1981-1985 GNP Growth*

Average Annual GNP Growth Rates, Percent

Bulgaria
1.9 -- Constant Deliveries 1980-85
1.9 -- Halved Deliveries by 1985

Czecho-
slovakia
1.0
-0.2

German
Democratic
Republic
1.9
0.8

Hungary
1.2
-0.2

Romania
0.4
0.3

Poland
1.8
1.3

* Comparison of effects of holding Soviet oil deliveries constant and cutting
deliveries steadily to half the projected 1980 level by 1985.

On a per-capita basis, the situation is even worse as per capita GNP almost stagnates in most East European countries in this scenario, and a slow decline in living standards is a distinct possibility. Bulgaria seems capable of maintaining respectable although lower growth rates through the early 1980s. However, Bulgaria now has the lowest per capita GNP in Eastern Europe, and rapid growth during the 1970s may have created expectations for continued improvement that two percent growth is unlikely to fulfill.

These projections are probably somewhat optimistic because I assume that (a) Soviet energy deliveries will match current plans, (b) the real price of imported oil does not rise, and (c) East European exports to the West can grow faster than GNP growth in the West and in Eastern Europe itself. The assumption that real investment rates will not rise over the next five years is consistent with plans in most countries to hold investment down in an effort to relieve some of the building pressure on private consumption. Any rise in investment, while improving the capital stock picture, is also likely to aggravate an already tight consumption situation with adverse consequences for labor productivity.

The growth scenarios shown in Figure 1 probably are also somewhat on the high side because they do not fully reflect the drag on growth that may come from restricted non-energy imports from the West. The assumed debt-service ratio constraint on hard currency trade reflects the likelihood that either internal or external pressures will hold down the accumulation of debt. The growth projections also assume an attempt to maintain imports of Western food as well as industrial goods and raw materials other than fuels at some minimum acceptable level in relation to economic activity. Unless these countries manage to do more belt-tightening than I now see likely, growth prospects will deteriorate further because of import constraint problems. The estimates in Figure 1, however, do not attempt to take this additional factor into account.

Figure 1 also shows what East European growth might be under an alternative situation in which imported energy supplies fully meet residual energy requirements. As I have already noted, however, these rates of growth imply unrealistically high levels of borrowing to finance imports of Western oil. The difference between growth limited and not limited by energy shortages might be viewed as the sacrifice imposed by hard currency constraints. The remaining retardation in growth — that is, the difference between historical rates and projections without an energy constraint — is due to other factors such as slower growth in the labor force and the capital stock. In the case of Czechoslovakia, 0.8 of a percentage point of the drop in growth (2.8 to 2.0 percent) can be attributed to non-energy factors and 1.0 percentage point (2.0 to 1.0) to the projected energy shortfall.

Figure Al

Eastern Europe: Flow Diagram
for Analytical Framework

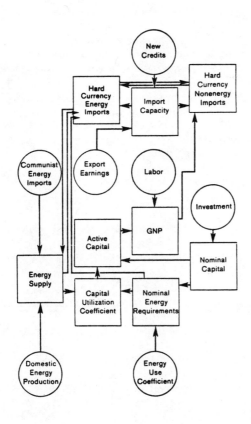

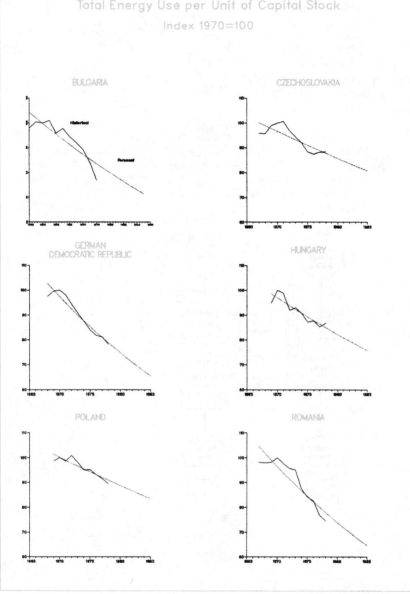

Total Energy Use per Unit of Capital Stock
Index 1970=100

Sensitivity to Changes in Soviet Oil Deliveries

The basic projections of GNP growth assumed — in line with Soviet statements — that annual Soviet oil deliveries to Eastern Europe will remain at their 1980 levels through 1985. The eventual level of Soviet deliveries to the six countries remains highly uncertain, however, so I have also considered a bleaker scenario in which the Soviets halve their oil exports to Eastern Europe by 1985. If Soviet oil production falls by 1985 to the 10-11 million barrels per day range that I now see likely, the opportunity cost of maintaining even constant exports to Eastern Europe may be prohibitive. In such a case, reductions of the magnitude assumed here may be one of the few options available to the Soviets to ease their own economic situation.[1]

In this scenario, East European GNP growth in 1981-85 falls from an average of 1.2 percent to 0.6 percent per year.[2] However, some countries are relatively independent of Soviet oil exports while others are markedly vulnerable (see Figure 2). Romania, for example, is hurt little by a halving of Soviet oil deliveries, because it represents such a small portion of total energy supplies, whereas growth rates in Czechoslovakia, Hungary, and the GDR would be sharply depressed. Bulgaria, however, is able to make up on the hard-currency market for the Soviet shortfall by greatly expanded borrowing in the West. This, of course, assumes that Bulgaria would have access to Western credits and would use them up to the liberal debt-service ceiling which I have assumed. The implications for per capita GNP are even more pronounced. With lower Soviet oil deliveries, per capita GNP is stagnant or falling for all countries in the region and living standards might actually drop.

To some degree, the impact of lower Soviet oil deliveries is understated in these calculations. Other fuels could not be substituted for gasoline or diesel fuel or even easily for fuel oil in the short run, but these structural effects have not been considered in the analysis. Poland, for example, depends (as of 1980) on oil for only 15 percent of energy consumption. However, since petroleum products are critical in key sectors of the economy, I am understating the consequences of a shortage.

---

[1] This possibility was developed in an earlier OER-CIA paper on the Soviet Union, *Simulations of Soviet Growth Options to 1985*, ER 79-10131, March 1979.

[2] These calculations assume that East European exports cannot be diverted from the Soviet Union to the West as Soviet oil deliveries fall. This reflects the limited Western market for most East European goods exported to the Soviets. It also reflects the likelihood that lower Soviet oil exports would be accompanied by reduced credits to, not reduced imports from, Eastern Europe.

Prospects for Staving Off the Slowdown

The uncertainty associated with economic prospects for Eastern Europe is great, and the confidence one has in any projection diminishes quickly as the forecast horizon is extended. In particular, the potential for social and political change, managerial-technological innovations, and transformation of productive factors increases greatly as the time is extended.

Without exception, the East European governments realize that the economic outlook is worse than at any time since the 1950s. They probably hope to keep GNP growth at a respectable level – and their peoples pacified – by trying to:

- push exports harder in hard currency markets and minimize necessary imports for hard currency;
- finance current account deficits with both Western and Soviet credits;
- persuade the USSR to change its mind about energy deliveries as East European shortfalls become larger;
- find OPEC countries willing to barter oil for manufactures, arms, and technical assistance;
- improve the efficiency with which energy is used; and
- accelerate rates of increase in productivity.

Even in combination these approaches are unlikely to prevent the near-stagnation projected above. Certain countries may be able to achieve a somewhat better hard currency export growth over the next 5 years than the 3 percent real growth I have assumed, but trade would then absorb an increasing share of domestic output. Meanwhile, the continuing Soviet demand for higher quality goods in exchange for raw materials impedes efforts to supply the Western market. The capacity to import oil from the West would rise if other hard currency imports can be scaled down. Yet essential non-energy imports – industrial materials, machinery, spare parts, and grain – are either in very short supply or have no good substitutes. On the debt side, the projections, which permit sustained debt-service ratios remains from well over 100 percent in Poland to 50 percent in the other countries, probably are on the high size and leave little room for more use of credit than I have assumed.

Finally, the extent of the projected economic slowdown in Eastern Europe depends on whether the rhetorical emphasis placed on raising productivity can be translated into near-term results. Likely curbs on investment mean slower improvements in the average quality of the capital stock, and access to Western technology will diminish because of trade difficulties. As for labor productivity, the prospect of slower growth or even stagnation in per-capita consumption would sap work incentives. There is little reason, then, to see a likely way out of the poor growth prospects facing Eastern Europe in either improved productivity or better trade performance.

This paper uses a common analytical framework to assess prospects for economic growth in each country in Eastern Europe. The framework had to meet two important criteria. First, it had to be supported by the data base available for each of the six East European countries, which meant that it had to be consistent with the "lowest common denominator" from the data standpoint. Second, it had to maintain the essential linkages among productive factors (including energy), the level of economic activity, and the hard currency balance-of-payments in each country. Thus the framework ensures that projections of GNP for each country are consistent with both energy and hard currency constraints.

A flowchart of the important components and linkages in our general country framework is represented in Figure A1. Rectangles represent endogenously determined variables and circles represent exogenous variables.

This analytical framework generates values for variables in the following categories:

- *Production*. GNP is computed as a function of employment and the active capital stock.
- *Capital Formation*. Total investment, both domestically produced and imported, is the source of additions to the capital stock.
- *Energy Balance*. The model generates forecasts of total energy requirements and total energy supplies. The ratio of these two variables is used to estimate the effective or active portion of the capital stock.
- *Hard Currency Energy Imports*. Affordable energy imports from the West are calculated consistent with projected balance-of-payments accounts.
- *Hard Currency Balance of Payments*. East European trade with the West is described by calculations of imports, new borrowing, hard currency principal repayments, interest payments, and the debt-service ratio.

These projections from the model reflect our assumptions about the following variables:

- *Employment*. Employment growth is based on projections of working age population and is exogenous to the model.
- *Energy Supplies*. Domestic energy production, energy imports from communist countries, and energy exports are estimated outside of the model.
- *Balance of Payments*. Hard currency export earnings are considered to be principally demand driven and therefore exogenous. We also assume likely values for the interest rate, average maturity of the debt, and a debt-service ratio ceiling.

The functional relationships among the variables are summarized in Table A1. These equations define the endogenous variables and the linkages connecting them and the exogenous variables. Table A2 shows the energy assumptions underlying the growth projections. The analytical framework can be summarized in the five sections indicated in Table A1:

* *Production*: We use a Cobb-Douglas production function to generate estimates of GNP from projections of employment and active capital stock, which is simply nominal capital stock adjusted for utilization (equation 1). The utilization rate of the nominal capital stock is determined by the ratio of energy availability to energy requirements (equation 2).

* *Capital Formation*: An identity calculates this year's capital stock from last year's capital stock and net capital formation (equation 3). Net additions to the capital stock are generated from estimates of total investment and the assumed rate of retirement of the capital stock (equation 4). Investment in fixed assets is assumed to be constant in real terms throughout the projection period. Although historical investment functions can be estimated statistically, they do not appear applicable for medium term projections. Most East European countries seem resigned to no real growth in fixed investment due to both reduced imports from the West and increasing pressure to allocate somewhat larger shares of national income to private consumption.

* *Energy Balance*: Total energy supply in each of the countries is the sum of domestic production, net imports from communist countries (essentially Soviet deliveries), and the net imports that can be purchased for hard currency on the world market (equations 5-10). The balance-of-payments accounts determine how much import capacity will be available for hard currency energy purchases. Energy requirements are computed from the capital stock and projections of the average energy intensity of capital (equation 11). Thus, we implicitly assume that energy and capital are complementary factors of production. The energy requirement per unit of the capital stock is extrapolated from the historical trend (equation 12). Figure A2 shows historical and projected trends in energy use per unit of capital stock in each of the countries.

* *Hard Currency Energy Imports*: The capacity to import energy from the West is influenced by a number of factors. It not only depends on export earnings, new borrowings, and the structure and size of the debt; it also depends on competing needs to import non-energy goods (equation 13). Our basic assumption is that hard currency will be allocated to energy imports only after debt-service obligations have been met and minimum levels of non-energy imports have been satisfied. The volume of affordable hard currency energy imports is calculated from this residual import capacity and assumed future oil prices (equation 14). Future oil prices are assumed constant in real terms starting at $30 per barrel in 1980.

* *Hard Currency Balance-of-Payments Accounts*: Total debt is determined from an accounting relationship as the prior year's debt plus new borrowings minus principal repayments (equation 15). The debt-service

ratio is calculated as the ratio of payments on interest and principal to total export earnings, including earnings from invisibles (equation 16). New borrowings (equation 13) are limited by an upper constraint on the debt-service ratio: 90 percent for Poland and 50 percent for the other countries. Principal repayments are a function of total debt, the fraction of total debt which is medium and long term, and the average maturity of the debt (equation 17). Interest obligations depend on the size of the debt, the distribution of the debt between commercial credits and officially backed credits, and the respective interest rates on the two types of borrowing (equation 18). Minimum non-energy imports from the West depend upon the level of GNP (equation 19).

Table A1

Summary of Equations

Production:

1. Log (Gross National Product) $= a + b \times$ log (active capital stock) $+ (1-b) \times$ log (employment)
2. Active capital stock $=$ (nominal capital stock) $\times$ (energy available/ nominal energy requirement)

Capital Formation:

3. Nominal capital stock $=$ nominal capital stock (t-1) $+$ net capital formation
4. Net capital formation $= n \times$ investment $- (0.02 \times$ nominal capital stock (t-1)

Energy Balance:

5. Coal available $=$ coal production $+$ coal imports $-$ coal exports
6. Gas available $=$ gas production $+$ gas imports $-$ gas exports
7. Primary electricity available $=$ primary electricity production $+$ electricity imports $-$ electricity exports
8. Oil available $=$ oil production $+$ oil imports $-$ oil exports
9. Oil imports $=$ oil imports from communist countries $+$ oil imports for hard currency
10. Total energy available $=$ coal available
    $+$ gas available
    $+$ electricity available
    $+$ oil available
11. Nominal energy requirements $=$ nominal capital stock $\times$ energy use per unit of capital
12. log (energy use per unit of capital) $= e + f$ (time)

Hard Currency Energy Imports:

13. Value of energy imports for hard currency = merchandise export earnings + invisibles earnings + new borrowings - interest payments - principal repayments - minimum non-energy hard currency imports

14. Volume of oil imports for hard currency = value of oil imports for hard currency/hard currency oil price

Hard Currency Balance-of-Payments

15. Debt = debt (t-1) + gross financing - principal repayments

16. Debt service ratio = (interest payments + principal repayments)/ (merchandise export earnings + invisibles earnings)

17. Principal repayments = (share of debt which is medium and long term) × (debt (t-1)/average maturity of medium and long term debt)

18. Interest payments = debt (t-1) × [(share of debt commercial × commercial interest rate) + (share of debt non-commercial × non-commercial interest rate)]

19. Minimum non-energy hard currency imports = minimum non-energy hard currency imports (t-1) × [gross national product/ gross national product (t-1)]

Table A2

Eastern Europe: Summary of Energy Assumptions
(thousand barrels per day)

	Bulgaria		Czechoslovakia		German Democratic Republic	
	1980	1985	1980	1985	1980	1985
Domestic Production						
Coal	125	150	928	940	1073	1100
Gas	1	1	13	13	53	53
Primary Electricity	53	100	28	60	65	95
Oil	3	3	2	2	0	0
Imports from the Soviet Union						
Coal	88	88	43	43	56	56
Gas	75	97	177	177	106	106
Primary Electricity	39	45	12	15	1	15
Oil	300	300	384	384	380	380
Total Energy Exports	4	4	104	104	82	82

	Hungary		Poland		Romania	
	1980	1985	1980	1985	1980	1985
Domestic Production						
Coal	140	140	2570	3180	180	270
Gas	101	98	120	120	600	575
Primary Electricity	1	40	13	13	50	60
Oil	40	40	7	7	234	200
Imports from the Soviet Union						
Coal	11	11	13	13	7	7
Gas	62	62	90	137	21	21
Primary Electricity	42	50	8	15	0	0
Oil	210	210	337	337	20	20
Total Energy Exports	47	47	699	754	166	131

Implications for the West, Including Defense, of CMEA Energy Prospects

Friedemann Müller

I. Assumptions

Before attempting to draw any conclusions about the implications of CMEA energy prospects for the West, I would like to present a few assumptions that will be the necessary basis for my explanations. This area will be discussed in depth in papers that will have been presented earlier in this colloquium, but that are not available to me at this time.

My assumptions are summarized within the following six theses:

1. A decline in Soviet oil production during the 1980s is expected. This argument focuses not so much on the question of existing reserves as on how much can be produced by available technological and capital means. The decline might be less than the baseline in the CIA (1979) study[2], since the earlier CIA prediction for 1980 was too pessimistic (it was, however, the closest one to reality that was available in 1977). Production of 520 million tons of oil in the Soviet Union in 1990 would mean an average 1.4 percent annual decrease in production during the 1980s.

2. Natural gas production in the Soviet Union might still increase at a relatively high growth rate. The most important limiting factor could be the construction of the necessary pipeline systems. The current stagnation in Soviet steel production could lead to a lack of pipes that could only be filled by imports from the West. But during the 1980s East-West trade will probably depend more on political decisions than it did during the 1970s. An annual Soviet Union economic growth of between 5 and 6 percent could be a possibility if Western pipes and pumps are available.

3. No fast recovery from the current decline in Soviet Union coal production is expected. The high need for infrastructure, especially in the field of transportation, and the poor quality of unexploited coal make production increases less feasible, but nevertheless indispensable. This could lead to a very slow production growth rate of about 1 percent annually.

4. Growth rates in nuclear power should be as high as 20 percent per year. But the original target for 1990 (100-110 GW) is unattainable. If 90 GW are achieved by 1990, about 6 percent of Soviet energy production could be covered by nuclear energy (in comparison to 1 percent in 1980). The combined assumptions of the above four energy sources imply a 2 percent annual growth in Soviet energy production during the 1980s.

5. In spite of the comparably high waste of energy, there is no essential potential for energy conservation in the Soviet Union. The share of unproductive private energy consumption is very low and has to increase. The current unfavorable productivity development in the industrial sector and the growing distance for raw material transport hinder extensive conservation measures. The 1985 plan predicts a 17 percent (medium line) increase in the production of oil, gas, and coal[3]. If nuclear power is included, the planned growth rate for energy production is higher. The planned growth rate in national income is 19 percent (medium line). Since exports are announced not to grow as fast and GNP growth is less than national income growth[4], the relation between energy consumption growth and GNP growth, as it is assumed by the Soviet leadership, is not below 1.

6. The energy production growth in Eastern Europe that amounted to an average annual rate of 2.1 percent between 1970 and 1979 will fall below 2 percent per year during the 1980s. Energy conservation is not expected to be much more successful there than in the Soviet Union, according to the experiences between 1975 and 1978[5]. Since growing energy imports from outside of CMEA regions are to be excluded for financing reasons, the Soviet Union will have to deliver more energy to Eastern Europe than the amount that was promised in 1979 (which implied a stable delivery on the 1980 basis up to 1985) if a disastrous development is to be prevented. Romania's drastic fall in oil production leads to an even additional demand without increasing the supply of these countries.

II. Implications for East-West Trade

1. Soviet-West Trade

Soviet energy exports to the West played a central role in the dynamic development of East-West trade during the 1970s, as is shown in Table 1.

TABLE 1
The Share of Energy in Soviet Exports
Toward OECD Countries
(in billion rubles)

Exporter				growth p.a.	
Soviet Union	1973	1975	1979	1979/73	1979/75
Importer OECD					
Total export	3.744	6.127	12.504	22.2	19.5
Energy export	1.319	3.176	8.535	36.5	28.0
Non-energy export	2.425	2.951	3.969	8.6	7.7
Importer Western Europe					
Total export	2.959	5,284	11.168	24.8	20.6
Energy export	1.243	2.954	8.207	37.0	29.1
Non-energy export	1.716	2.331	2.962	9.5	6.2
Importer EEC					
Total export	2.123	3.321	7.818	24.3	23.9
Energy export	0.787	1.792	5.517	38.4	32.5
Non-energy export	1.336	1.529	2.301	9.5	10.8

Source: *Vneshniaia Torgovlia SSSR,* 1973, 1975, 1979.

If one divides overall Soviet exports to the West into energy exports (oil, gas, coal, excluding others like electricity) and non-energy exports it becomes obvious that the main share of export growth is related to the energy export. During the 1973-1979 period, energy exports to the OECD countries increased by an annual average growth rate of 36.5 percent, while non-energy exports grew by no more than 8.6 percent. About the same growth relation exists in exports to Western Europe and the EEC (Table 1).

The consequence of this was a growing share of energy exports in overall exports.

TABLE 2
Share of Energy Sources in Soviet
Exports to OECD Countries (%)

	1973	1975	1979
Overall exports	100.0	100.0	100.0
Energy	35.2	51.8	68.3
Oil	31.4	46.8	58.4
Natural gas	0.5	1.5	7.7
Coal	3.3	3.6	2.1

Source: *Vneshniaia Torgovlia SSSR,* different years.

In 1979, more than two-third of Soviet exports to the West were energy products; 58 percent of the overall export revenue was related to oil exports alone. The share of natural gas in overall exports is growing fast, but the revenues are still less than one-seventh of the oil revenues.

Considering the structure of non-energy exports, the slow productivity improvements, and the low demand growth in Western countries, it cannot be expected that non-energy exports from the Soviet Union will grow by a higher rate than during the 1970s. This rate will probably be even lower during the 1980s. That means that the loss of oil exports cannot be balanced by non-energy exports. High growth rates in coal exports can also be excluded. This leaves natural gas as the only real alternative to balance decreasing oil exports. According to an OECD study, natural gas exports to the West might be somewhere between 26 and 48 billion m³ in 1990 (25 billion m³ in 1980)[6]. Jonathan Stern predicts 54.5 m³ exports to the West in 1990, which means a little more than twice as much as in 1980[7]. A CIA study expects 48 billion m³ in 1985[8]. If the project for a pipeline from Yamal peninsula to Western Europe is agreed upon soon[9], it should be possible that 60 to 70 billion m³ of natural gas will be exported to Western Europe in 1990. Without such an agreement, which includes Western credits of $10 to $15 billion and equipment delivery of about the same amount, the Soviet Union should not be able to increase exports by more than 100 percent.

If the price for natural gas increases 2.6-fold up to 1990 (which is equivalent to an annual price increase of 10 percent), a 70 billion m³ gas export to the West could compensate for the monetary loss of 1979 oil exports. But even then no nominal export growth in energy would be reached, which means that Soviet real exports to OECD countries would decrease.

Exports to OECD countries are not the only way the Soviet Union may earn hard currency. Some of its exports to Third World countries and to Yugoslavia (18 percent of total Soviet exports go to these countries) are also paid for in hard currencies. In addition, gold sales, services, and a share of arms sales are not included in the Soviet foreign trade statistics. According to a CIA study, total hard currency revenues were 49 percent higher in 1978 than export revenues to OECD countries[10]. On the other hand, the availability to the Soviet Union of hard currency for imports is reduced by its debt payments toward Western banks and credits to Eastern European countries, especially Poland. Total elimination of Soviet oil exports would obviously mean a reduction in imports, at least in real terms.

For financing reasons, it seems absolutely impossible that the Soviet Union will become a net importer of oil. If, for example, the Soviet Union had to import 1 million b/d of oil in 1990, it would mean the loss of the entire revenue of 60 billion m³ natural gas exports due the USSR under the assumption of a constant price relation between oil and natural gas during the 1980s. This would lead to an enormous reduction of non-oil imports, probably down to one-third in real terms. This example should show that not only are Soviet net oil imports absolutely improbable, but also that net exports below the current exports to Eastern European countries of at least 1.6 million b/d are not to be expected. From the viewpoint of efficiency of importing Western high technology and capital investment goods, it seems more probable that the Soviet Union will maintain a certain amount of oil exports to the West, say .5 million b/d, to gain further participation in Western technological development and capital investment availability, even if this leads to a further reduction of energy in domestic consumption.

Energy is not the only growth-limiting factor in the Soviet economy. The stagnating steel production, the lack of transportation capacity, the low investment growth in connection with low productivity growth and stagnating labor availability, and finally the high share of unproductive military expenditures in the GNP may lead to an economic growth that is lower than 2 percent. This in turn could, because of the then low energy consumption growth, allow an ongoing export not only of energy as a whole, but also, to a small extent, of oil.

A reduction of oil exports to the West is not only probable, it has been announced several times by the Soviet Union[11]. A loss of 1 million b/d of oil to the West (in 1979 the Soviet Union exported 1.2 million b/d) corresponds to about .4 percent of the estimated import needs of Western countries in 1990. This is not a negligible amount considering the general insecurities in future oil supplies, but in comparison to an OPEC output decrease of 8.5 million b/d within 12 months (from October 1979 to October 1980)[12], this loss within a decade should be manageable.

Western European dependence on Soviet energy exports is not expected to increase to any significant degree. In 1977 6.6 percent of energy consumption in Western Europe was imported from the Soviet Union and Poland; more than half of it was related to Soviet oil[13]. Coal dependence, which extended to 8.5 percent in 1977 Western European consumption (6.2 percent of EEC consumption) is not too dangerous because of the high degree of self-supply in Western Europe.

The crucial point is the debate over Western European dependence on Soviet natural gas. This dependence could increase fom 7.4 percent in 1977 (4.2 percent in EEC) to 16-18 percent in 1990 if the Soviet Union delivers 70 billion m³ to Western Europe. Besides Austria, with its almost total dependence on Soviet natural gas, West Germany, which is especially engaged in providing credits and equipment for pipeline construction, projects a 30 percent dependence on Soviet natural gas. But a dependence on natural gas does not seem to be as sensitive as in the case of oil, although natural gas cannot be stored as easily as oil and coal. Unlike the oil supply, there is a high self supply in Western Europe in natural gas of 80-90 percent, which in 1990 will still be around 70 percent. Secondly, there is a good chance for a short term balancing of regional shortages among West European countries in case of a cut in Soviet deliveries. Thirdly, some industrial consumers are obliged to substitute natural gas by other energy sources within a very short time. In the case of West Germany this concerns about 15% of the gas consumption and this share has an increasing tendency. Finally, in comparison with the alternatives, a dependence on Soviet natural gas does not seem to be an unbearable risk. In opposition to other natural gas suppliers like Algeria, or possibly later again Iran, there exists a mutual dependence with the Soviet Union that obliges her, more than Western European countries, to present herself as a reliable trade partner. A total cutting of natural gas deliveries would happen only in extreme circumstances. In other words, this instrument could only be used in a situation where energy regulations allow a drastic reduction in private and sectoral industrial consumption.

In contrast to Soviet trade with the West, Eastern Europe's trade with this region is not dominated by energy goods[14]. Only about 20 percent of total Eastern European exports to the West are energy related; Polish coal accounts for more than half of this and oil products from Romania for about one quarter. Romania has been a net importer of oil since 1976, but it has refinery capacity for much more than its domestic consumption, which leads to the export of Romanian oil products to the West that are based on imported oil. This export volume has, however, been declining since 1976. It can be expected that the dominant role of Polish coal will be intensified in future Eastern energy exports to the West. The volume of future exports will be determined less by Western demand than by Polish production capacity though this is now in danger because of the current labor unrest. Between 1973 and 1978, these Polish exports grew in real terms by approximately 4 percent, in monetary terms by almost 20 percent per year, and amounted to about 30 percent in total Polish export volume to the West.

Eastern European energy imports should not play any significant role on the world market, although these countries have been urged by the Soviet Union to cover their needs more and more by imports from outside the CMEA. Between 1973 and 1978, Eastern European oil imports (excluding Romania) from outside the CMEA area grew only from .15 to .19 million b/d. In 1978, Romania alone imported .26 million b/d, but exported approximately .2 million b/d. Net imports of all Eastern European countries (including Romania) amounted to .18 million b/d in 1977[15]. All of these countries are especially sensitive to price rises in hard currency trade, since they have not succeeded in keeping their exports to the hard currency areas as high as their import needs. This has resulted in a very high indebtment[16] and a low flexibility in increasing the monetary amount of their imports. Considering the 1979/1980 price rises and expected further increases, oil imports of the Eastern European countries from outside the CMEA can hardly be increased during the 1980s. Taking into account that these countries will not import any other sources of energy from outside the CMEA area and that Poland especially will continue to export coal to the West, the Eastern European countries will continue to be net energy exporters to the world market outside the CMEA. But neither Eastern European oil imports nor its coal exports will have a pronounced influence on Western energy supplies.

The critical issue in the CMEA energy situation on trade between Eastern Europe and the West is related to the unfavorable outlook for Eastern European economies caused by their difficult domestic energy situations. Between 1973 and 1979, for example, the cost for energy imported from the Soviet Union[17] grew more than 5-fold (from 1.37 billion Rb to 7.0 billion Rb)[18]. Although the price increases inside the CMEA took effect more smoothly than on the world market, due to the five-year moving average system, and CMEA energy prices might be only 50-60 percent of the 1981 world market price, a growshare of the Eastern European GNP, especially machinery, has to be paid for to balance the stagnating or very slightly increasing energy deliveries. In 1973, energy accounted for 18.5 percent of the total cost of Eastern European imports from the Soviet Union; by 1979 this had increased to 38 percent[19]. This tendency will continue, since the sharp increase in world market energy prices during the 1979-1980 period has not yet fully affected price increases within the CMEA.

Price rises in energy, the low productivity growth in Eastern Europe, the threatening stagnating energy delivery from the Soviet Union, and the exclusion of higher energy imports from outside the CMEA for financing reasons create depressing constraints on Eastern European economies, especially on their ability to cope with Western demand in international trade and cooperation. There is a high potential for energy conservation in Eastern Europe since these countries need twice as much energy per produced GNP unit than Western European countries do[20]. However, this potential can obviously only be used in a substantial way if reform of the economic system takes place and energy-saving technologies find more application there. Much depends on the current change in Poland. If this occurs in a way that will encourage the other Eastern European countries to carry out reforms leading to decentralization of decisions, and if the Soviet Union supports such a change through further deliveries in the raw material field, growth rates in the GNP and in economic relations with the West could be reached in spite of energy shortage.

III. Political and Defense Aspects

1. Influence on Economic Growth and Military Expenditure

The influence of the energy situation on economic growth is only to be indicated here. As mentioned earlier, it seems improbable that during the 1980s the economic growth rate in the CMEA will be higher than the energy consumption growth rate. The volume of energy consumption, on the other hand, is influenced not only by energy production but also by the net trade. Exports from the Soviet Union to the West are expected to decrease, and Soviet exports to Eastern Europe could increase very slowly. In no case will total Soviet energy exports increase by more than its production growth rate. This means that if Soviet energy production grows by 2 percent annually, consumption can grow by very little more than 2 percent. The same growth rate could be assumed by overall economic growth. Energy availability, however, is not the only growth-limiting factor. This makes predictions about the dependence of economic growth on energy availability difficult in two ways. First, if economic growth is lower than, for instance, 2 percent because of poor productivity development, a shortage in steel, general availability of investment means, and labor potential, more energy could be available than would be necessary to meet this growth rate. Secondly, low economic growth could even further lower Soviet energy production, which could lead to a mutual decelerating effect on energy production and economic growth.

If economic growth stablizes at 2 percent, this will have a certain impact on military expenditures. During the 1970s, military expenditure growth in the Soviet Union has probably not deviated too much from GNP growth. According to the CIA, military expenditures grew during the 1970s with an average growth rate of 3 percent (in constant dollars[21]), while the average GNP growth (in constant dollars) amounted to 3.7 percent during the same period[22]. Some estimations of Soviet military expenditure rates are considerably higher, especially if calculated in rubles. William Lee assumes even a 10-11 percent annual growth rate during the period between 1970 and 1980 in constant rubles[23]. (The CIA assumes a 4-5 percent growth rate in constant rubles.) All relevant sources (including several alternatives published by the U.S. Arms Control and Disarmament Agency[24]) estimated growth rates in military expenditures that were lower in the second half of the 1970s than in the first half, but that were more stable than the declining GNP growth rates. There is an obvious relation between a long-term GNP growth and growth in military expenditures, but this does not mean that the Soviet Union will not be able to keep military expenditure growth higher than GNP growth over a decade. If, in 1980, the share of military expenditures in the Soviet GNP is 14 percent, and its GNP grows by an annual rate of 2 percent while military expenditures increase by 3 percent by 1990 its share in the GNP will be 15.4 percent. This is not an unbearable change. The energy problem alone does not create unsolvable problems for the growth of the military budget. But if the energy problem is seen as a part of an economic crisis, the military budget might be included in reform considerations. However, during the 1960s the reduction of the military burden on the economy was a reform option that was not chosen[25]. There is no evidence for a more urgent need to choose this option today, especially since Soviet international influence and power after the 1960s have been more and more concentrated on military means.

2. The Middle East and Global Energy Supply

The lack of energy in the Soviet Union will not lead to a major economic breakdown or to an inability to continue the military buildup according to the Soviet Union's own perception of the necessity of military expenditures. However, the availability of a certain share of Middle East oil sources to the Soviet Union would solve a lot of problems. If one assumes a decrease in Soviet oil production from 12 million b/d to 10.4 million b/d by 1990, access to the present unused capacity of Iranian oil production (approximately 3 million b/d[26]) alone could preserve a further growth in Soviet oil consumption, while the rest of the world would have to cope with a declining supply. The cost of running the Iranian oil production would amount to only a small fraction of the cost of exploiting new oil fields in the Soviet Union. Costs for transportation to the consumption centers in the Soviet Union would be lower also, because of shorter distances and geographic advantages. For these reasons, it seems probable that in such a hypothetical case the Soviet Union would reduce domestic production efforts because the resultant investment savings could then be transferred to other sectors that have influence on economic growth. Considering high growth rates with natural gas and very high growth rates with nuclear power, a stable production of 12 million b/d (including the assumed Soviet production in Iran at an amount of 3 million b/d) could still allow a 3 percent growth in energy consumption, which would give a favorable outlook for overall economic growth. If the Soviet Union could get influence over more than the Iranian oil fields, this would lead to a major impact on world oil supply and prices. According to a Stanford University estimate, interruption of Persian Gulf oil deliveries would create the following GNP losses in the United States and Western Europe[27].

Interruption	% GNP Loss	
	U.S.A.	Western Europe
6 m b/d for 6 months	2	3
9 m b/d for 12 months	5	7
18 m b/d for 12 months	13	22

This estimate was based on normal deliveries from the Persian Gulf states of 18 million b/d, which is said to be 35 percent of the non-communist world oil supply. In October 1980 actual deliveries to the West were 14.6 million b/d; this in fact was 35 percent of the total non-communist world supply, which amounted to 41.7 million b/d at that time[28] because of a sharp decline in OPEC oil production during 1980.

If the Soviet Union were to gain influence over an essential share of Persian Gulf oil fields, another major economic impact could be expected. The Soviet Union could get attractive trade partners in most of the Third World countries if she offered to supply them with oil. This could more than compensate for the Soviet loss in reputation after the Afghanistan invasion. In the long-term view, this could lead to a very close embrace of selected Third World countries by the Soviet Union.

However, it must be stated that the crucial energy situation within the Soviet Union does not create an additional option to extend its influence in the Middle East area. It might, however, produce an additional Soviet interest in this region and it could provoke a more risky behavior in Soviet foreign policy. Regardless of the instability of this region, which is related to its different conflict levels (Arab-Israeli conflict, Afghanistan, Islamic revolution, oil production, price fixing and distribution), the Soviet Union could be interested in keeping these conflicts alive, waiting for a chance to promote the establishment of a favorite political party as a ruling power in one of these countries. It is surely in the Western interest to deter Soviet military intervention in the Middle East by military means (Carter Doctrine, January 1980); Western security aspects must additionally include an incentive to reduce Soviet interests in a continuing instability in this region. A Western security policy must also counteract the tendency toward a worldwide oil supply shortage with all its destabilizing and explosive factors.

An approach to this component of a security policy could be a package that combines an offer to the Soviet Union for more cooperation in exploiting Soviet energy resources with a code of conduct that obliges her not to intervene in Middle East domestic affairs. The expert for Western European affairs with the Central Committee of the Communist Party of the Sorviet Union, Portugalov, proposed in February 1980 to combine discussions about cooperation in the energy field at an all-European energy conference (including the United States and Canada) with a common guarantee for the oil routes through the Straits of Hormuz[29]. It cannot, of course, be in the interest of the Western countries to extend the Soviet influence in this region, but it is in the Western interest that the Soviet Union chooses an option of responsible behavior in this crisis area in general, and in the field of future oil supply and secure distribution especially. The more attractive a Western offer for cooperation in exploiting Soviet energy sources would be to the Soviet Union, the better the chance that she will accept, that the Middle East will not be an area of her interference, and the more she could be hurt in case of a violation of this agreement by cancelling this cooperation. Neither the Western energy problem nor the threatening danger from various levels of the Middle East crisis can be mitigated by refusing cooperation in energy exploitation within the Soviet Union, nor could this refusal probably lead to a negative effect on the future military strength of the Soviet Union. On the other hand, the ongoing heavy interest of the Soviet Union in intensified cooperation in the energy field could indicate that this puts the West into a strong bargaining position.

3. Dependence and Detente

The West does not have much leverage to convince the Soviet Union that responsible behavior, in the sense of a common effort to reduce tensions in crisis areas, would be in its own self-interest. Energy cooperation, however, could be a compelling factor. The West has a relative abundance of what the Soviet Union needs to exploit its reserves, namely capital and technology. The West, on the other hand, needs a higher worldwide production in energy, especially in oil, to prevent a global gap between demand and supply and to counteract cripling price increases. But even with a drastic Western help, the Soviet energy production would not be high enough to become a real influential power on the world energy market. Up to 1990, Western investment aid would not influence the Soviet oil output very much, and after 1990 the Soviet oil production would still have to struggle to meet the domestic and CMEA need. There is no reason to believe that the Soviet economy will do better during the 1990s in providing enough investment goods for energy production, even if Western technology is available.

The Soviet role in world natural gas supply could become more dominant than its role in the world oil market. But there is no comparable single natural gas market like the world oil market. Gas deliveries are to a strong degree tied to the existing pipeline nets. The natural gas market is more similar to a couple of bilateral monopolies than to a market where a worldwide balance of supply and demand can be managed or at least indicated on one spot market. This lowers the chance to influence the world energy market as a gas supplier to a large degree. The reason that Western European dependence is limited, even in case of a 15-20 percent share of the consumption delivered by the Soviet Union, was explained earlier.

However, Western economic aid to the Soviet energy production program could become an influential power on Soviet behavior toward the West. Arthur Meyerhoff writes:

> Because of the lack of technology the USSR must use foreign countries to help find oil. To do this, the country must begin the granting of foreign contracts in 1980 and it will take 10 to 15 years to bring the USSR to self-sufficiency in 1990-95 . . . If foreign influences . . . are to be excluded . . . the USSR will have to catch up on its own. This will mean 20 to 30 years of new research and development, and self-sufficiency will not be gained until 2000-10[30].

In contrast to Meyerhoff, I am convinced that the Soviet Union will never become a net importer either in oil or in overall energy because, considering the trade balance problem, the option of importing energy does not exist. But the necessity to remain a self-supplier has led the Soviet Union to become even more dependent on the West.

In contrast to, for instance, grain trade where the trade volume is to be fixed every year depending on the harvest of the purchaser, cooperation in such fields as energy production is dependent on long-term experiences of the partners with each other, and on a basic confidence that both sides wish to keep this cooperation for the long term and do not try to get short-term gains in the sense of a zero-sum-game. Since the Soviet Union depends more on the long-term stability of this cooperation than the West, it can be expected that she would respect agreements about stabilizing behavior in crisis areas if these agreements were linked to the energy cooperation agreement.

There is no reason why the Western countries should fear to lose anything if they would agree to an all-European energy conference. Since the Soviet Union put so much prestige into the proposal of this conference she wants it to succeed. This gives the Western countries a good chance to reach their goals of stabilizing crisis areas, especially in the Middle East.

If this kind of linkage policy is called a continuation of the detente process, which it is at least in the sense that it brings to bear basic agreements of the Helsinki Final Act of 1975, it has to be made clear that this policy does not contradict a policy of military strength; it certainly is not a substitution for it. But even if such a policy of common interest and common responsibility for keeping regional conflicts in the Third World areas on the lowest possible level improves the condintions for arms control negotiations, this does not mean a weakening of Western position.

References

1. The author is grateful to Maureen Madden for her invaluable help in the preparation of this paper.
2. National Foreign Assessment Center, *Simulations of Soviet Growth Options to 1985*, ER 79-10131, Washington, D.C., March 1979.
3. *Ekonomicheskaia Gazeta*, No. 49, December 1980, p. 6.
4. According to CIA estimations of Soviet GNP between 1970 and 1979, GNP growth was .76 times as high as National Income growth (Soviet Statistics). Sources: National Foreign Assessment Center, *Handbook of Economic Statistics 1980*, ER 80-10452, Washington, D.C., October 1980, and *Narodnoe khoziaistvo SSSR v 1979*, Moscow 1980.
5. In contrast to all Western countries, the relation between energy consumption and GNP did not diminish between 1973 or 1975 and 1978. Although the available data on energy consumption (*U.N. World Energy Supplies 1973-1978*, New York, 1979, or the CIA *Handbook*) and GNP (*World Bank Atlas*, CIA *Handbook*) are not absolutely reliable, the tendency to a worsening or stagnating efficiency of energy use (if the relation of energy consumption to GNP is accepted as a rough measure) in the CMEA countries is obvious, while in Western countries energy consumption did not grow half as fast as GNP.
6. Cf. Michael Roeskau, "Perspektiven der Energieproduktion Osteuropas," in *Energiewirtschaft*, Vol. 3, No. 1, 1980, pp. 41-45.
7. Jonathan Stern, *Soviet Natural Gas Development to 1990*, Lexington Books, Lexington, Mass., 1980.
8. National Foreign Assessment Center, *Simulation of Soviet Growth Options to 1985*, ER 79-10131, Washington, C.D., March 1979, p. 6.
9. Negotiations on the financing terms seem likely to be resolved in 1981. Cf. *The Wall Street Journal*, February 2, 1981.
10. Cf. National Foreign Assessment Center, *Estimating Soviet and East European Hard Currency Debt*, ER 80-10327, Washington, D.C., June 1980, p. 16.
11. Cf., for instance, *Los Angeles Times*, February 3, 1981.
12. Cf. *Petroleum Intelligence Weekly*, October 27, 1980, p. 11.
13. Cf. United Nations, *World Eı ergy Supplies 1973-1978*, New York, 1979.
14. Cf. *OECD Statistics of Foreign Trade 1977*, Series C, Paris, 1980.
15. Cf. *U.N. World Energy Supplies 1973-1978*, New York, 1979; and Ethan S. Burger, *Eastern Europe and Oil. The Soviet Dilemma*, The Rand Corporation, Santa Monica, California, P-6368, October 1979.
16. At the end of 1979, the hard currency debt volume of the Eastern European countries amounted to approximately $50 billion, which was almost twice the export volume of these countries to hard currency areas in 1979 ($25.5 billion).
17. Cf. *Vneshniaia Torgovlia SSSR, 1973, 1979*, Moscow, 1974 and 1980.
18. This increase is calculated in relatively stable ruble prices; in dollar prices it would be considerably more.
19. Cf. *Vneshniaia Torgovlia SSSR*, Moscow, different volumes.
20. According to sources mentioned in footnote 4.
21. Cf. National Foreign Assessment Center, *Soviet and U.S. Defense Activities 1970-79: A Dollar Cost Comparison*, SR 80-10005, Washington, C.D., January 1980.
22. Cf. National Foreign Assessment Center, *Handbook of Economic Statistics 1980*, ER 80-10452, Washington, D.C., October 1980, p. 24.
23. William T. Lee, *Soviet Defense Expenditures in an Era of SALT*, United States Strategic Institute, USSI Report 79-1, Washington, D.C., 1979, p. 10.

24. Cf. the Annual Reports of the United States Arms Control and Disarmament Agency, *World Military Expenditures and Arms Transfer.*
25. Cf. Abraham Becker, "Sustaining the Burden of Soviet Defense: Some Political-Economic Factors", unpublished conference paper, The Rand Corporation, Santa Monica, California, August 1980, p..50ff.
26. Cf. *Petroleum Intelligence Weekly*, December 22, 1980, p. 11.
27. See Henry Rowan, "Western Economies and the Gulf War," *The Wall Street Journal*, october 2, 1980.
28. See *Petroleum Intelligence Weekly*, December 22, 1980, p. 11.
29. See *Le Monde,* Mars-2, 1980, p. 1.
30. Arthur Meyerhoff, "Soviet Petroleum: History, Technology, Geology, Reserves, Potential and Policy", Discussion Paper, Association of American Geographers, Washington, D.C., June 1980, p. 142.

Summing Up
NATO Economics Colloquium 1981
'CMEA: Energy, 1980-1990'

Jeremy L. Russell

It would have been extremely surprising, and even worrying, if a colloquium of this nature, bringing together as it did a great many well informed people from a large number of countries, should have found itself in complete agreement on a multifaceted, complicated and partially unquantified subject such as the energy situation in the European COMECON countries.

That there were significant points over which experts disagreed was probably healthy in that it highlighted those areas to which greater attention should be directed in the future, and it also demonstrated that there are certain aspects of the COMECON energy scene, for example the size of Soviet oil reserves and ultimate oil production potential, which are simply not known. They should not be allowed to form the basis for major western policy decisions without considerable refinement.

The colloquium was extremely fortunate to have been addressed by so many distinguished speakers, recognized western authorities on different aspects of COMECON energy. Unfortunately, it was not possible in the time available for summing up to remind those present of more than a few of the more important things which came out in the papers and which were discussed during the two and a half days proceedings. It is hoped that what follows is an acceptable distillation of the main messages, and it is hoped that authors will forgive the writer if less than full justice has been done to their own contributions.

Before the colloquium assembled many people were probably grappling to find answers to the following questions:

Do the COMECON countries have energy problems too?;
How serious are these and can they be solved domestically
or with help from outside COMECON;

Are COMECON energy problems likely to exacerbate the
energy problems faced by the rest of the world? — or,
alternatively, could Soviet energy resources be expected
to alleviate the global energy situation to any extent?;

Are the smaller COMECON countries' energy problems
such as to increase tensions within COMECON or with the
Soviet Union? — And is the Soviet oil situation really so bad
that it could cause the Soviet Union to take steps to secure
supplies of energy from countries outside COMECON?

It was felt that people received sufficient at the colloquium to be able to
answer these questions. On the journey to enlightenment, the colloquium
looked at the COMECON energy situation in the global perspective. In the
industrialized countries of the West, primary energy requirements may, if
the objectives to which these countries are committed during this decade
are achieved, increase at a rate of less than 2 per cent per annum, while in
the developing countries a steep increase in energy requirements is to be
expected with growth rates in non-OPEC developing countries in the order
of 5-6 per cent per annum. However, there is little expectation that OPEC's
annual oil production will ever again exceed the 30 million barrel per day
mark, and OPEC's oil exports might well decrease at a rate close to the
reduction of oil demand in industrialized consumer countries. As a result of
this, tight market conditions are likely to continue to prevail. Against this
background, European COMECON has a potential for remaining a net
energy exporter, although this will involve a basic shift in the structure of
those exports — with natural gas replacing oil as the predominant export
item. Availability of Soviet oil for exports to the West seems likely to
decline, at least during the next 5 years, while there is considerable
potential for increased Soviet natural gas exports, particularly to Western
Europe which will be pursuing an energy diversification policy away from
oil. The serious problems facing the energy-poor European COMECON
countries if their growing oil requirements are not to be met by increased
Soviet deliveries, has been generally recognized. It means that they will be
obliged to try to secure oil on the hard currency market at a time when their
own hard currency situations are extremely tight and when the availability
of oil on the world market will also be tight.

The colloquium examined sectoral aspects of COMECON energy demand
in the 1980s and took notice of the dominant role in energy consumption
that industrial production plays in the COMECON countries and thus the
expectations for energy saving and wastereduction which industry will have
to fulfil. The colloquium recalled the historical, ideological and resources

endowment reasons why many of the COMECON countries have depended so much more upon coal, and its conversion to electricity, than upon hydrocarbons, although the share of the latter in the overall COMECON fuels/energy balance has been increasing in recent decades. A trend towards even greater electrification on the basis of a rapid growth in nuclear power, particularly in the smaller COMECON countries, is seen as inevitable, and the development of energy-efficient co-generation and district heating schemes will suit the living patterns and government policies in these countries, although structural problems are increasingly being encountered.

Energy demand for agriculture will become an increasing priority and consumption in this sector is expected to grow at an annual rate considerably in excess of that for the economy as a whole, during the 1980s in several countries where the energy intensity of agriculture will increase. In contrast to industry and agriculture, there is the modest demand of the transport sector which uses, on a per capita basis, but a fraction of the energy consumed in the same sector in West Europe. The undeveloped state of private motoring and trucking is seen as the chief cause.

For the future, the further modernization of the still backward household energy sector is considered essential, and the modernization of energy used by the rural population is seen as an urgent task. In general, the production and distribution of energy and its processing and conversion into more flexible and valuable forms is seen as placing incrasing demands on both the capital and scientific resources of COMECON, and the energy resource base itself, since a growing energy input is required to achieve these very goals. The financial constraints faced by COMECON countries in bringing about energy efficient changes in the economy are considerable, as are the problems arising from the worsening labor shortage which will require the further application of mechanical energy in the economies. Co-generation, based on coal, is scheduled to be an important energy development in the western part of the COMECON area, but atomic co-generation plants will hardly make an imporession before the 1990s. The smaller COMECON countries are not seen as having any significant reserves of oil saving capabilities, and this enhances the value which increased deliveries of Soviet natural gas will have for their economies.

Following these broader analyses, consideration was given to solid fuels, which are increasingly looked to in COMECON for power generation and as a substitute for fuel oil, particularly in the Soviet Union, as oil supply generally becomes constrained and emphasis is increased upon lightening the oil refining barrel. And yet, just when coal should have been playing an increasingly important part in the Soviet Union, production has started to falter. There is clearly no resource-base limitation on Soviet coal production although there are enormous geographical and logistic constraints. New production from more easterly situated coal fields has not kept pace with the depletion of the older, more westerly fields where mines have to go deeper than ever, with attendant increases in costs and physical effort. In

COMECON as a whole, the tendency is for an increasingly tight supply of hard coal, and for a slow but steady expansion of lower-grade brown coal production. In the Soviet Union, future coal capacity expansion will have to be concentrated for hard coal in the Kuznetsk Basin, and the strip brown coal mines of Ekibastuz and Kansk-Achinsk. The current Soviet 5 year plan target for coal production, in a similar range as that targeted for the previous 5 year plan, still appears very optimistic, since major mine construction effort will be required just to slow the decrease in mine output in, particularly, the Donets Basin, from which the Soviet Union supplies substantial parts of the coal imports of Bulgaria, Czechoslovakia, East Germany and Hungary. Exports may increasingly have to come from Kuznetsk and Ekibastuz, further to the East, and, while production costs here are lower than in Donetsk this will increase the already serious burden on the railways, since coal represents about 20 percent of all Soviet rail loadings and the average length of haul has grown sharply in recent years. The Soviets place considerable importance on the potential of coal-by-wire projects, the siting of power-intensive industries near the mines, as well as the construction of extra-high voltage transmissions lines.

In the smaller European COMECON countries, where coal still represents nearly 60 percent of the fuels budget, there seems little room for production expansion in view of the limited reserves position, even in Poland, where there are of course labor and other problems. In view of the difficulties in achieving growth in coal production both in Eastern Europe and the Soviet Union, recourse is being sought in the accelerated development of nuclear power generation.

The colloquium examined the prospects for oil production, supply and demand in COMECON. On the production side, in spite of a new, promising, find in Poland, and a stable output projection for Hungary, the future of oil production in the smaller COMECON countries seems likely to remain bleak, with even Romania's position likely to deteriorate during the decade. As far as Soviet oil is concerned, there is perhaps excessive concentration by Western observers upon this sector of the fuels/energy industry. Of course, oil has played the dominant role in Soviet foreign trade relations both within COMECON and with the rest of the world, and there are security aspects which cannot be ignored. However, the dangers of speculation can be great and the numerical basis for such speculation, for example about the size of Soviet oil reserves, just does not exist. One of the main causes of speculation by the West over this whole problem is a restrictive Soviet information policy on what is inevitably a sensitive matter. A decisive question for Soviet oil is — when Soviet production growth will reach its limit and enter the period X form which it will decline. Soviet oil production is clearly slowing, and critics point to methods of production as being primarily to blame. The well-density, for example, has been extended too rapidly in order to obtain favorable results in too short a time, and this has reduced the scope of the exploitable reserves. If this policy is continued, then Soviet oil production could probably soon reach its maximum and begin to decline, but if the extent of production drilling is reduced, it should be possible to increase oil production further without excessive investment. Indeed, lower rates of growth in oil production may not be primarily due to a shortage of capital but to the inefficient use of that capital. A substantial dependence upon Western technology cannot be deduced from the scarce data available, and for all the difficulties in the oil industry, the Soviet Union has not been induced to increase its import of oil drilling equipment significantly over the past 5 or 6 years.

Regarding Soviet reserves, there is a clear lack of hard evidence to support either pessimistic or optimistic assessments, which could both lead to wrong economic and political conclusions. However, the quantity of oil likely to be in place does not seem to predetermine a reduction of oil production during this decade and while the proven reserves may be of uncertain size, the potential for new discoveries remains rather large.

There is a growing competition for available funds between the oil and the gas industries, and the oil industry is unlikely to receive such favorable increases in investment as it has enjoyed in the past. A slow-down of Soviet oil production seems hardly to be in the West's best interest, and perhaps the West should therefore be prepared to supply the new technical equipment required by the Soviet Union. In any case, the sooner the Soviet Union succeeds in replacing its foreign exchange earnings from oil exports by earnings from gas, the sooner it will be able to devote more attention to oil conservation.

It is already too late for any new, more remotely located Arctic or East Siberian major oil discovery to have any direct impact upon the Soviet production level, until at least the early 1990s, and, in the same way, even massive western cooperation in the development of Soviet energy resources, supposing it were possible to negotiate and sign agreement on a major scheme in the very near future, would not contribute significantly until the next decade. In five years time or so Samotlor and other first-generation West Siberian fields will begin to decline, and by 1990s, if no major new fields are discovered in the area, the production profile will resemble the current profile of the Volga-Urals region and all-Union production will not be able to compensate for decline in its two major provinces and so will decline also.

On the demand side in the Soviet Union, where over 55 percent of energy is consumed by industry, oil is being phased out of the energy intensive sectors, not by price, but by allocation. Nevertheless, oil demand in the Soviet Union will tend to grow at about twice the annual growth in oil supply, assuming that the economy meets its plan targets. A slower economic advance might alleviate the pressure upon oil.

In the smaller COMECON countries, with the exception of Romania, oil occupies a remarkably low share of the fuels/energy balance, and while the Soviet Union has sufficient flexibility in its primary energy mix to substitute for oil, the others have little or no such flexibility. Oil demand there is expected to increase by about 18 percent by 1985, making a total demand of some 120 million tones minimum although usage of oil would undoubtedly be much higher if oil supplies were going to be easier.

Looking at COMECON as a whole, not only is the oil export surplus expected to decline, but the import of non-COMECON crude should increase to at least 35 million tonnes by mid-decade. Exports to the hard currency area could drop to only half the 1980 level although, for the Soviet Union, this loss of volume would be compensated by higher dollar prices and by gas exports.

The six smaller COMECON members will undoubtedly have to face severely constrained oil supplies. They have been caught up in the global oil problem before they have really entered the oil age, particularly East Germany, Poland and Czechoslovakia. Imports of energy intensive goods and technology will have to be sharply curtailed or else these countries are going to have to double their export capabilities. Whatever happens they are going to have to pay a lot more for their oil wherever it comes from.

The colloquium's attention was turned to the question of the cost of Soviet oil and, although the long-run marginal cost of Soviet oil is rising very rapidly, it still seems to be some way below 'world' oil prices. The Soviet Union is obliged, in view of the high cost of oil elsewhere, to produce oil from new fields under very unfavorable climatic and geological conditions, with a consequently rising long-run marginal cost. Even so, the Soviet Union as an oil exporter has suffered less from the rising long-run marginal cost that it has gained from the rising price on the world market, and so it is still well worthwhile for it to produce oil both for home consumption and for export. The immense cost of new pipeline construction may put the advantage of building long east-to-west pipelines into serious question by the middle of the decade, and there is some indication that Soviet planners intend to let the domestic price of oil rise towards world levels. The Soviet Union is, for the time being at least, a relatively low-cost producer and, since marginal production is probably being exported, exports might logically be expected to be cut as marginal costs rise further.

The colloquium then considered the fuel with a bright future in COMECON—natural gas. The rapidly growing share of gas in the fuels/energy balance in the new five year plan is very significant, particularly in view of the growing share of Siberia in total Soviet output. Investment in the Soviet gas industry is seen by Soviet planners as being more economically effective than that in the oil industry. The extremely strong Soviet position of possessing around one third of world proven gas reserves is well known as is the growing inaccessibility of these reserves and the awesome problems facing the Soviet gas industry in developing the production and transportation infrastructures required to bring the gas the long distances from Siberia to the markets in the West of the country and abroad. The Soviet gas production target for the current five year plan may be rather ambitious, particularly if fulfilment has to depend entirely upon domestic equipment resources, but they may be expected to reach the lower end of the range. A key factor in the Soviet capability to achieve its planned target will be Soviet access to large diameter pipelines and to compressor stations, a considerable proportion of which will have to come from the West. Nevertheless, gas is destined to be the major incremental contributor both to the Soviet and to the overall COMECON energy balance in the 1980s, when it will not only be expected to compensate for faltering production of other fuels but also to compensate for an expected decline in Soviet oil exports as a major hard currency earner. In this connection, if the Yamburg export project for West Europe does not come about, then it will be very interesting to see if the Soviet Union diverts effort away from gas in order to maintain oil exports. Yamburg is a very difficult deposit in any case, while Urengoy seems even bigger than previously foreseen, and so another alternative would be to divert the effort from Yamburg to further development of Urengoy.

It is very doubtful whether Soviet natural gas will, on its own, be able to fill all COMECON's energy gaps or, indeed, Soviet hard currency earning requirements, if other energy forms fall dramatically short of production targets.

As a result of the discussion on the fossil fuels sectors the colloquium expressed bewilderment about the ability of Soviet planners so persistently to get their published longer-term production targets 'wrong'. However, it was felt that Soviet plans are mainly designed for internal consumption and that outsiders tend to attach too much significance and sanctity to Soviet plans and thus tend to over-dramatize Soviet failures or successes in meeting planned targets.

The colloquium directed its thoughts to the supply and demand of electrical energy in COMECON in the 1980s. COMECON has essentially a self-sufficient electricity system, although production is likely to continue to have problems in meeting demand as a result not only of changes in the fuel base but also of the geographical gap between sources of energy supply and areas of demand, and there is a need to expand electrical generating capacity for use during peak load periods in the principal areas of demand. COMECON electric power planners are looking to an expansion of gas turbine and pumped-storage capacity, and to the increasing use of inerconnections between power supply systems. The concentration of demand in the Western areas of COMECON and the availability of supplies in more Eastern parts, particularly of the Soviet Union, will give rise to a growing Westward flow of electricity both within the Soviet Union and between the Soviet Union and Eastern Europe, although this will depend upon successful installation of extra-high-voltage lines from lignite-fired power stations near Ekibastuz and Kansk-Achinsk, and an expanding network of lines feeding nuclear power from projected stations near to Soviet Western borders.

Although there is considererable potential for Soviet hydroelectricity development, particularly in Siberia, this will have to be used mainly locally, in power-intensive industries such as aluminium production.

In view of the many transportation problems associated with the exploitation of the more Easterly situated coal deposits and natural gas fields, nuclear energy seems to be the sole major source of incremental base-load electricity generating capacity in the European part of the Soviet Union as well as in Eastern Europe. Reactor manufacturing capacity is thought likely to be a bottleneck until the plant at Volgodonsk reaches its designed capacity of eight 1000 MW units a year, but at present there seems likely to be substantial underfulfillment of plant manufacture plans and therefore of nuclear power generation plans. Nuclear power stations in the European part of the USSR are due to be interconnected via a 750 kV grid which will allow for large inter-system electricity transfers and will serve for the transfer of electricity between, for example, the power systems of the Western Soviet Union and those of Eastern Europe, facilitated by the time difference of 2 hours. Although nuclear generating capacity in Eastern Europe is scheduled to increase substantially during the decade, most East European electricity generation is likely to continue to be based on solid fuels at least until the end of this century. The increasing stress on nuclear power in COMECON raises problems with respect to the transportation of nuclear fuel from the Soviet Union to Eastern Europe, the disposal of spent fuel and the choice of suitable nuclear power station sites.

The colloquium looked at problems and perspectives of COMECON energy transport systems and the critical situation on the railways, particularly for coal transport, which seems unlikely to be overcome in the foreseeable future and which will clearly affect coal usage. On the other hand, the electricity transport system is likely to be developed at a rate sufficient to prevent distribution being a constraint upon its usage. The transport of hydrocarbons within COMECON is still dogged by pipeline problems and it is rather doubtful whether the Soviet Union can, for both technical and financial reasons, construct the necessary large diameter throughputs for it to be able to achieve its production targets. Furthermore, the distribution of oil products from refineries, particularly over rather short distances, could surely be done more efficiently by more smaller diameter pipelines, thus freeing-up considerable capacity on the railways. It is clear that the Soviet Union will be giving priority to furnishing COMECON with adequate supplies of hydrocarbons even though this will require a huge outlay of equipment, manpower and finance on a COMECON-wide scale. By contrast, coal and lignite are only treated on a regional basis by each of the COMECON countries in the light of their domestic needs, production capabilities and prospects. It is surprising therefore that the Soviet Union, particularly in view of its longer term need to boost solid fuel production, is doing very little about developing a railway system commensurate with its future needs. The adequate westward transmission of coal-by-wire is by no means assured and is probably not economically justified. The concentratin on hydrocarbon transporation will result in higher energy prices for the Soviet economy while the disorganization of other transportation systems, deprived of the necessary investment, will be exacerbated and will generate a snowball effect on all sectors of the economy.

The final sector of the colloquium considered the interface between the energy situations within European COMECON countries and those outside starting with the energy factor in East/West relations. This presented a great deal of food for thought, and emphasized the fundamental reorientation in thinking on the question of East/West energy interdependence which is likely to be necessary during this decade and into the next. From a United States perspective there may be a case for the integration of commercial and economic potential as an integral part of American policy towards the Soviet Union in a narrower sense, and, in a broader context, as a feature of an Alliance strategy for dealing with the COMECON bloc. Economic difficulties could persuade the Kremlin leadership to follow a more conciliatory line in international politics, particularly if it could be made clear to them that such a shift in national security policy were a prerequisite to increased economic intercourse with the West. However, in considering the scope, advantages and disadvantages of trade with the Soviet Union the colloquium was reminded of the divergence of views between the United States and its allies over these issues. Particularly when energy issues are considered, this divergence reflects the reality of international energy trends and the increasing dependence of the industrialized democracies upon energy imports. For Europe and Japan, energy trade with the Soviet Union represents a rational diversification of their import suppliers, whereas the United States, which takes little Soviet energy but sells large quantities of grain and technology to the Soviet Union, tends to view the Soviet-American relationship as the focal point of the East/West competition. The split amongst the allies in energy trade policy vis a vis the Soviet Union essentially reflects the differing stakes which the nations involved perceive. There is also disagreement over the extent to which Western technology and equipment actually does benefit the Soviet economy, although in certain narrow sectors it undoubtedly does. Western energy technology could, for example, alleviate several bottlenecks in Soviet production industries. The main question is how vital for the energy industries Western technology actually is.

The colloquium examined the whole question of the application of Western economic leverage on the Eastern bloc and the arguments for and against, but it also looked at the opposite side of that question, namely the potential for Soviet economic leverage upon the West, based primarily on potential future Soviet energy exports. The colloquium was alerted to the implications of energy policies for the cohesion of both the Western and Eastern alliances and the fact that after 1990, the West could increasingly feel the pressure to respond to Soviet coercive and persuasive measures arising from the potential power which the Soviet Union's future energy and mineral wealth and the growing dependence of Western nations upon Soviet deliveries will combine to give it. The Soviet Union is the most self-sufficient industrial power in terms of strategic minerals and is also a major supplier of precious metals to the West. Indeed, the possession of these critical minerals in conjunction with energy fuels could leave the Soviet Union as the world's primary resource base. Increasingly the allies are going to be in growing competition for scarce resources.

The colloquium felt that the development of a coherent Western energy relationship with the COMECON countries must become a major topic for both economic and security discussion in an appropriate forum representing the industrialized democracies of the West. The West may become involved in joint projects that would establish Siberia as the basis of an all-European (and Japanese) energy system, detaching West Europe and Tokyo somewhat from American influence and leaving Moscow in a position of great influence in the allocation of a significant share of global energy supplies. The industrialized democracies will require vigorously to implement effective national energy targets to reduce their collective dependence upon energy imports, and they will have to co-operate effectively in the case of sudden supply disruptions or shifts in global energy distribution patterns. The establishment of a common position with respect to dealing with COMECON must be pursued, particularly with regard to technology transfer, long-range energy ventures and supply interdependency.

While it is understandable that COMECON energy relationships with the industrialized countries of the West should have been of primary significance for the members of the colloquium, it was felt important to remember that countries in the developing world also have a direct interest in what COMECON has to offer or is likely to need in the way of energy and energy related items. The colloquium therefore focused upon the forms and the dimension of Soviet and East European trade and co-operation in energy with third world economies. By the mid 1970s COMECON had intensified energy relations with many third world countries, with the Soviet Union becoming a major petroleum supplier to some of them and the smaller COMECON countries entering into a variety of arrangements, mainly of a bilateral clearing nature, with the Arab OPEC countries and with Iran, aimed at diversifying oil imports and reducing dependence upon Soviet oil. Although Soviet oil exports to third world countries never represented more than a small share — some 4 percent maximum — of total Soviet oil exports, if Soviet oil exports have peaked then it is likely that the Kremlin's ability to profit from the opportunities arising out of third world interest in taking oil from the Soviet Union in preference to or in addition to supplies form elsewhere is going to be limited. the Soviet Union will probably concentrate its oil exports in a relatively small number of strategically located countries, such as India, Turkey and Morocco, while it is likely that it will also try to secure special economic terms from these countries, for example oil-for-grain barter agreements, etc. For the other COMECON countries, recent political and economic developments in the Gulf, particularly in Iran and Iraq — two major suppliers of their non-Soviet imports in the past—have made considerable difficulties for COMECON's plans to further diversify supplies, and the rapid increase in prices has hit these hard-currency-short countries at a particularly bad time. Since the mid 1970s there has been a shift away from bilateral clearing towards hard-currency settlement in East/South trade, which has thus become closer in structure and form to North/South economic relations. In relations with the COMECON countries, the developing countries have become locked into the same role, as importers of manufactures and exporters of primary products, that they have so deplored in their relations with the developed countries of the West.

Scope for extension of COMECON energy assistance to third world countries is limited by the availability of skilled labor and other resources urgently required for projects back home within COMECON. Furthermore, slower rates of growth in COMECON, added to regional commitments and the need to balance trade with the Soviet Union while reducing payments imbalances with the West, make uncertain the extent to which the smaller East European countries can greatly expand exports to third world countries aimed at securing additional volumes of increasingly highly priced oil. Unless the smaller COMECON countries can obtain greatly increased credit it is quite possible that they will not actually be in a position to contribute to a worsening of any global oil shortage through substantial increases in their own offtakes of third world oil. On the other hand, the Soviet Union could, with its greater hard currency purchasing ability, further strengthen its economic grip on the other COMECON countries by securing increasing third world supplies for them. Whatever happens with other fuels, the smaller COMECON countries are going to have to learn how to make do with a severely constrained oil supply situation, and their economic dependency upon the Soviet Uion will continue and increase.

The colloquium was reminded that there is a great deal of energy contained in grain, pipe and machinery and the increasing imports of these commodities should be assessed in terms of the overall energy trade.

In view of a constrained COMECON energy situation it was felt necessary to look at whether there is any likelihood of Research and Development in the Soviet Union or its allies leading to a breakthrough in energy production in the foreseeable future. The substitution of other energy sources such as coal, gas, or nuclear power for oil, as its supply tightens, requires the creation of new, or the upgrading of old, technologies and equipment for the production, processing and transport of the alternative fuels, while energy conservation aimed at bringing down the heat rate also involves the design and commercialization of new technologies. The East European countries are likely to remain heavily dependent both upon Soviet energy itself and, in a very large part of their energy sector technology, upon Soviet technology, even in the nuclear power and electric power generating sectors.

In the Soviet Union, energy R and D organizations tend to be somewhat more effective than the average in that country although this probably does not mean that they can innovate effectively, and the Soviet Union has had a conspicuous lack of success in developing, for example, a domestically reproducible gas compressor. Soviet R and D, furthermore, is often not steadily and continuously promoted in a particular field and crash programmes attempt to telescope the R and D process, resulting in too little intermediate testing of ideas, processes and concepts, or adaptation of research directions of fit the real needs. In short, Soviet R and D is not good at commercializing and applying the technology it develops. There is a common R and D failure to come up with the phased and co-ordinated development of systems as a whole, and R and D in the Soviet Uion is strongly influenced by a strategic point of view, with effort often focused only on selected elements in a given situation. The Soviet R and D system is unlikely to be effective at developing conservation technologies since it will neglect all but the most visible possibilities which get targeted by people at the top. There is great inertia and insensitivity in many R and D organizations, arising from assigned specializations and the prevalence of institutional rather than project financing, while centrally imposed stragetic views play an important role in energy policy and the research and development efforts that support it. Central attention is crucial if an idea is ever to advance along the development spectrum, and in Soviet R and D too many parameters tend to be fixed in advance while ideas tend to be put into metal and concrete too soon. Auxiliary equipment is not developed at the same time or to the same degree as the main projects under development.

The end users of Soviet R and D, the industrial ministries, have limited motivation and freedom to reject technologies that are not commercially appealing to them, particularly when decisions on that technology have come from the top, and there is a reduced chance that foreign competition can supersede a domestically developed technology except possibly in the form of technology transfer, but only when the domestic program turns out to be a flagrant failure. It is therefore unlikely, in spite of considerable success in heavy electrical power generation R and D programs, that the Soviet Union will achieve the kind of dramatic breakthroughs in any given technological area that could tilt the balance of economic advantages decisively one way or the other in any of the major energy choices. It does not, for example, seem realistic to expect breakthroughs in the technology of coal conversion or in power transmission such as would give Kansk-Achinsk coal a dominant place in the solution of the energy deficit of the European USSR, and the technological challenges facing the Soviet Union are such that it will not easily out-grow its needs for Western technology.

The colloquium examined the linkages between Soviet energy issues and economic growth prospects for the 1980s and considered whether or not the Soviet Union can remain a major exporter of energy overall. There is a possibility that Soviet economic growth during the 1980s will, in addition to constraints imposed by demographic, labor shortage and capital stock developments, be energy-constrained, particularly if Soviet oil production falls to the levels predicted by the CIA. In such a case, the Soviet Union could well be unable to adjust the energy consuming capital stock fast enough to accommodate a changing energy supply mix. Furthermore, the Soviet Union might deliberately become a net importer of oil in order to try and relieve some of the pressure on domestic oil use although this would severely reduce the Soviet capability to import Western machinery and industrial goods. The Soviet eleventh five year plan energy production guidelines are much more optimistic than this, however, and if they are actually fulfilled then economic modeling indicates that Soviet economic growth would not be energy-constrained, and the Soviet Union could therefore remain a net oil exporter to the hard currency area. If problems in the domestic Soviet energy supply do develop, then the possibility arises that, for opportunity-cost reasons, the Soviet Union might have to slash energy exports to its East European allies in order to avoid negative effects on its own economic growth and its trading position with the West. This is clearly an area which needs to be watched carefully in future years.

The colloquium also examined the linkages between energy and the economic growth rates in the smaller COMECON countries of Eastern Europe. Here, the rising cost and uncertainty of supply of energy is seen as seriously complicating East European economic growth prospects — already constricted by sluggish productivity growth and declining increments to the labor force. Economic models indicate that, unless the Soviet Union further increases deliveries of energy, the other European COMECON countries could require over 50 million tons of non-communist oil by 1985 if they are to reach growth potentials, and the cost of this could amount to over half the region's hard currency earnings. In view of the numerous constraints on hard currency earning capabilities of East European countries, particularly in Poland which is virtually bankrupt, non-communist oil imports may in fact be limited to nearer 25 million tons per annum and economic growth will therefore be energy-constrained so that standards of living could stagnate or even fall in some countries. Per capital GNP could actually decline in Hungary, Czechoslovakia and Poland, but in any event economic growth rates in Eastern Europe will be significantly lower over the next five years than they have been during the 1970s, and little or no growth in real investment seems possible in the immediate future. A more optimistic scenario would have to involve an exceptionally high borrowing from the West and an unacceptably high debt service ratio.

In the final session the colloquium examined the implications for the West, including defense, of COMECON energy prospects. For financing reasons if for no other, it seems absolutely impossible that the Soviet Union will become a net importer of oil in the 1980s, and no sharp reduction of Soviet oil exports to the East European countries below the current 80 million ton per annum level is considered likely either. Soviet economic growth could perhaps be even lower than 2 per cent per annum, with a resulting lower growth in energy consumption that could possibly allow Soviet energy exports to continue at their present levels, including even oil.

Oil exports to hard currency areas are, however, almost certain to decline and this could mean a loss of approximately 4 percent of the estimated import needs of Western countries in 1990. West European dependence upon Soviet energy exports need not necessarily grow, since increasing dependency on Soviet natural gas exports is likely to be balanced by a reduction in oil dependency. Dependence on natural gas was not seen by the colloquium as so sensitive as dependence upon oil, in view of the high level of self-supply in West European gas. There surely exists a mutual, albeit a non simultaneous, dependence between Western Europe and the Soviet Union in respect of natural gas supply, in view of the Soviet Union's apparent on-going requirement for Western finance, technology and industrial goods, and a total cutting off of gas by the Soviet Union could only be an ultimate weapon.

East European oil imports or coal exports are unlikely to have a pronounced influence upon Western energy supplies during this decade, but the critical issue in the COMECON energy situation as far as its impact upon trade is concerned is the unfavorable outlook for the East European economies, and a consequent reduction in their capability to import non-energy goods and services from the West. Energy constraint in the Soviet Union is not seen by some Europeans as leading either to a major economic breakdown or to an inability to continue the military build up, although there is some economic attraction to COMECON if the Soviet Union can secure an availability of Middle Eastern oil either for its own or for its allies' use.

The Soviet energy situation itself is not considered sufficiently serious to oblige the Soviet Union to extend its influence in the Middle East although it could well produce an additional Soviet interest in the area. Could it be in the Western interest to pursue a security policy that combines an offer to the Soviet Union for more co-operation in exploiting Soviet energy resources with a code of conduct that would oblige the Soviet Union not to intervene in Middle East domestic affairs? Would such a policy work? The more attractive such a Western offer for energy co-operation, the greater the chance that the Soviet Union would accept it and choose an option of responsible behavior in this general crisis area. The colloquium recognized, however, that there might be a great many reasons why the Soviet Union might decide to ignore any such code. A Western refusal to co-operate in energy exploitation within the Soviet Union would do nothing, however, to mitigate either the West's energy problems or the threat of crisis in the Middle East, and would be unlikely to have a negative effect on the future military strength of the Soviet Union. On the other hand, even substantial Western assistance in the Soviet energy field will not boost Soviet energy production to the point where it could significantly effect the world energy market. The Soviet Union's desire and need to be self-sufficient in energy may have resulted in its becoming more dependent upon the West, and so perhaps the West has less to fear from pursuing a co-operative policy in respect of Soviet energy developments.

Throughout the colloquium there did seem to be a slight difference in approach to COMECON energy matters manifested by both presenters and participants who came from different sides of the Atlantic. Mainly, these differences concerned the degree of seriousness which should be attached to the problems facing the Soviet oil industry and the implications for both Eastern and Western foreign policy initiatives. These implications must surely merit deeper discussion. European speakers tended to see these problems as significantly less serious than did those from North America. Similarly, European participants tended to be more in favor of co-operation with COMECON in the development of energy resources than did their colleagues from the United States. Perhaps there was in general a tendency to underestimate what the Soviet Union can achieve with or without western assistance, but perhaps also the tendency to overestimate the options open to the smaller East European countries.

The colloquium, however, seemed to agree that the smaller COMECON countries really do face substantial economic problems as a result of energy supply constraints and that these problems will deepen during the 1980s. Apart from the provision of even more credits however, these seems little which the West can do to help these countries and the prospect for East/West trade does not therefore seem very good. On the other hand, their energy problems seem unlikely to exacerbate those of the Western industrialized countries even though tensions within COMECON will undoubtedly be increased.

The colloquium was felt to have greatly assisted the understanding of the complexities both of the COMECON energy situation itself and of different peoples' approaches to it within the framework of Western analysis and evaluation. Finally, this colloquium guided people to look beyond the conventional controversy over how much Western financial and technical co-operation in energy might or might not benefit the COMECON countries, to where the West's own best interests might lie. The colloquium agreed that the COMECON countries may have their own energy problems but, when all is said and done, the Soviet bloc is by comparison with the industrialized West substantially less dependent upon others, and this must enable them to remain rather aloof form the energy related conflicts which affect the rest of the world. Whether they like it or not, the COMECON countries and their people have an ability for belt-tightening considerably greater than that which the industrialized Western countries seem prepared to countenance. The colloquium also agreed that the need for the creation of a coherent Western policy on energy relations with COMECON is now pressing and the time available for more deliberation of these issues is short.